THE DEAD LUCKY

PUBLISHER

— ✕

IMAGE COMICS, INC. • Robert Kirkman: Chief Operating Officer • Erik Larsen: Chief Financial Officer • Todd McFarlane: President • Marc Silvestri: Chief Executive Officer • Jim Valentino: Vice President • Eric Stephenson: Publisher / Chief Creative Officer • Nicole Lapalme: Vice President of Finance • Leanna Caunter: Accounting Analyst • Sue Korpela: Accounting & HR Manager • Matt Parkinson: Vice President of Sales & Publishing Planning • Lorelei Bunjes: Vice President of Digital Strategy • Dirk Wood: Vice President of International Sales & Licensing • Ryan Brewer: International Sales & Licensing Manager • Alex Cox: Director of Direct Market Sales • Chloe Ramos: Book Market & Library Sales Manager • Emilio Bautista: Digital Sales Coordinator • Jon Schlaffman: Specialty Sales Coordinator • Kat Salazar: Vice President of PR & Marketing • Deanna Phelps: Marketing Design Manager • Drew Fitzgerald: Marketing Content Associate • Heather Doornink: Vice President of Production • Drew Gill: Art Director • Hilary DiLoreto: Print Manager • Tricia Ramos: Traffic Manager • Melissa Gifford: Content Manager • Erika Schnatz: Senior Production Artist • Wesley Griffith: Production Artist • Rich Fowlks: Production Artist • IMAGECOMICS.COM

DETAILS

—

THE DEAD LUCKY, VOL. 1. March 2023. Published by Image Comics, Inc. Office of publication: PO BOX 14457, Portland, OR 97293. Copyright © 2023 Melissa Flores & French Carlomagno. All rights reserved. Contains material originally published in single magazine form as THE DEAD LUCKY #1-6. "The Dead Lucky," its logos, and the likenesses of all characters herein are trademarks of Melissa Flores & French Carlomagno, unless otherwise noted. "Image" and the Image Comics logos are registered trademarks of Image Comics, Inc. No part of this publication may be reproduced or transmitted, in any form or by any means (except for short excerpts for journalistic or review purposes), without the express written permission of Melissa Flores & French Carlomagno, or Image Comics, Inc. All names, characters, events, and locales in this publication are entirely fictional. Any resemblance to actual persons (living or dead), events, or places, without satirical intent, is coincidental. Printed in the USA. For international rights, contact: foreignlicensing@imagecomics.com. ISBN: 978-1-5343-2466-4.

LOGOS

BLACK MARKET NARRATIVE

THE DEAD LUCKY

```
TERMINAL                                    _  ×

GHOST:~ admin$ CollectionProfiler
Volume:
     No.: 001
     Title: The Good Die Young.
```

```
CREDITS                           _  ×

login: admin
password:
last login: Wed Mar 22 09:00:00 from 127.0.0.1
welcome to GHOST

GHOST:~ admin$ ls -1 files/users
     writer                    melissa_flores
     artist                    french_carlomagno
     colorist                  mattia_iacono
     color·assistant/issue004  luca_mattioni
     letterer                  becca_carey

     production·artist         wesley_griffith
     suit·designer             federico_sabbatini
     robot·designer            stefano_simeone
     recipes                   sandra_winn
     creative·consultant       kyle_higgins
     designer&editor           michael_busuttil
```

```
TERMINAL                                                    _  ✕

────────────────────────────────────────────────────────────────

GHOST:~ admin$ SingleIssueProfiler
Issue:
    No.: 001
    Title: The Good Die Young.
```

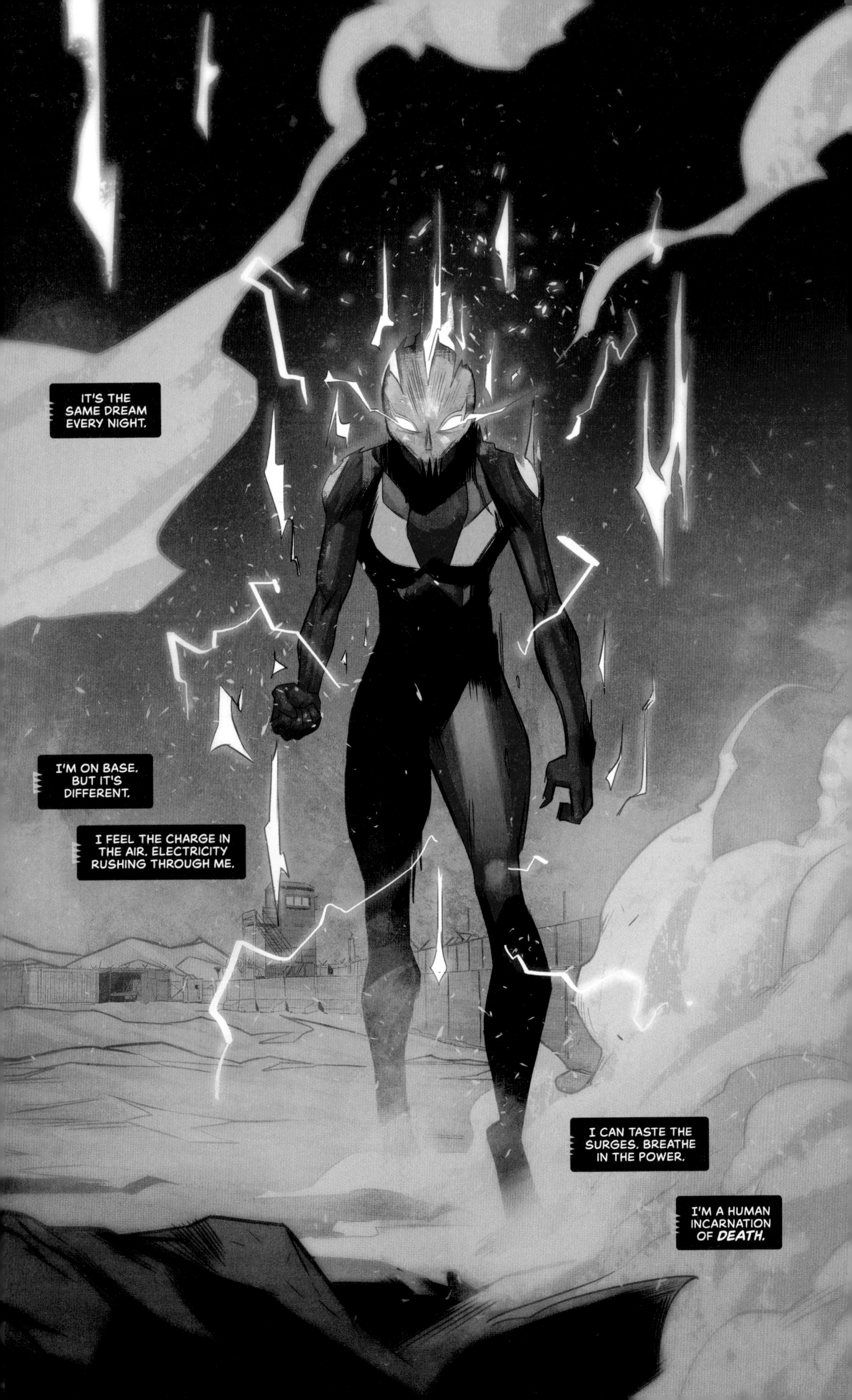
IT'S THE SAME DREAM EVERY NIGHT.
I'M ON BASE. BUT IT'S DIFFERENT.
I FEEL THE CHARGE IN THE AIR. ELECTRICITY RUSHING THROUGH ME.
I CAN TASTE THE SURGES. BREATHE IN THE POWER.
I'M A HUMAN INCARNATION OF *DEATH.*

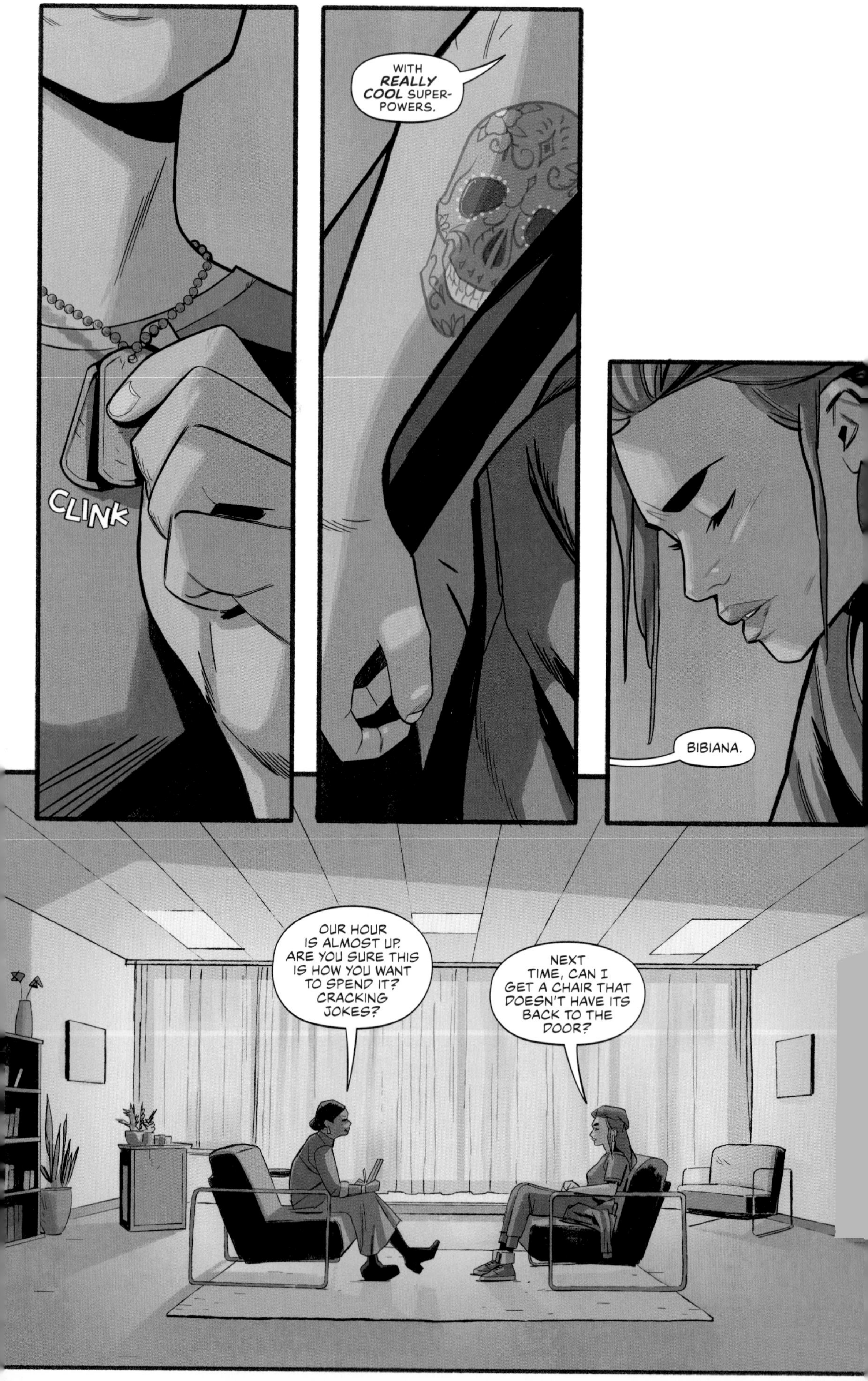
CLINK
WITH REALLY COOL SUPER-POWERS.
BIBIANA.
OUR HOUR IS ALMOST UP. ARE YOU SURE THIS IS HOW YOU WANT TO SPEND IT? CRACKING JOKES?
NEXT TIME, CAN I GET A CHAIR THAT DOESN'T HAVE ITS BACK TO THE DOOR?

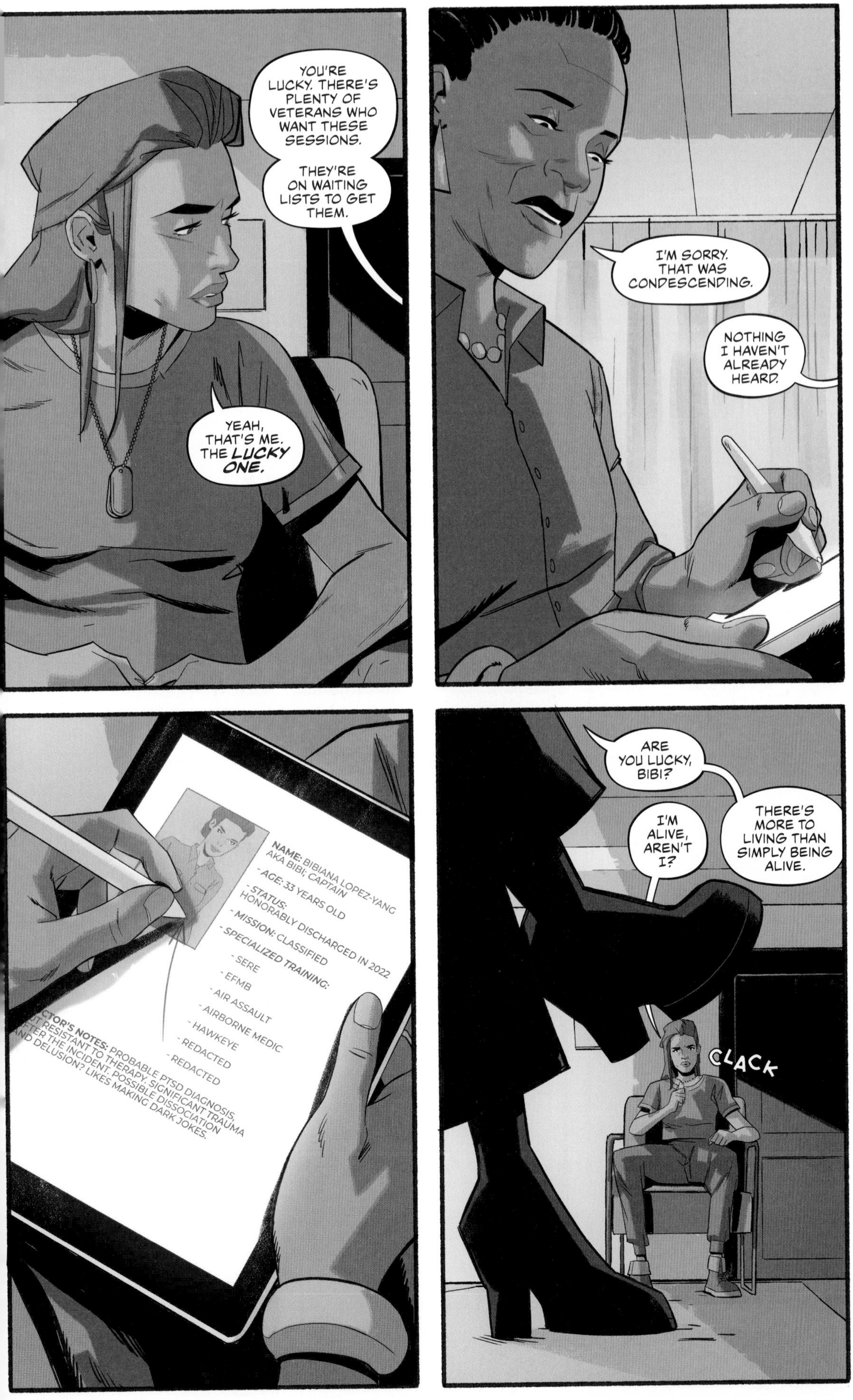
YOU'RE LUCKY. THERE'S PLENTY OF VETERANS WHO WANT THESE SESSIONS.
THEY'RE ON WAITING LISTS TO GET THEM.
YEAH, THAT'S ME. THE *LUCKY ONE.*
I'M SORRY. THAT WAS CONDESCENDING.
NOTHING I HAVEN'T ALREADY HEARD.
NAME: BIBIANA LOPEZ-YANG AKA BIBI; CAPTAIN
- **AGE:** 33 YEARS OLD
- **STATUS:** HONORABLY DISCHARGED IN 2022
- **MISSION:** CLASSIFIED
- **SPECIALIZED TRAINING:**
- SERE
- EFMB
- AIR ASSAULT
- AIRBORNE MEDIC
- HAWKEYE
- REDACTED
- REDACTED
CTOR'S NOTES: PROBABLE PTSD DIAGNOSIS,
UT RESISTANT TO THERAPY. SIGNIFICANT TRAUMA
TER THE INCIDENT. POSSIBLE DISSOCIATION
ND DELUSION? LIKES MAKING DARK JOKES.
ARE YOU LUCKY, BIBI?
I'M ALIVE, AREN'T I?
THERE'S MORE TO LIVING THAN SIMPLY BEING ALIVE.
CLACK

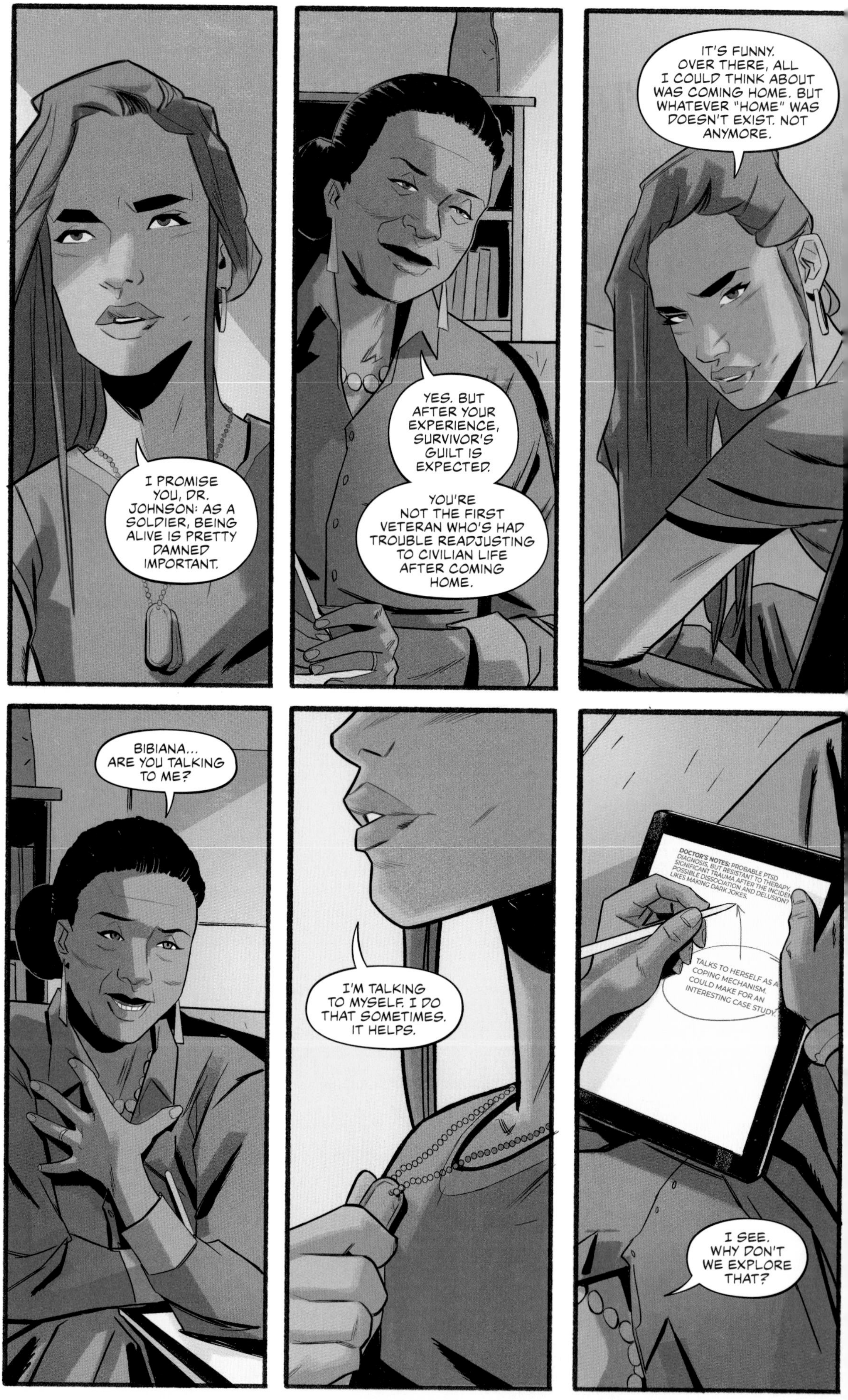
I PROMISE YOU, DR. JOHNSON: AS A SOLDIER, BEING ALIVE IS PRETTY DAMNED IMPORTANT.
YES. BUT AFTER YOUR EXPERIENCE, SURVIVOR'S GUILT IS EXPECTED.
YOU'RE NOT THE FIRST VETERAN WHO'S HAD TROUBLE READJUSTING TO CIVILIAN LIFE AFTER COMING HOME.
IT'S FUNNY. OVER THERE, ALL I COULD THINK ABOUT WAS COMING HOME. BUT WHATEVER "HOME" WAS DOESN'T EXIST. NOT ANYMORE.
BIBIANA... ARE YOU TALKING TO ME?
I'M TALKING TO MYSELF. I DO THAT SOMETIMES. IT HELPS.
DOCTOR'S NOTES: PROBABLE PTSD DIAGNOSIS, BUT RESISTANT TO THERAPY. SIGNIFICANT TRAUMA AFTER THE INCIDEN POSSIBLE DISSOCIATION AND DELUSION? LIKES MAKING DARK JOKES.
TALKS TO HERSELF AS A COPING MECHANISM. COULD MAKE FOR AN INTERESTING CASE STUDY.
I SEE. WHY DON'T WE EXPLORE THAT?

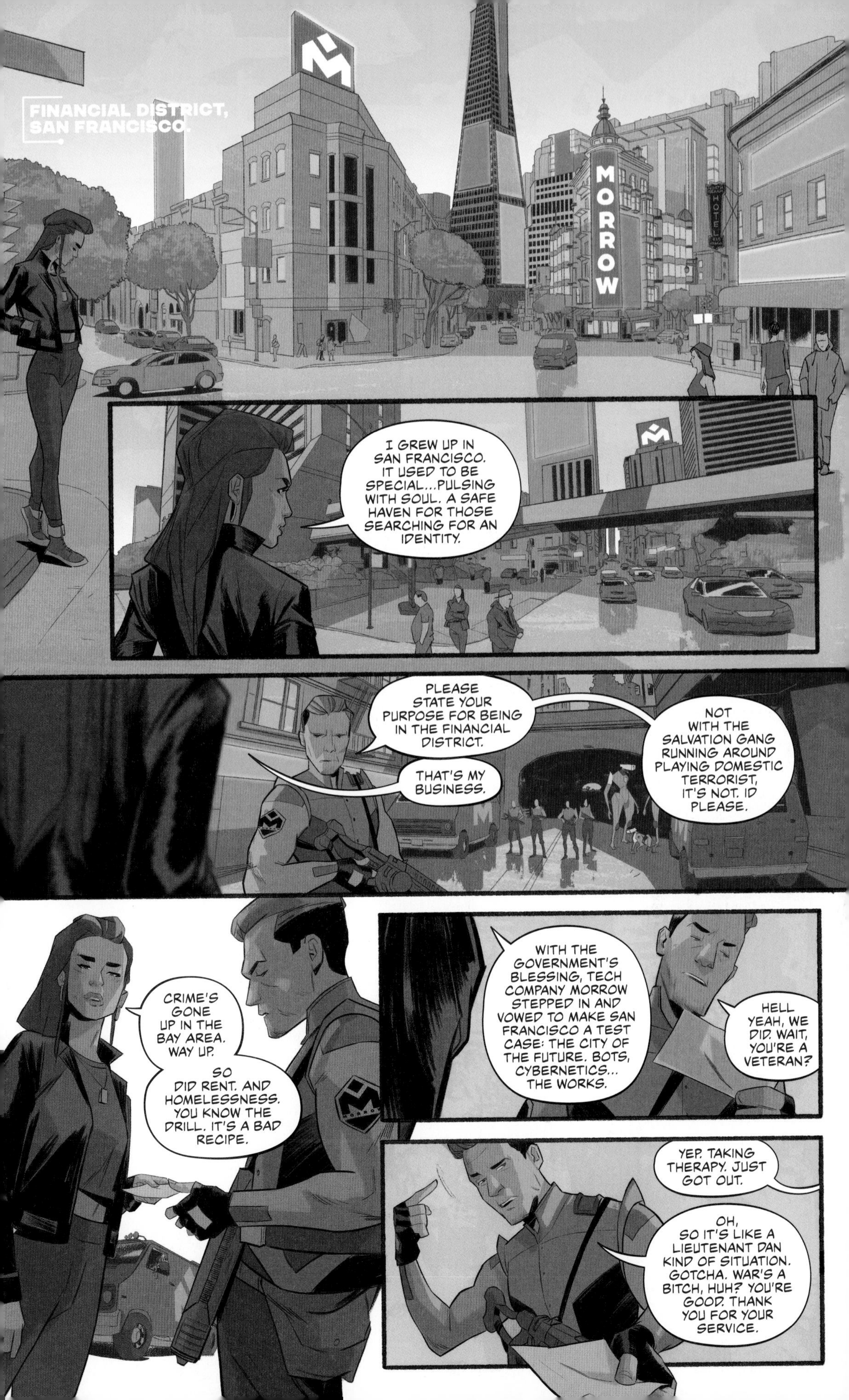
FINANCIAL DISTRICT, SAN FRANCISCO.
MORROW
HOTEL
I GREW UP IN SAN FRANCISCO. IT USED TO BE SPECIAL...PULSING WITH SOUL. A SAFE HAVEN FOR THOSE SEARCHING FOR AN IDENTITY.
PLEASE STATE YOUR PURPOSE FOR BEING IN THE FINANCIAL DISTRICT.
THAT'S MY BUSINESS.
NOT WITH THE SALVATION GANG RUNNING AROUND PLAYING DOMESTIC TERRORIST, IT'S NOT. ID PLEASE.
CRIME'S GONE UP IN THE BAY AREA. WAY UP.
SO DID RENT. AND HOMELESSNESS. YOU KNOW THE DRILL. IT'S A BAD RECIPE.
WITH THE GOVERNMENT'S BLESSING, TECH COMPANY MORROW STEPPED IN AND VOWED TO MAKE SAN FRANCISCO A TEST CASE: THE CITY OF THE FUTURE. BOTS, CYBERNETICS... THE WORKS.
HELL YEAH, WE DID. WAIT, YOU'RE A VETERAN?
YEP. TAKING THERAPY. JUST GOT OUT.
OH, SO IT'S LIKE A LIEUTENANT DAN KIND OF SITUATION. GOTCHA. WAR'S A BITCH, HUH? YOU'RE GOOD. THANK YOU FOR YOUR SERVICE.

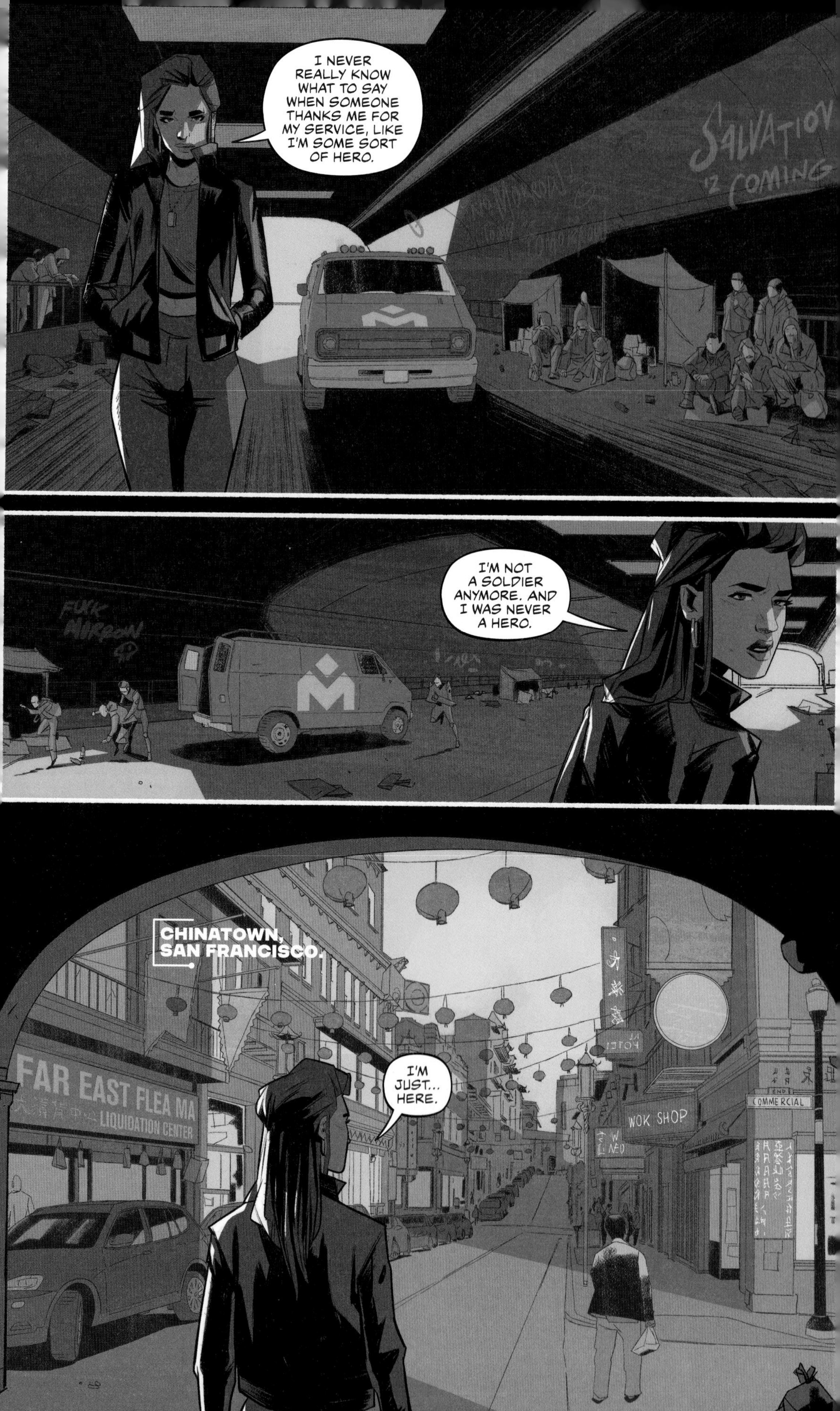

I NEVER REALLY KNOW WHAT TO SAY WHEN SOMEONE THANKS ME FOR MY SERVICE, LIKE I'M SOME SORT OF HERO.
I'M NOT A SOLDIER ANYMORE. AND I WAS NEVER A HERO.
CHINATOWN, SAN FRANCISCO.
FAR EAST FLEA MA
LIQUIDATION CENTER
I'M JUST... HERE.
WOK SHOP
COMMERCIAL

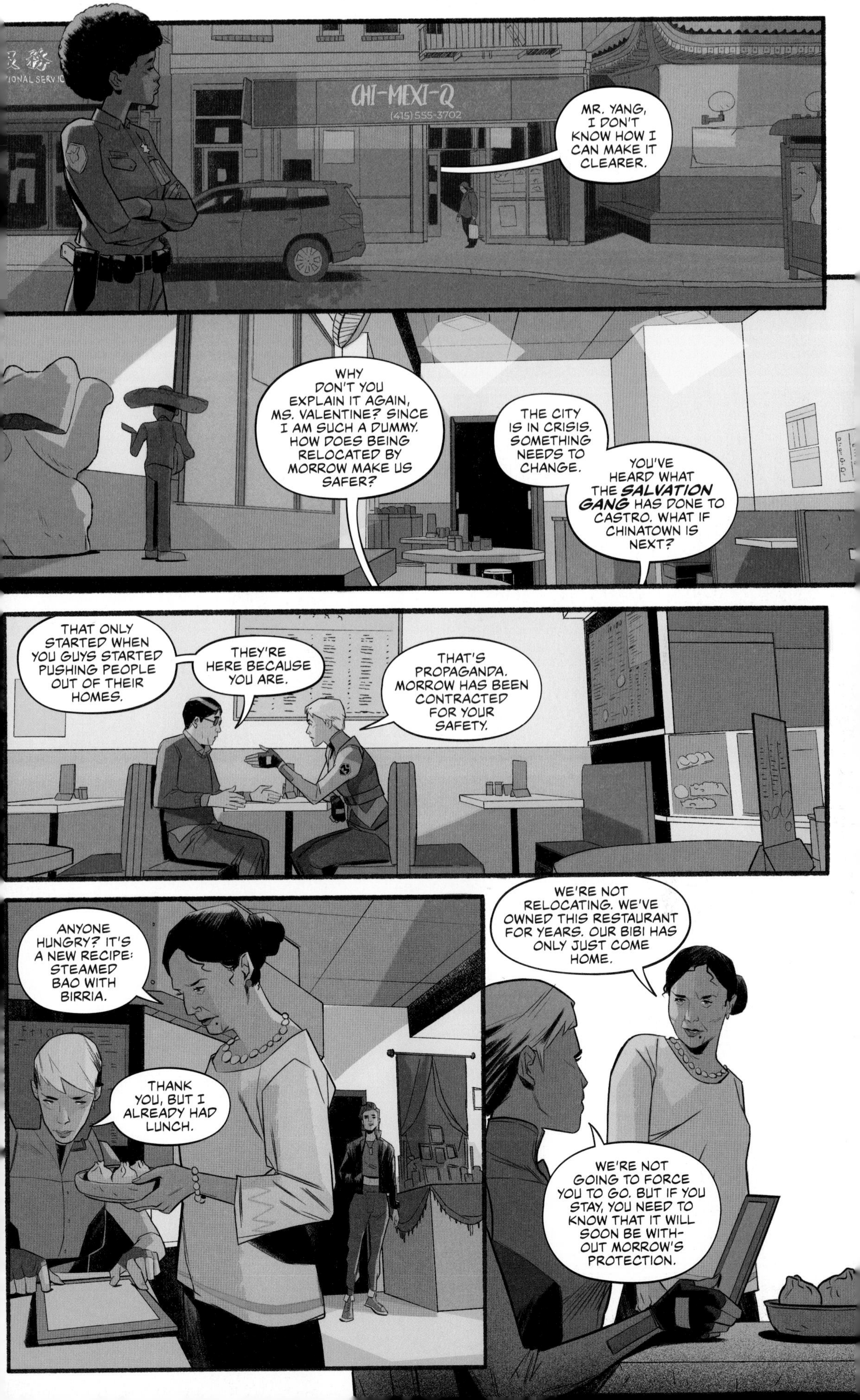

CHI-MEXI-Q
(415) 555-3702
MR. YANG, I DON'T KNOW HOW I CAN MAKE IT CLEARER.
WHY DON'T YOU EXPLAIN IT AGAIN, MS. VALENTINE? SINCE I AM SUCH A DUMMY. HOW DOES BEING RELOCATED BY MORROW MAKE US SAFER?
THE CITY IS IN CRISIS. SOMETHING NEEDS TO CHANGE.
YOU'VE HEARD WHAT THE SALVATION GANG HAS DONE TO CASTRO. WHAT IF CHINATOWN IS NEXT?
THEY'RE HERE BECAUSE YOU ARE.
THAT ONLY STARTED WHEN YOU GUYS STARTED PUSHING PEOPLE OUT OF THEIR HOMES.
THAT'S PROPAGANDA. MORROW HAS BEEN CONTRACTED FOR YOUR SAFETY.
ANYONE HUNGRY? IT'S A NEW RECIPE: STEAMED BAO WITH BIRRIA.
THANK YOU, BUT I ALREADY HAD LUNCH.
WE'RE NOT RELOCATING. WE'VE OWNED THIS RESTAURANT FOR YEARS. OUR BIBI HAS ONLY JUST COME HOME.
WE'RE NOT GOING TO FORCE YOU TO GO. BUT IF YOU STAY, YOU NEED TO KNOW THAT IT WILL SOON BE WITHOUT MORROW'S PROTECTION.

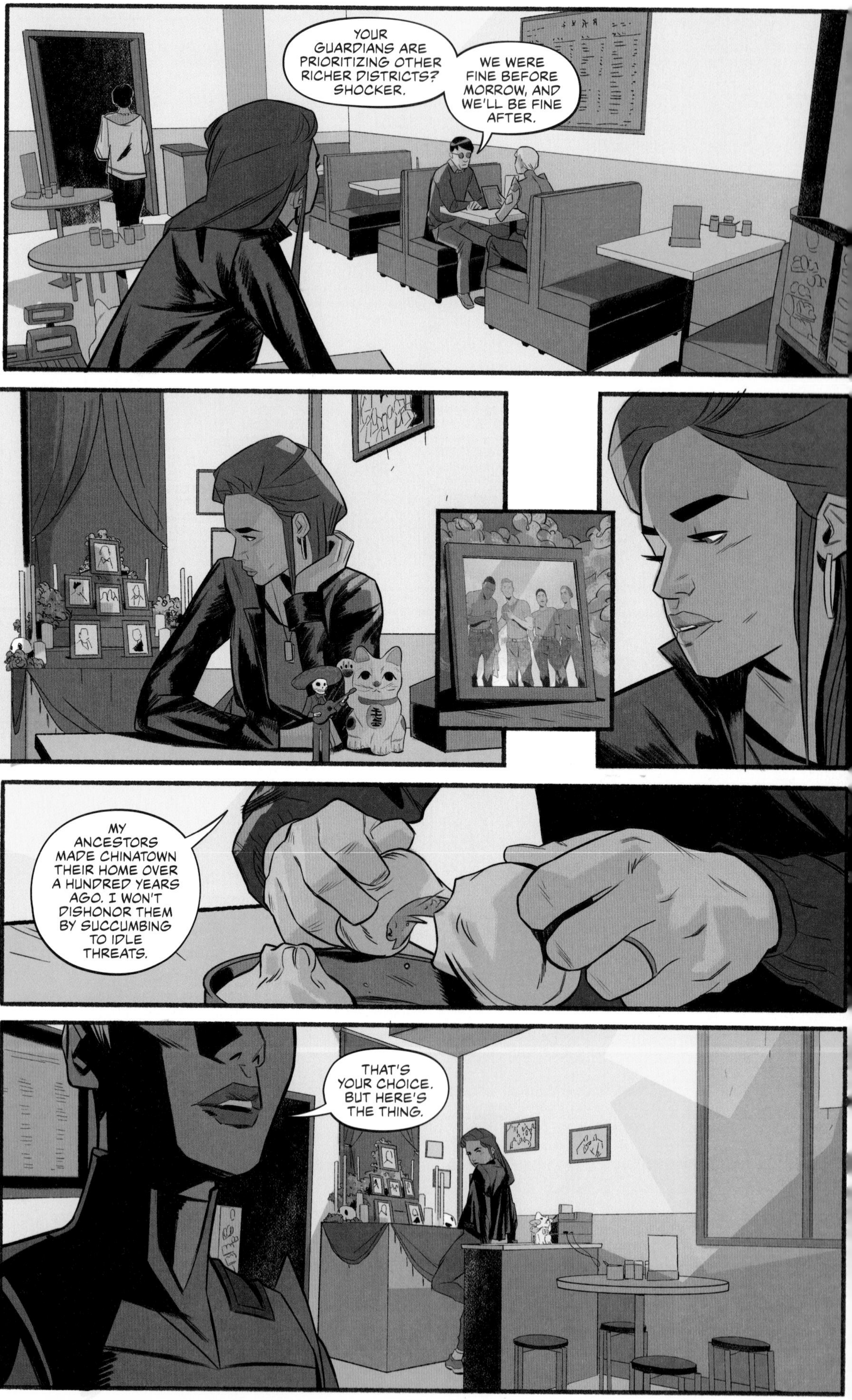
YOUR GUARDIANS ARE PRIORITIZING OTHER RICHER DISTRICTS? SHOCKER.
WE WERE FINE BEFORE MORROW, AND WE'LL BE FINE AFTER.
MY ANCESTORS MADE CHINATOWN THEIR HOME OVER A HUNDRED YEARS AGO. I WON'T DISHONOR THEM BY SUCCUMBING TO IDLE THREATS.
THAT'S YOUR CHOICE. BUT HERE'S THE THING.

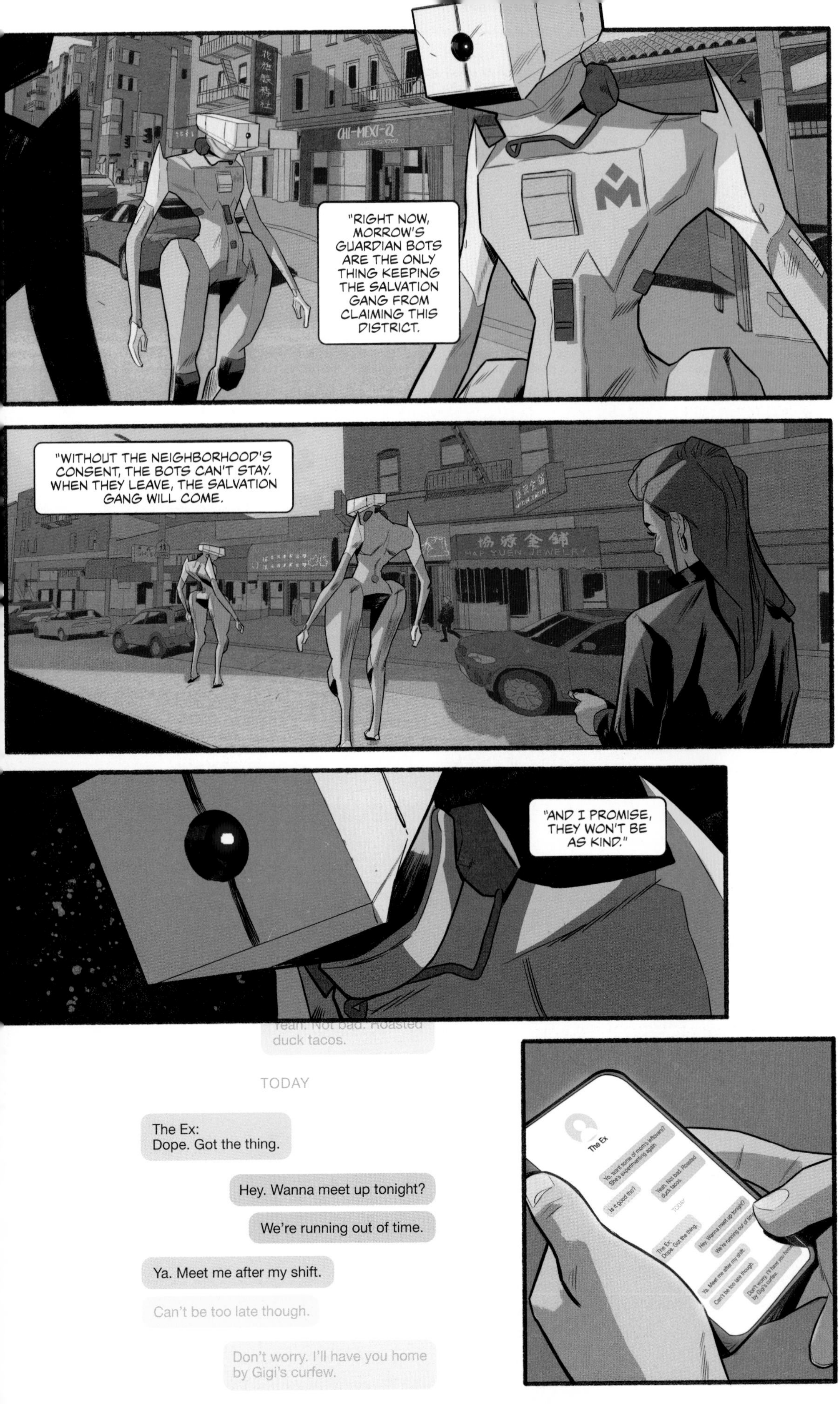
CHI-MEXI-Q
"RIGHT NOW, MORROW'S GUARDIAN BOTS ARE THE ONLY THING KEEPING THE SALVATION GANG FROM CLAIMING THIS DISTRICT.
"WITHOUT THE NEIGHBORHOOD'S CONSENT, THE BOTS CAN'T STAY. WHEN THEY LEAVE, THE SALVATION GANG WILL COME.
協源金舖
HAP YUEN JEWELRY
"AND I PROMISE, THEY WON'T BE AS KIND."
Yeah. Not bad. Roasted duck tacos.
TODAY
The Ex:
Dope. Got the thing.
Hey. Wanna meet up tonight?
We're running out of time.
Ya. Meet me after my shift.
Can't be too late though.
Don't worry. I'll have you home by Gigi's curfew.

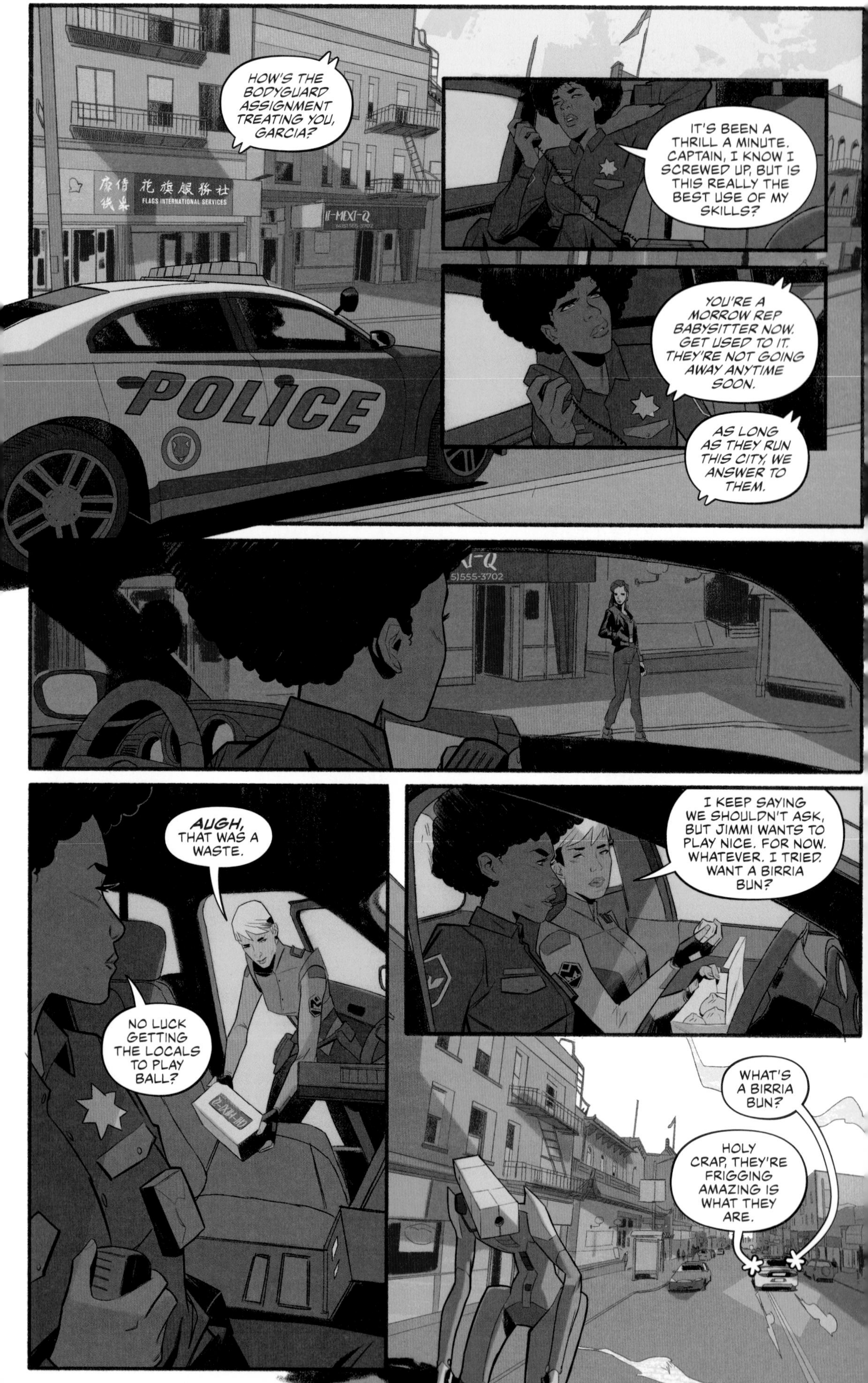
HOW'S THE BODYGUARD ASSIGNMENT TREATING YOU, GARCIA?
花旗服務社
FLAGS INTERNATIONAL SERVICES
POLICE
IT'S BEEN A THRILL A MINUTE. CAPTAIN, I KNOW I SCREWED UP, BUT IS THIS REALLY THE BEST USE OF MY SKILLS?
YOU'RE A MORROW REP BABYSITTER NOW. GET USED TO IT. THEY'RE NOT GOING AWAY ANYTIME SOON.
AS LONG AS THEY RUN THIS CITY, WE ANSWER TO THEM.
AUGH, THAT WAS A WASTE.
NO LUCK GETTING THE LOCALS TO PLAY BALL?
I KEEP SAYING WE SHOULDN'T ASK, BUT JIMMI WANTS TO PLAY NICE. FOR NOW. WHATEVER. I TRIED. WANT A BIRRIA BUN?
WHAT'S A BIRRIA BUN?
HOLY CRAP, THEY'RE FRIGGING AMAZING IS WHAT THEY ARE.

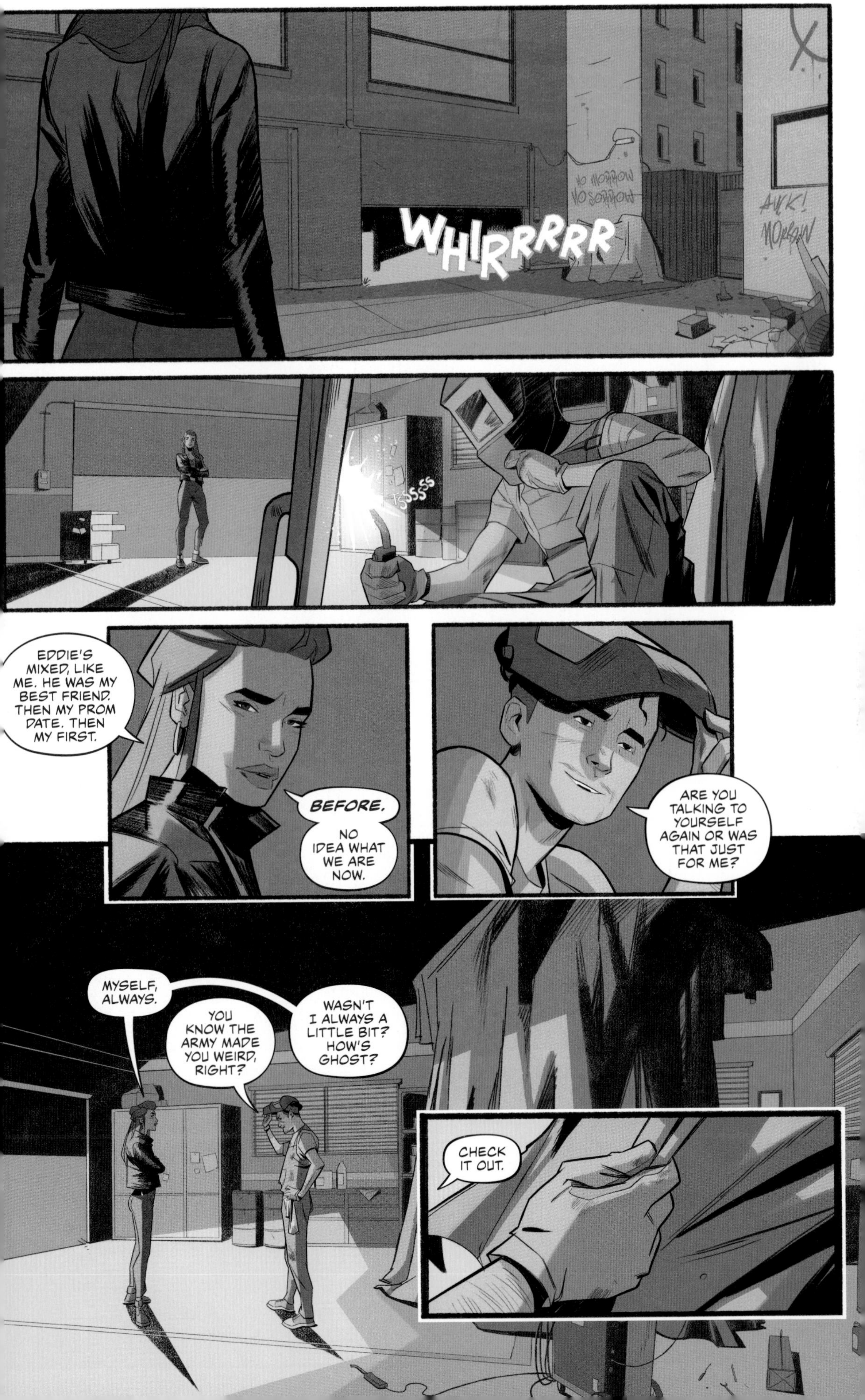
NO MORROW
NO SORROW
WHIRRRRR
AUK!
MORROW
TSSSSS
EDDIE'S MIXED, LIKE ME. HE WAS MY BEST FRIEND. THEN MY PROM DATE. THEN MY FIRST.
BEFORE.
NO IDEA WHAT WE ARE NOW.
ARE YOU TALKING TO YOURSELF AGAIN OR WAS THAT JUST FOR ME?
MYSELF, ALWAYS.
YOU KNOW THE ARMY MADE YOU WEIRD, RIGHT?
WASN'T I ALWAYS A LITTLE BIT? HOW'S GHOST?
CHECK IT OUT.

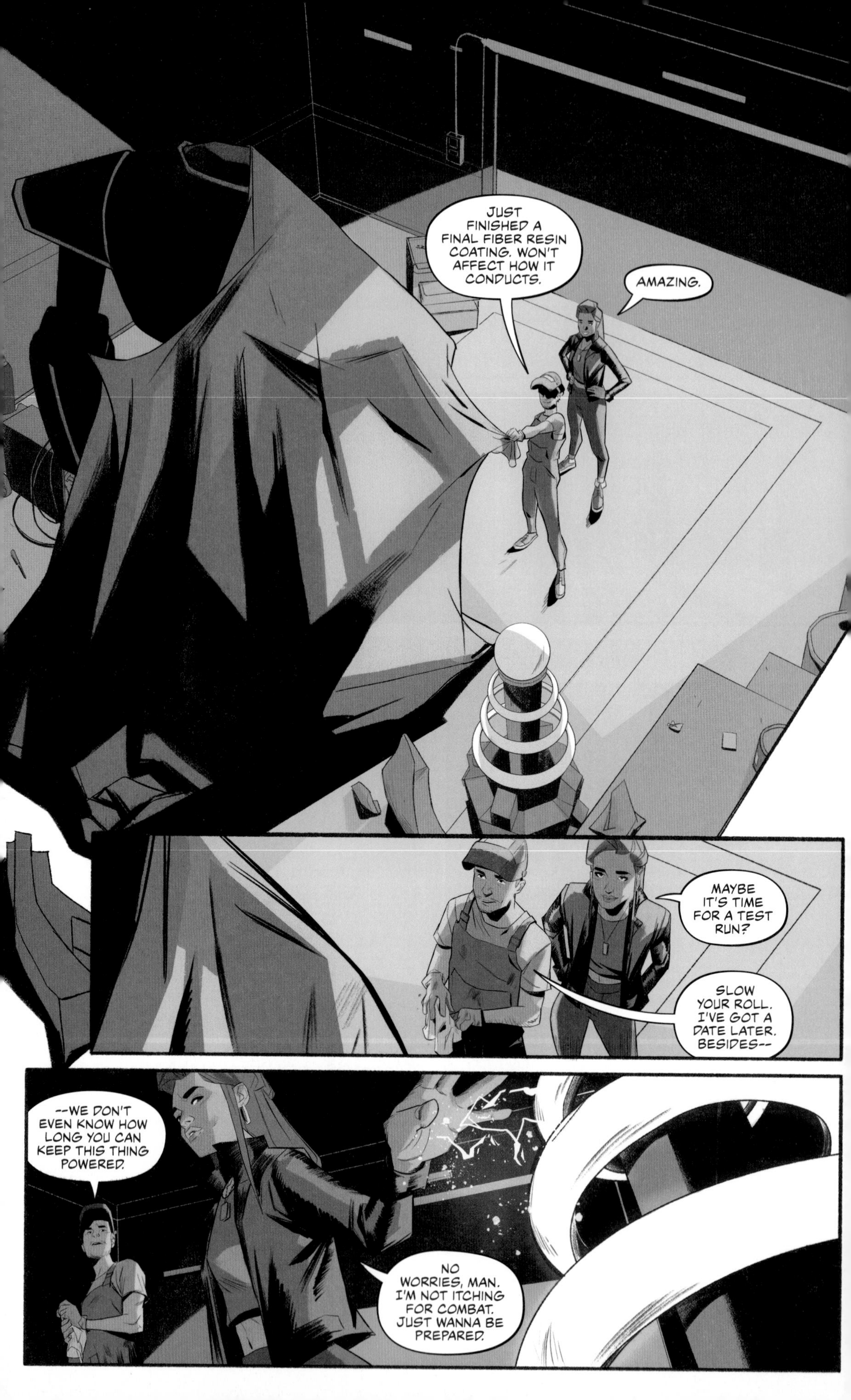
JUST FINISHED A FINAL FIBER RESIN COATING. WON'T AFFECT HOW IT CONDUCTS.
AMAZING.
MAYBE IT'S TIME FOR A TEST RUN?
SLOW YOUR ROLL. I'VE GOT A DATE LATER. BESIDES--
--WE DON'T EVEN KNOW HOW LONG YOU CAN KEEP THIS THING POWERED.
NO WORRIES, MAN. I'M NOT ITCHING FOR COMBAT. JUST WANNA BE PREPARED.

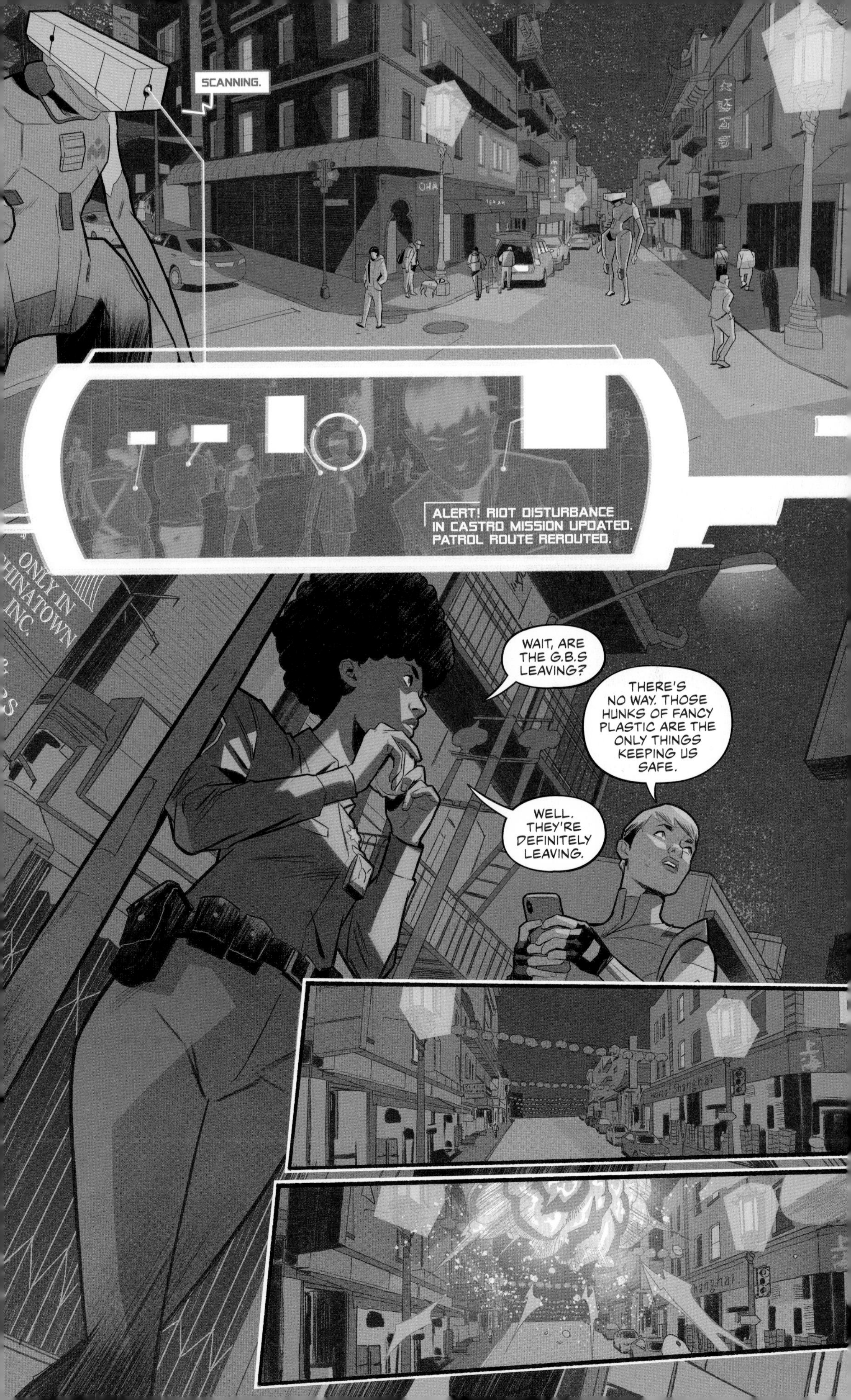
SCANNING.
ALERT! RIOT DISTURBANCE IN CASTRO MISSION UPDATED. PATROL ROUTE REROUTED.
WAIT, ARE THE G.B.S LEAVING?
THERE'S NO WAY. THOSE HUNKS OF FANCY PLASTIC ARE THE ONLY THINGS KEEPING US SAFE.
WELL. THEY'RE DEFINITELY LEAVING.

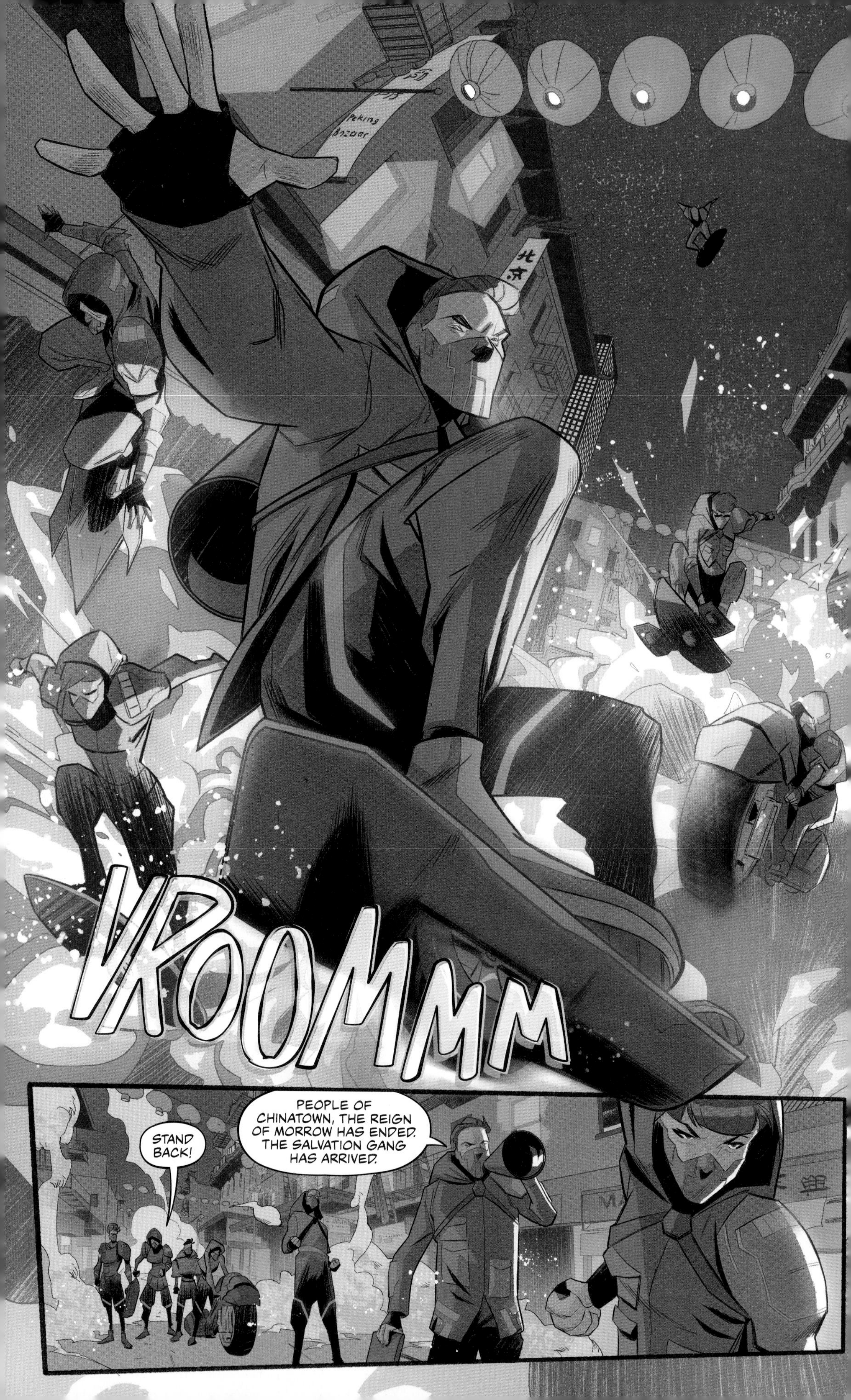
Peking Bazaar
北京
VROOMMM
STAND BACK!
PEOPLE OF CHINATOWN, THE REIGN OF MORROW HAS ENDED. THE SALVATION GANG HAS ARRIVED.

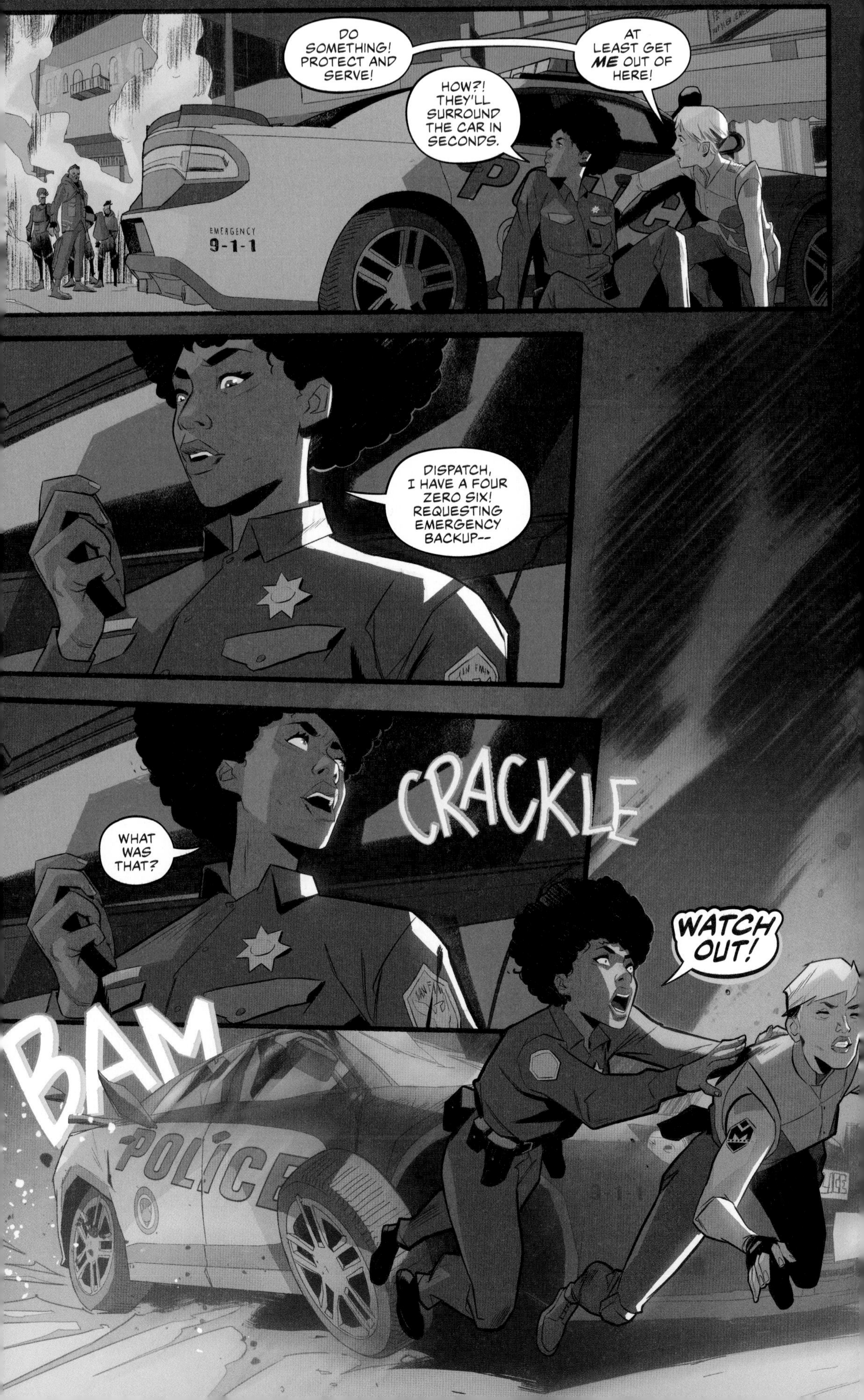

DO SOMETHING! PROTECT AND SERVE!
AT LEAST GET ME OUT OF HERE!
HOW?! THEY'LL SURROUND THE CAR IN SECONDS.
EMERGENCY 9-1-1
DISPATCH, I HAVE A FOUR ZERO SIX! REQUESTING EMERGENCY BACKUP--
CRACKLE
WHAT WAS THAT?
WATCH OUT!
BAM
POLICE

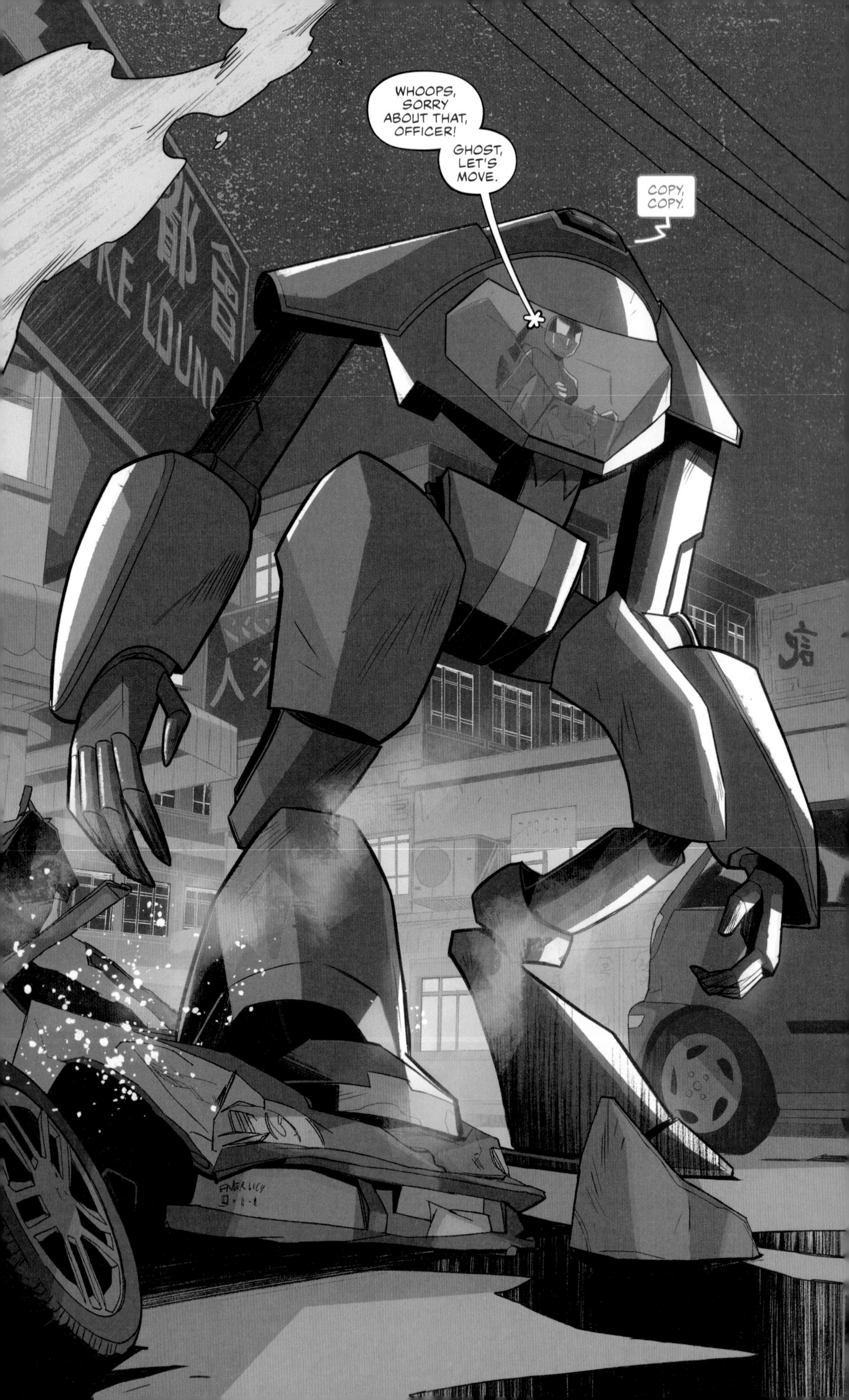
WHOOPS, SORRY ABOUT THAT, OFFICER!
GHOST, LET'S MOVE.
COPY, COPY.

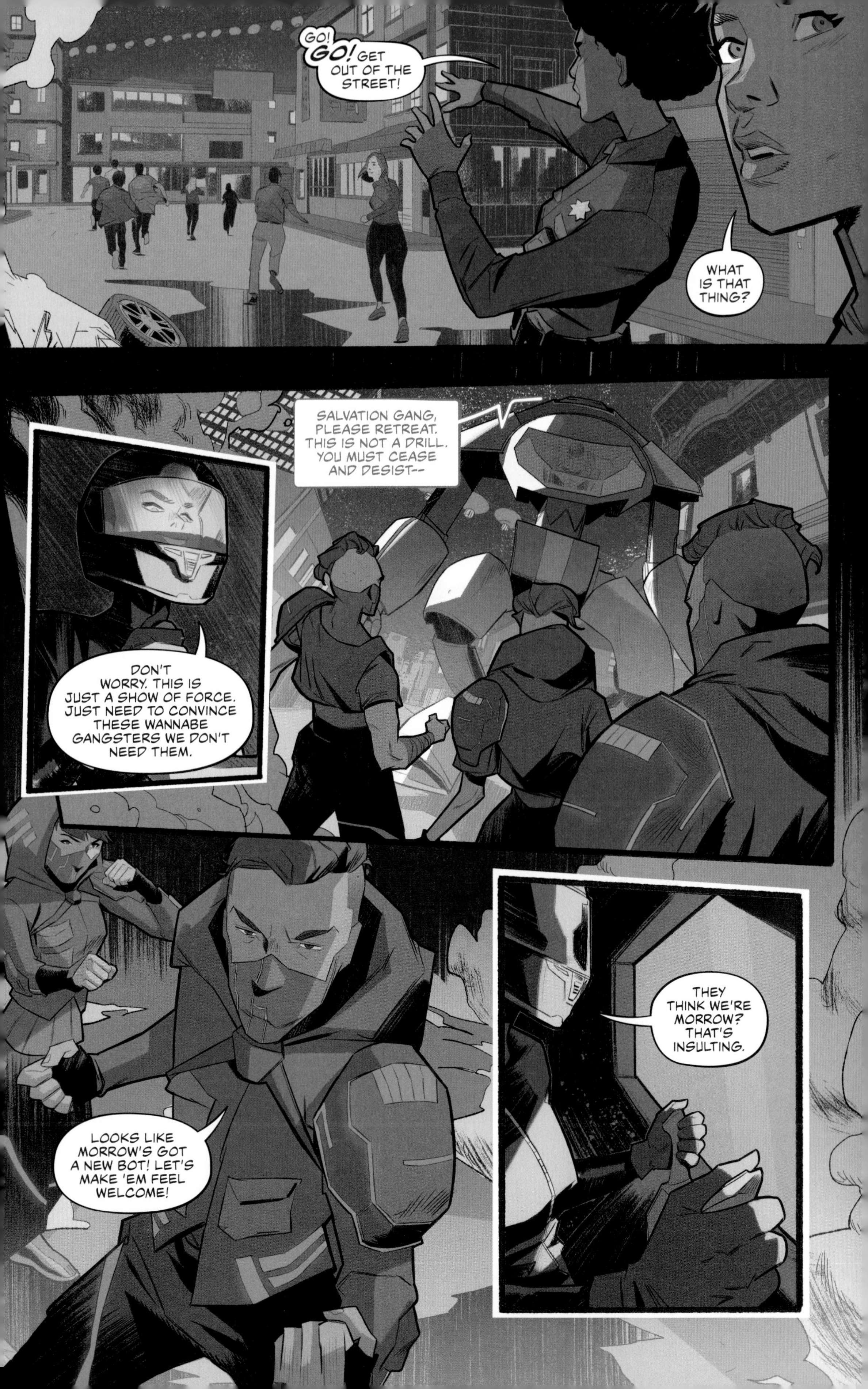
GO! GO! GET OUT OF THE STREET!
WHAT IS THAT THING?
SALVATION GANG, PLEASE RETREAT. THIS IS NOT A DRILL. YOU MUST CEASE AND DESIST--
DON'T WORRY. THIS IS JUST A SHOW OF FORCE. JUST NEED TO CONVINCE THESE WANNABE GANGSTERS WE DON'T NEED THEM.
LOOKS LIKE MORROW'S GOT A NEW BOT! LET'S MAKE 'EM FEEL WELCOME!
THEY THINK WE'RE MORROW? THAT'S INSULTING.

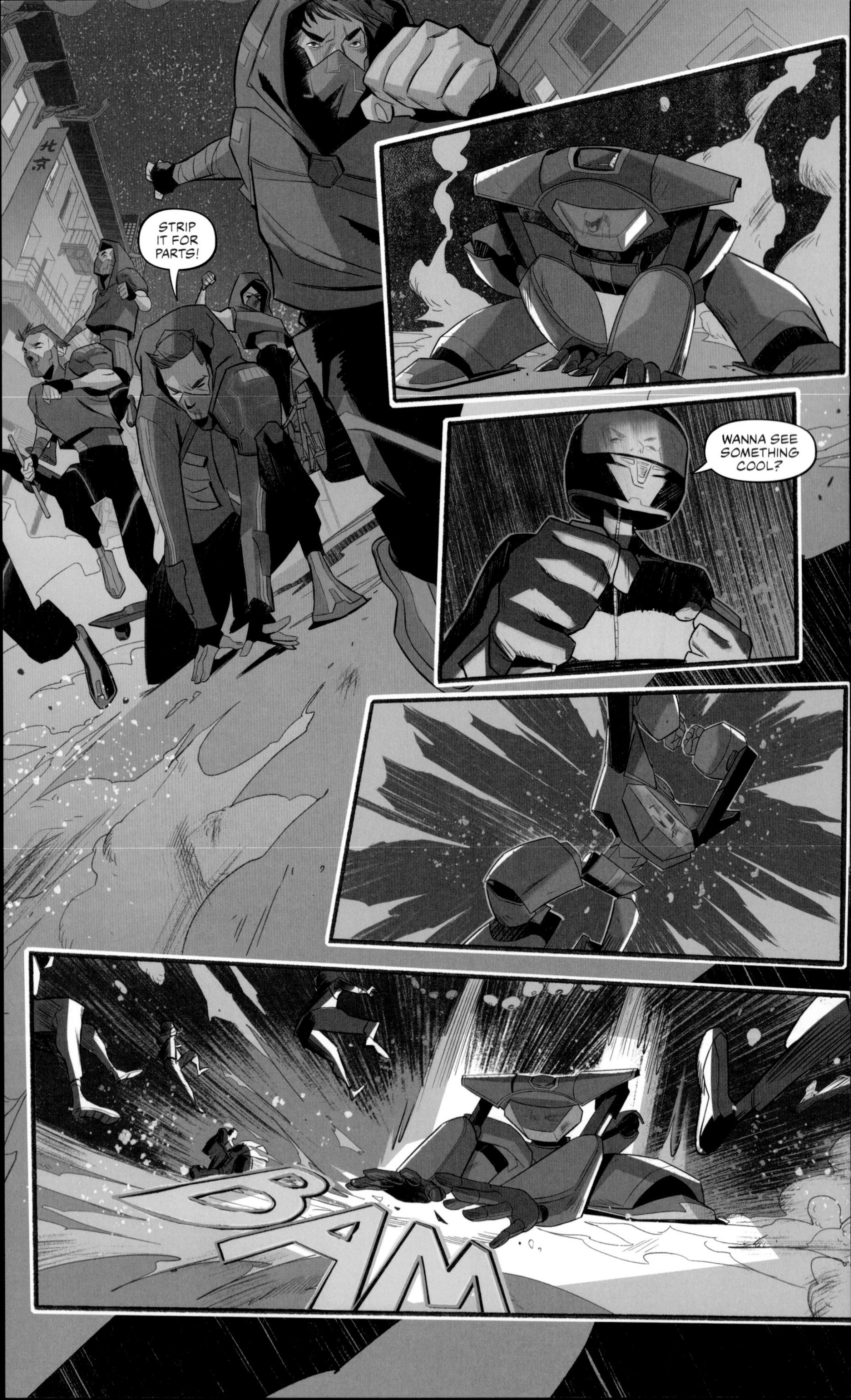
STRIP IT FOR PARTS!
WANNA SEE SOMETHING COOL?
BAM

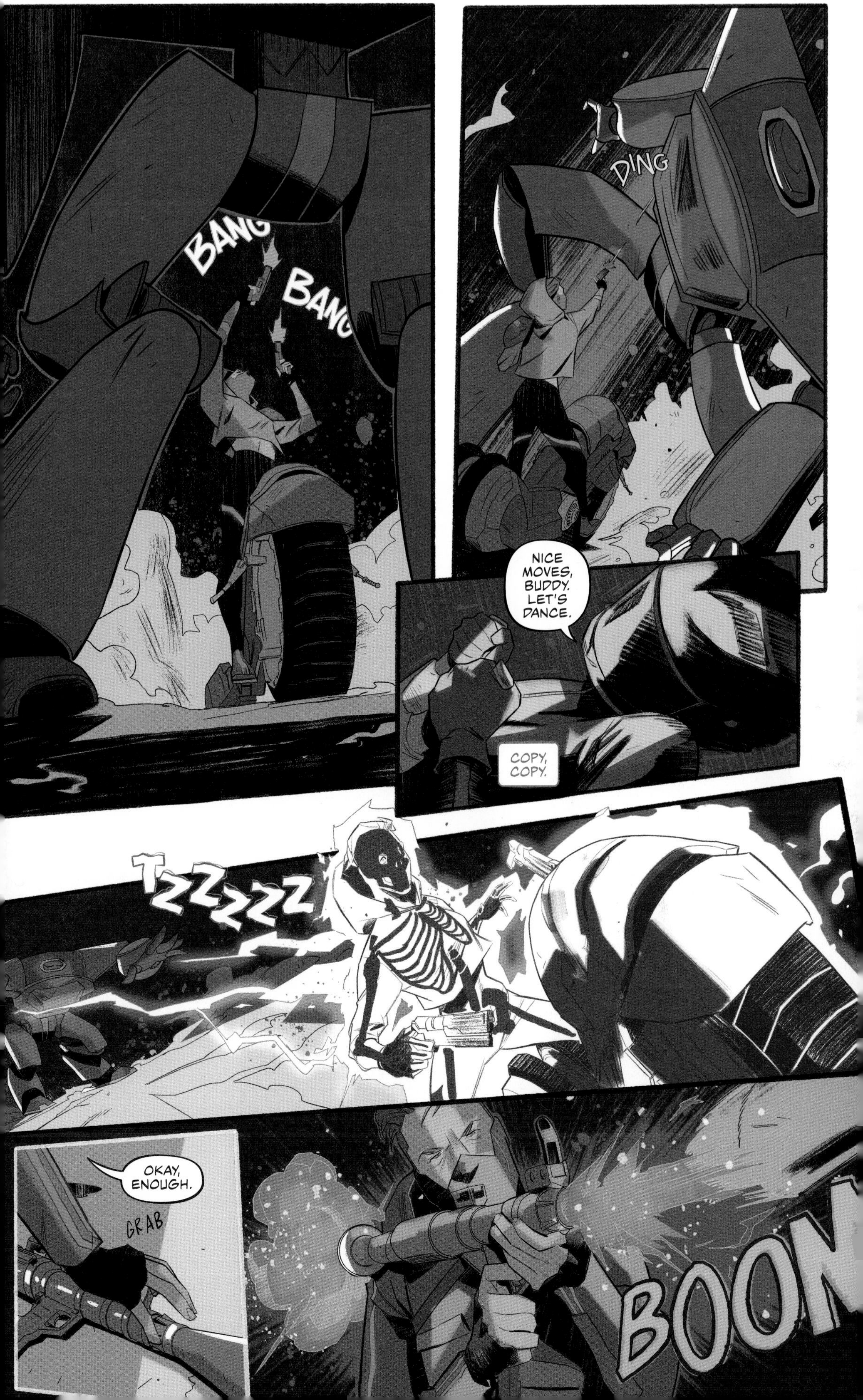
BANG
BANG
DING
NICE MOVES, BUDDY. LET'S DANCE.
COPY, COPY.
TZZZZZZ
OKAY, ENOUGH.
GRAB
BOOM

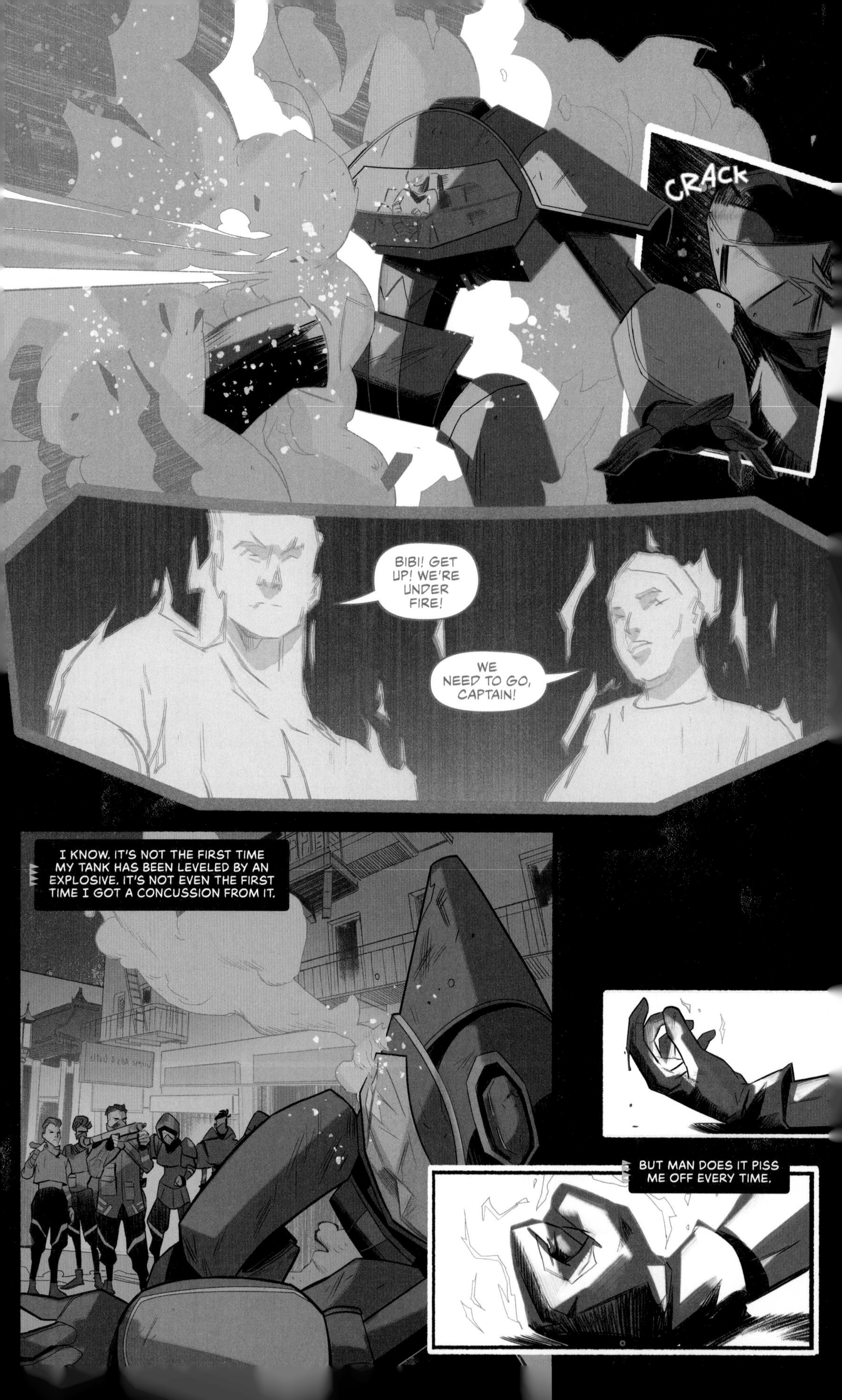
CRACK
BIBI! GET UP! WE'RE UNDER FIRE!
WE NEED TO GO, CAPTAIN!
I KNOW. IT'S NOT THE FIRST TIME MY TANK HAS BEEN LEVELED BY AN EXPLOSIVE. IT'S NOT EVEN THE FIRST TIME I GOT A CONCUSSION FROM IT.
BUT MAN DOES IT PISS ME OFF EVERY TIME.

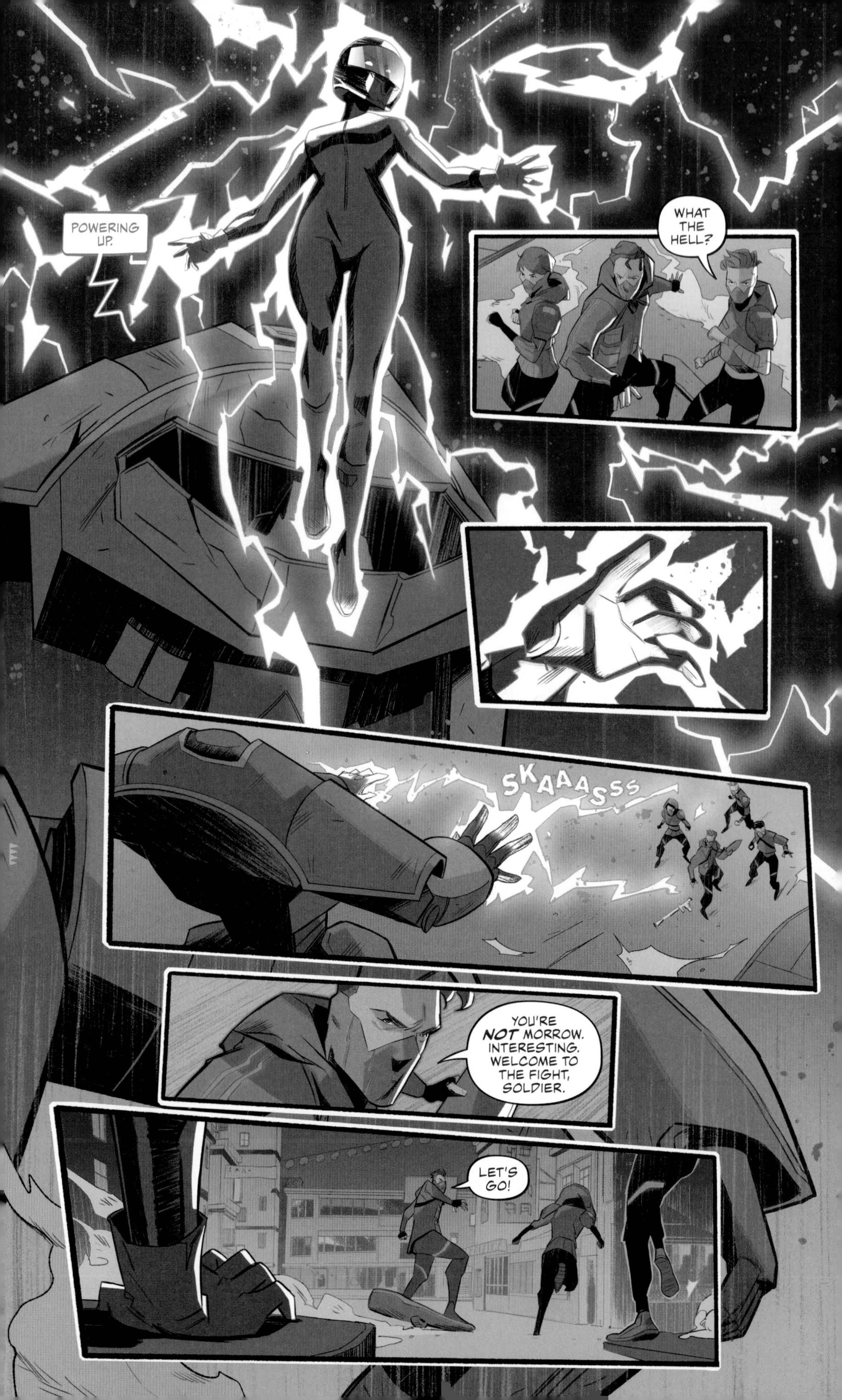
POWERING UP.
WHAT THE HELL?
SKAAASSS
YOU'RE **NOT** MORROW. INTERESTING. WELCOME TO THE FIGHT, SOLDIER.
LET'S GO!

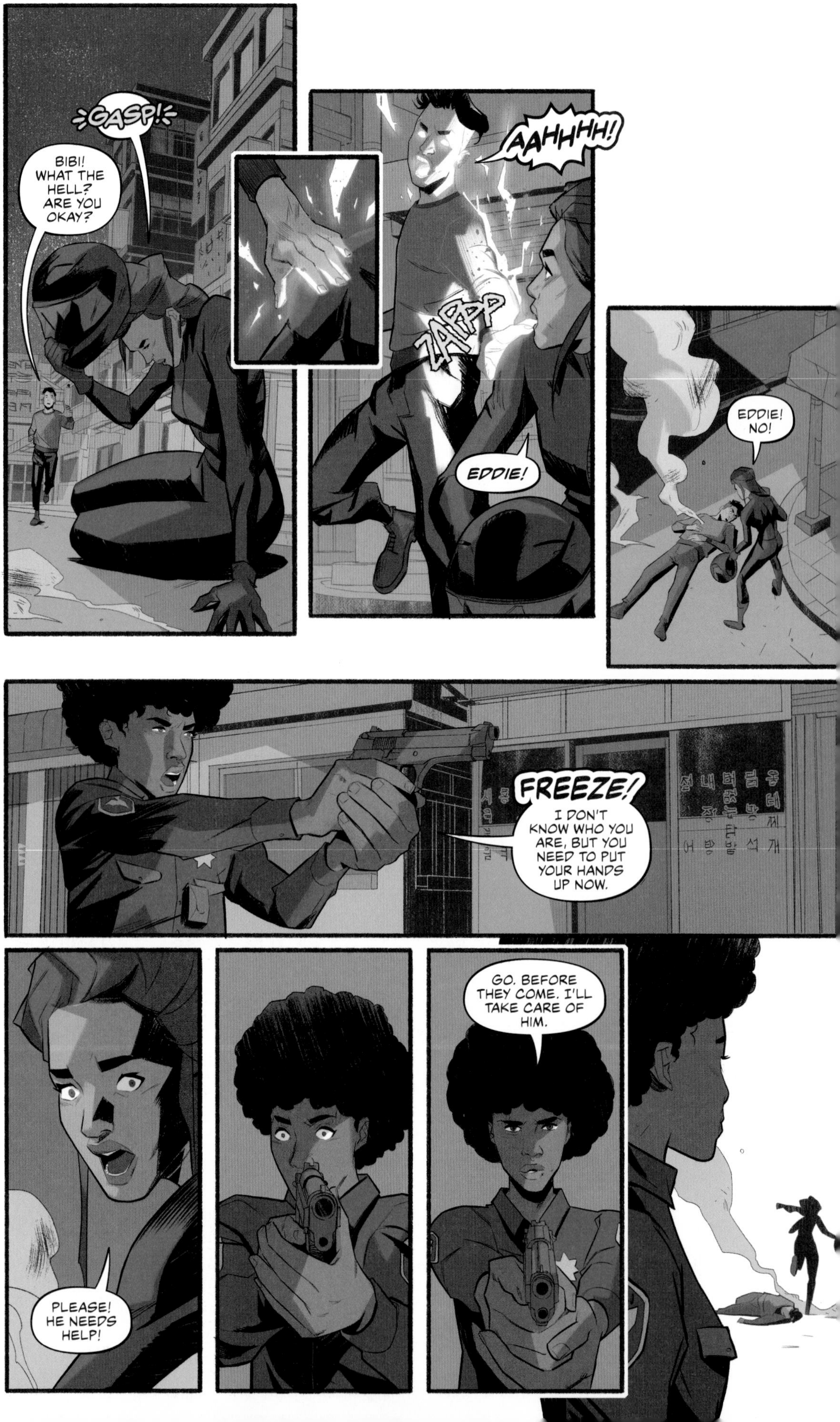
BIBI! WHAT THE HELL? ARE YOU OKAY?
GASP!
AAHHHH!
ZAPPP
EDDIE!
EDDIE! NO!
FREEZE!
I DON'T KNOW WHO YOU ARE, BUT YOU NEED TO PUT YOUR HANDS UP NOW.
PLEASE! HE NEEDS HELP!
GO. BEFORE THEY COME. I'LL TAKE CARE OF HIM.

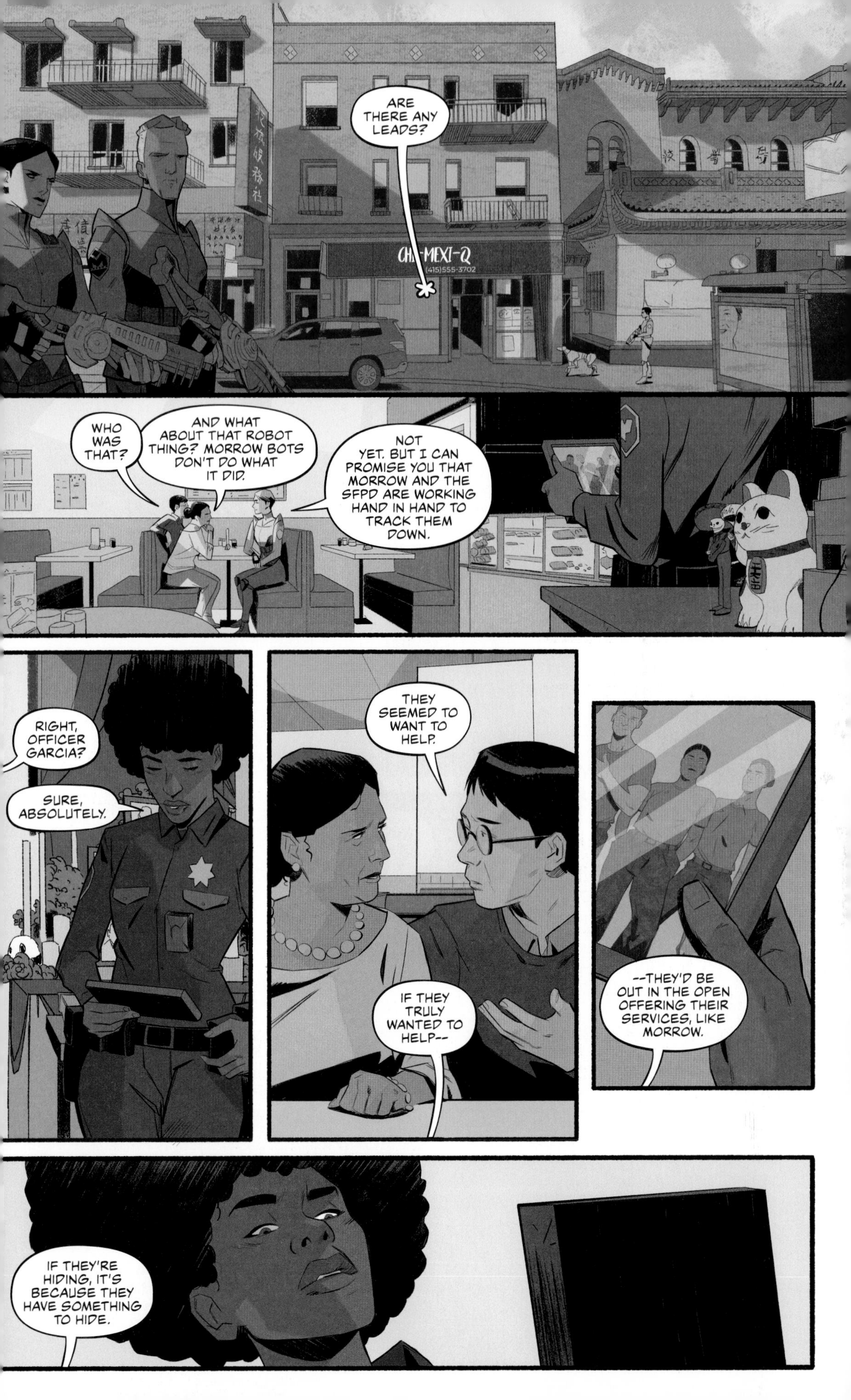

ARE THERE ANY LEADS?
CHI-MEXI-Q
(415)555-3702
WHO WAS THAT?
AND WHAT ABOUT THAT ROBOT THING? MORROW BOTS DON'T DO WHAT IT DID.
NOT YET. BUT I CAN PROMISE YOU THAT MORROW AND THE SFPD ARE WORKING HAND IN HAND TO TRACK THEM DOWN.
RIGHT, OFFICER GARCIA?
SURE, ABSOLUTELY.
THEY SEEMED TO WANT TO HELP.
IF THEY TRULY WANTED TO HELP--
--THEY'D BE OUT IN THE OPEN OFFERING THEIR SERVICES, LIKE MORROW.
IF THEY'RE HIDING, IT'S BECAUSE THEY HAVE SOMETHING TO HIDE.

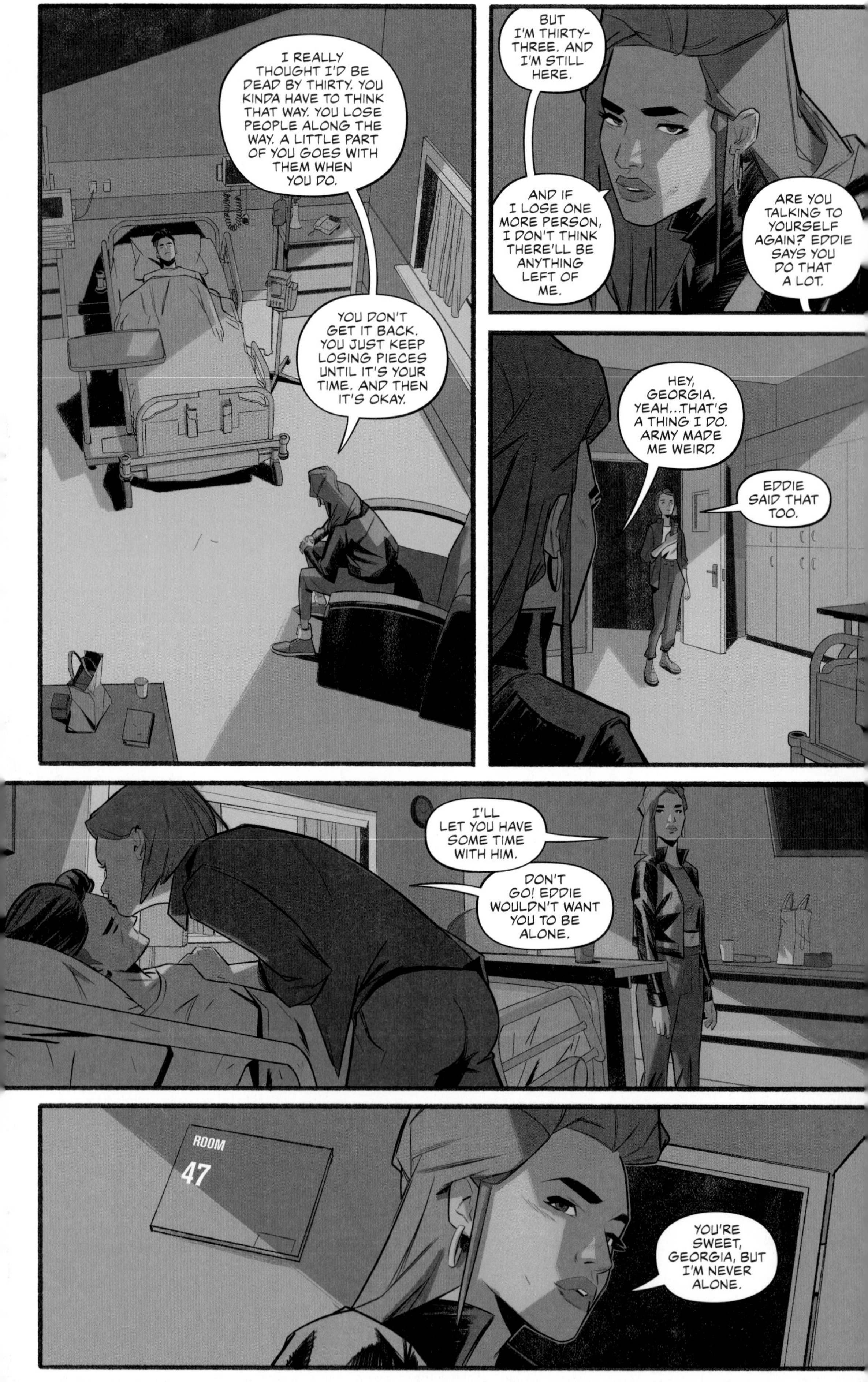
I REALLY THOUGHT I'D BE DEAD BY THIRTY. YOU KINDA HAVE TO THINK THAT WAY. YOU LOSE PEOPLE ALONG THE WAY. A LITTLE PART OF YOU GOES WITH THEM WHEN YOU DO.
YOU DON'T GET IT BACK. YOU JUST KEEP LOSING PIECES UNTIL IT'S YOUR TIME. AND THEN IT'S OKAY.
BUT I'M THIRTY-THREE. AND I'M STILL HERE.
AND IF I LOSE ONE MORE PERSON, I DON'T THINK THERE'LL BE ANYTHING LEFT OF ME.
ARE YOU TALKING TO YOURSELF AGAIN? EDDIE SAYS YOU DO THAT A LOT.
HEY, GEORGIA. YEAH...THAT'S A THING I DO. ARMY MADE ME WEIRD.
EDDIE SAID THAT TOO.
I'LL LET YOU HAVE SOME TIME WITH HIM.
DON'T GO! EDDIE WOULDN'T WANT YOU TO BE ALONE.
ROOM
47
YOU'RE SWEET, GEORGIA, BUT I'M NEVER ALONE.

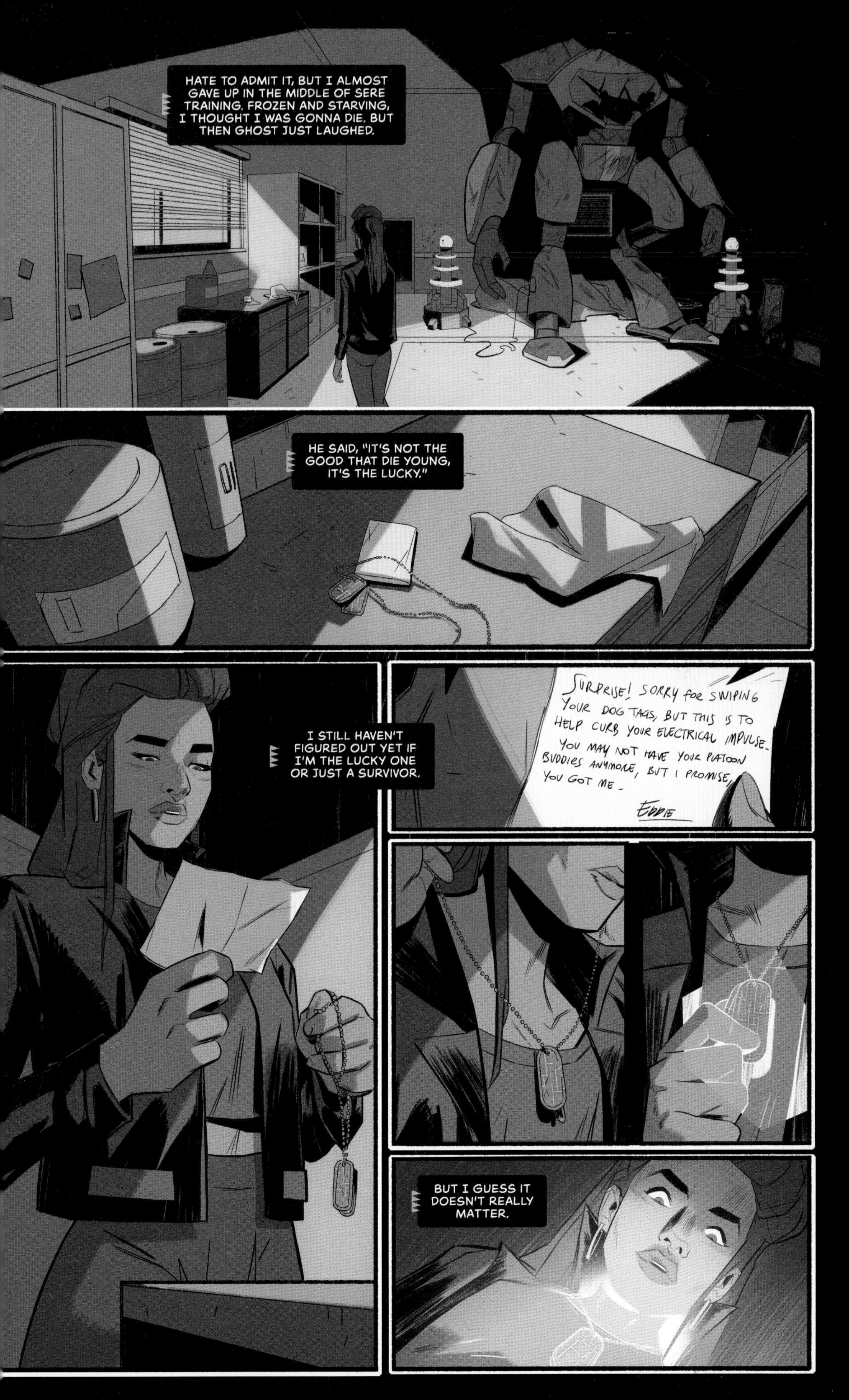
HATE TO ADMIT IT, BUT I ALMOST GAVE UP IN THE MIDDLE OF SERE TRAINING. FROZEN AND STARVING, I THOUGHT I WAS GONNA DIE. BUT THEN GHOST JUST LAUGHED.
HE SAID, "IT'S NOT THE GOOD THAT DIE YOUNG, IT'S THE LUCKY."
I STILL HAVEN'T FIGURED OUT YET IF I'M THE LUCKY ONE OR JUST A SURVIVOR.
SURPRISE! SORRY FOR SWIPING YOUR DOG TAGS, BUT THIS IS TO HELP CURB YOUR ELECTRICAL IMPULSE. YOU MAY NOT HAVE YOUR PLATOON BUDDIES ANYMORE, BUT I PROMISE, YOU GOT ME -
EDDIE
BUT I GUESS IT DOESN'T REALLY MATTER.

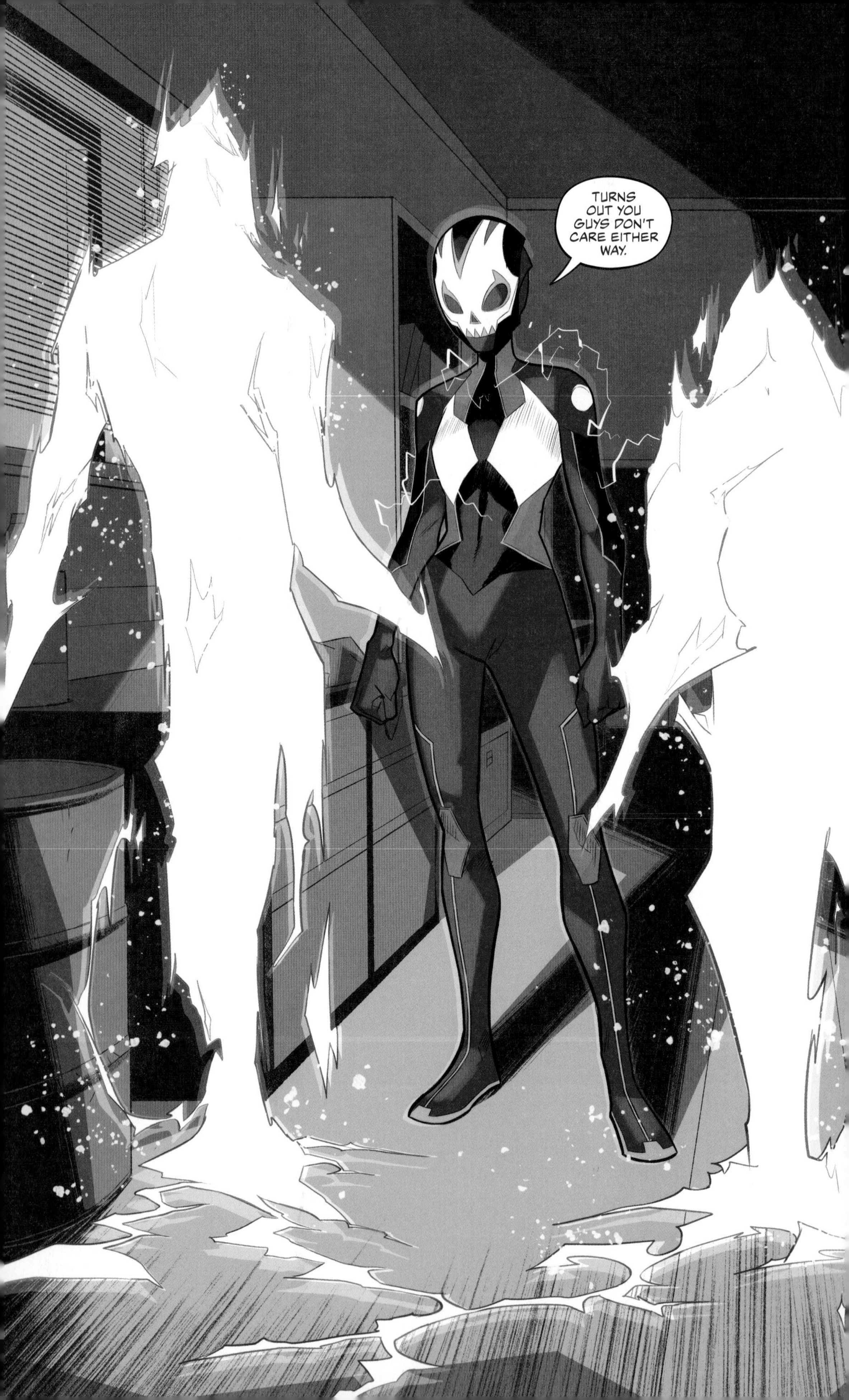
TURNS OUT YOU GUYS DON'T CARE EITHER WAY.

```
TERMINAL                                                    _  ×
─────────────────────────────────────────────────────────────────

GHOST:~ admin$ SingleIssueProfiler
Issue:
    No.: 002
    Title: This is Trauma.
```

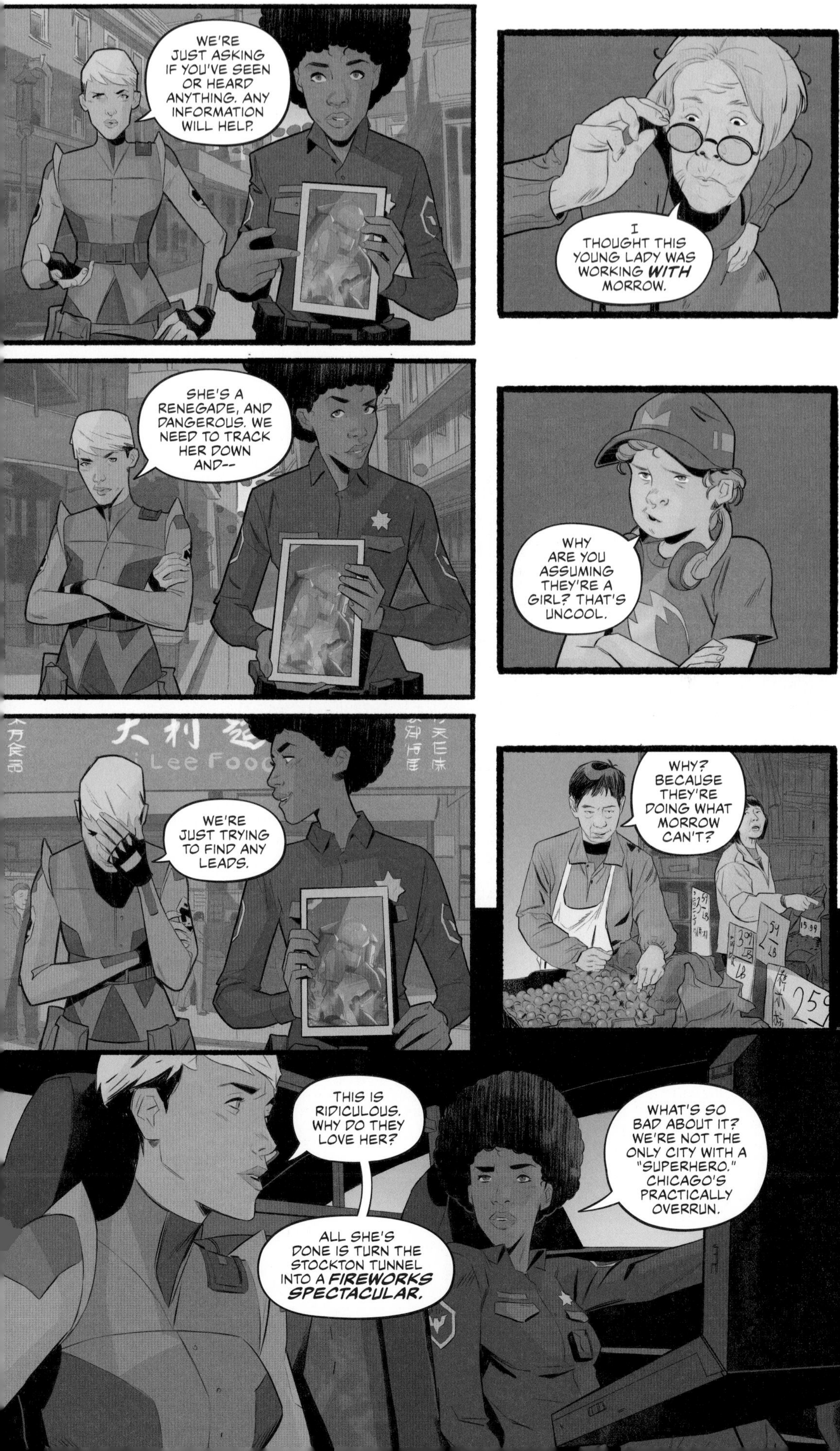
WE'RE JUST ASKING IF YOU'VE SEEN OR HEARD ANYTHING. ANY INFORMATION WILL HELP.
I THOUGHT THIS YOUNG LADY WAS WORKING **WITH** MORROW.
SHE'S A RENEGADE, AND DANGEROUS. WE NEED TO TRACK HER DOWN AND--
WHY ARE YOU ASSUMING THEY'RE A GIRL? THAT'S UNCOOL.
WE'RE JUST TRYING TO FIND ANY LEADS.
WHY? BECAUSE THEY'RE DOING WHAT MORROW CAN'T?
THIS IS RIDICULOUS. WHY DO THEY LOVE HER?
ALL SHE'S DONE IS TURN THE STOCKTON TUNNEL INTO A ***FIREWORKS SPECTACULAR.***
WHAT'S SO BAD ABOUT IT? WE'RE NOT THE ONLY CITY WITH A "SUPERHERO." CHICAGO'S PRACTICALLY OVERRUN.

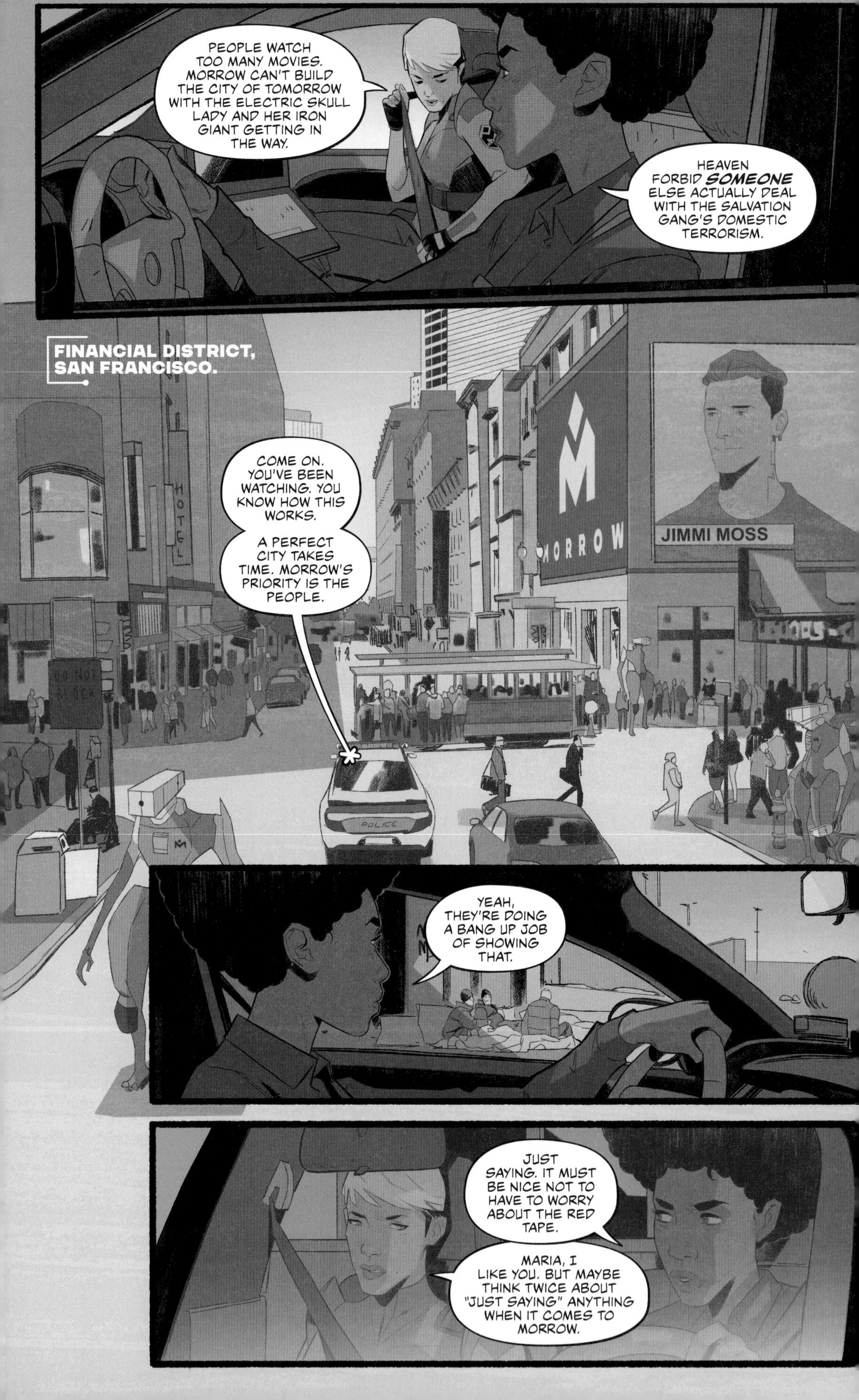
PEOPLE WATCH TOO MANY MOVIES. MORROW CAN'T BUILD THE CITY OF TOMORROW WITH THE ELECTRIC SKULL LADY AND HER IRON GIANT GETTING IN THE WAY.
HEAVEN FORBID *SOMEONE* ELSE ACTUALLY DEAL WITH THE SALVATION GANG'S DOMESTIC TERRORISM.
FINANCIAL DISTRICT, SAN FRANCISCO.
COME ON. YOU'VE BEEN WATCHING. YOU KNOW HOW THIS WORKS.
A PERFECT CITY TAKES TIME. MORROW'S PRIORITY IS THE PEOPLE.
MORROW
JIMMI MOSS
HOTEL
POLICE
YEAH, THEY'RE DOING A BANG UP JOB OF SHOWING THAT.
JUST SAYING. IT MUST BE NICE NOT TO HAVE TO WORRY ABOUT THE RED TAPE.
MARIA, I LIKE YOU. BUT MAYBE THINK TWICE ABOUT "JUST SAYING" ANYTHING WHEN IT COMES TO MORROW.

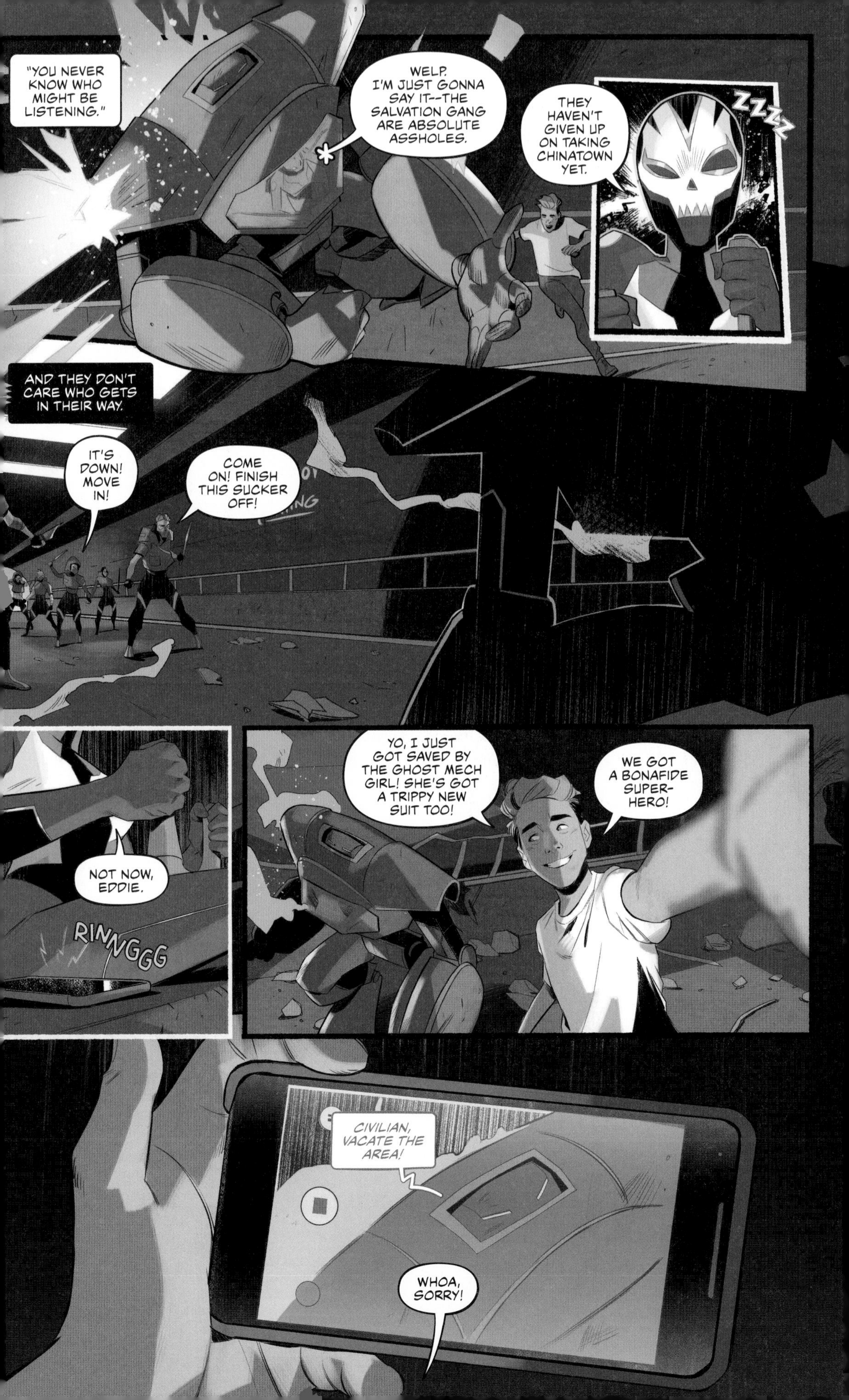
"YOU NEVER KNOW WHO MIGHT BE LISTENING."
WELP. I'M JUST GONNA SAY IT--THE SALVATION GANG ARE ABSOLUTE ASSHOLES.
THEY HAVEN'T GIVEN UP ON TAKING CHINATOWN YET.
ZZZZ
AND THEY DON'T CARE WHO GETS IN THEIR WAY.
IT'S DOWN! MOVE IN!
COME ON! FINISH THIS SUCKER OFF!
NOT NOW, EDDIE.
RINNGGG
YO, I JUST GOT SAVED BY THE GHOST MECH GIRL! SHE'S GOT A TRIPPY NEW SUIT TOO!
WE GOT A BONAFIDE SUPER-HERO!
CIVILIAN, VACATE THE AREA!
WHOA, SORRY!

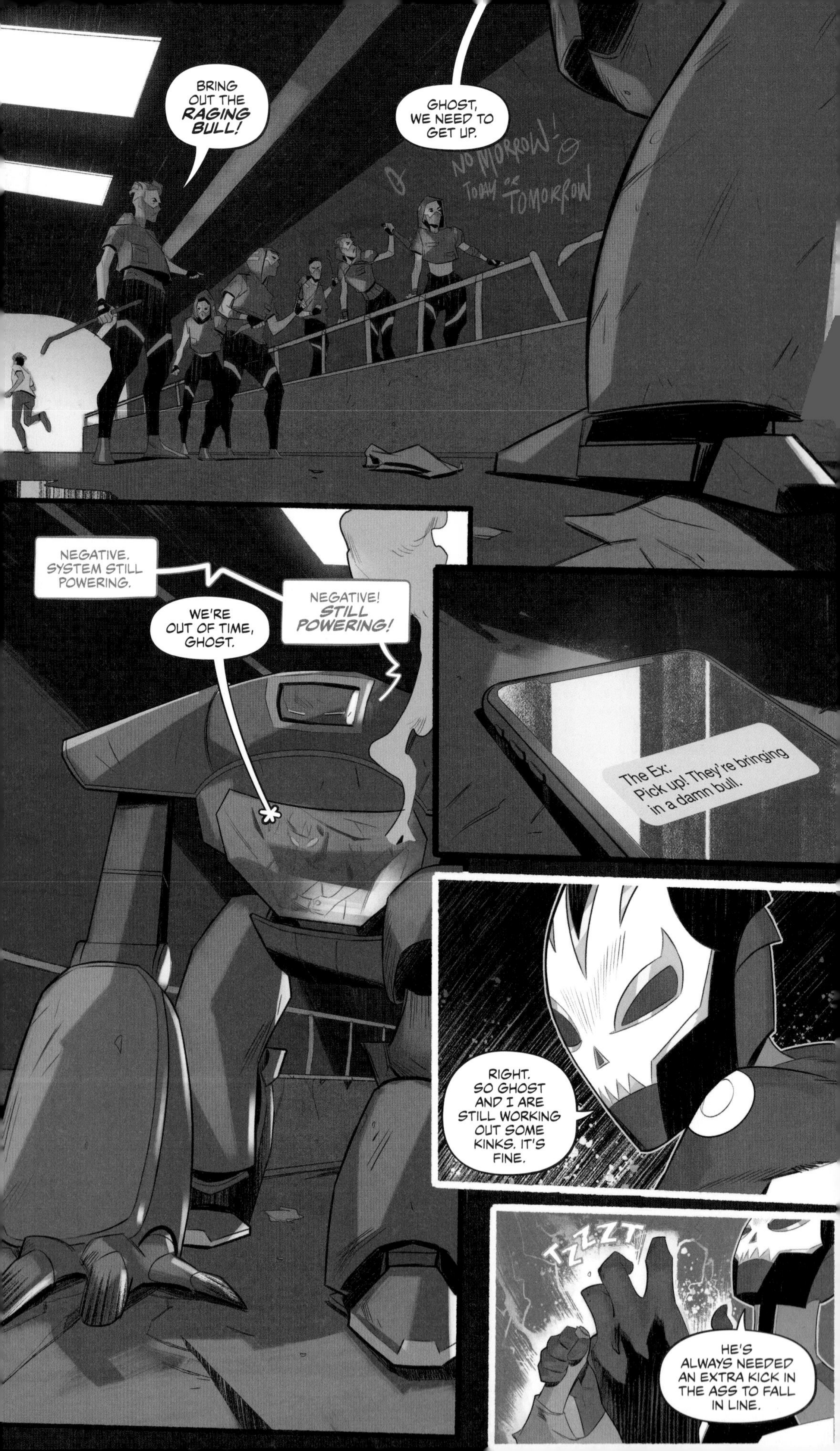
BRING OUT THE RAGING BULL!
GHOST, WE NEED TO GET UP.
NO MORROW!
TODAY OR TOMORROW
NEGATIVE. SYSTEM STILL POWERING.
WE'RE OUT OF TIME, GHOST.
NEGATIVE! STILL POWERING!
The Ex:
Pick up! They're bringing in a damn bull.
RIGHT. SO GHOST AND I ARE STILL WORKING OUT SOME KINKS. IT'S FINE.
TZZZT
HE'S ALWAYS NEEDED AN EXTRA KICK IN THE ASS TO FALL IN LINE.

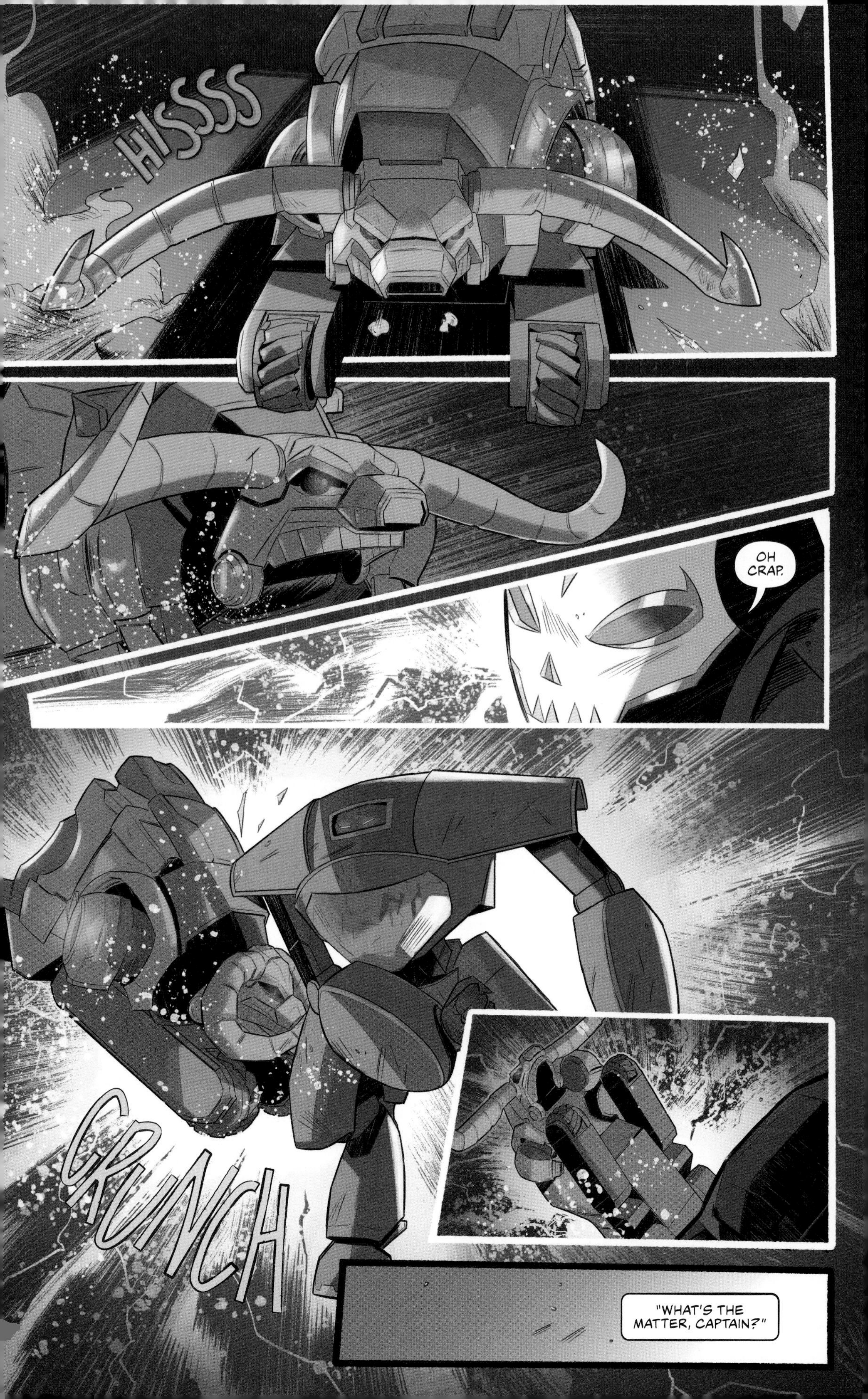
HISSSS
OH CRAP.
CRUNCH
"WHAT'S THE MATTER, CAPTAIN?"

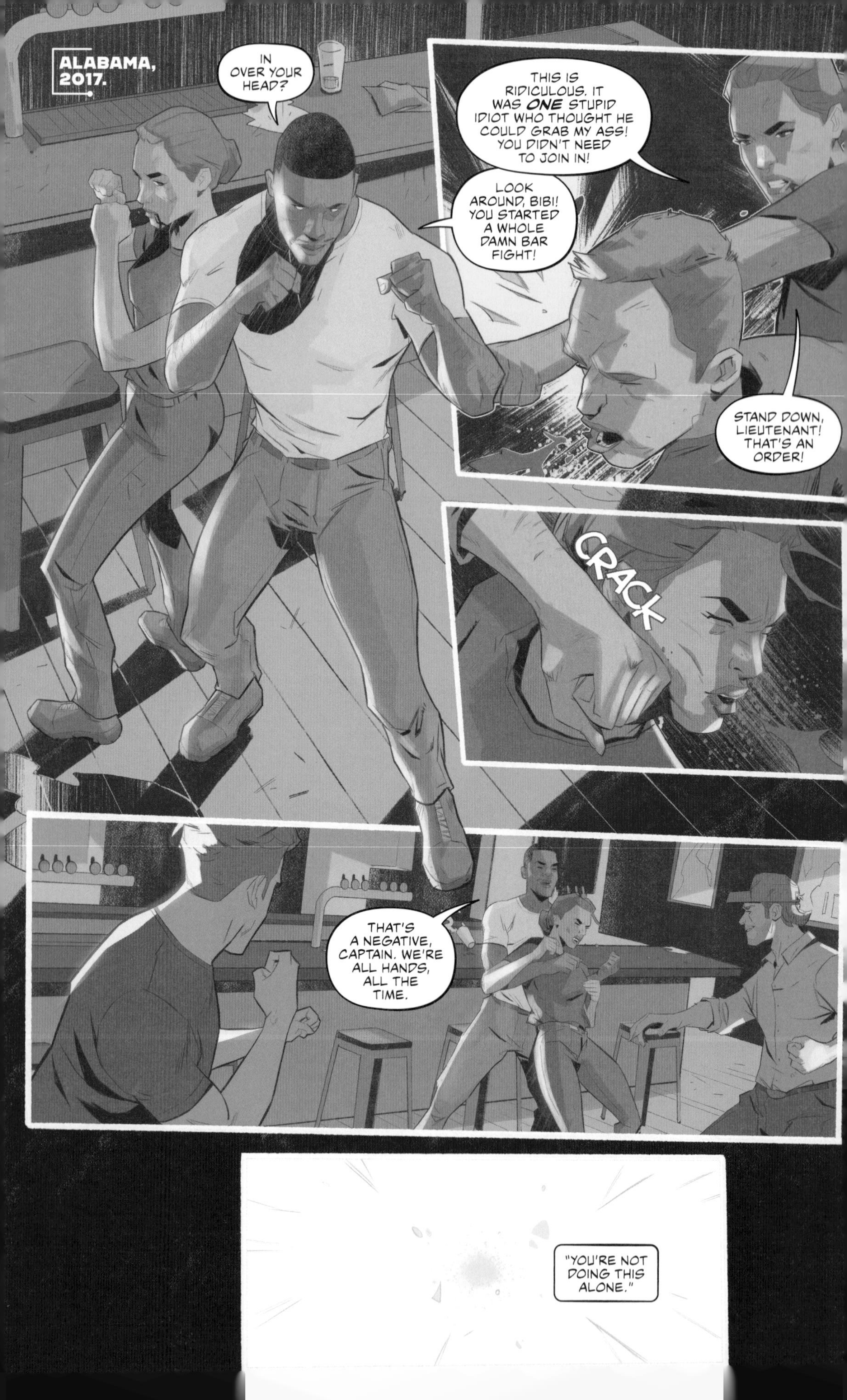

ALABAMA, 2017.
IN OVER YOUR HEAD?
THIS IS RIDICULOUS. IT WAS *ONE* STUPID IDIOT WHO THOUGHT HE COULD GRAB MY ASS! YOU DIDN'T NEED TO JOIN IN!
LOOK AROUND, BIBI! YOU STARTED A WHOLE DAMN BAR FIGHT!
STAND DOWN, LIEUTENANT! THAT'S AN ORDER!
CRACK
THAT'S A NEGATIVE, CAPTAIN. WE'RE ALL HANDS, ALL THE TIME.
"YOU'RE NOT DOING THIS ALONE."

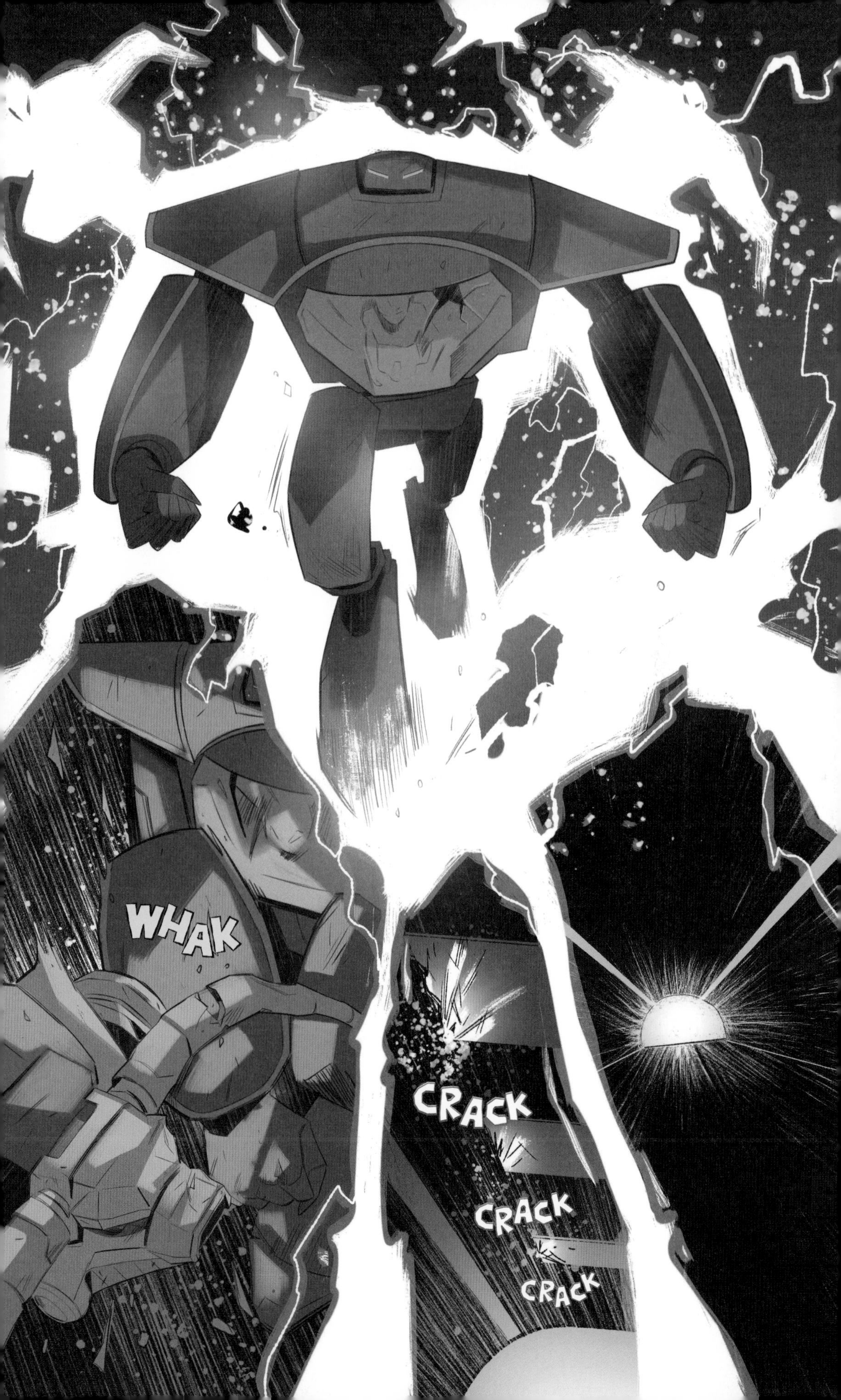
WHAK
CRACK
CRACK
CRACK

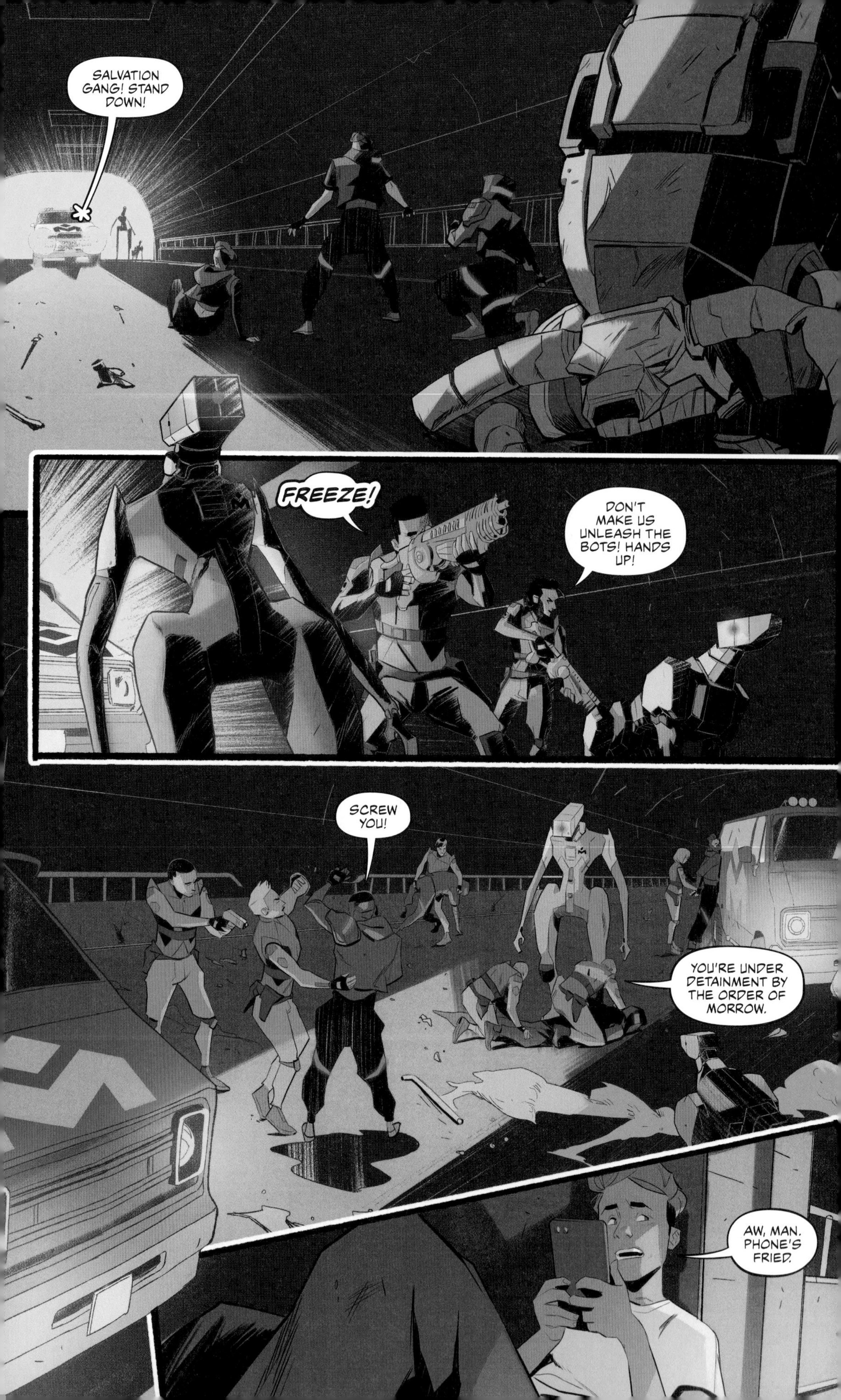
SALVATION GANG! STAND DOWN!
FREEZE!
DON'T MAKE US UNLEASH THE BOTS! HANDS UP!
SCREW YOU!
YOU'RE UNDER DETAINMENT BY THE ORDER OF MORROW.
AW, MAN. PHONE'S FRIED.

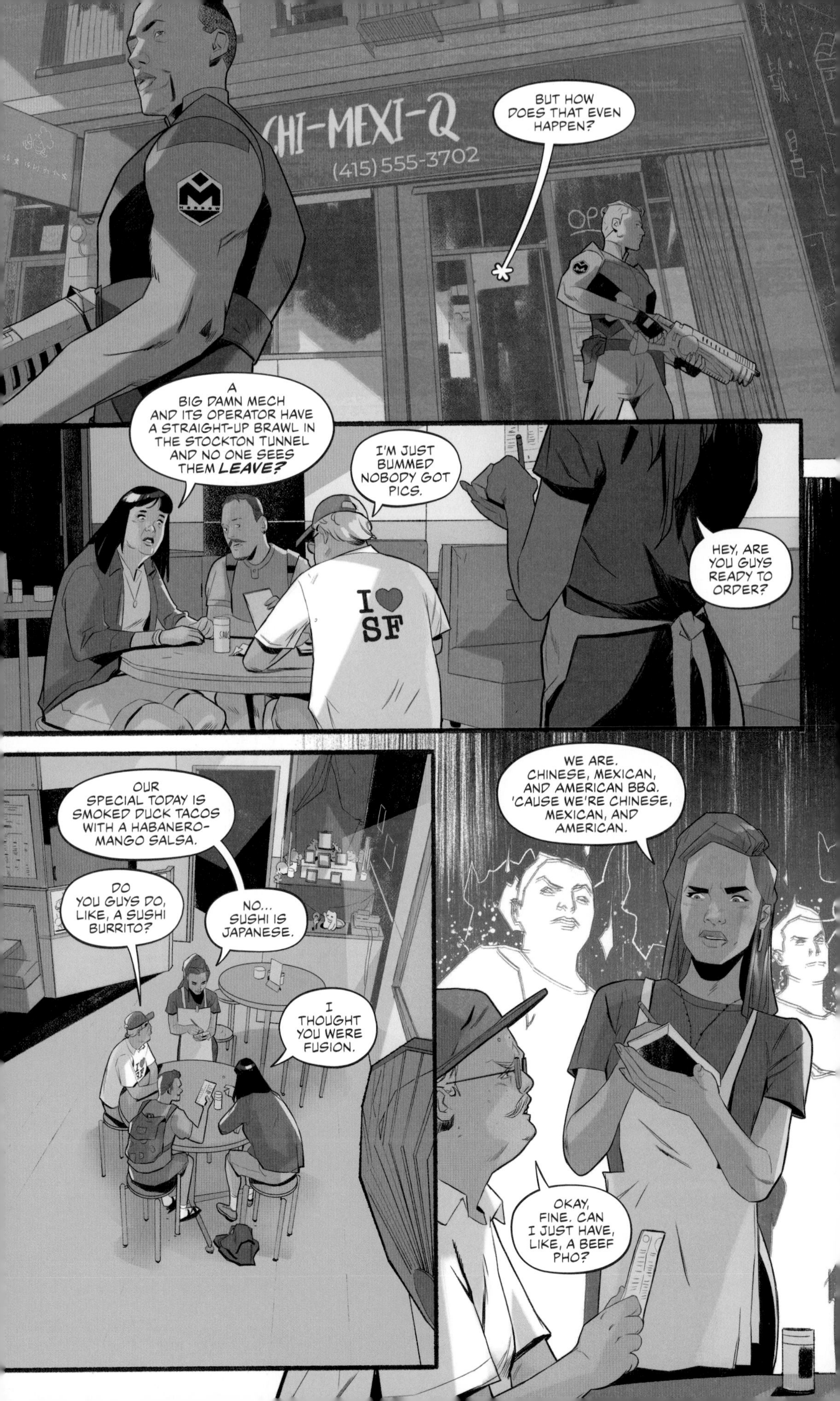

CHI-MEXI-Q
(415) 555-3702
MORROW
BUT HOW DOES THAT EVEN HAPPEN?
A BIG DAMN MECH AND ITS OPERATOR HAVE A STRAIGHT-UP BRAWL IN THE STOCKTON TUNNEL AND NO ONE SEES THEM LEAVE?
I'M JUST BUMMED NOBODY GOT PICS.
I ♥ SF
HEY, ARE YOU GUYS READY TO ORDER?
OUR SPECIAL TODAY IS SMOKED DUCK TACOS WITH A HABANERO-MANGO SALSA.
DO YOU GUYS DO, LIKE, A SUSHI BURRITO?
NO... SUSHI IS JAPANESE.
I THOUGHT YOU WERE FUSION.
WE ARE. CHINESE, MEXICAN, AND AMERICAN BBQ. 'CAUSE WE'RE CHINESE, MEXICAN, AND AMERICAN.
OKAY, FINE. CAN I JUST HAVE, LIKE, A BEEF PHO?

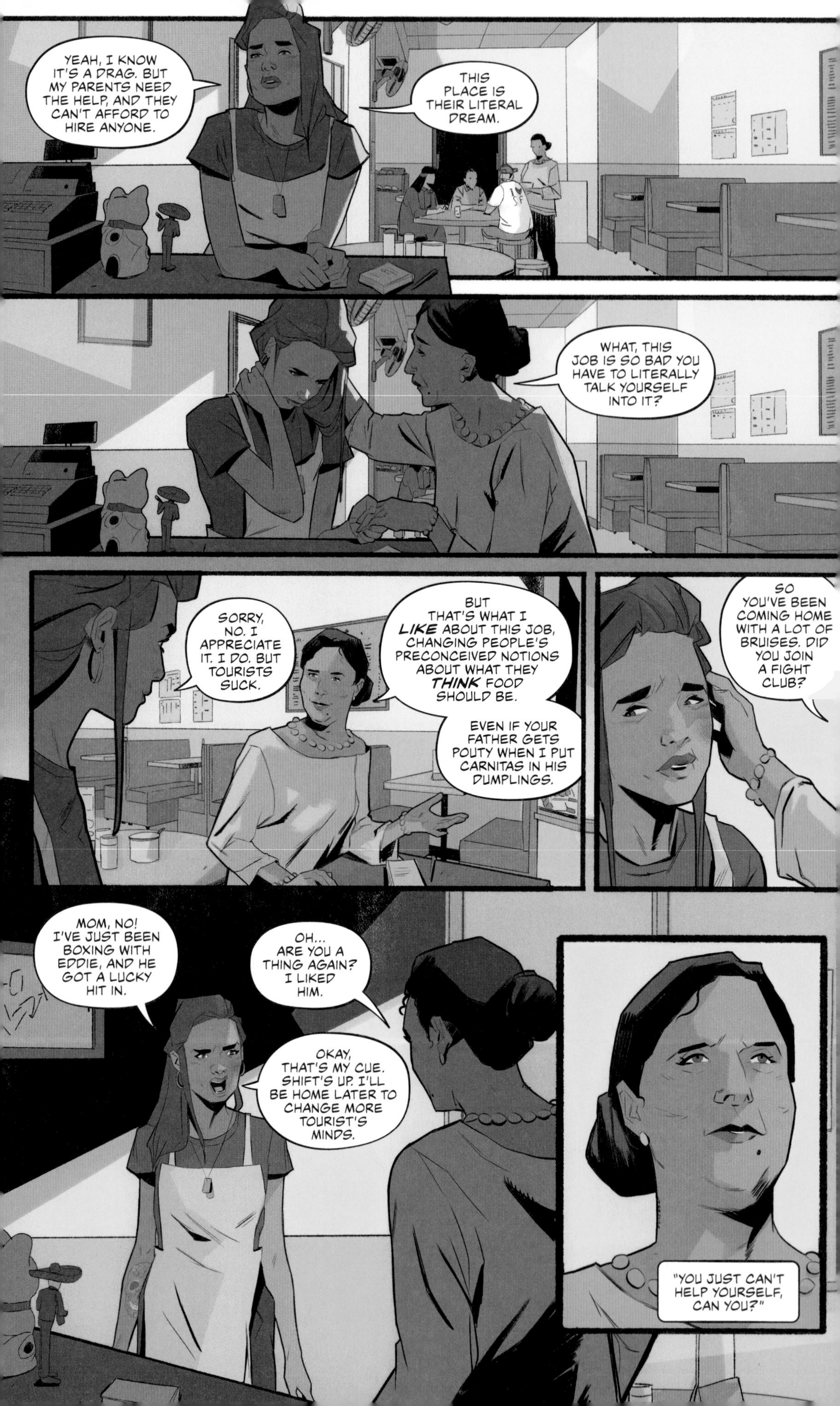
YEAH, I KNOW IT'S A DRAG. BUT MY PARENTS NEED THE HELP, AND THEY CAN'T AFFORD TO HIRE ANYONE.
THIS PLACE IS THEIR LITERAL DREAM.
WHAT, THIS JOB IS SO BAD YOU HAVE TO LITERALLY TALK YOURSELF INTO IT?
SORRY, NO. I APPRECIATE IT. I DO. BUT TOURISTS SUCK.
BUT THAT'S WHAT I LIKE ABOUT THIS JOB, CHANGING PEOPLE'S PRECONCEIVED NOTIONS ABOUT WHAT THEY THINK FOOD SHOULD BE.
EVEN IF YOUR FATHER GETS POUTY WHEN I PUT CARNITAS IN HIS DUMPLINGS.
SO YOU'VE BEEN COMING HOME WITH A LOT OF BRUISES. DID YOU JOIN A FIGHT CLUB?
MOM, NO! I'VE JUST BEEN BOXING WITH EDDIE, AND HE GOT A LUCKY HIT IN.
OH... ARE YOU A THING AGAIN? I LIKED HIM.
OKAY, THAT'S MY CUE. SHIFT'S UP. I'LL BE HOME LATER TO CHANGE MORE TOURIST'S MINDS.
"YOU JUST CAN'T HELP YOURSELF, CAN YOU?"

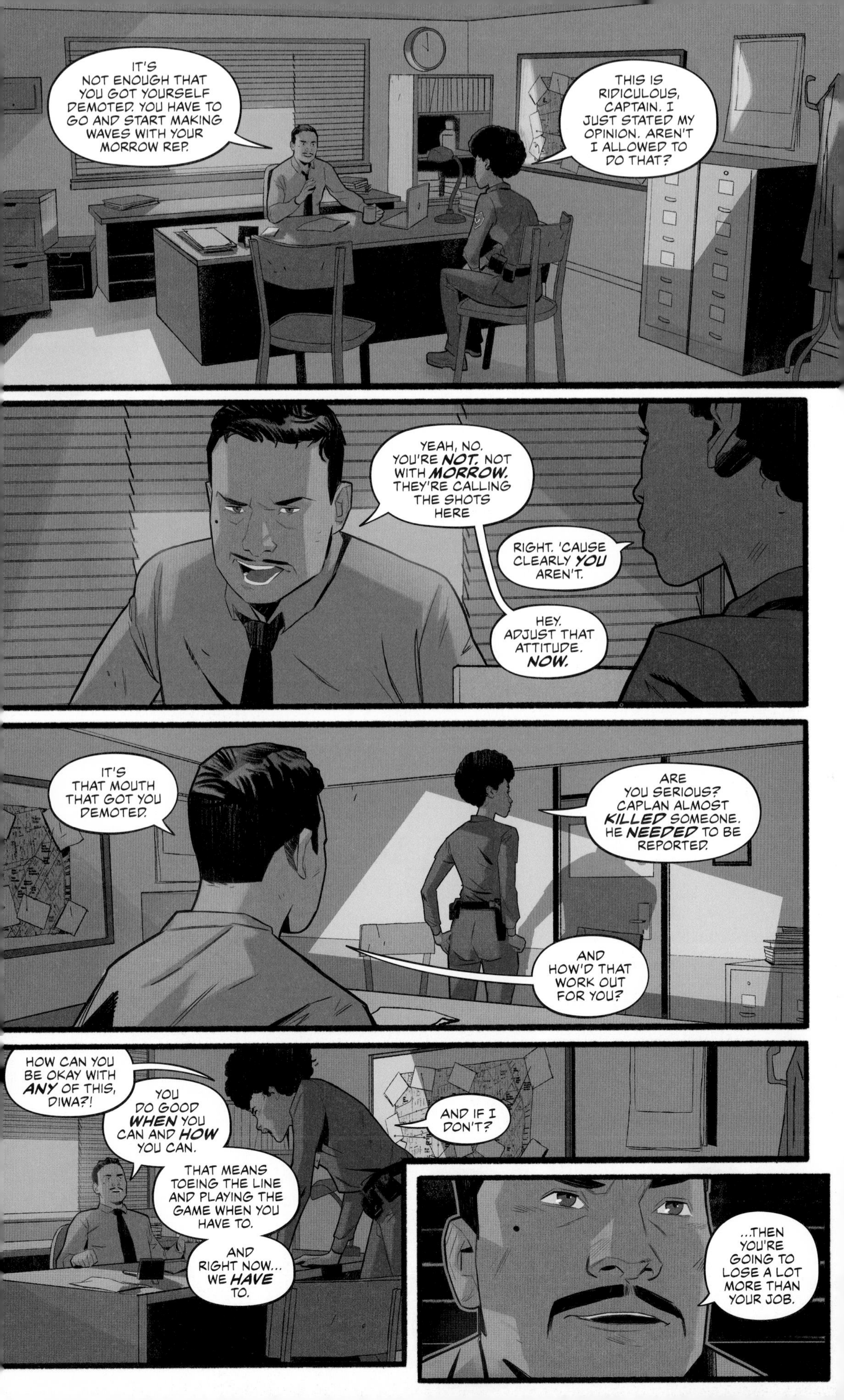
IT'S NOT ENOUGH THAT YOU GOT YOURSELF DEMOTED. YOU HAVE TO GO AND START MAKING WAVES WITH YOUR MORROW REP.
THIS IS RIDICULOUS, CAPTAIN. I JUST STATED MY OPINION. AREN'T I ALLOWED TO DO THAT?
YEAH, NO. YOU'RE NOT. NOT WITH MORROW. THEY'RE CALLING THE SHOTS HERE
RIGHT. 'CAUSE CLEARLY YOU AREN'T.
HEY. ADJUST THAT ATTITUDE. NOW.
IT'S THAT MOUTH THAT GOT YOU DEMOTED.
ARE YOU SERIOUS? CAPLAN ALMOST KILLED SOMEONE. HE NEEDED TO BE REPORTED.
AND HOW'D THAT WORK OUT FOR YOU?
HOW CAN YOU BE OKAY WITH ANY OF THIS, DIWA?!
YOU DO GOOD WHEN YOU CAN AND HOW YOU CAN.
THAT MEANS TOEING THE LINE AND PLAYING THE GAME WHEN YOU HAVE TO.
AND RIGHT NOW... WE HAVE TO.
AND IF I DON'T?
...THEN YOU'RE GOING TO LOSE A LOT MORE THAN YOUR JOB.

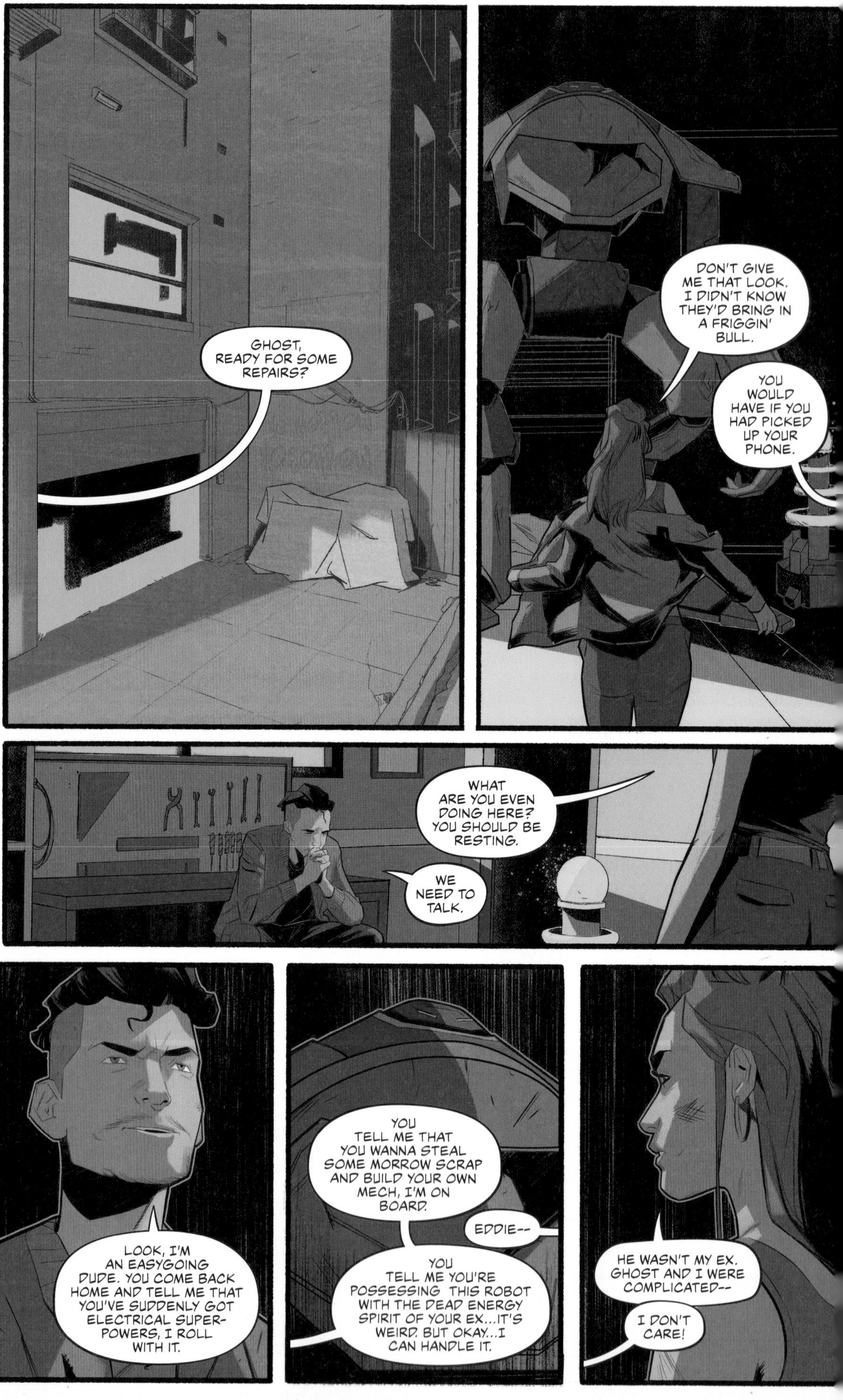
GHOST, READY FOR SOME REPAIRS?
DON'T GIVE ME THAT LOOK. I DIDN'T KNOW THEY'D BRING IN A FRIGGIN' BULL.
YOU WOULD HAVE IF YOU HAD PICKED UP YOUR PHONE.
WHAT ARE YOU EVEN DOING HERE? YOU SHOULD BE RESTING.
WE NEED TO TALK.
LOOK, I'M AN EASYGOING DUDE. YOU COME BACK HOME AND TELL ME THAT YOU'VE SUDDENLY GOT ELECTRICAL SUPER-POWERS, I ROLL WITH IT.
YOU TELL ME THAT YOU WANNA STEAL SOME MORROW SCRAP AND BUILD YOUR OWN MECH, I'M ON BOARD.
EDDIE--
YOU TELL ME YOU'RE POSSESSING THIS ROBOT WITH THE DEAD ENERGY SPIRIT OF YOUR EX...IT'S WEIRD. BUT OKAY...I CAN HANDLE IT.
HE WASN'T MY EX. GHOST AND I WERE COMPLICATED--
I DON'T CARE!

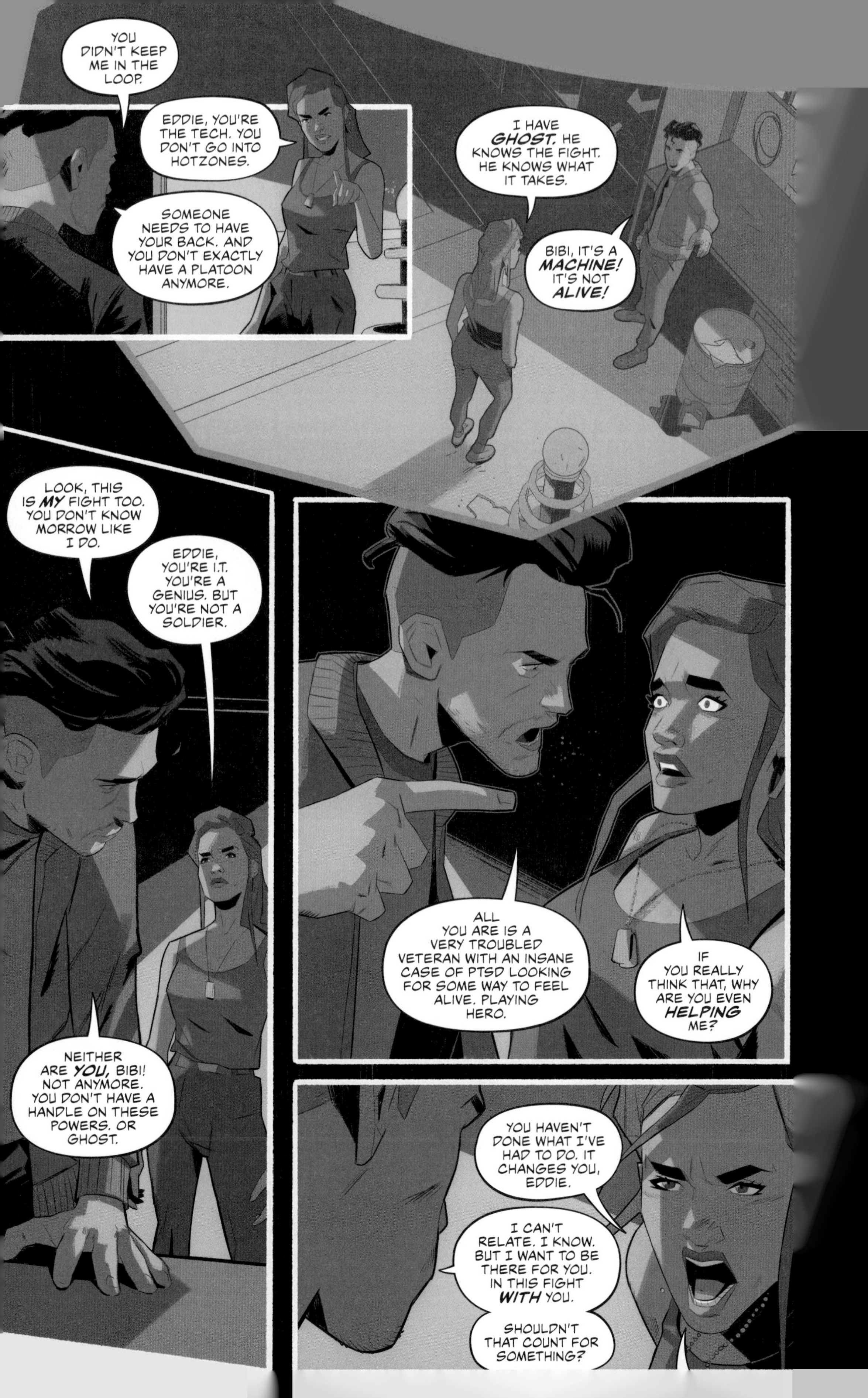
YOU DIDN'T KEEP ME IN THE LOOP.
EDDIE, YOU'RE THE TECH. YOU DON'T GO INTO HOTZONES.
SOMEONE NEEDS TO HAVE YOUR BACK. AND YOU DON'T EXACTLY HAVE A PLATOON ANYMORE.
I HAVE GHOST. HE KNOWS THE FIGHT. HE KNOWS WHAT IT TAKES.
BIBI, IT'S A MACHINE! IT'S NOT ALIVE!
LOOK, THIS IS MY FIGHT TOO. YOU DON'T KNOW MORROW LIKE I DO.
EDDIE, YOU'RE I.T. YOU'RE A GENIUS. BUT YOU'RE NOT A SOLDIER.
NEITHER ARE YOU, BIBI! NOT ANYMORE. YOU DON'T HAVE A HANDLE ON THESE POWERS. OR GHOST.
ALL YOU ARE IS A VERY TROUBLED VETERAN WITH AN INSANE CASE OF PTSD LOOKING FOR SOME WAY TO FEEL ALIVE. PLAYING HERO.
IF YOU REALLY THINK THAT, WHY ARE YOU EVEN HELPING ME?
YOU HAVEN'T DONE WHAT I'VE HAD TO DO. IT CHANGES YOU, EDDIE.
I CAN'T RELATE. I KNOW. BUT I WANT TO BE THERE FOR YOU. IN THIS FIGHT WITH YOU.
SHOULDN'T THAT COUNT FOR SOMETHING?

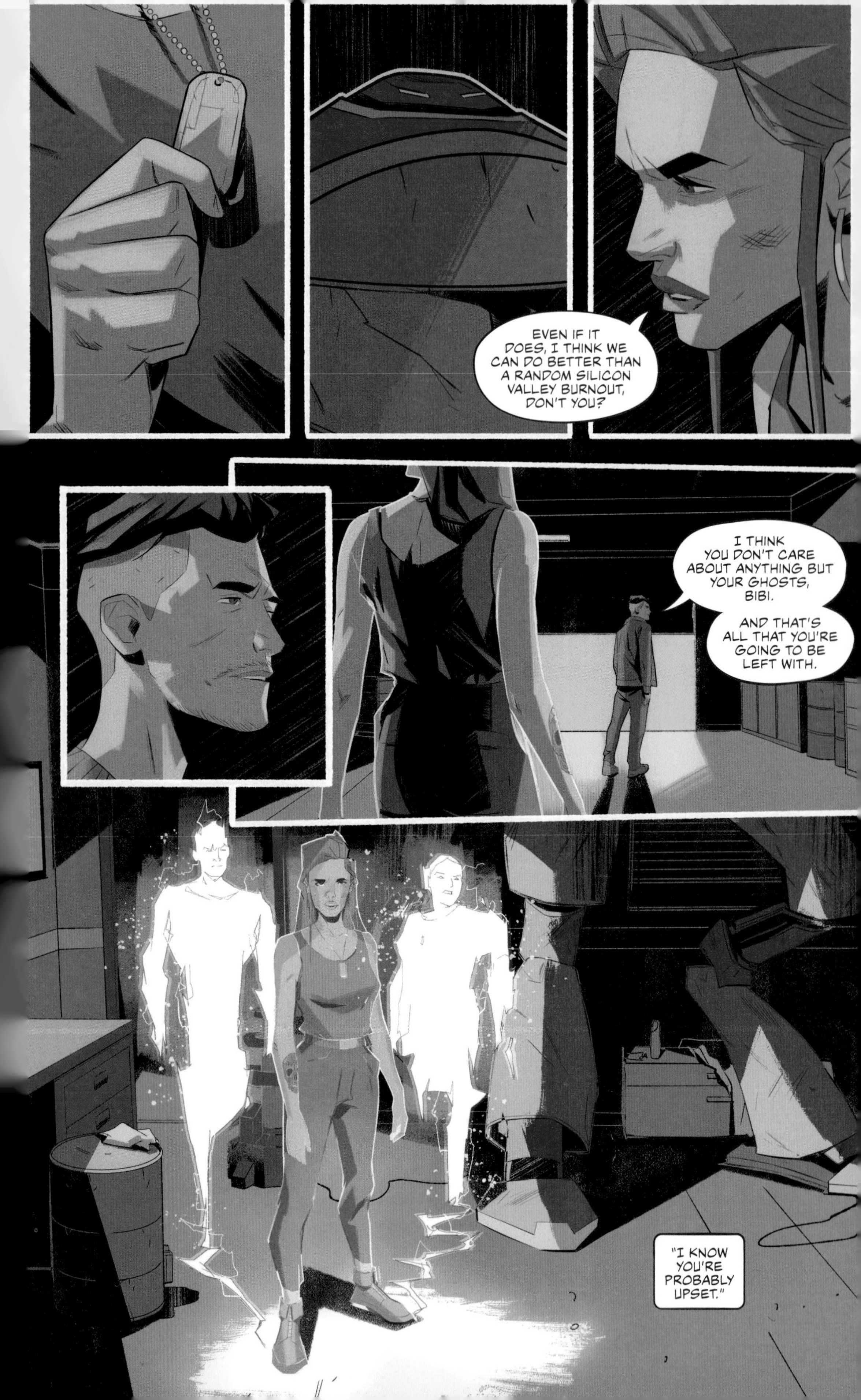
EVEN IF IT DOES, I THINK WE CAN DO BETTER THAN A RANDOM SILICON VALLEY BURNOUT, DON'T YOU?
I THINK YOU DON'T CARE ABOUT ANYTHING BUT YOUR GHOSTS, BIBI.
AND THAT'S ALL THAT YOU'RE GOING TO BE LEFT WITH.
"I KNOW YOU'RE PROBABLY UPSET."

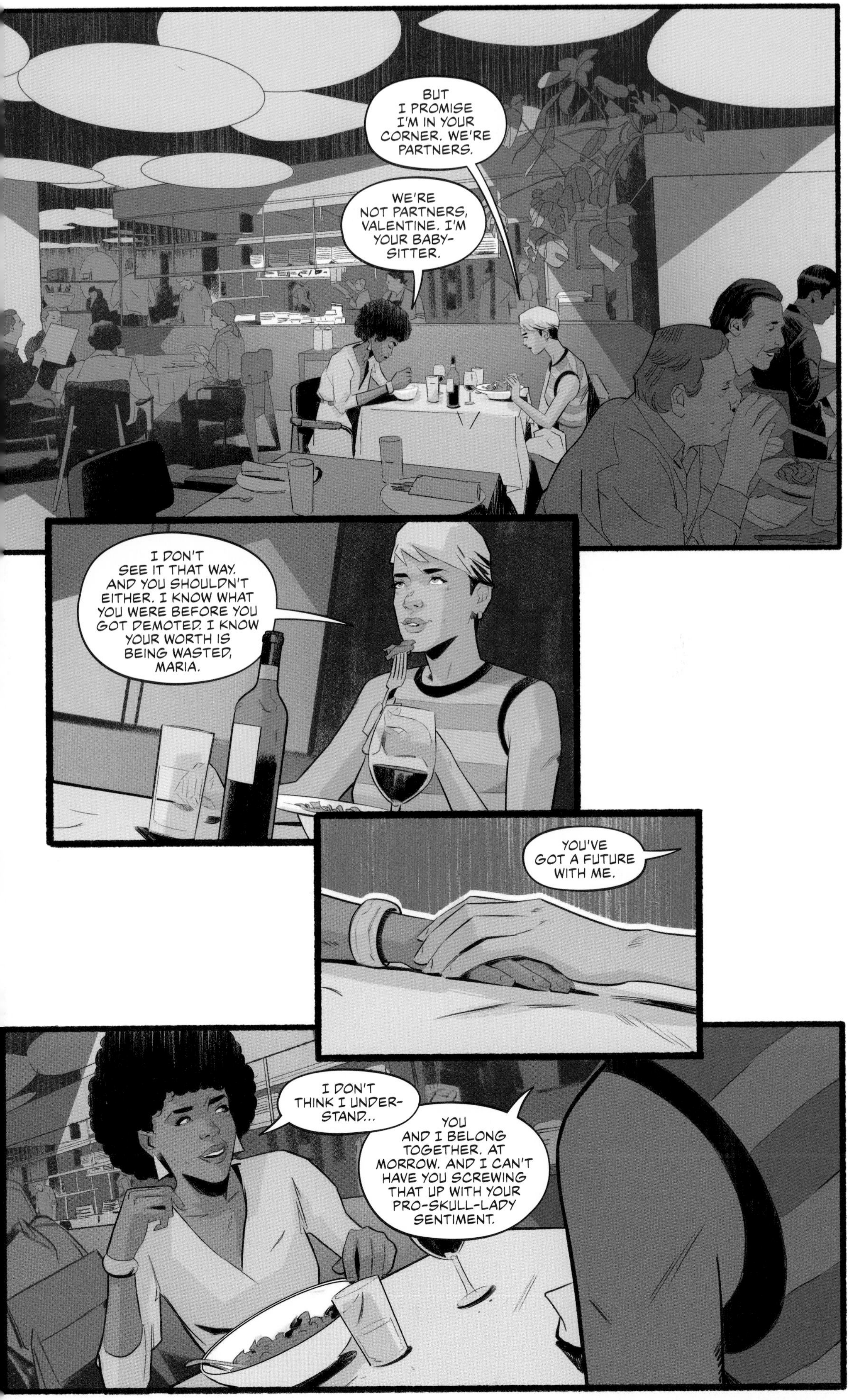
BUT I PROMISE I'M IN YOUR CORNER. WE'RE PARTNERS.
WE'RE NOT PARTNERS, VALENTINE. I'M YOUR BABY-SITTER.
I DON'T SEE IT THAT WAY. AND YOU SHOULDN'T EITHER. I KNOW WHAT YOU WERE BEFORE YOU GOT DEMOTED. I KNOW YOUR WORTH IS BEING WASTED, MARIA.
YOU'VE GOT A FUTURE WITH ME.
I DON'T THINK I UNDER-STAND...
YOU AND I BELONG TOGETHER. AT MORROW. AND I CAN'T HAVE YOU SCREWING THAT UP WITH YOUR PRO-SKULL-LADY SENTIMENT.

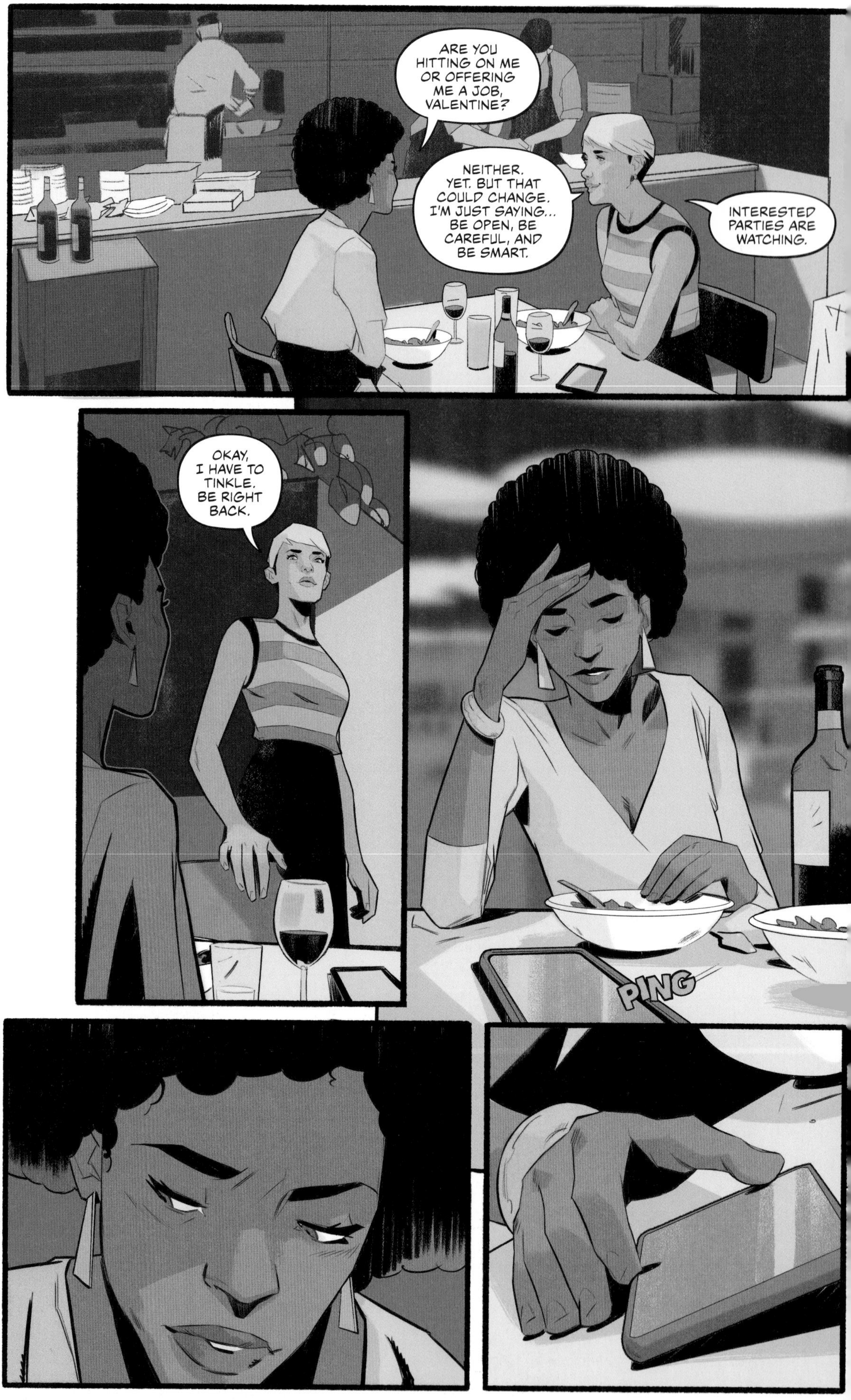
ARE YOU HITTING ON ME OR OFFERING ME A JOB, VALENTINE?
NEITHER. YET. BUT THAT COULD CHANGE. I'M JUST SAYING... BE OPEN, BE CAREFUL, AND BE SMART.
INTERESTED PARTIES ARE WATCHING.
OKAY, I HAVE TO TINKLE. BE RIGHT BACK.
PING

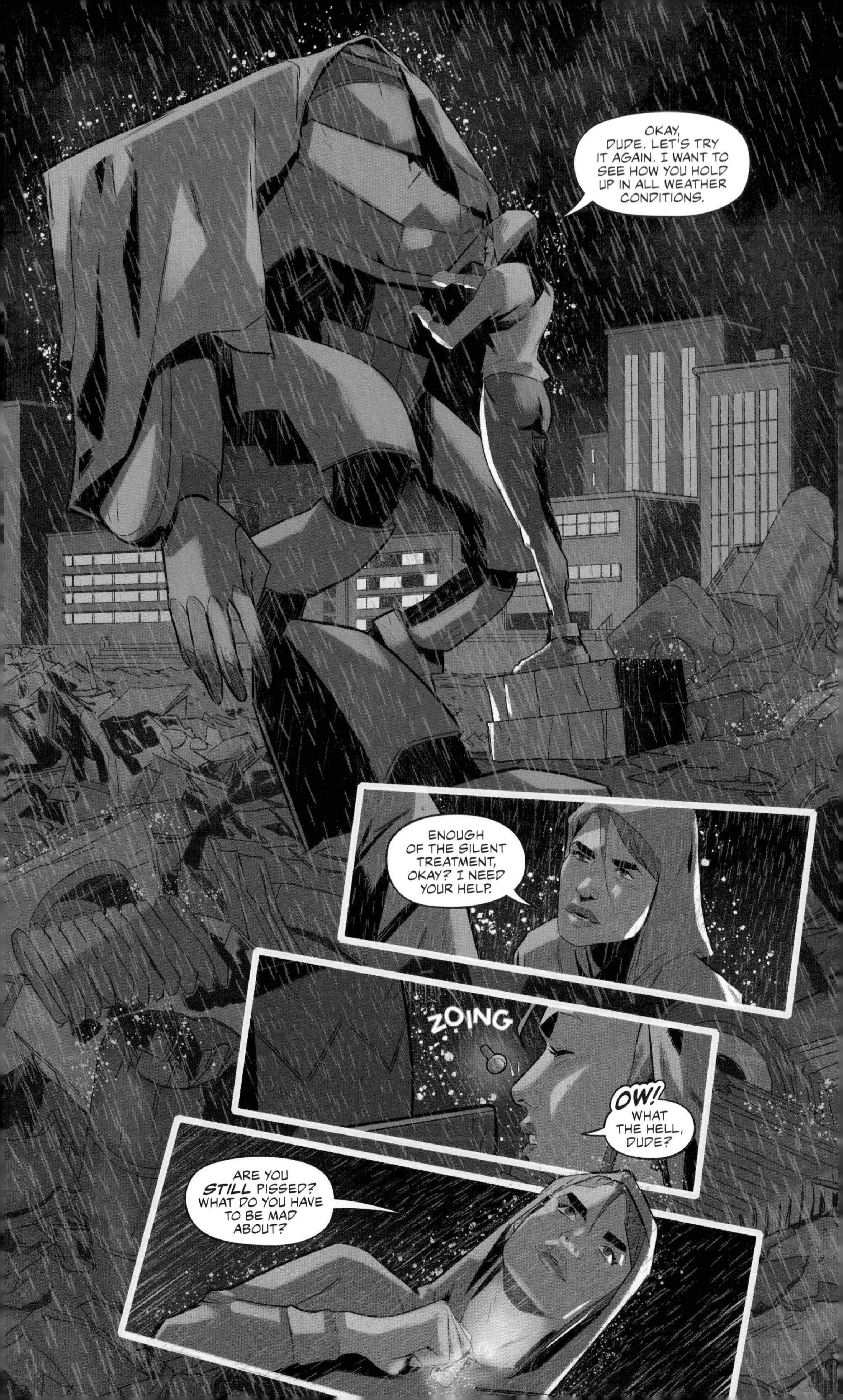
OKAY, DUDE. LET'S TRY IT AGAIN. I WANT TO SEE HOW YOU HOLD UP IN ALL WEATHER CONDITIONS.
ENOUGH OF THE SILENT TREATMENT, OKAY? I NEED YOUR HELP.
ZOING
OW! WHAT THE HELL, DUDE?
ARE YOU STILL PISSED? WHAT DO YOU HAVE TO BE MAD ABOUT?

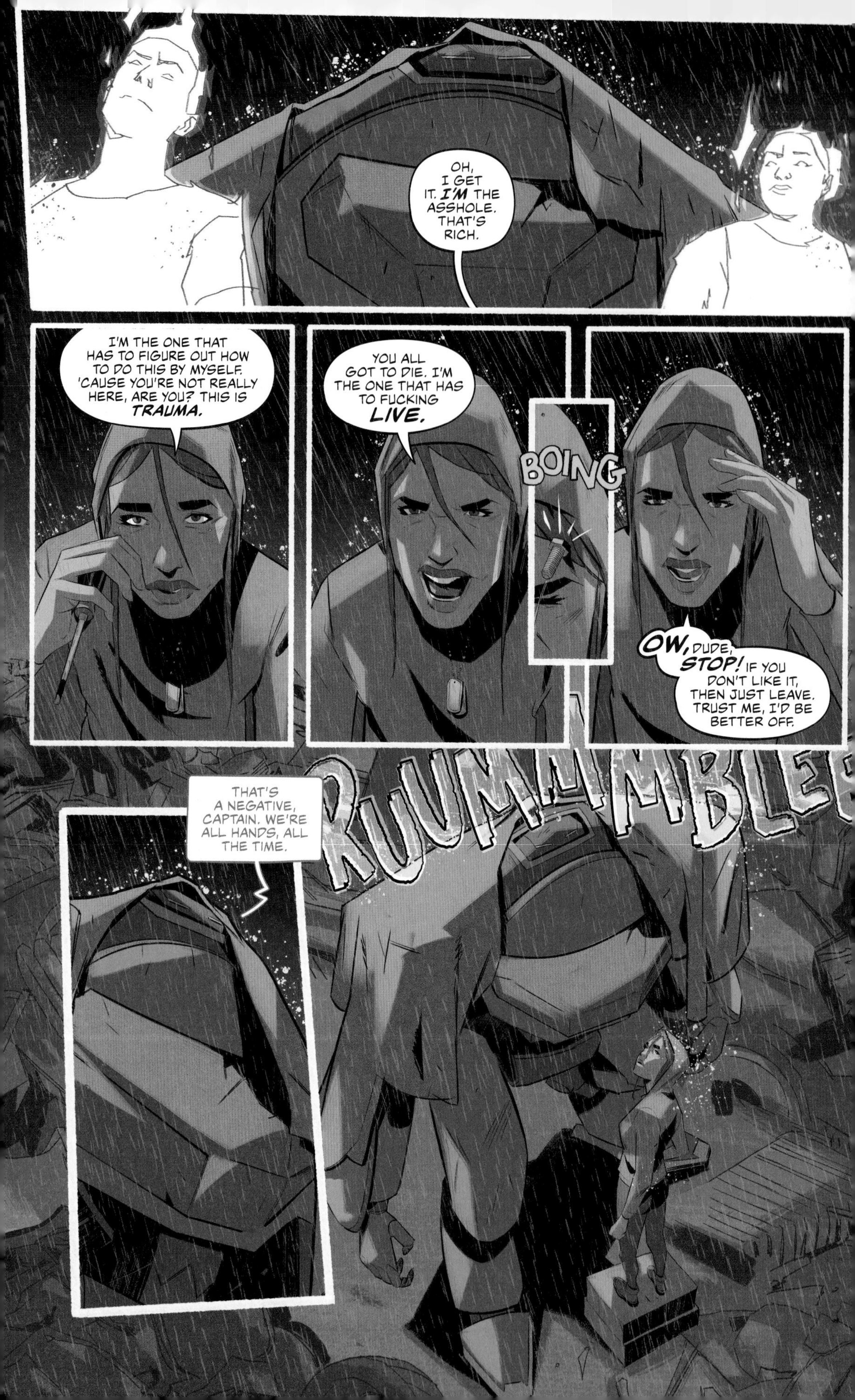

OH, I GET IT. I'M THE ASSHOLE. THAT'S RICH.
I'M THE ONE THAT HAS TO FIGURE OUT HOW TO DO THIS BY MYSELF. 'CAUSE YOU'RE NOT REALLY HERE, ARE YOU? THIS IS TRAUMA.
YOU ALL GOT TO DIE. I'M THE ONE THAT HAS TO FUCKING LIVE.
BOING
OW, DUDE, STOP! IF YOU DON'T LIKE IT, THEN JUST LEAVE. TRUST ME, I'D BE BETTER OFF.
THAT'S A NEGATIVE, CAPTAIN. WE'RE ALL HANDS, ALL THE TIME.
RUUMMMBLE

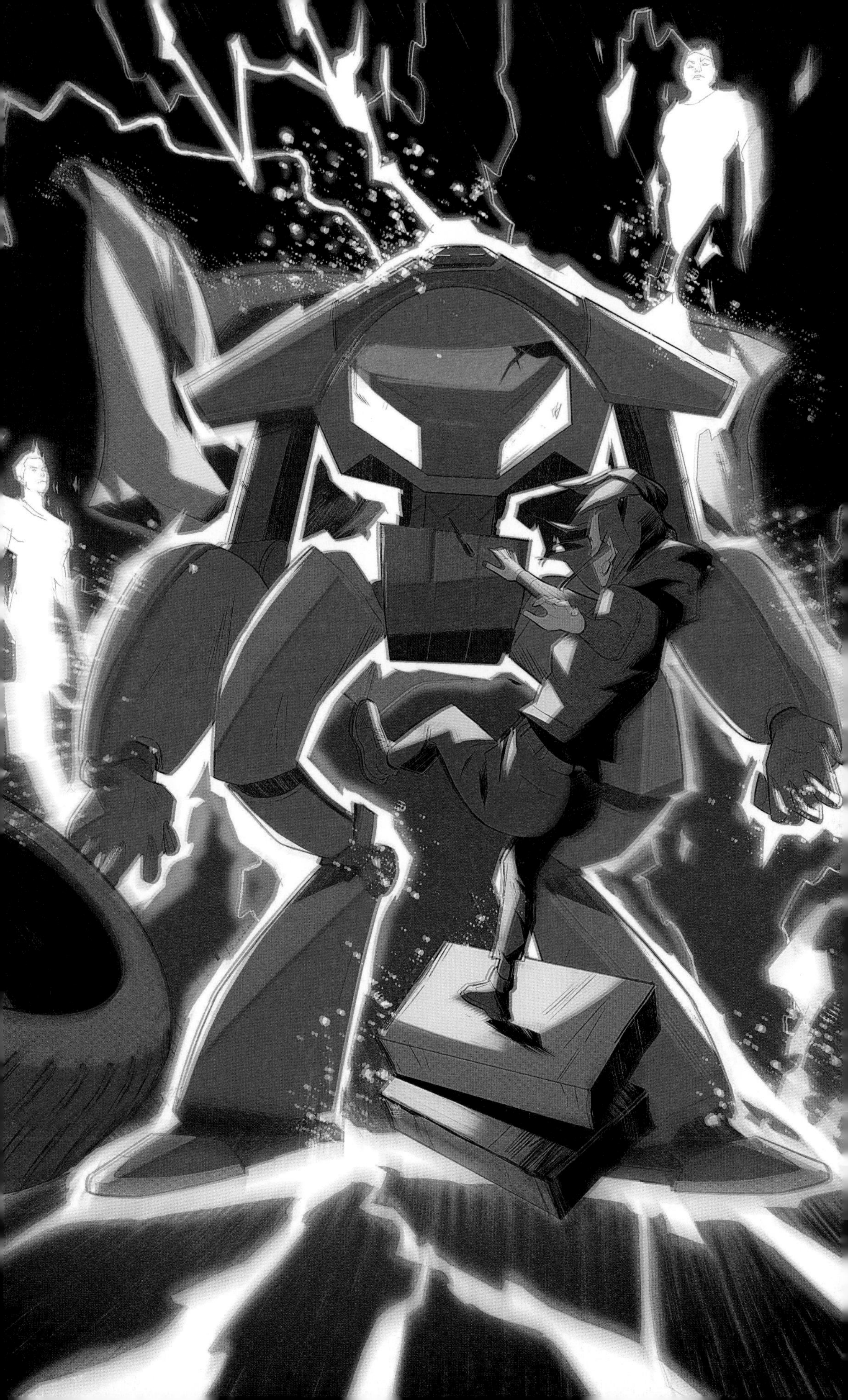

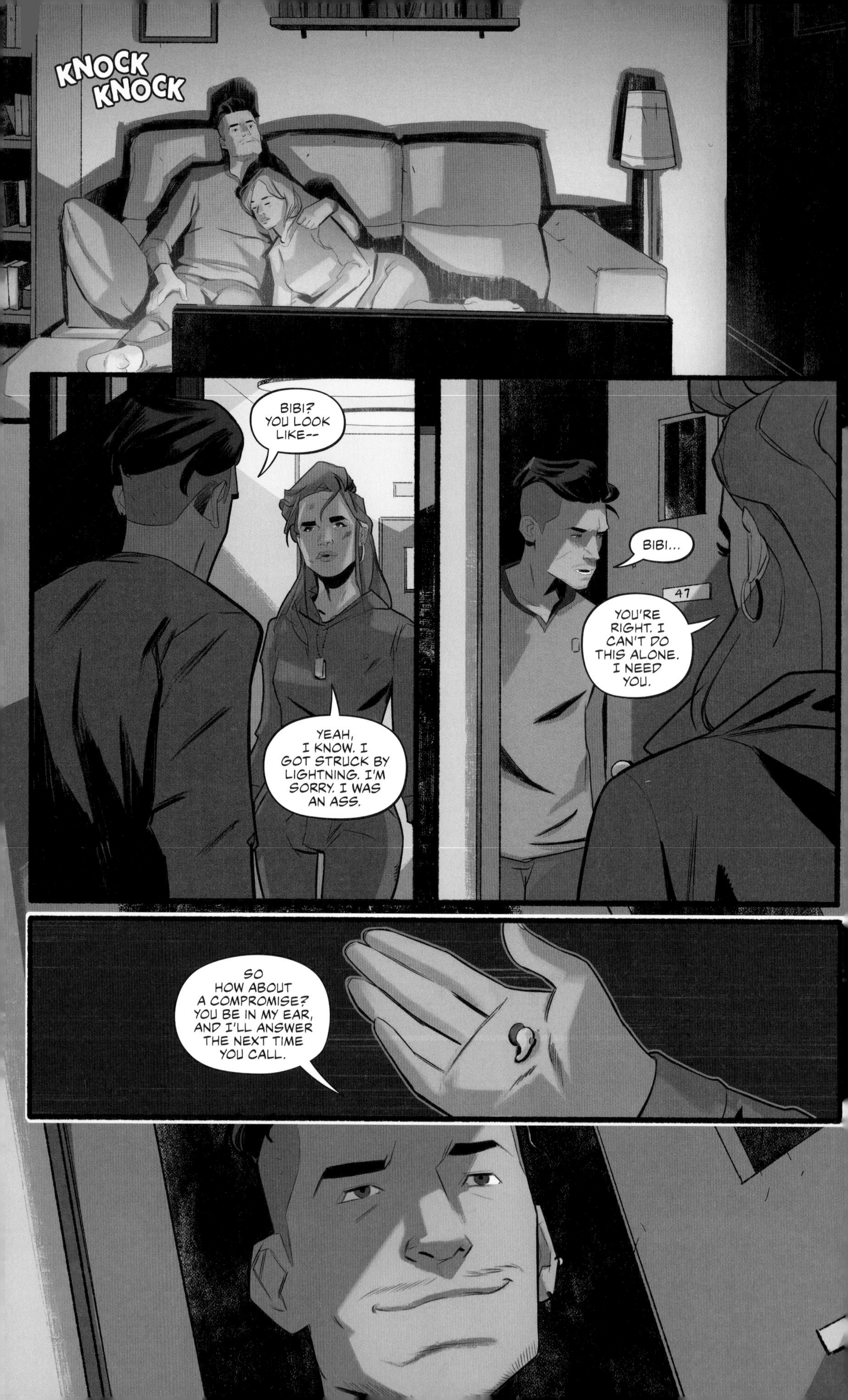
KNOCK KNOCK
BIBI? YOU LOOK LIKE--
YEAH, I KNOW. I GOT STRUCK BY LIGHTNING. I'M SORRY. I WAS AN ASS.
BIBI...
YOU'RE RIGHT. I CAN'T DO THIS ALONE. I NEED YOU.
47
SO HOW ABOUT A COMPROMISE? YOU BE IN MY EAR, AND I'LL ANSWER THE NEXT TIME YOU CALL.

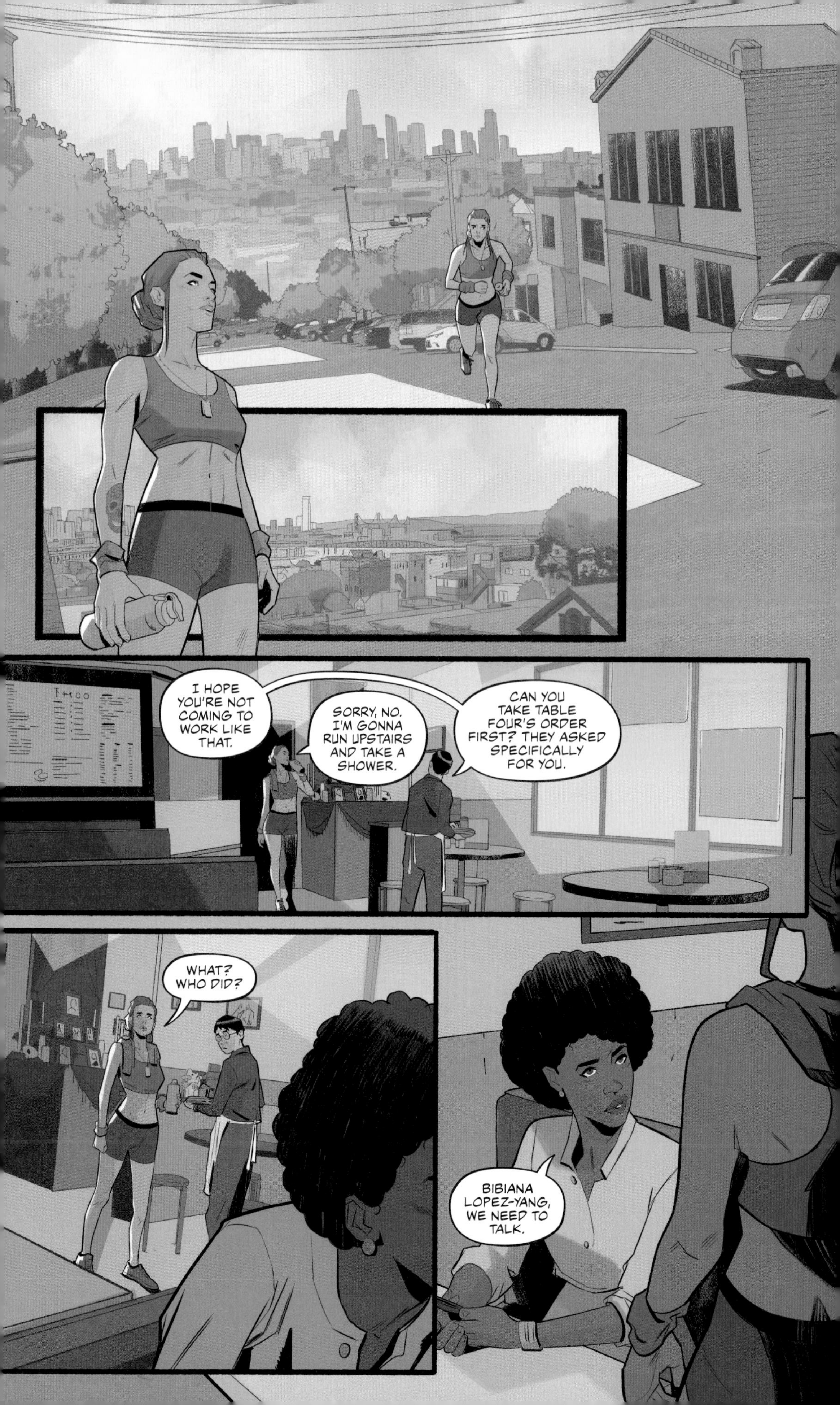

I HOPE YOU'RE NOT COMING TO WORK LIKE THAT.
SORRY, NO. I'M GONNA RUN UPSTAIRS AND TAKE A SHOWER.
CAN YOU TAKE TABLE FOUR'S ORDER FIRST? THEY ASKED SPECIFICALLY FOR YOU.
WHAT? WHO DID?
BIBIANA LOPEZ-YANG, WE NEED TO TALK.

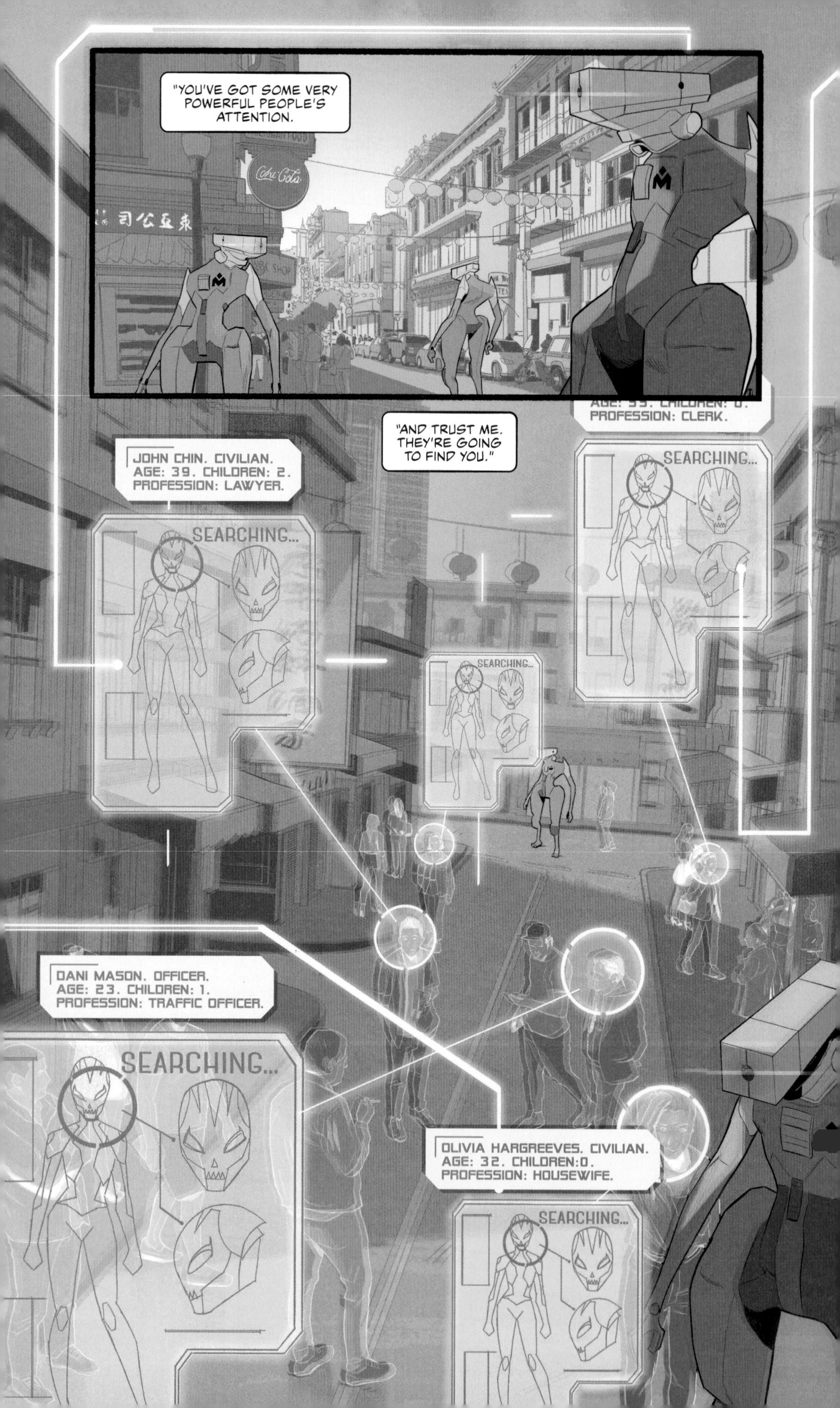
"YOU'VE GOT SOME VERY POWERFUL PEOPLE'S ATTENTION.
"AND TRUST ME. THEY'RE GOING TO FIND YOU."
JOHN CHIN. CIVILIAN. AGE: 39. CHILDREN: 2. PROFESSION: LAWYER.
SEARCHING...
SEARCHING...
PROFESSION: CLERK.
SEARCHING...
DANI MASON. OFFICER. AGE: 23. CHILDREN: 1. PROFESSION: TRAFFIC OFFICER.
SEARCHING...
OLIVIA HARGREEVES. CIVILIAN. AGE: 32. CHILDREN:0. PROFESSION: HOUSEWIFE.
SEARCHING...

TERMINAL   — ✕

GHOST:~ admin$ SingleIssueProfiler
Issue:
    No.: 003
    Title: The Dead Don't Want Me.

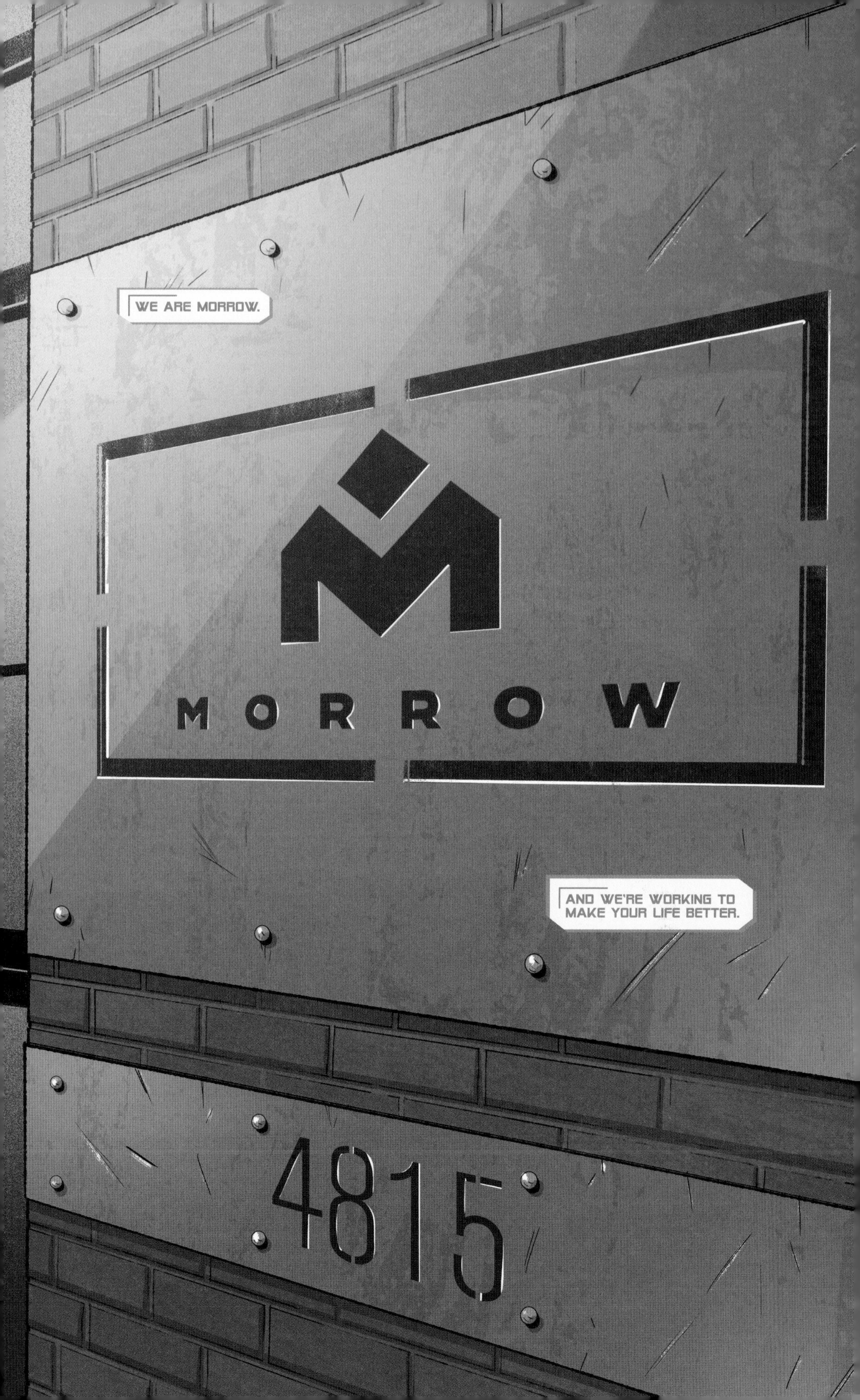
WE ARE MORROW.
MORROW
AND WE'RE WORKING TO MAKE YOUR LIFE BETTER.
4815

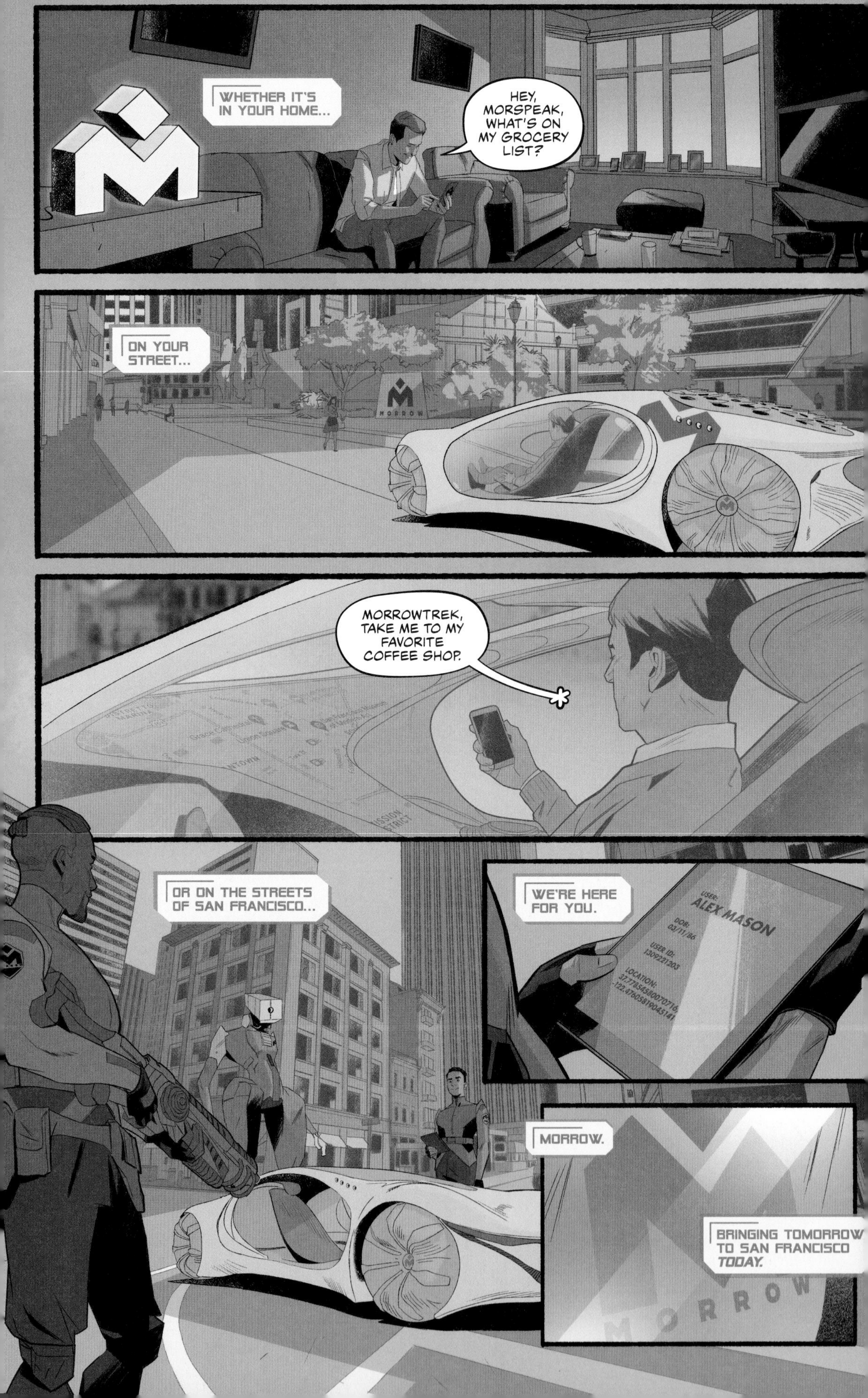
WHETHER IT'S IN YOUR HOME...
HEY, MORSPEAK, WHAT'S ON MY GROCERY LIST?
ON YOUR STREET...
MORROW
MORROWTREK, TAKE ME TO MY FAVORITE COFFEE SHOP.
OR ON THE STREETS OF SAN FRANCISCO...
WE'RE HERE FOR YOU.
USER:
ALEX MASON
DOB:
03/11/86
USER ID:
1309221203
LOCATION:
37.77854580070716
-122.47605819045141
MORROW.
BRINGING TOMORROW TO SAN FRANCISCO *TODAY.*
MORROW

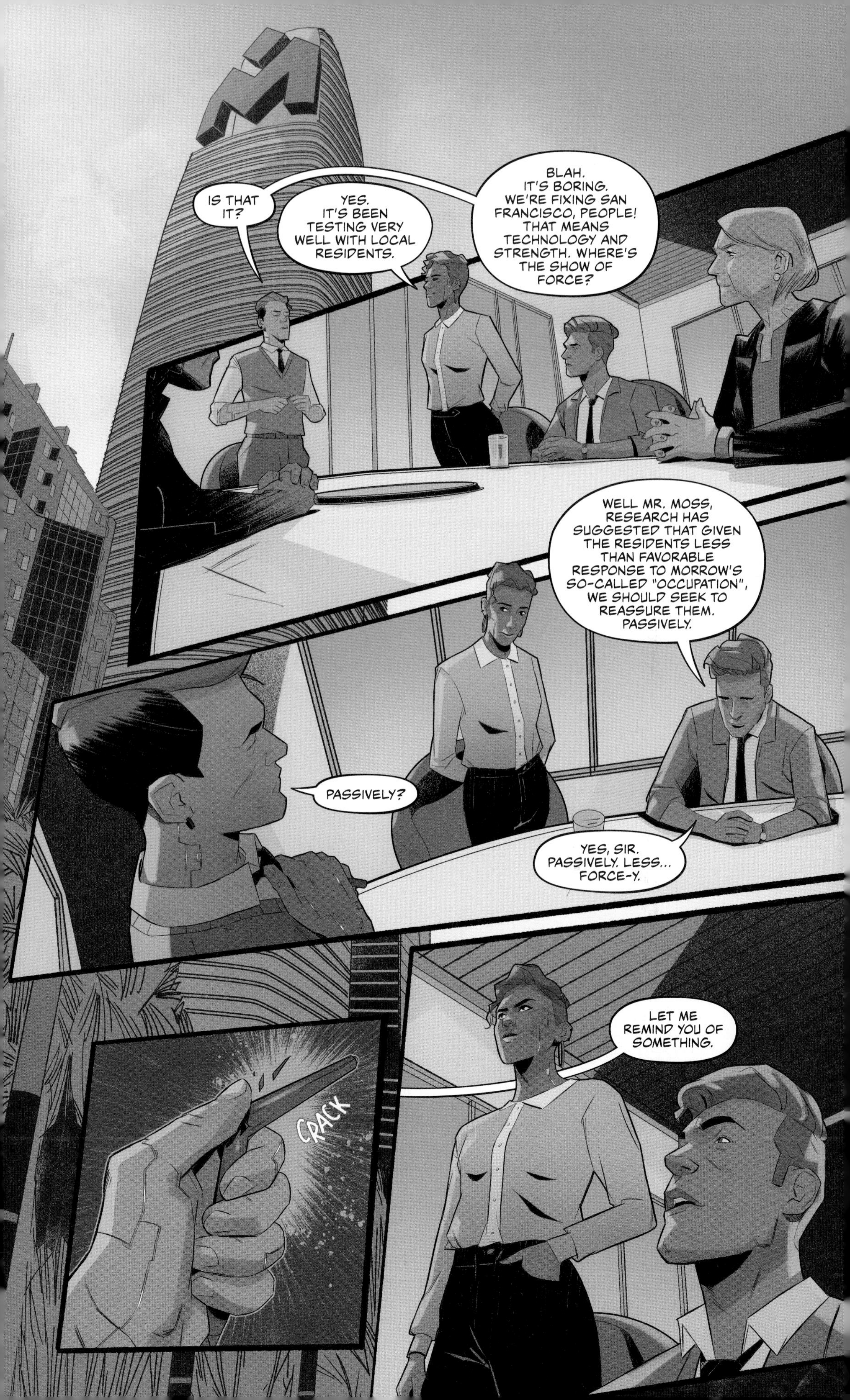
IS THAT IT?
YES. IT'S BEEN TESTING VERY WELL WITH LOCAL RESIDENTS.
BLAH. IT'S BORING. WE'RE FIXING SAN FRANCISCO, PEOPLE! THAT MEANS TECHNOLOGY AND STRENGTH. WHERE'S THE SHOW OF FORCE?
WELL MR. MOSS, RESEARCH HAS SUGGESTED THAT GIVEN THE RESIDENTS LESS THAN FAVORABLE RESPONSE TO MORROW'S SO-CALLED "OCCUPATION", WE SHOULD SEEK TO REASSURE THEM. PASSIVELY.
PASSIVELY?
YES, SIR. PASSIVELY. LESS... FORCE-Y.
CRACK
LET ME REMIND YOU OF SOMETHING.

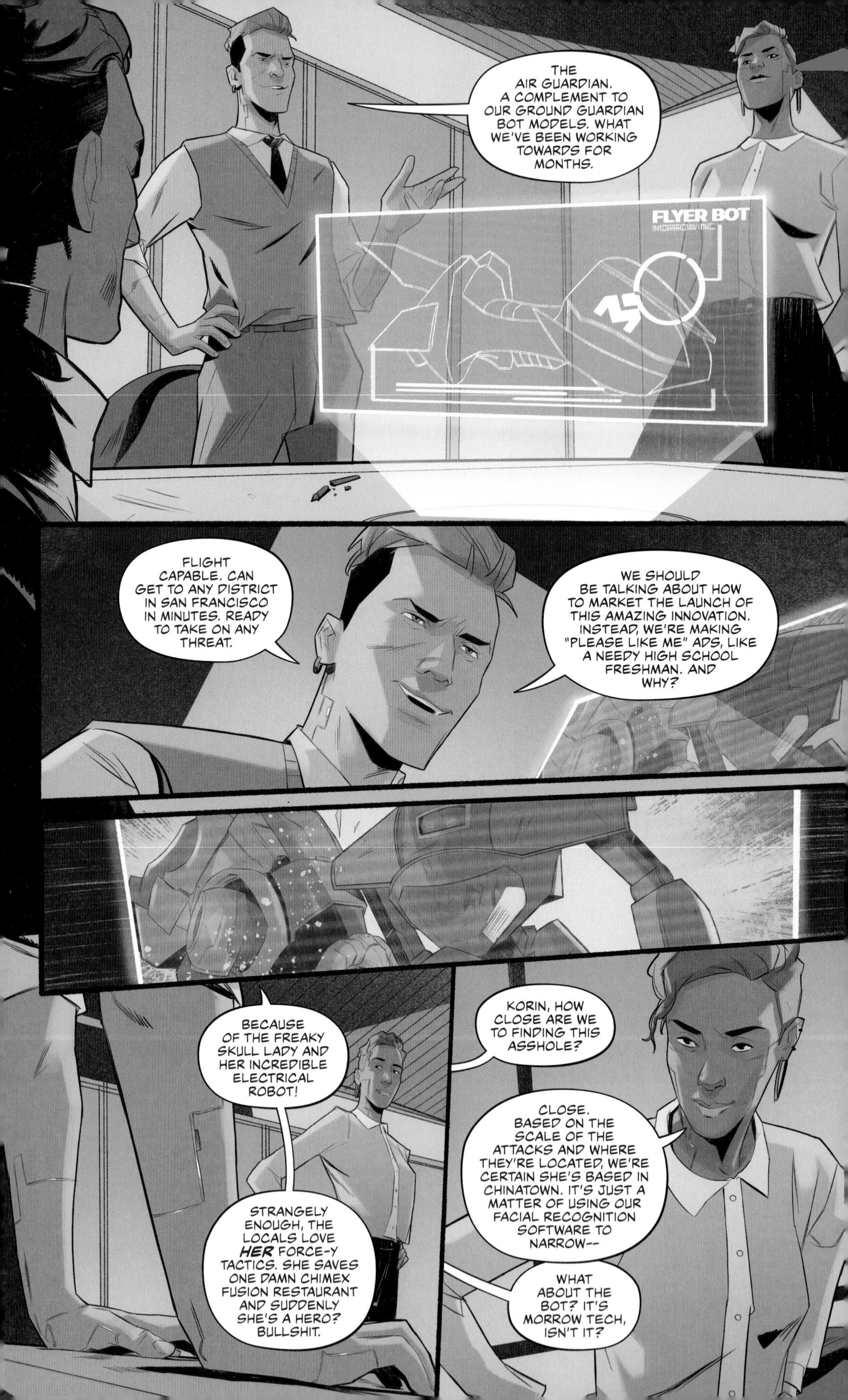
THE AIR GUARDIAN. A COMPLEMENT TO OUR GROUND GUARDIAN BOT MODELS. WHAT WE'VE BEEN WORKING TOWARDS FOR MONTHS.
FLYER BOT
MORROW INC.
FLIGHT CAPABLE. CAN GET TO ANY DISTRICT IN SAN FRANCISCO IN MINUTES. READY TO TAKE ON ANY THREAT.
WE SHOULD BE TALKING ABOUT HOW TO MARKET THE LAUNCH OF THIS AMAZING INNOVATION. INSTEAD, WE'RE MAKING "PLEASE LIKE ME" ADS, LIKE A NEEDY HIGH SCHOOL FRESHMAN. AND WHY?
BECAUSE OF THE FREAKY SKULL LADY AND HER INCREDIBLE ELECTRICAL ROBOT!
STRANGELY ENOUGH, THE LOCALS LOVE **HER** FORCE-Y TACTICS. SHE SAVES ONE DAMN CHIMEX FUSION RESTAURANT AND SUDDENLY SHE'S A HERO? BULLSHIT.
KORIN, HOW CLOSE ARE WE TO FINDING THIS ASSHOLE?
CLOSE. BASED ON THE SCALE OF THE ATTACKS AND WHERE THEY'RE LOCATED, WE'RE CERTAIN SHE'S BASED IN CHINATOWN. IT'S JUST A MATTER OF USING OUR FACIAL RECOGNITION SOFTWARE TO NARROW--
WHAT ABOUT THE BOT? IT'S MORROW TECH, ISN'T IT?

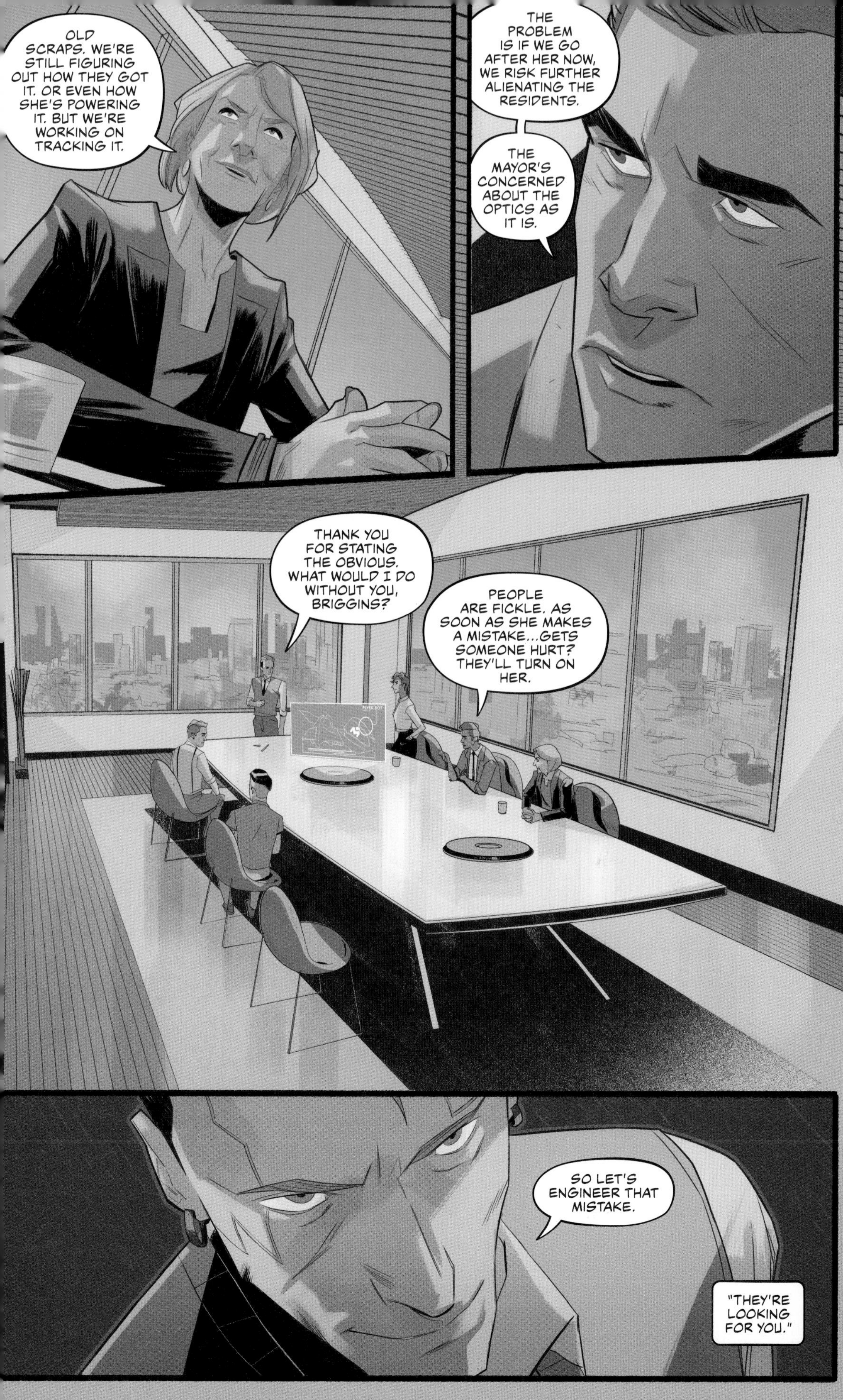
OLD SCRAPS. WE'RE STILL FIGURING OUT HOW THEY GOT IT. OR EVEN HOW SHE'S POWERING IT. BUT WE'RE WORKING ON TRACKING IT.
THE PROBLEM IS IF WE GO AFTER HER NOW, WE RISK FURTHER ALIENATING THE RESIDENTS.
THE MAYOR'S CONCERNED ABOUT THE OPTICS AS IT IS.
THANK YOU FOR STATING THE OBVIOUS. WHAT WOULD I DO WITHOUT YOU, BRIGGINS?
PEOPLE ARE FICKLE. AS SOON AS SHE MAKES A MISTAKE...GETS SOMEONE HURT? THEY'LL TURN ON HER.
SO LET'S ENGINEER THAT MISTAKE.
"THEY'RE LOOKING FOR YOU."

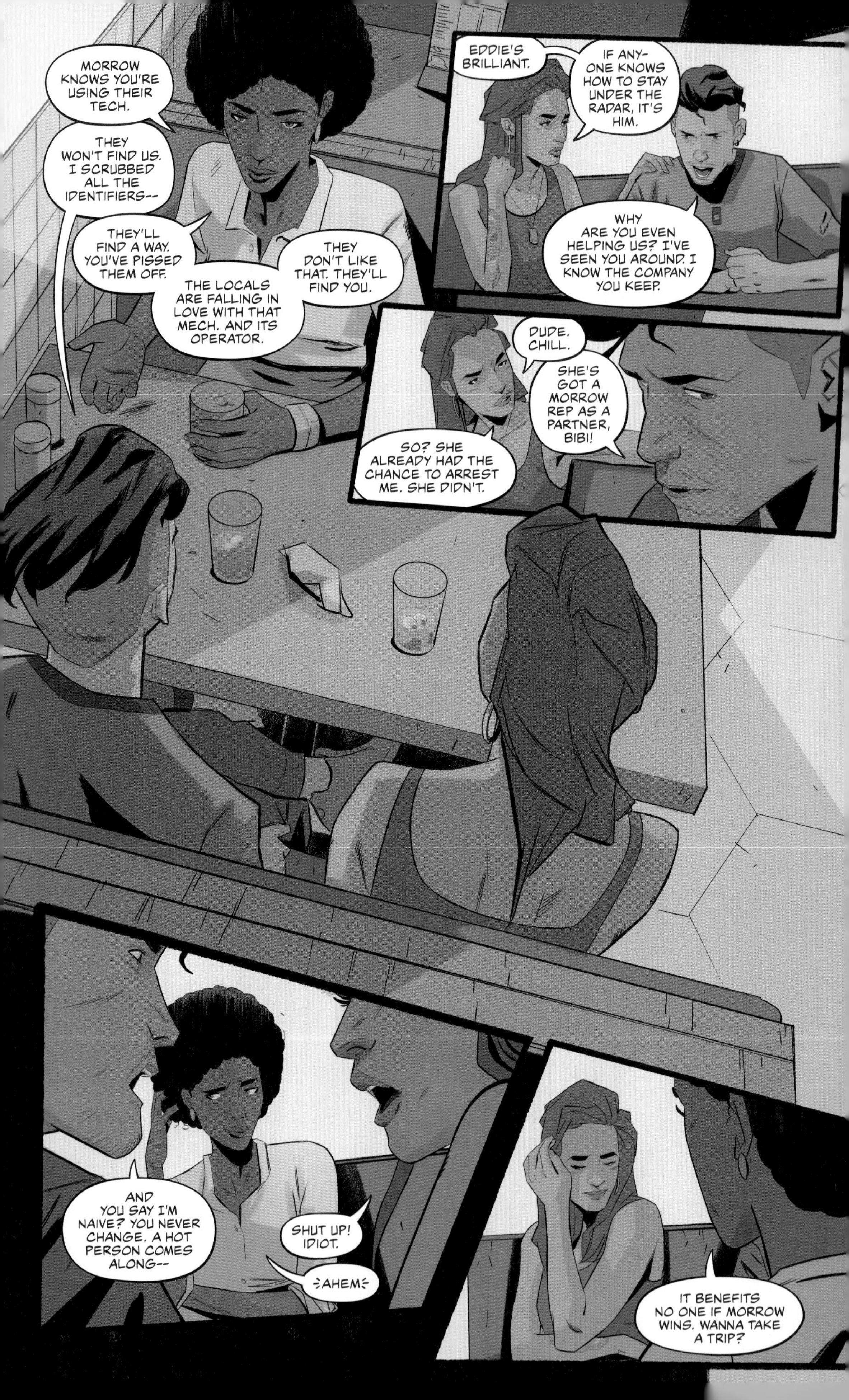
MORROW KNOWS YOU'RE USING THEIR TECH.
THEY WON'T FIND US. I SCRUBBED ALL THE IDENTIFIERS--
THEY'LL FIND A WAY. YOU'VE PISSED THEM OFF.
THE LOCALS ARE FALLING IN LOVE WITH THAT MECH. AND ITS OPERATOR.
THEY DON'T LIKE THAT. THEY'LL FIND YOU.
EDDIE'S BRILLIANT.
IF ANY-ONE KNOWS HOW TO STAY UNDER THE RADAR, IT'S HIM.
WHY ARE YOU EVEN HELPING US? I'VE SEEN YOU AROUND. I KNOW THE COMPANY YOU KEEP.
DUDE. CHILL.
SHE'S GOT A MORROW REP AS A PARTNER, BIBI!
SO? SHE ALREADY HAD THE CHANCE TO ARREST ME. SHE DIDN'T.
AND YOU SAY I'M NAIVE? YOU NEVER CHANGE. A HOT PERSON COMES ALONG--
SHUT UP! IDIOT.
AHEM
IT BENEFITS NO ONE IF MORROW WINS. WANNA TAKE A TRIP?

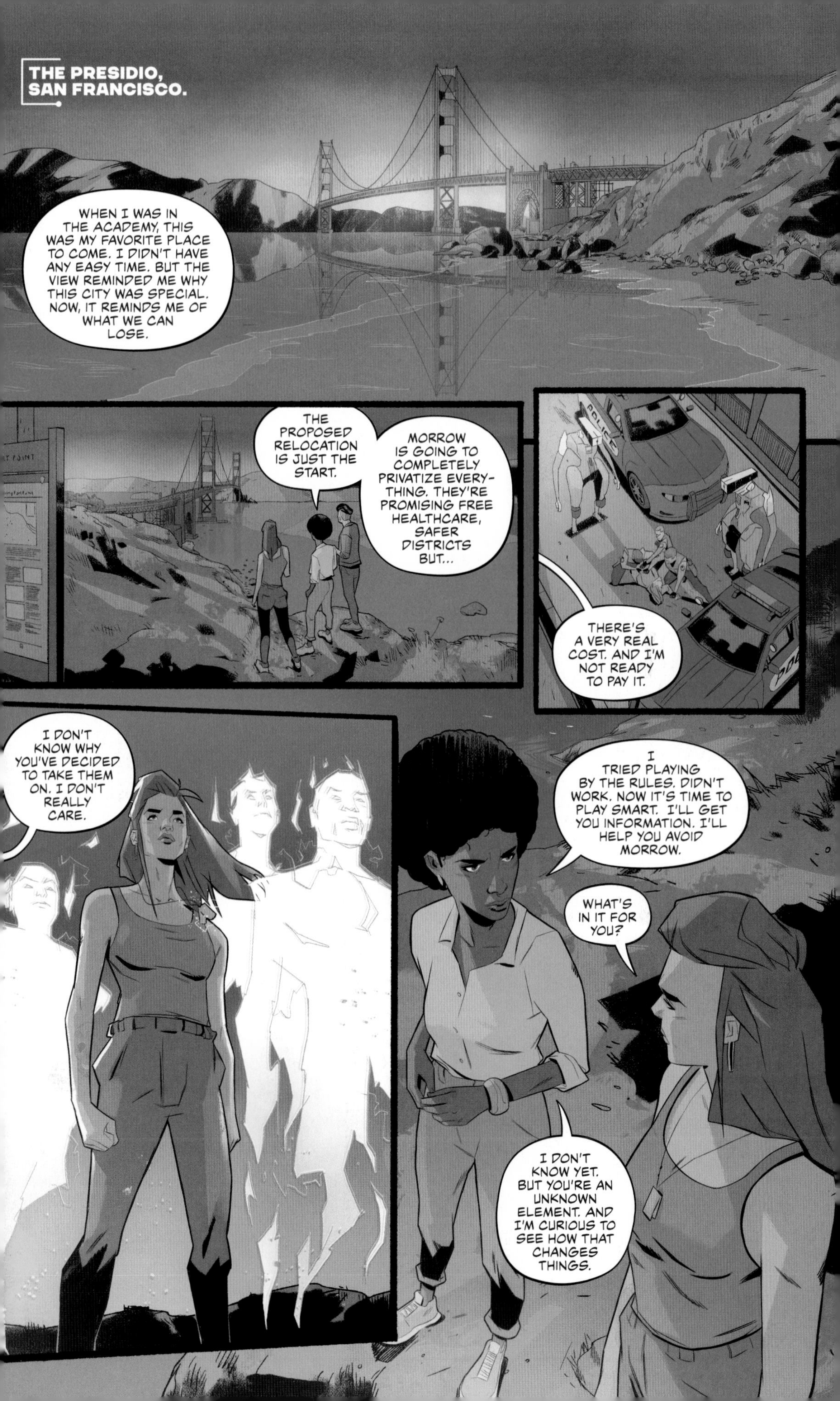
THE PRESIDIO, SAN FRANCISCO.
WHEN I WAS IN THE ACADEMY, THIS WAS MY FAVORITE PLACE TO COME. I DIDN'T HAVE ANY EASY TIME. BUT THE VIEW REMINDED ME WHY THIS CITY WAS SPECIAL. NOW, IT REMINDS ME OF WHAT WE CAN LOSE.
THE PROPOSED RELOCATION IS JUST THE START.
MORROW IS GOING TO COMPLETELY PRIVATIZE EVERY-THING. THEY'RE PROMISING FREE HEALTHCARE, SAFER DISTRICTS BUT...
THERE'S A VERY REAL COST. AND I'M NOT READY TO PAY IT.
I DON'T KNOW WHY YOU'VE DECIDED TO TAKE THEM ON. I DON'T REALLY CARE.
I TRIED PLAYING BY THE RULES. DIDN'T WORK. NOW IT'S TIME TO PLAY SMART. I'LL GET YOU INFORMATION. I'LL HELP YOU AVOID MORROW.
WHAT'S IN IT FOR YOU?
I DON'T KNOW YET. BUT YOU'RE AN UNKNOWN ELEMENT. AND I'M CURIOUS TO SEE HOW THAT CHANGES THINGS.

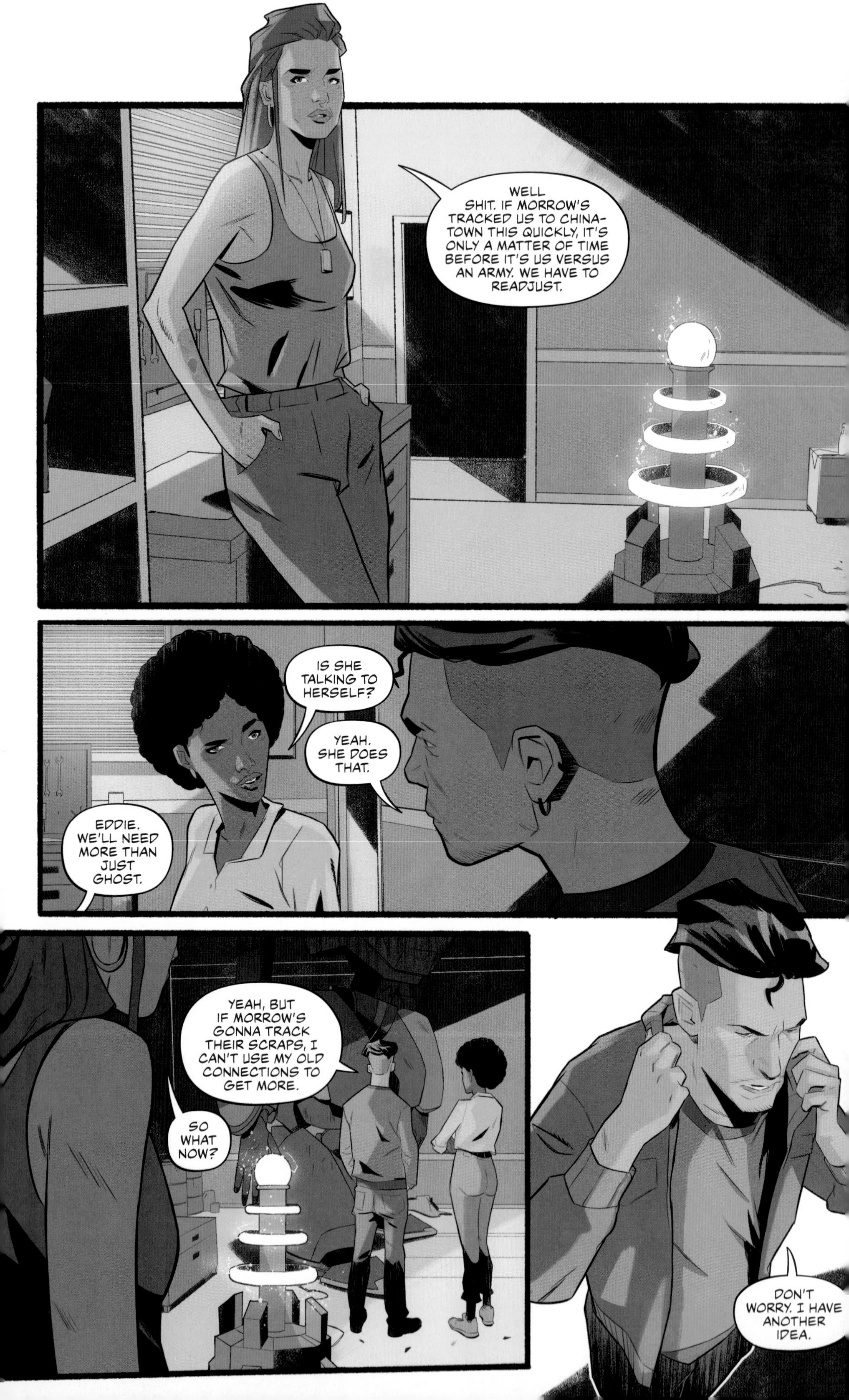
WELL SHIT. IF MORROW'S TRACKED US TO CHINA-TOWN THIS QUICKLY, IT'S ONLY A MATTER OF TIME BEFORE IT'S US VERSUS AN ARMY. WE HAVE TO READJUST.
IS SHE TALKING TO HERSELF?
YEAH. SHE DOES THAT.
EDDIE. WE'LL NEED MORE THAN JUST GHOST.
YEAH, BUT IF MORROW'S GONNA TRACK THEIR SCRAPS, I CAN'T USE MY OLD CONNECTIONS TO GET MORE.
SO WHAT NOW?
DON'T WORRY. I HAVE ANOTHER IDEA.

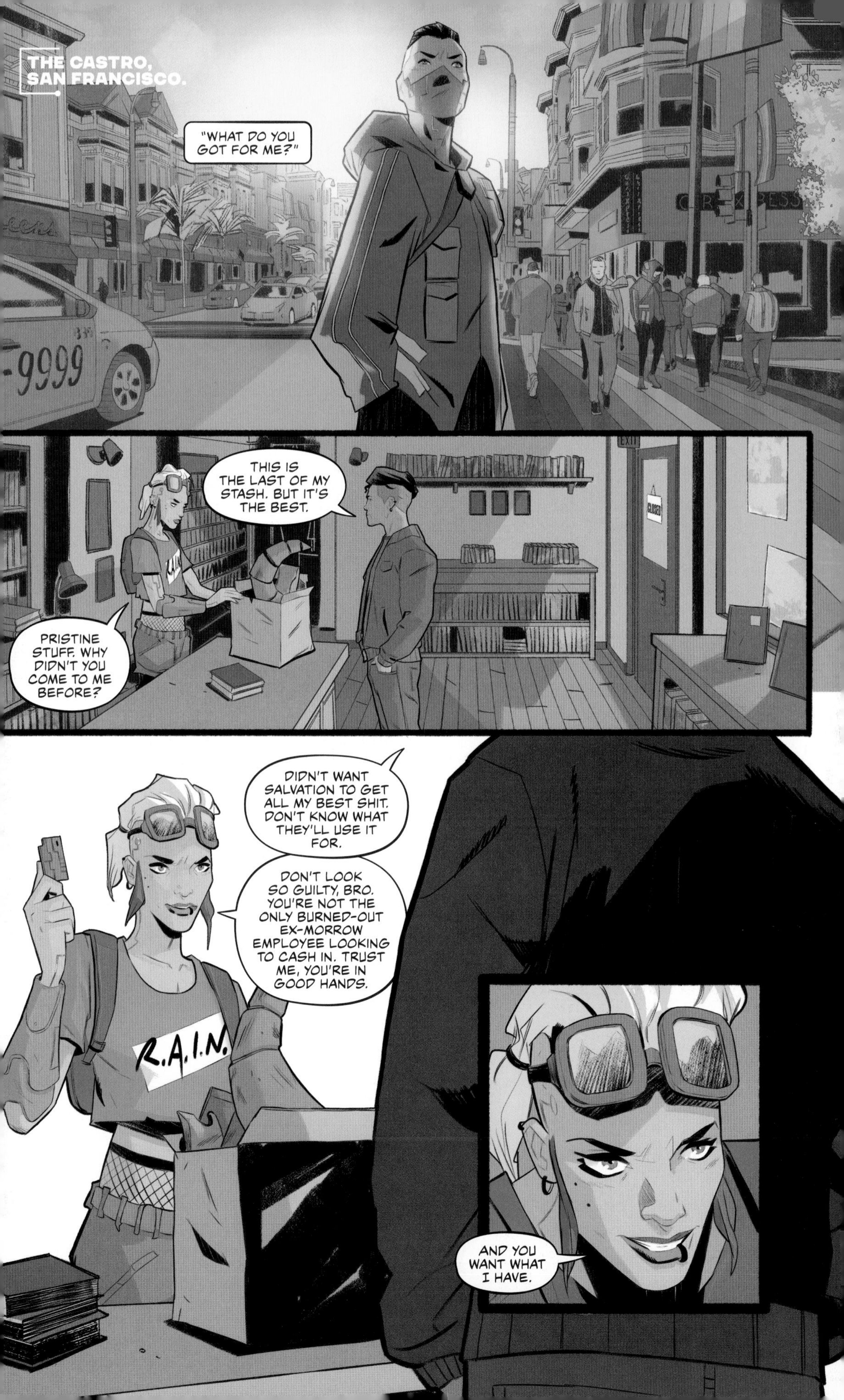
THE CASTRO, SAN FRANCISCO.
"WHAT DO YOU GOT FOR ME?"
-9999
THIS IS THE LAST OF MY STASH. BUT IT'S THE BEST.
PRISTINE STUFF. WHY DIDN'T YOU COME TO ME BEFORE?
EXIT
CLOSED
DIDN'T WANT SALVATION TO GET ALL MY BEST SHIT. DON'T KNOW WHAT THEY'LL USE IT FOR.
DON'T LOOK SO GUILTY, BRO. YOU'RE NOT THE ONLY BURNED-OUT EX-MORROW EMPLOYEE LOOKING TO CASH IN. TRUST ME, YOU'RE IN GOOD HANDS.
R.A.I.N.
AND YOU WANT WHAT I HAVE.

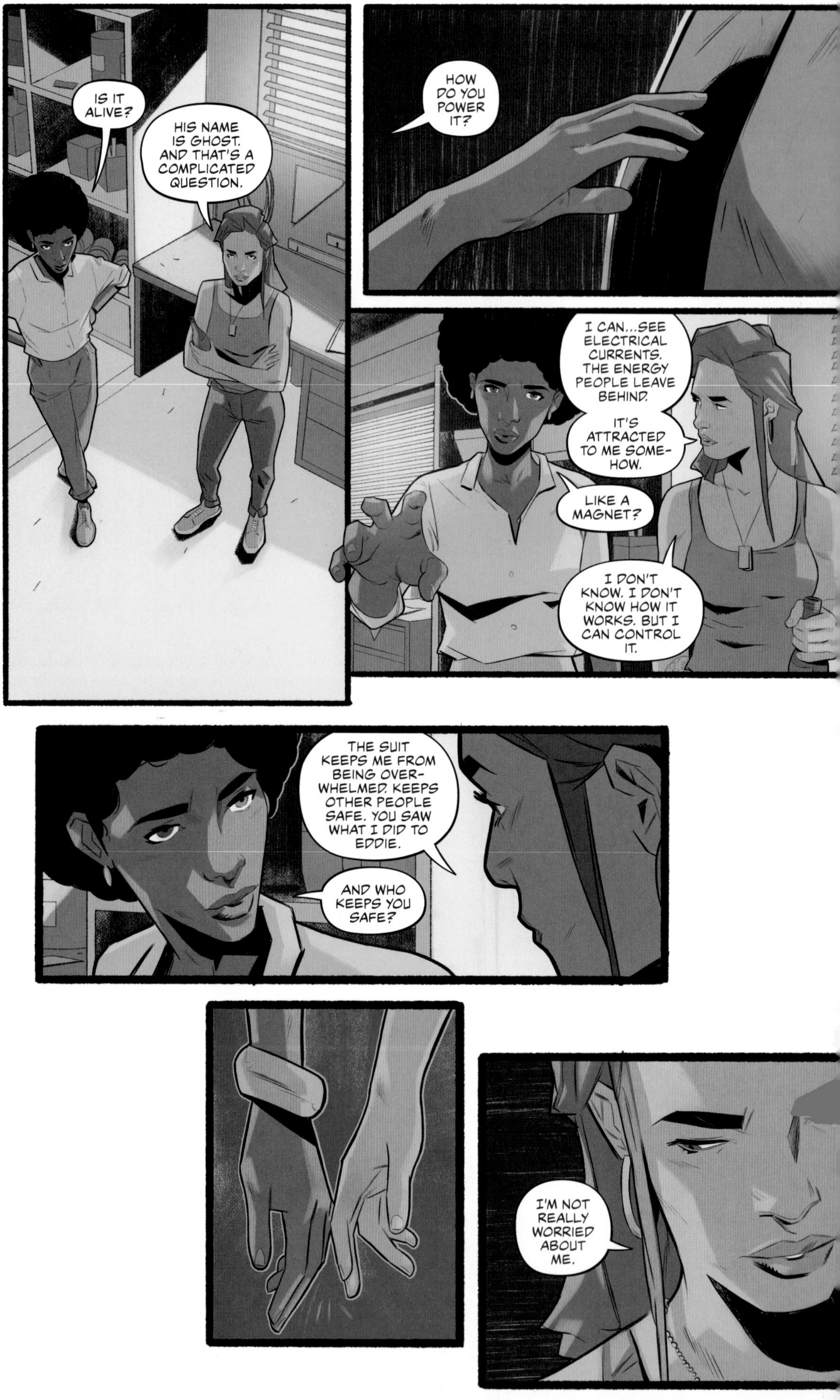
IS IT ALIVE?
HIS NAME IS GHOST. AND THAT'S A COMPLICATED QUESTION.
HOW DO YOU POWER IT?
I CAN...SEE ELECTRICAL CURRENTS. THE ENERGY PEOPLE LEAVE BEHIND.
IT'S ATTRACTED TO ME SOME-HOW.
LIKE A MAGNET?
I DON'T KNOW. I DON'T KNOW HOW IT WORKS. BUT I CAN CONTROL IT.
THE SUIT KEEPS ME FROM BEING OVER-WHELMED. KEEPS OTHER PEOPLE SAFE. YOU SAW WHAT I DID TO EDDIE.
AND WHO KEEPS YOU SAFE?
I'M NOT REALLY WORRIED ABOUT ME.

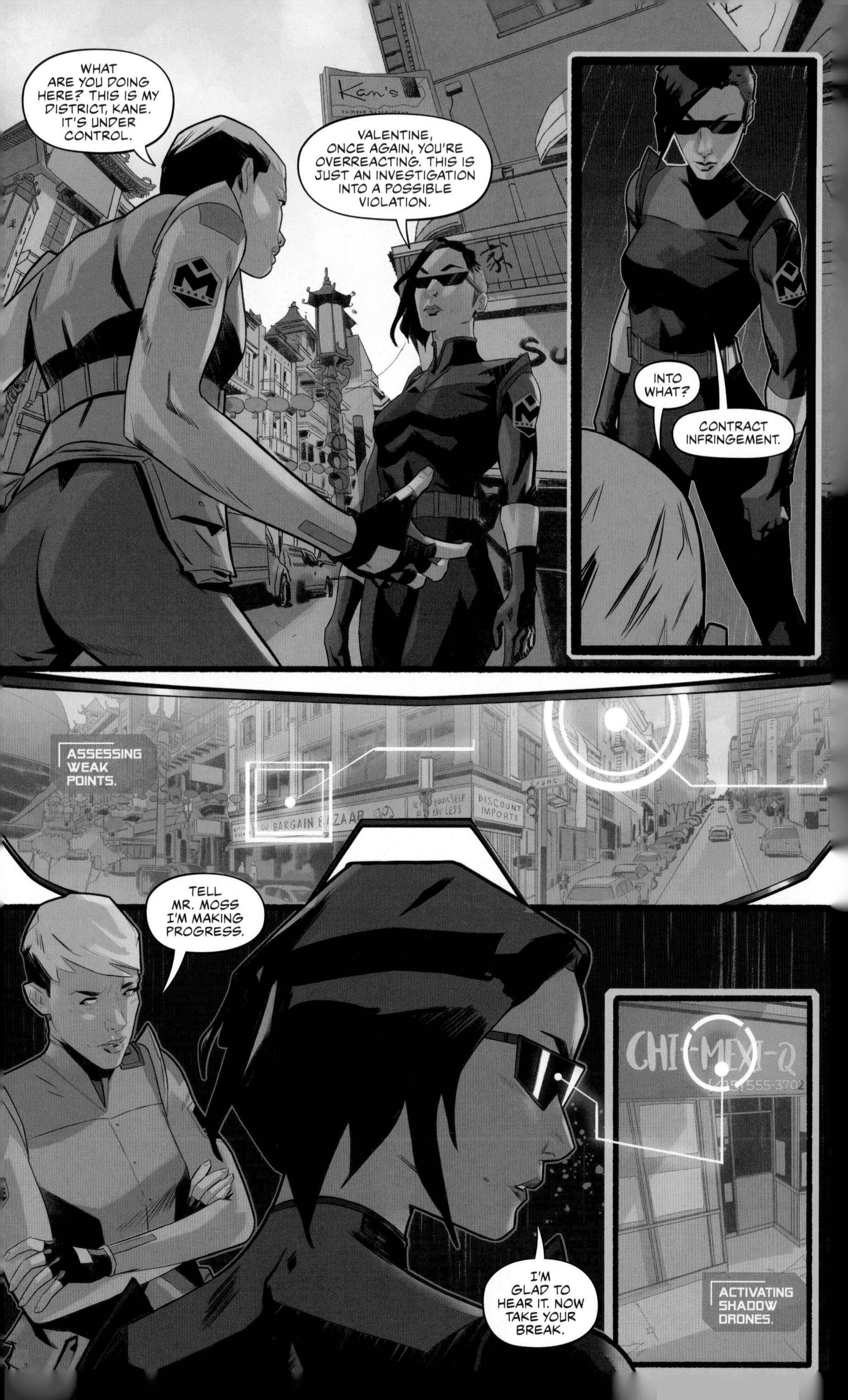
WHAT ARE YOU DOING HERE? THIS IS MY DISTRICT, KANE. IT'S UNDER CONTROL.
VALENTINE, ONCE AGAIN, YOU'RE OVERREACTING. THIS IS JUST AN INVESTIGATION INTO A POSSIBLE VIOLATION.
INTO WHAT?
CONTRACT INFRINGEMENT.
ASSESSING WEAK POINTS.
BARGAIN BAZAAR
DISCOUNT IMPORTS
TELL MR. MOSS I'M MAKING PROGRESS.
CHI-MEXI-Q
I'M GLAD TO HEAR IT. NOW TAKE YOUR BREAK.
ACTIVATING SHADOW DRONES.

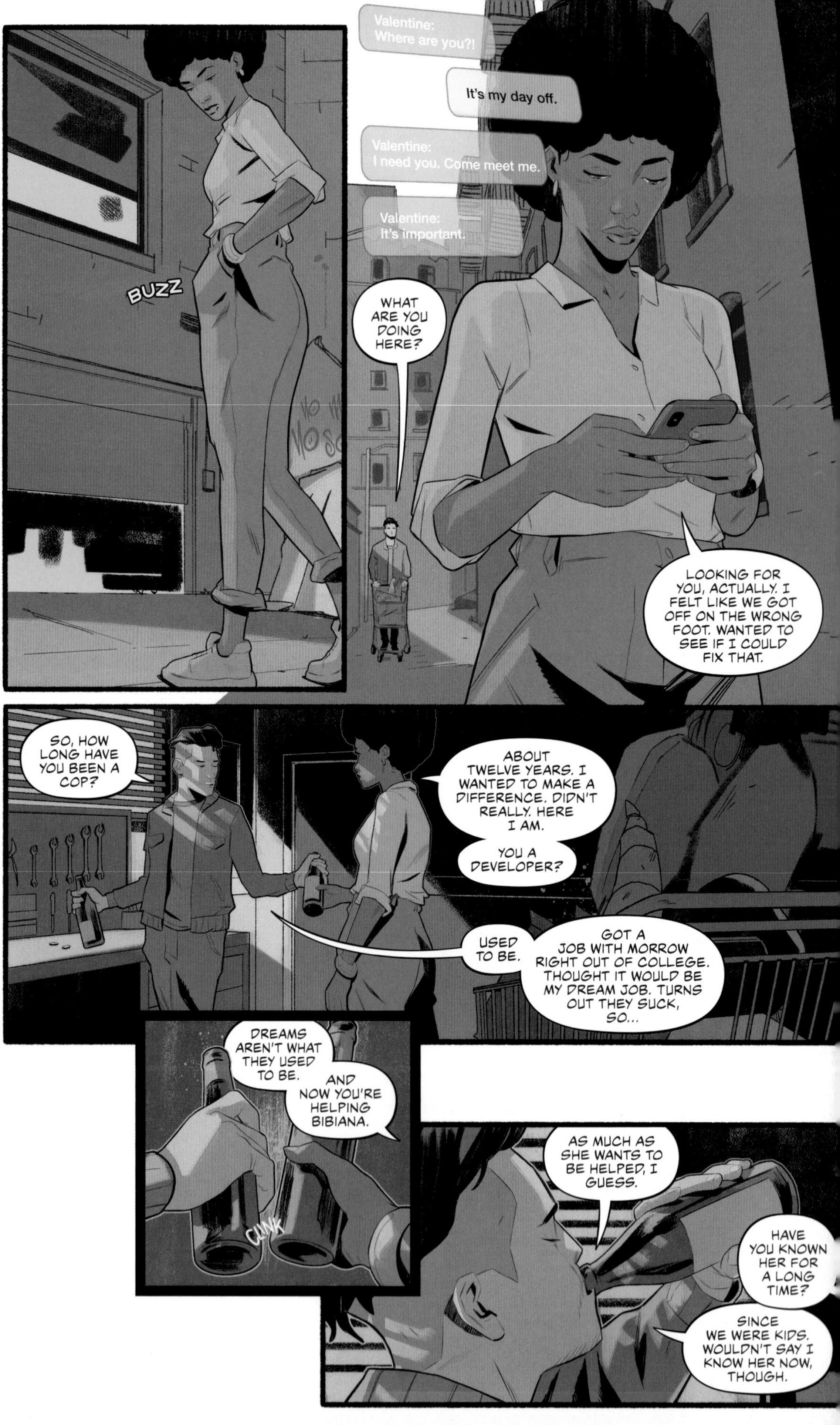
Valentine:
Where are you?!
It's my day off.
Valentine:
I need you. Come meet me.
Valentine:
It's important.
BUZZ
WHAT ARE YOU DOING HERE?
LOOKING FOR YOU, ACTUALLY. I FELT LIKE WE GOT OFF ON THE WRONG FOOT. WANTED TO SEE IF I COULD FIX THAT.
SO, HOW LONG HAVE YOU BEEN A COP?
ABOUT TWELVE YEARS. I WANTED TO MAKE A DIFFERENCE. DIDN'T REALLY. HERE I AM.
YOU A DEVELOPER?
USED TO BE.
GOT A JOB WITH MORROW RIGHT OUT OF COLLEGE. THOUGHT IT WOULD BE MY DREAM JOB. TURNS OUT THEY SUCK, SO...
DREAMS AREN'T WHAT THEY USED TO BE.
AND NOW YOU'RE HELPING BIBIANA.
CLINK
AS MUCH AS SHE WANTS TO BE HELPED, I GUESS.
HAVE YOU KNOWN HER FOR A LONG TIME?
SINCE WE WERE KIDS. WOULDN'T SAY I KNOW HER NOW, THOUGH.

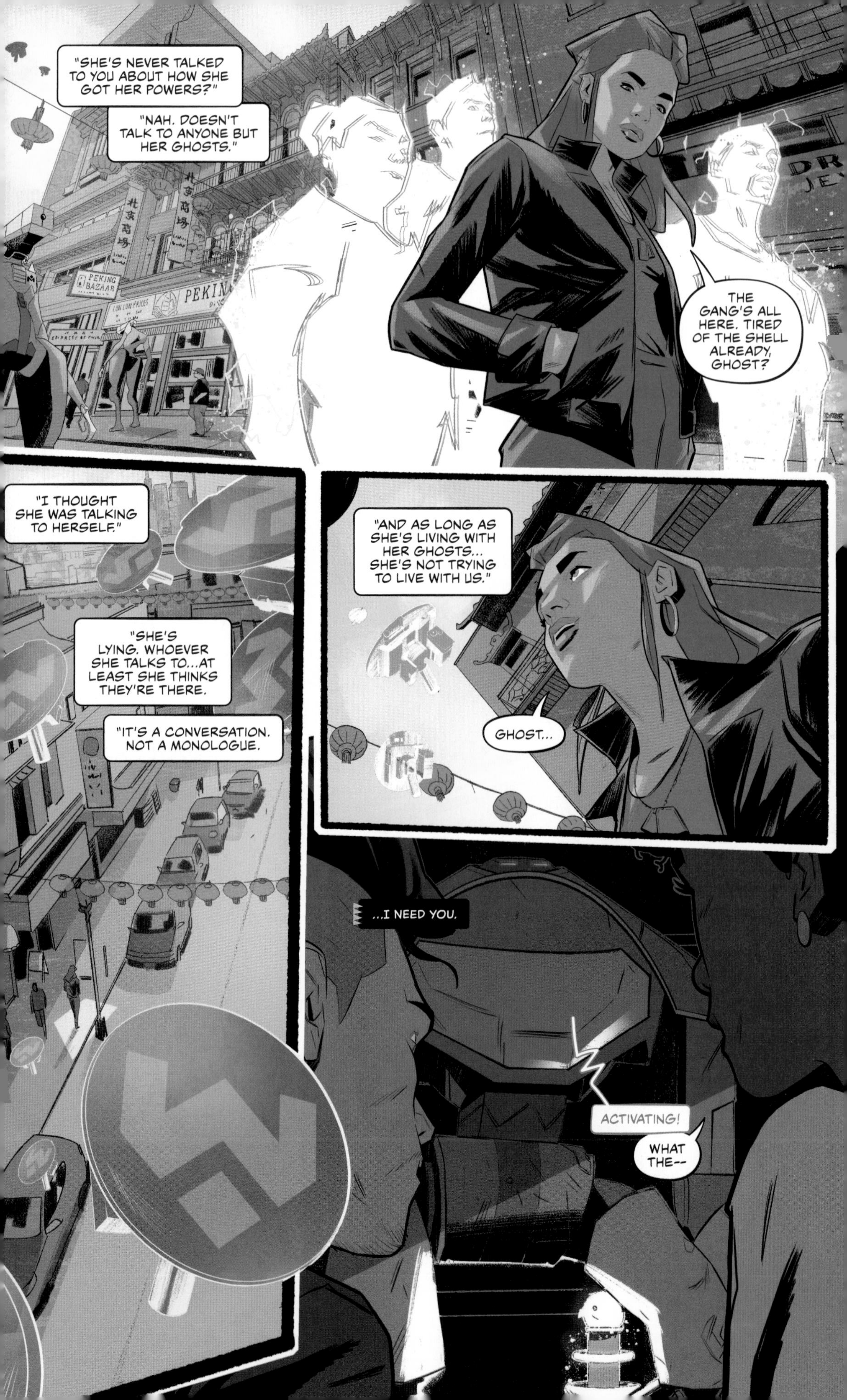
"SHE'S NEVER TALKED TO YOU ABOUT HOW SHE GOT HER POWERS?"
"NAH. DOESN'T TALK TO ANYONE BUT HER GHOSTS."
THE GANG'S ALL HERE. TIRED OF THE SHELL ALREADY, GHOST?
PEKING BAZAAR
"I THOUGHT SHE WAS TALKING TO HERSELF."
"SHE'S LYING. WHOEVER SHE TALKS TO...AT LEAST SHE THINKS THEY'RE THERE.
"IT'S A CONVERSATION. NOT A MONOLOGUE.
"AND AS LONG AS SHE'S LIVING WITH HER GHOSTS... SHE'S NOT TRYING TO LIVE WITH US."
GHOST...
...I NEED YOU.
ACTIVATING!
WHAT THE--

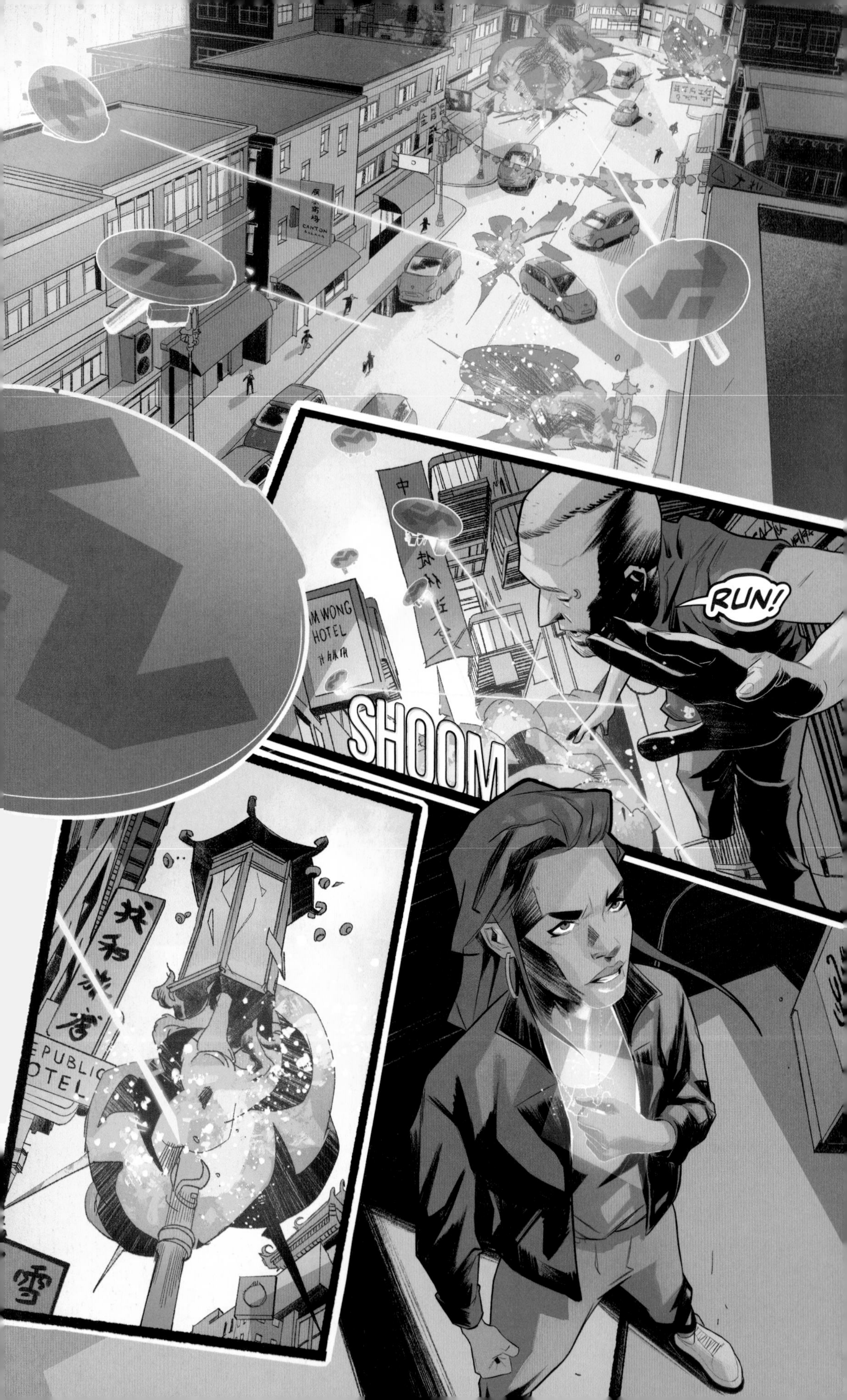
RUN!
SHOOM
M WONG
HOTEL
EPUBLIC
OTEL

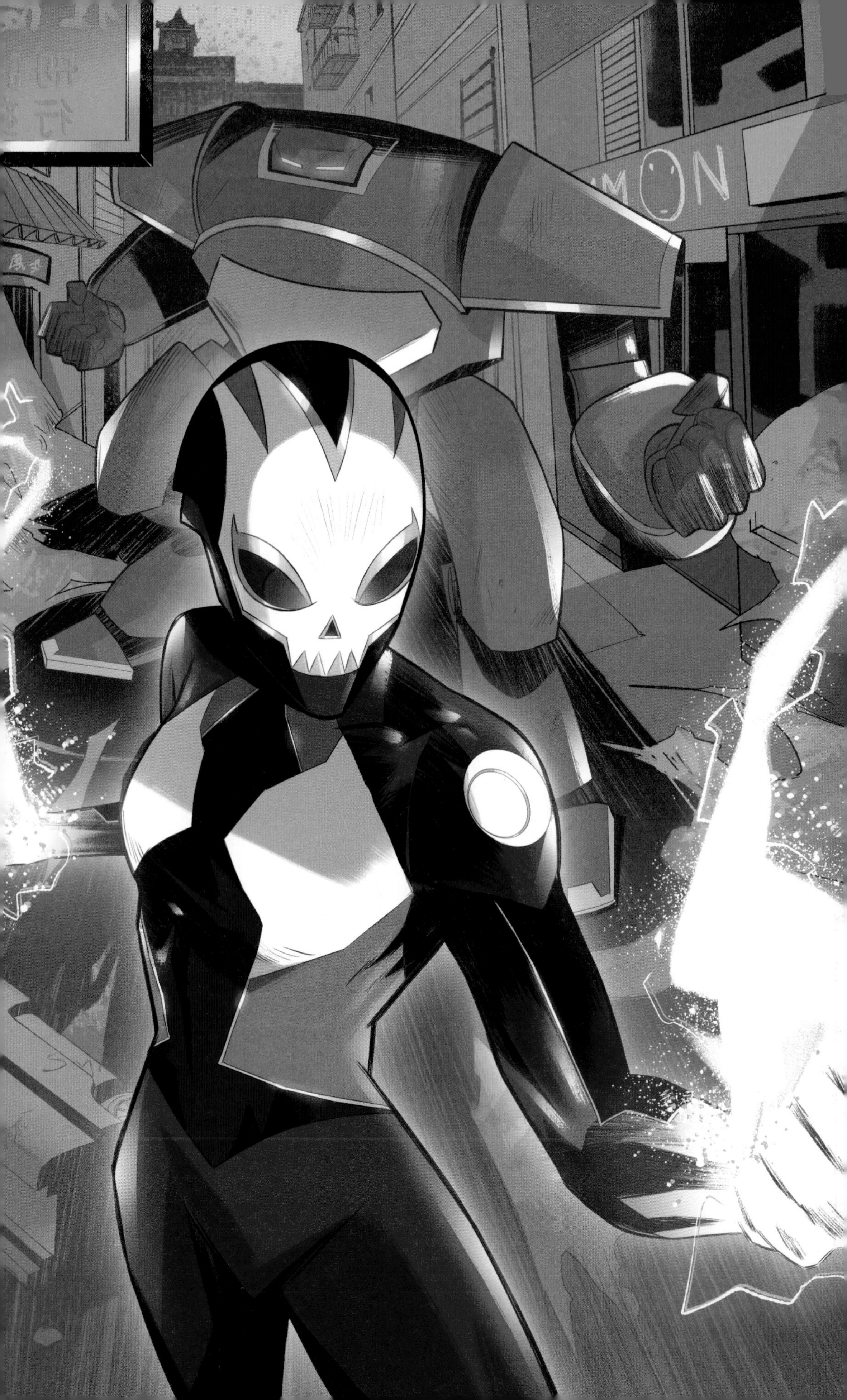
MON

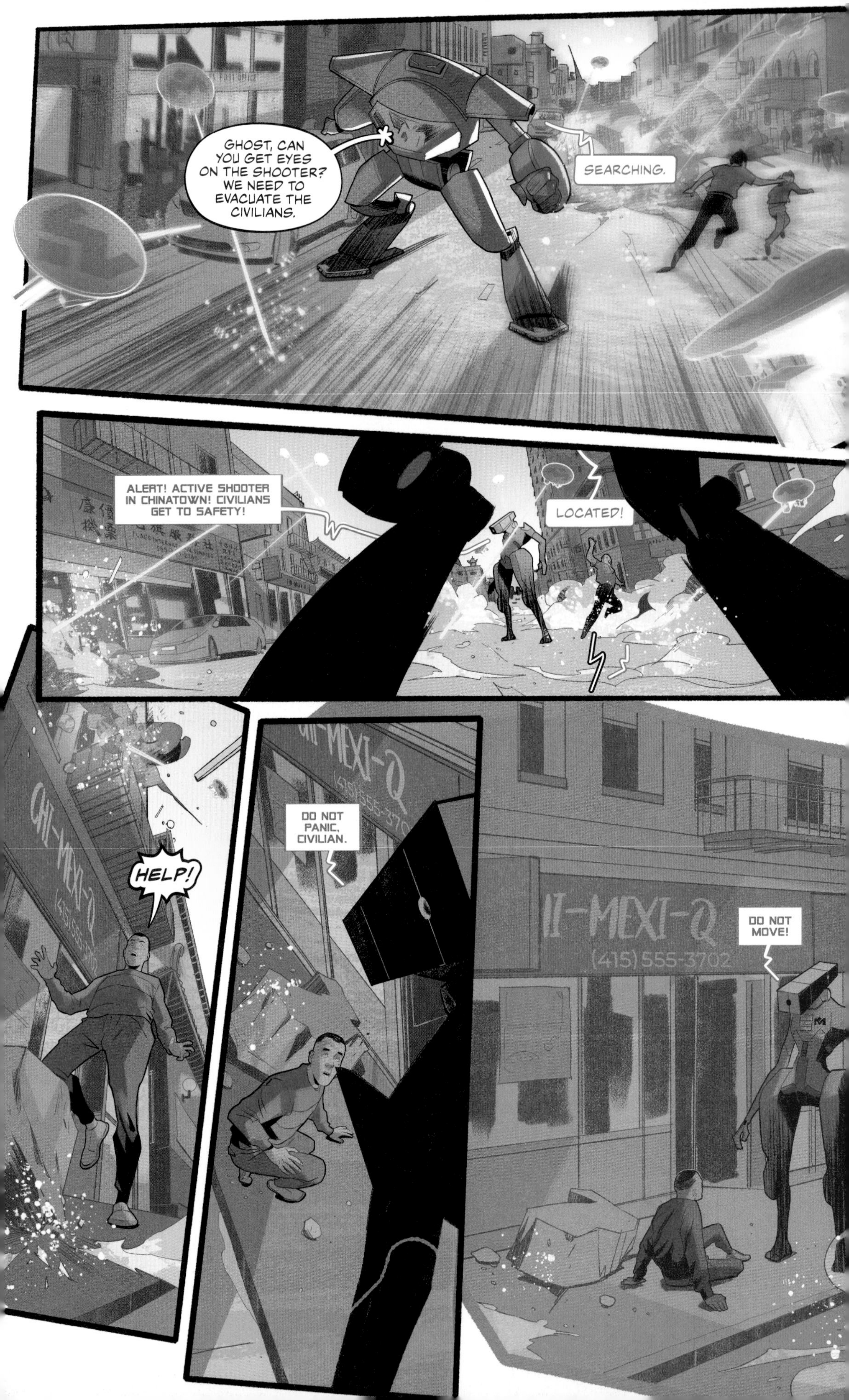
GHOST, CAN YOU GET EYES ON THE SHOOTER? WE NEED TO EVACUATE THE CIVILIANS.
SEARCHING.
ALERT! ACTIVE SHOOTER IN CHINATOWN! CIVILIANS GET TO SAFETY!
LOCATED!
HELP!
DO NOT PANIC, CIVILIAN.
II-MEXI-Q
(415) 555-3702
DO NOT MOVE!

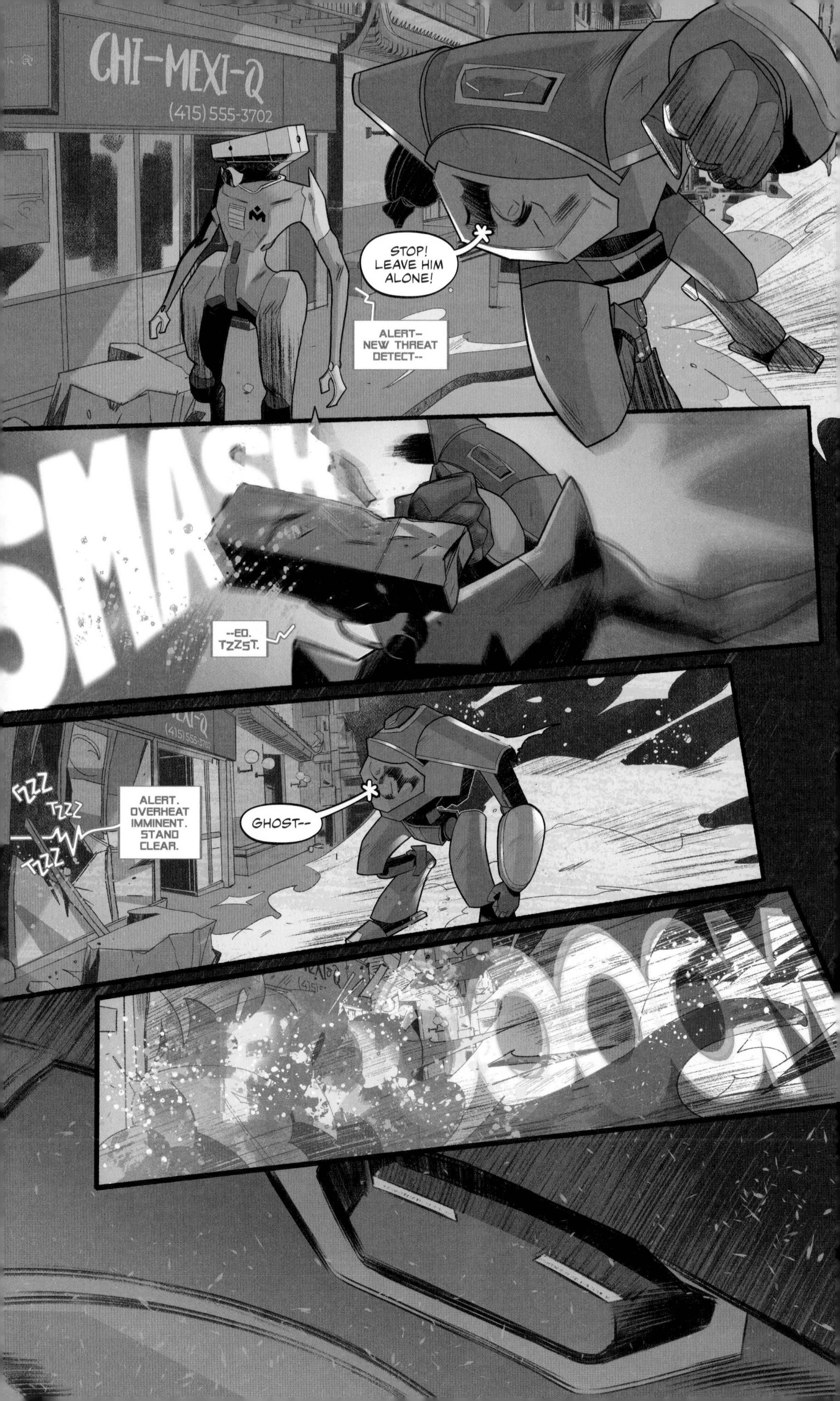
CHI-MEXI-Q
(415) 555-3702
STOP! LEAVE HIM ALONE!
ALERT- NEW THREAT DETECT--
SMASH
--ED. TZZST.
(415) 555-3702
TZZZ TZZZ TZZZ
ALERT. OVERHEAT IMMINENT. STAND CLEAR.
GHOST--
BOOOOM

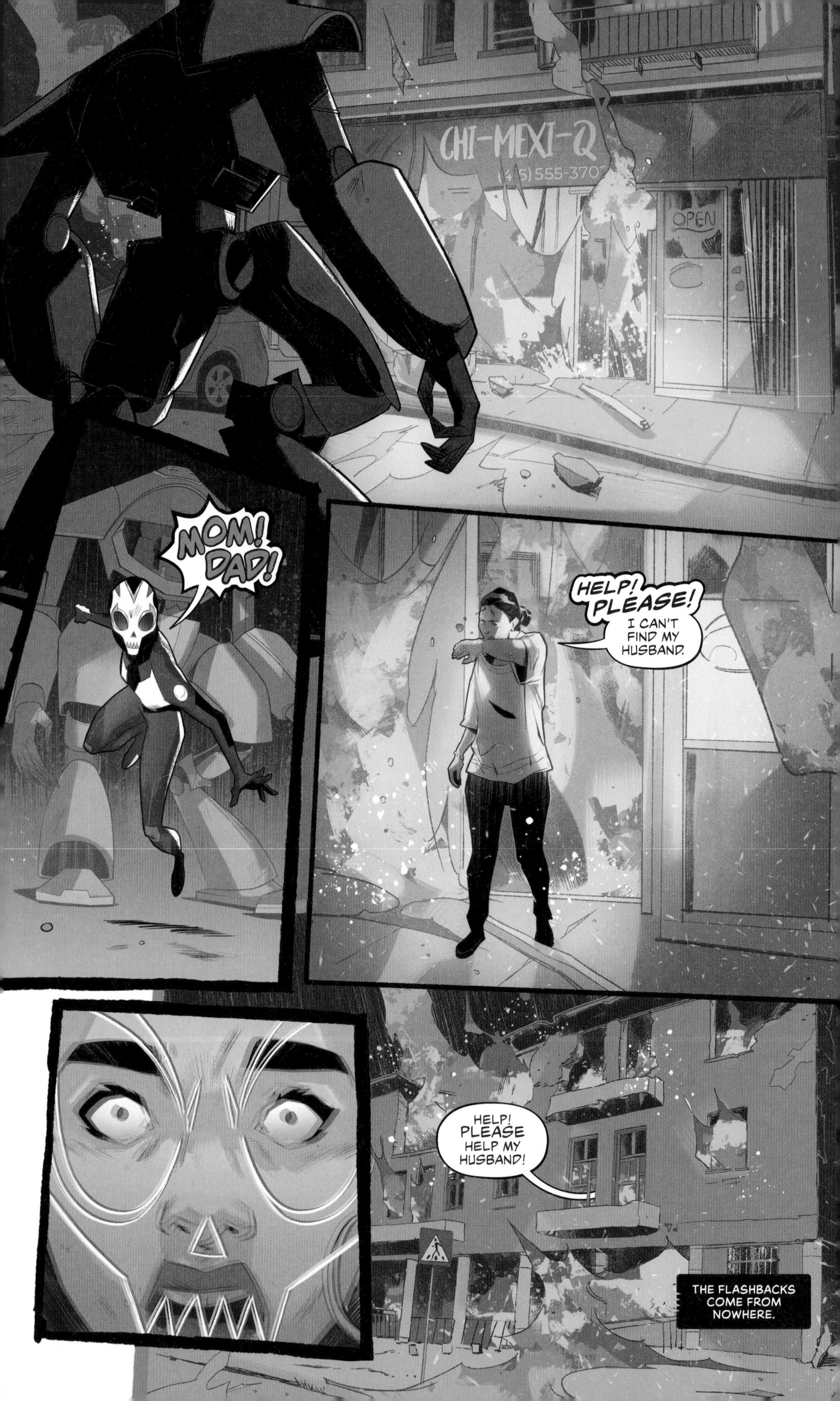

CHI-MEXI-Q
OPEN
MOM! DAD!
HELP! PLEASE! I CAN'T FIND MY HUSBAND.
HELP! PLEASE HELP MY HUSBAND!
THE FLASHBACKS COME FROM NOWHERE.

WITHOUT WARNING. WITHOUT QUESTION. I'M TRANSPORTED.

AND I REMEMBER.

PLEASE DON'T LEAVE HIM HERE!

HE'S ALREADY GONE, CAPTAIN!

CAPTAIN! WE HAVE TO MOVE!

WE SHOULD EVAC HIM TOO!

DAD!

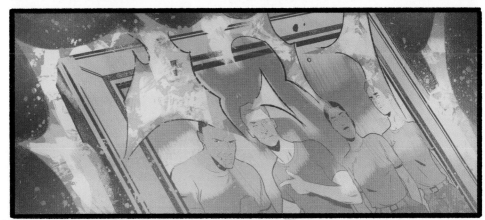

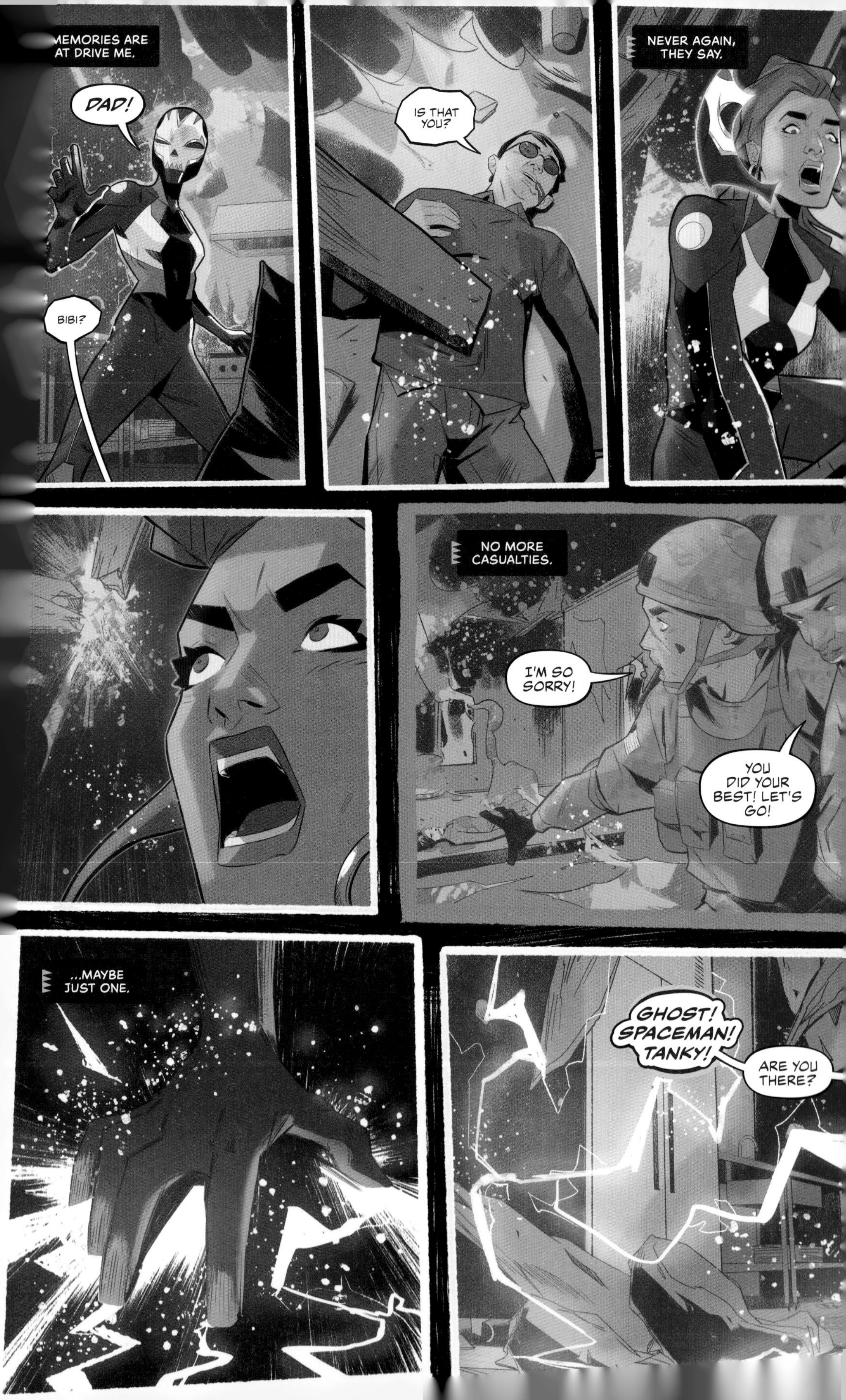
MEMORIES ARE
AT DRIVE ME.
DAD!
BIBI?
IS THAT YOU?
NEVER AGAIN, THEY SAY.
NO MORE CASUALTIES.
I'M SO SORRY!
YOU DID YOUR BEST! LET'S GO!
...MAYBE JUST ONE.
GHOST! SPACEMAN! TANKY!
ARE YOU THERE?

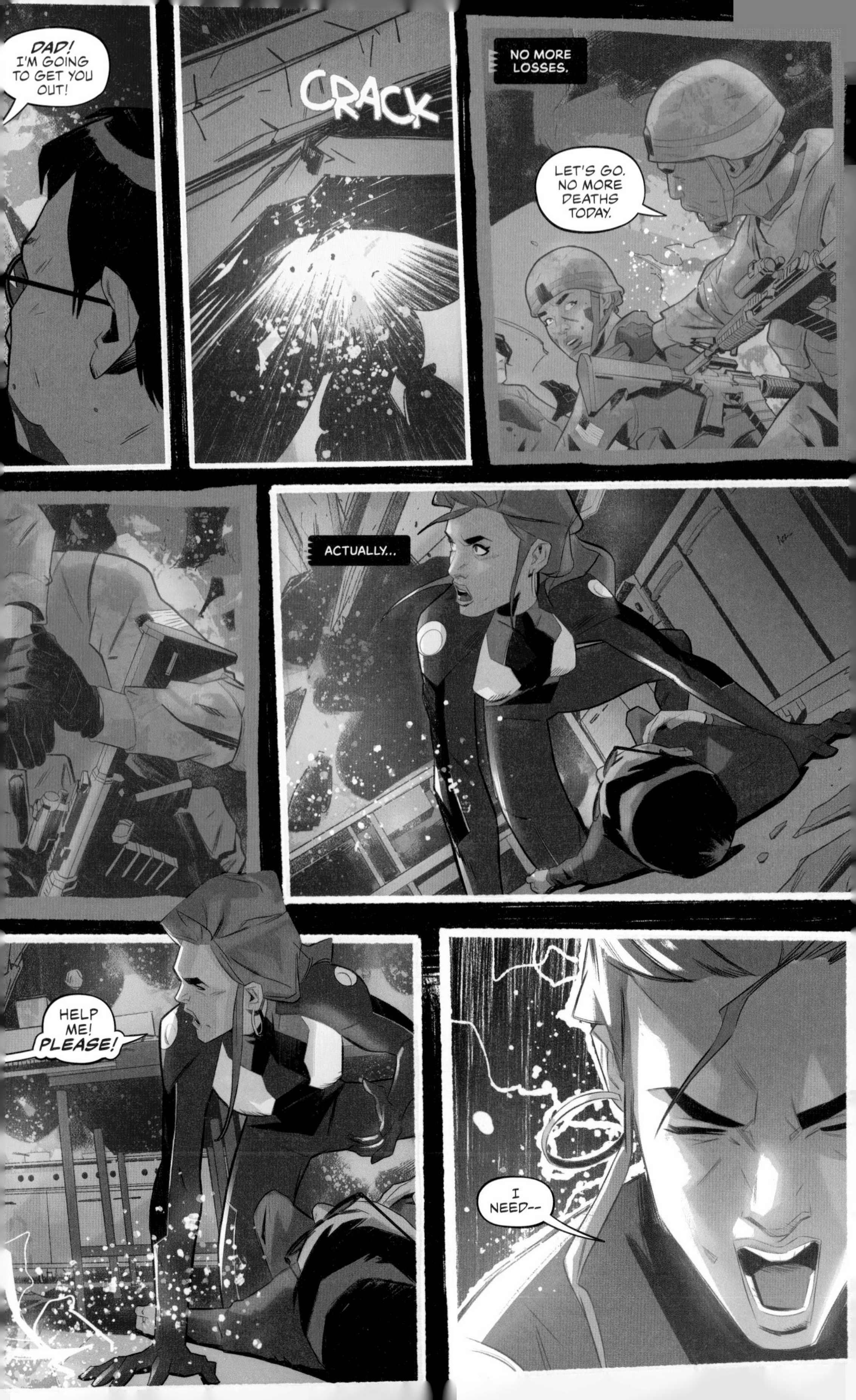
DAD! I'M GOING TO GET YOU OUT!
CRACK
NO MORE LOSSES.
LET'S GO. NO MORE DEATHS TODAY.
ACTUALLY...
HELP ME! PLEASE!
I NEED--

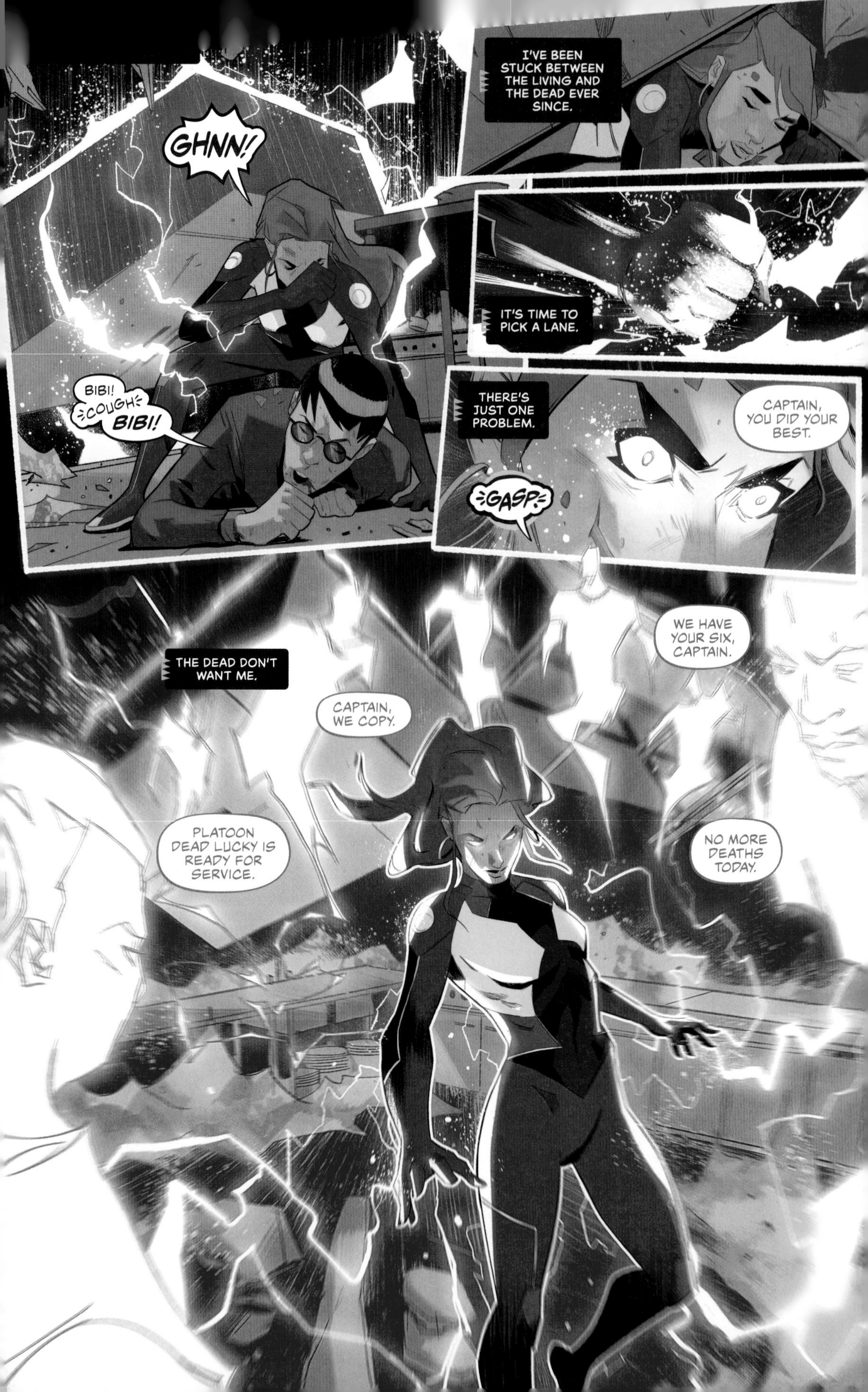
GHNN!
I'VE BEEN STUCK BETWEEN THE LIVING AND THE DEAD EVER SINCE.
IT'S TIME TO PICK A LANE.
BIBI! COUGH BIBI!
THERE'S JUST ONE PROBLEM.
CAPTAIN, YOU DID YOUR BEST.
GASP
THE DEAD DON'T WANT ME.
CAPTAIN, WE COPY.
WE HAVE YOUR SIX, CAPTAIN.
PLATOON DEAD LUCKY IS READY FOR SERVICE.
NO MORE DEATHS TODAY.

TERMINAL

```
GHOST:~ admin$ SingleIssueProfiler
Issue:
    No.: 004
    Title: They Sit Like Scars.
```

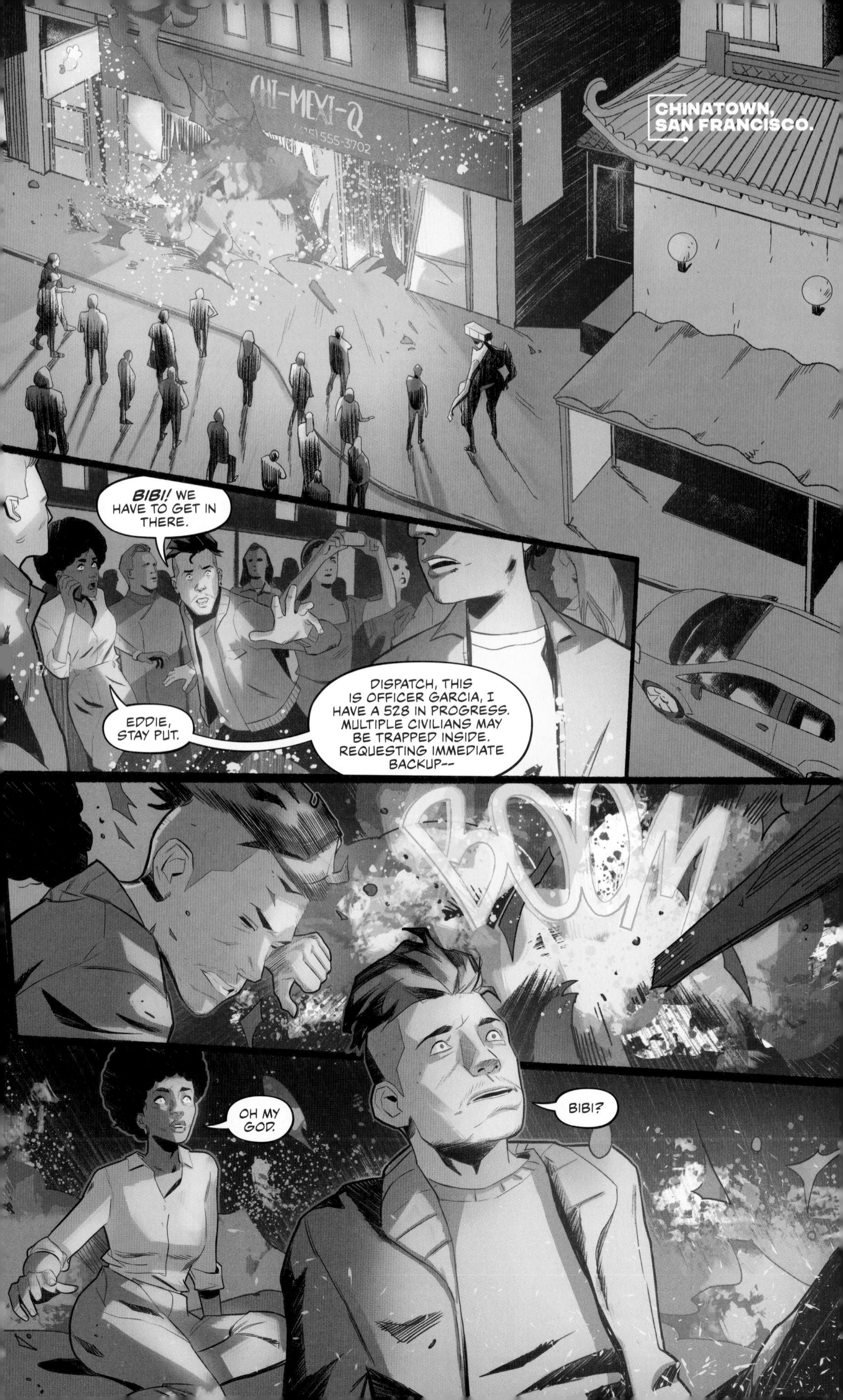
CHI-MEXI-Q
(415)555-3702
CHINATOWN, SAN FRANCISCO.
BIBI! WE HAVE TO GET IN THERE.
EDDIE, STAY PUT.
DISPATCH, THIS IS OFFICER GARCIA, I HAVE A 528 IN PROGRESS. MULTIPLE CIVILIANS MAY BE TRAPPED INSIDE. REQUESTING IMMEDIATE BACKUP--
BOOM
OH MY GOD.
BIBI?

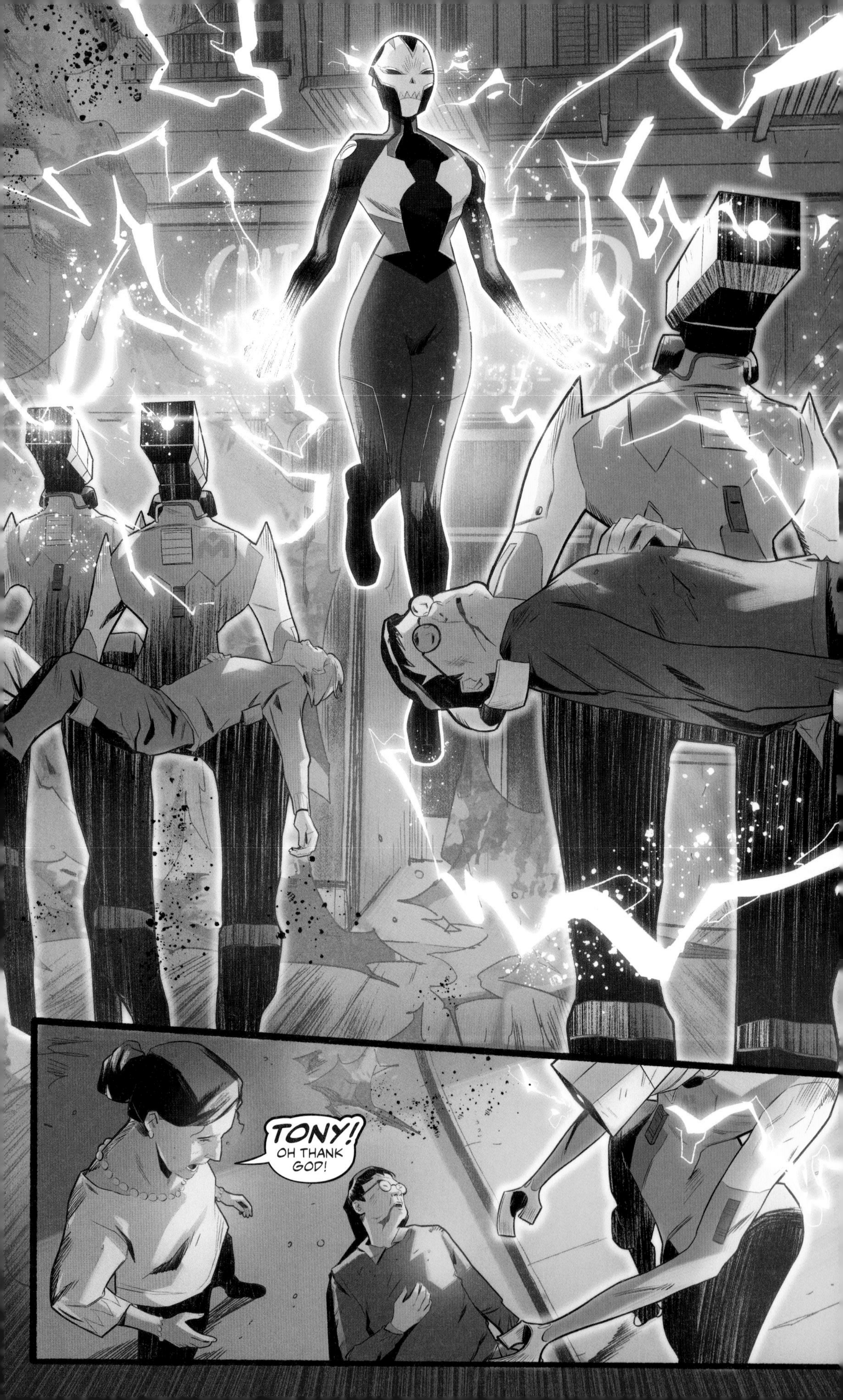
TONY! OH THANK GOD!

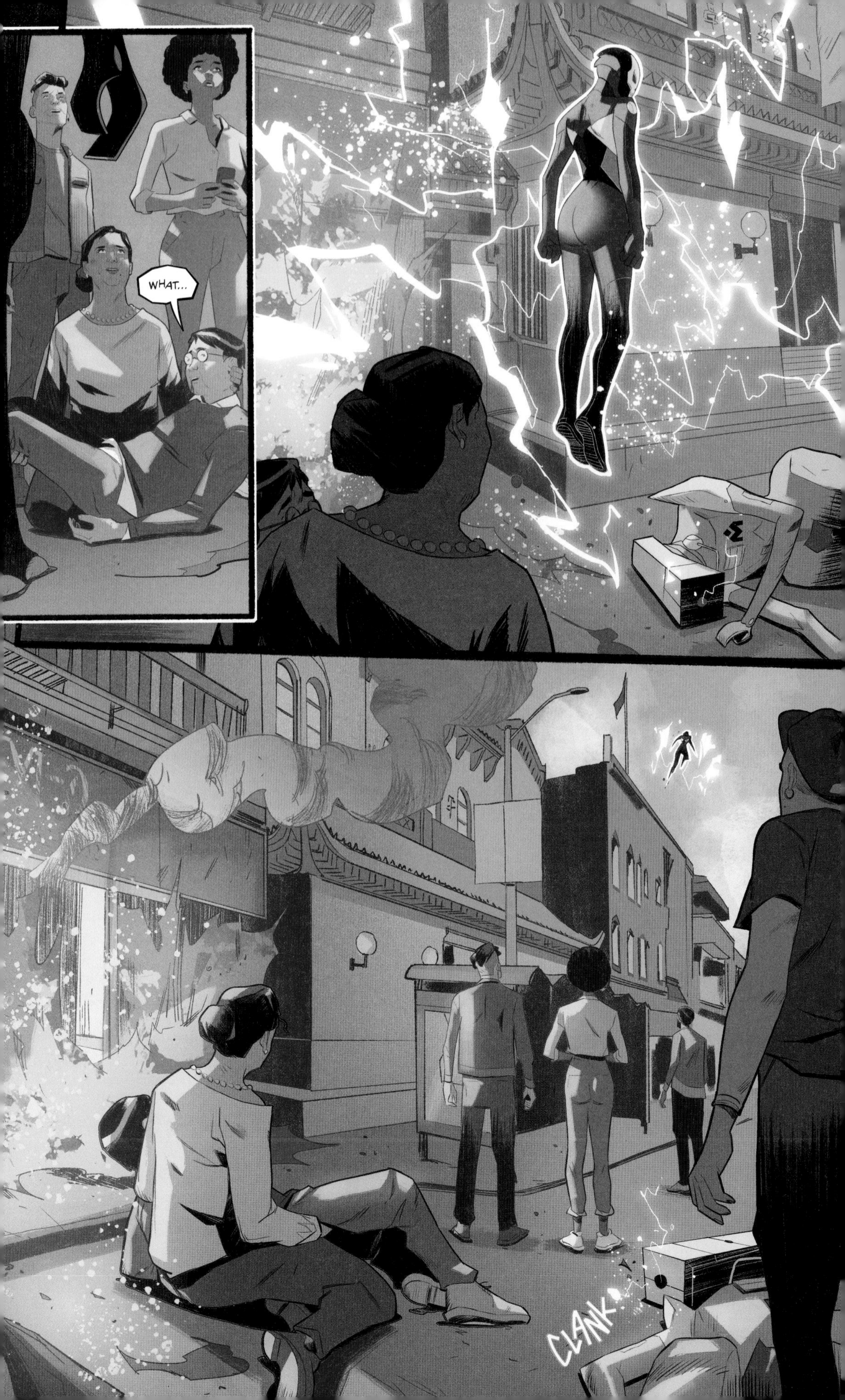
WHAT...
CLANK

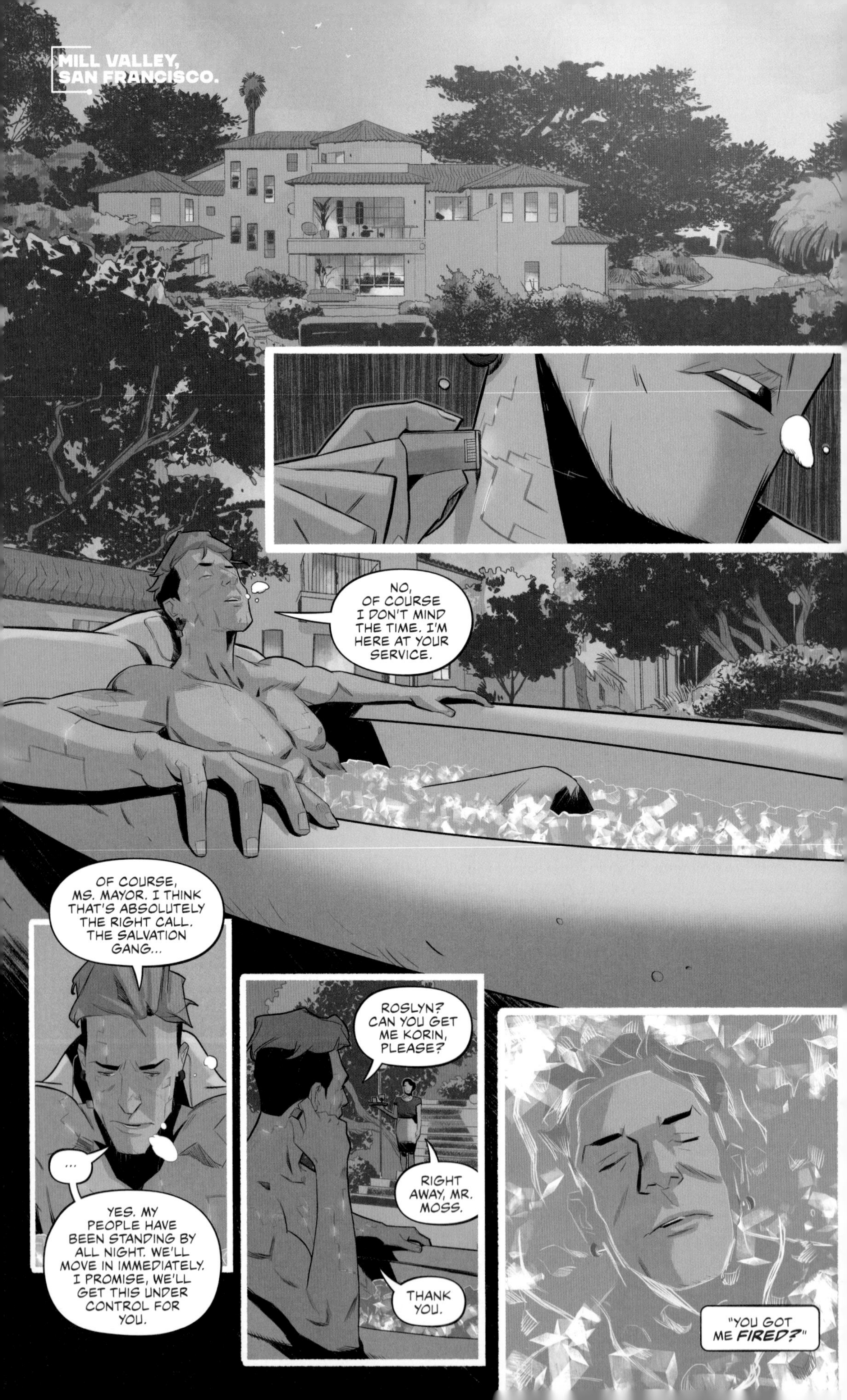
MILL VALLEY, SAN FRANCISCO.
NO, OF COURSE I DON'T MIND THE TIME. I'M HERE AT YOUR SERVICE.
OF COURSE, MS. MAYOR. I THINK THAT'S ABSOLUTELY THE RIGHT CALL. THE SALVATION GANG...
...
YES. MY PEOPLE HAVE BEEN STANDING BY ALL NIGHT. WE'LL MOVE IN IMMEDIATELY. I PROMISE, WE'LL GET THIS UNDER CONTROL FOR YOU.
ROSLYN? CAN YOU GET ME KORIN, PLEASE?
RIGHT AWAY, MR. MOSS.
THANK YOU.
"YOU GOT ME FIRED?"

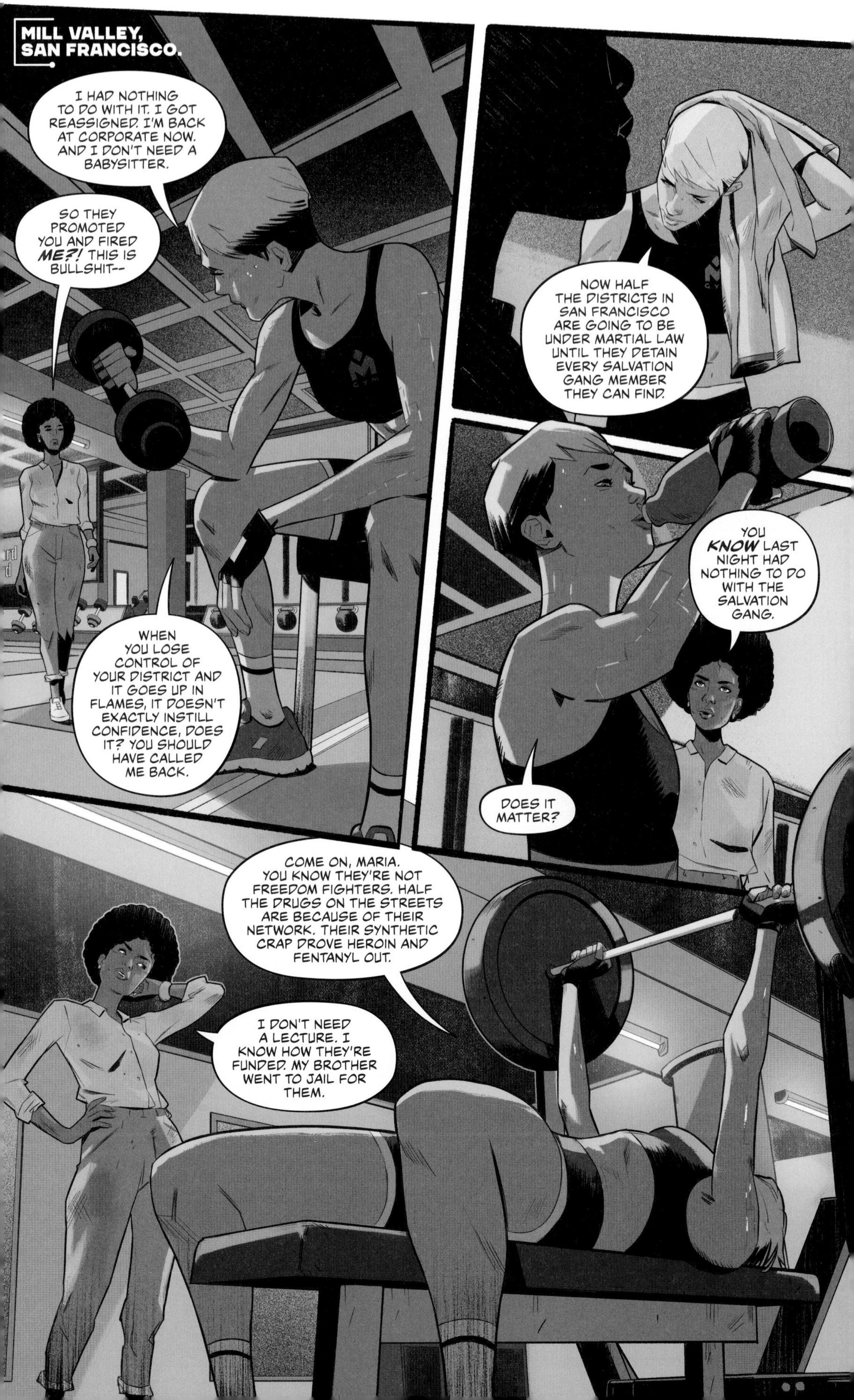
MILL VALLEY, SAN FRANCISCO.
I HAD NOTHING TO DO WITH IT. I GOT REASSIGNED. I'M BACK AT CORPORATE NOW. AND I DON'T NEED A BABYSITTER.
SO THEY PROMOTED YOU AND FIRED *ME?!* THIS IS BULLSHIT--
WHEN YOU LOSE CONTROL OF YOUR DISTRICT AND IT GOES UP IN FLAMES, IT DOESN'T EXACTLY INSTILL CONFIDENCE, DOES IT? YOU SHOULD HAVE CALLED ME BACK.
NOW HALF THE DISTRICTS IN SAN FRANCISCO ARE GOING TO BE UNDER MARTIAL LAW UNTIL THEY DETAIN EVERY SALVATION GANG MEMBER THEY CAN FIND.
YOU *KNOW* LAST NIGHT HAD NOTHING TO DO WITH THE SALVATION GANG.
DOES IT MATTER?
COME ON, MARIA. YOU KNOW THEY'RE NOT FREEDOM FIGHTERS. HALF THE DRUGS ON THE STREETS ARE BECAUSE OF THEIR NETWORK. THEIR SYNTHETIC CRAP DROVE HEROIN AND FENTANYL OUT.
I DON'T NEED A LECTURE. I KNOW HOW THEY'RE FUNDED. MY BROTHER WENT TO JAIL FOR THEM.

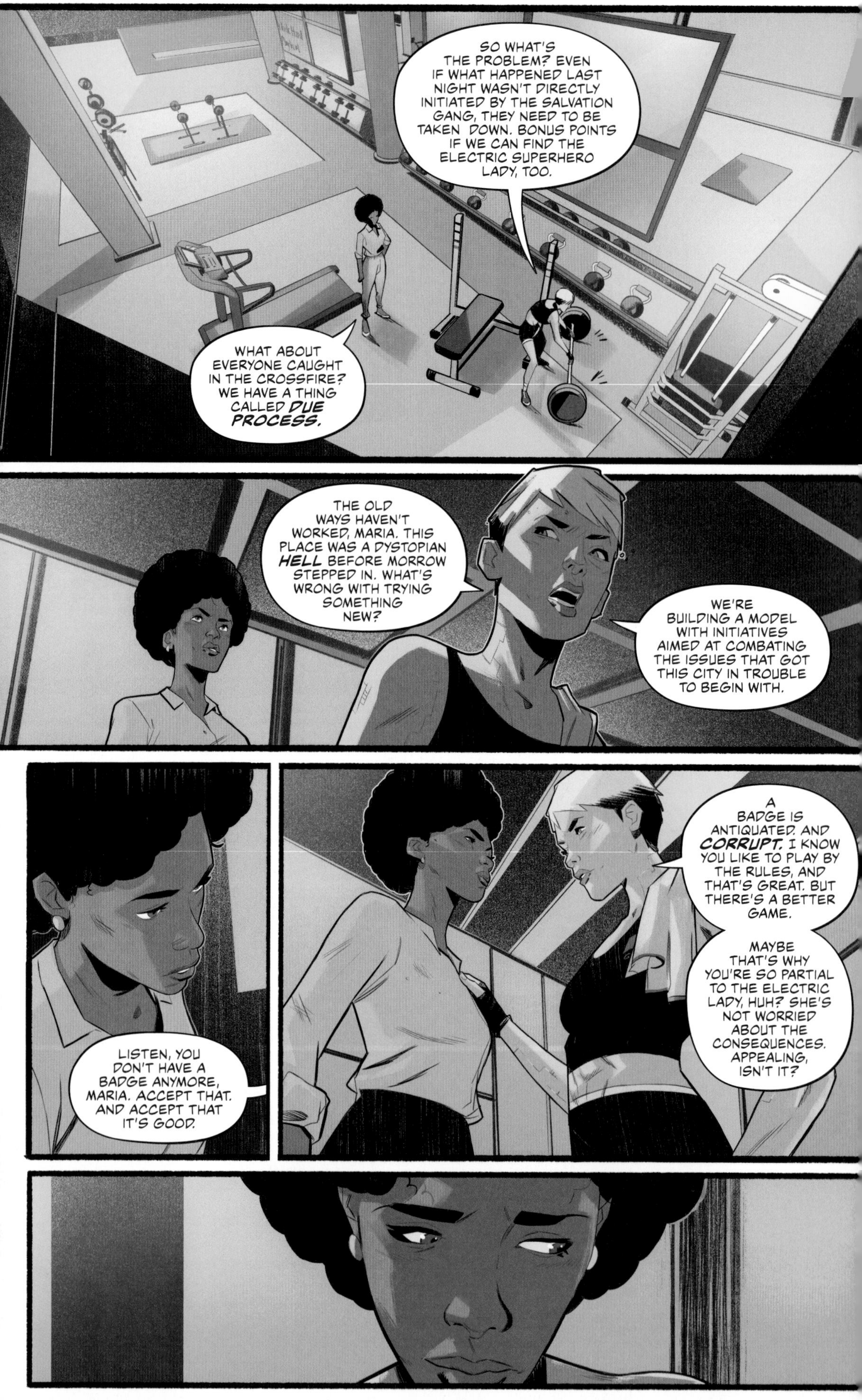

SO WHAT'S THE PROBLEM? EVEN IF WHAT HAPPENED LAST NIGHT WASN'T DIRECTLY INITIATED BY THE SALVATION GANG, THEY NEED TO BE TAKEN DOWN. BONUS POINTS IF WE CAN FIND THE ELECTRIC SUPERHERO LADY, TOO.
WHAT ABOUT EVERYONE CAUGHT IN THE CROSSFIRE? WE HAVE A THING CALLED *DUE PROCESS.*
THE OLD WAYS HAVEN'T WORKED, MARIA. THIS PLACE WAS A DYSTOPIAN *HELL* BEFORE MORROW STEPPED IN. WHAT'S WRONG WITH TRYING SOMETHING NEW?
WE'RE BUILDING A MODEL WITH INITIATIVES AIMED AT COMBATING THE ISSUES THAT GOT THIS CITY IN TROUBLE TO BEGIN WITH.
LISTEN, YOU DON'T HAVE A BADGE ANYMORE, MARIA. ACCEPT THAT. AND ACCEPT THAT IT'S GOOD.
A BADGE IS ANTIQUATED. AND *CORRUPT.* I KNOW YOU LIKE TO PLAY BY THE RULES, AND THAT'S GREAT. BUT THERE'S A BETTER GAME.
MAYBE THAT'S WHY YOU'RE SO PARTIAL TO THE ELECTRIC LADY, HUH? SHE'S NOT WORRIED ABOUT THE CONSEQUENCES. APPEALING, ISN'T IT?

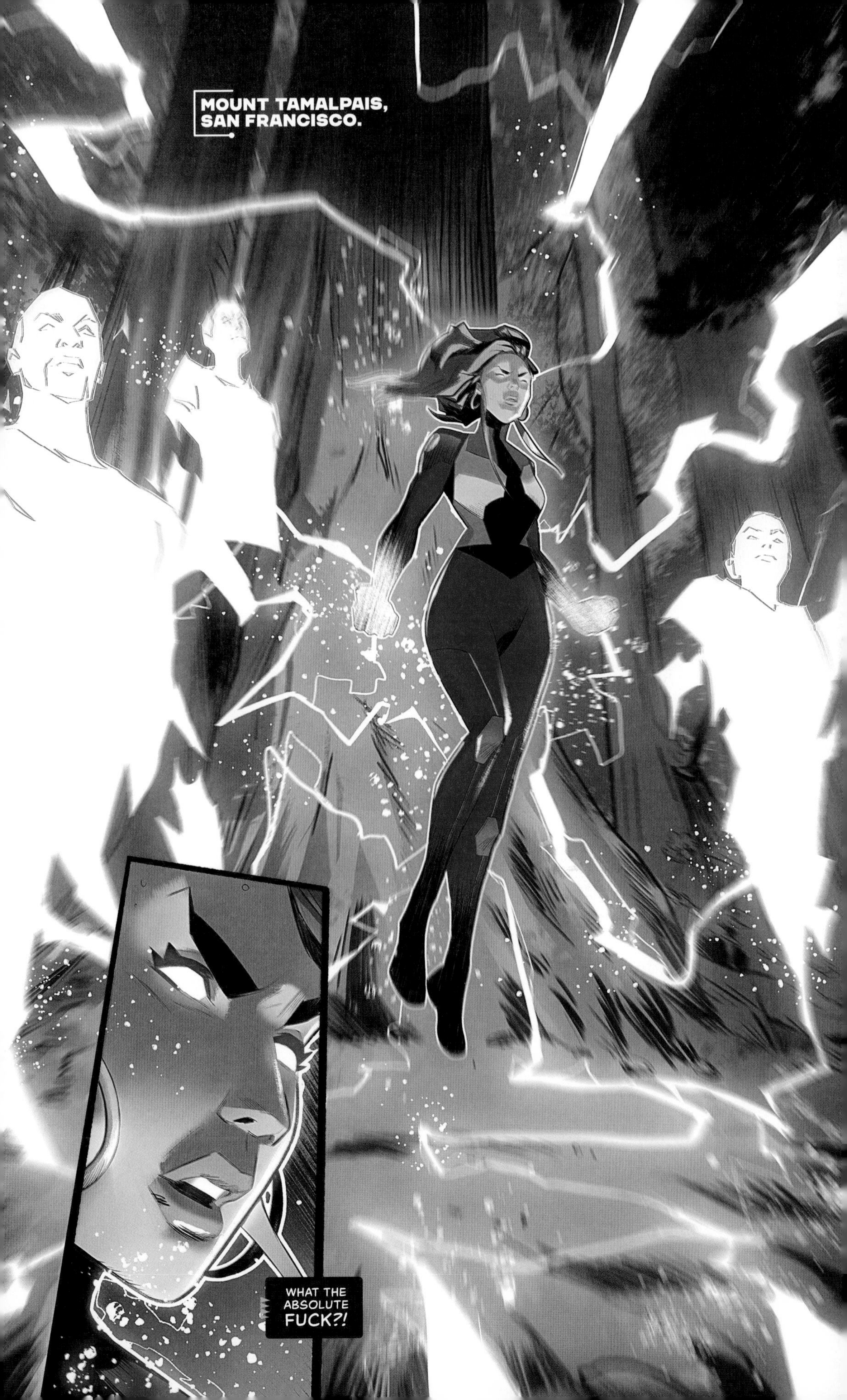
MOUNT TAMALPAIS,
SAN FRANCISCO.
WHAT THE ABSOLUTE FUCK?!

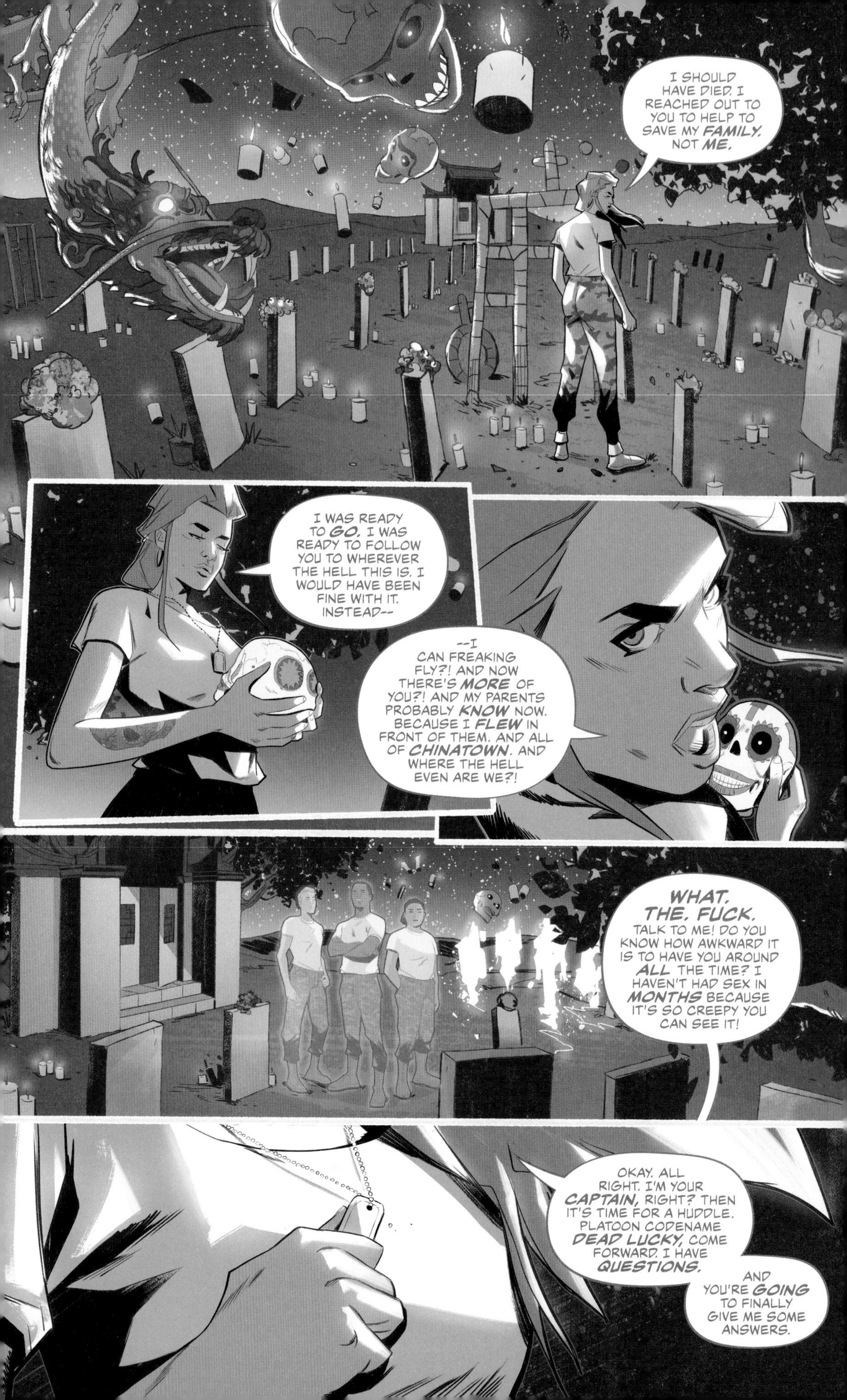
I SHOULD HAVE DIED. I REACHED OUT TO YOU TO HELP TO SAVE MY FAMILY. NOT ME.
I WAS READY TO GO. I WAS READY TO FOLLOW YOU TO WHEREVER THE HELL THIS IS. I WOULD HAVE BEEN FINE WITH IT. INSTEAD--
--I CAN FREAKING FLY?! AND NOW THERE'S MORE OF YOU?! AND MY PARENTS PROBABLY KNOW NOW. BECAUSE I FLEW IN FRONT OF THEM. AND ALL OF CHINATOWN. AND WHERE THE HELL EVEN ARE WE?!
WHAT. THE. FUCK.
TALK TO ME! DO YOU KNOW HOW AWKWARD IT IS TO HAVE YOU AROUND ALL THE TIME? I HAVEN'T HAD SEX IN MONTHS BECAUSE IT'S SO CREEPY YOU CAN SEE IT!
OKAY. ALL RIGHT. I'M YOUR CAPTAIN, RIGHT? THEN IT'S TIME FOR A HUDDLE. PLATOON CODENAME DEAD LUCKY, COME FORWARD. I HAVE QUESTIONS.
AND YOU'RE GOING TO FINALLY GIVE ME SOME ANSWERS.

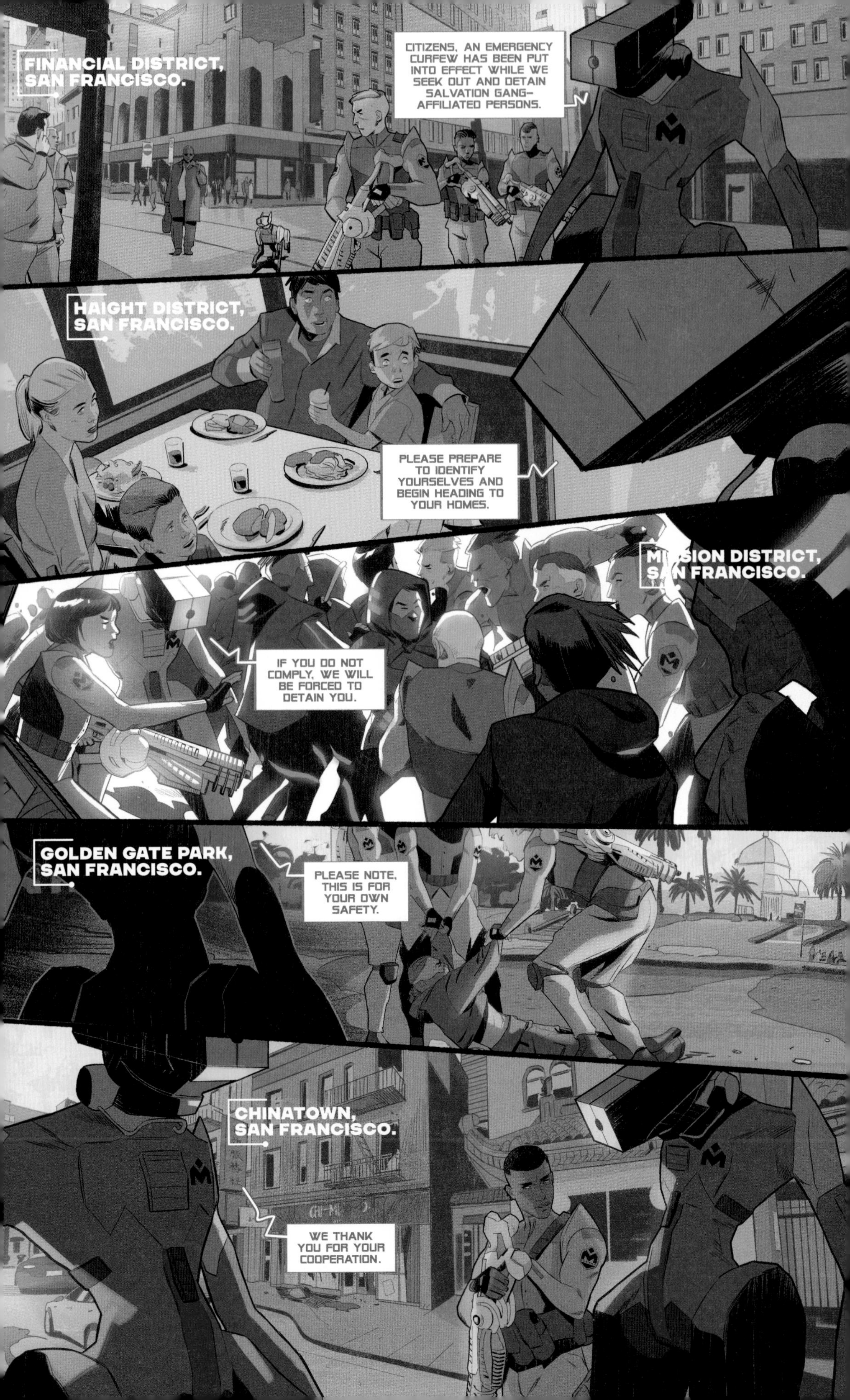
FINANCIAL DISTRICT, SAN FRANCISCO.
CITIZENS, AN EMERGENCY CURFEW HAS BEEN PUT INTO EFFECT WHILE WE SEEK OUT AND DETAIN SALVATION GANG-AFFILIATED PERSONS.
HAIGHT DISTRICT, SAN FRANCISCO.
PLEASE PREPARE TO IDENTIFY YOURSELVES AND BEGIN HEADING TO YOUR HOMES.
MISSION DISTRICT, SAN FRANCISCO.
IF YOU DO NOT COMPLY, WE WILL BE FORCED TO DETAIN YOU.
GOLDEN GATE PARK, SAN FRANCISCO.
PLEASE NOTE, THIS IS FOR YOUR OWN SAFETY.
CHINATOWN, SAN FRANCISCO.
WE THANK YOU FOR YOUR COOPERATION.

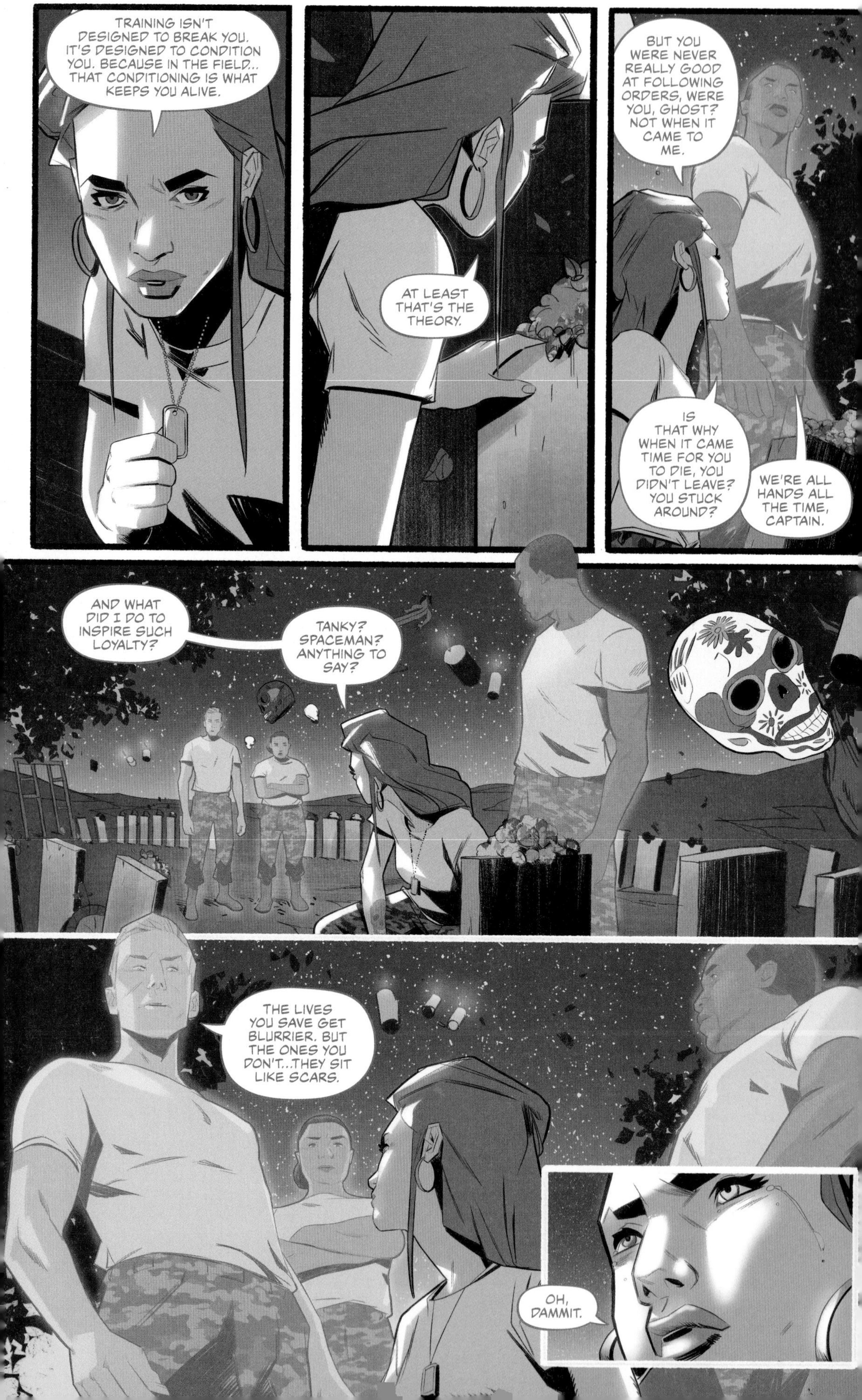
TRAINING ISN'T DESIGNED TO BREAK YOU. IT'S DESIGNED TO CONDITION YOU. BECAUSE IN THE FIELD... THAT CONDITIONING IS WHAT KEEPS YOU ALIVE.
AT LEAST THAT'S THE THEORY.
BUT YOU WERE NEVER REALLY GOOD AT FOLLOWING ORDERS, WERE YOU, GHOST? NOT WHEN IT CAME TO ME.
IS THAT WHY WHEN IT CAME TIME FOR YOU TO DIE, YOU DIDN'T LEAVE? YOU STUCK AROUND?
WE'RE ALL HANDS ALL THE TIME, CAPTAIN.
AND WHAT DID I DO TO INSPIRE SUCH LOYALTY?
TANKY? SPACEMAN? ANYTHING TO SAY?
THE LIVES YOU SAVE GET BLURRIER. BUT THE ONES YOU DON'T...THEY SIT LIKE SCARS.
OH, DAMMIT.

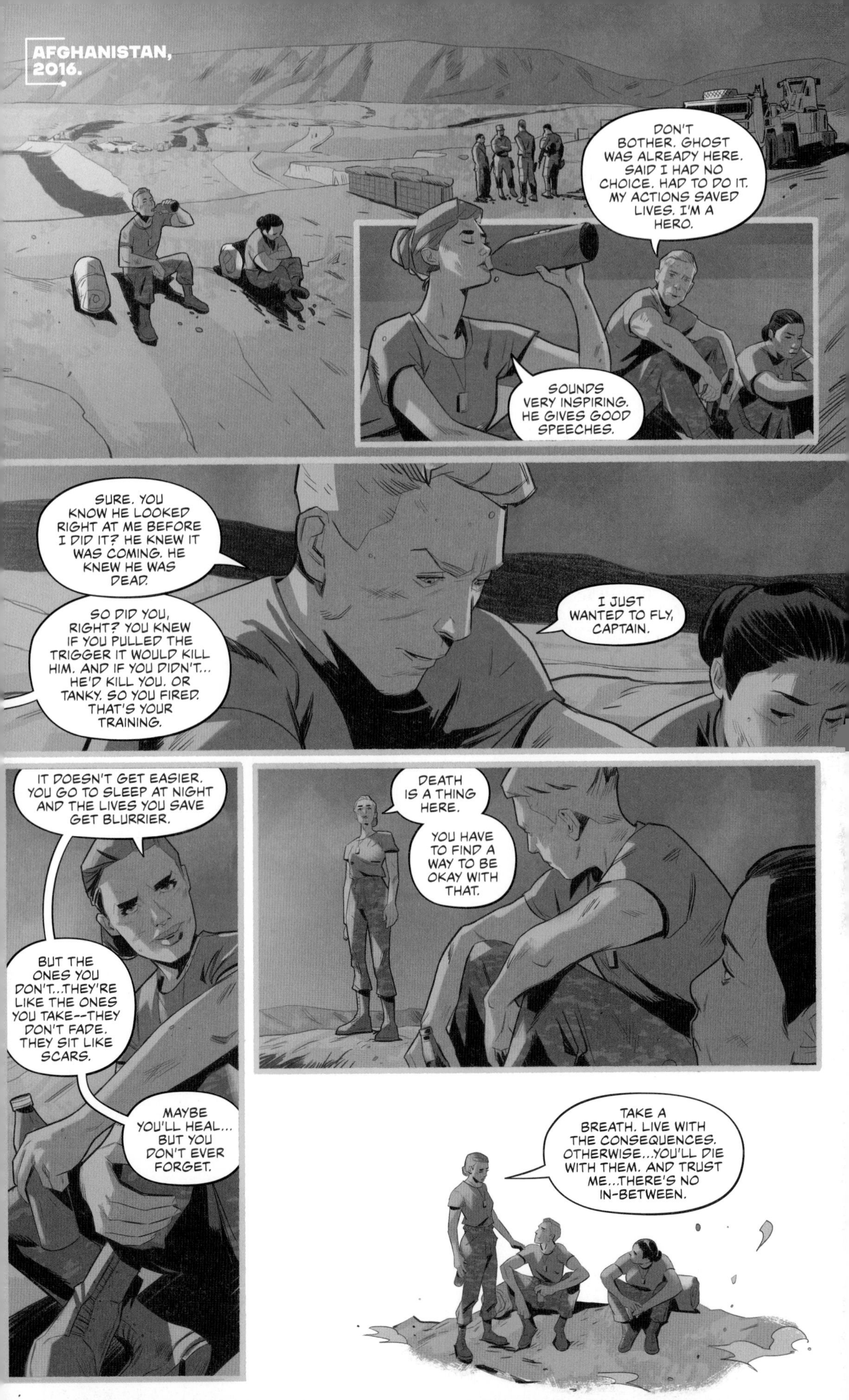
AFGHANISTAN, 2016.
DON'T BOTHER. GHOST WAS ALREADY HERE. SAID I HAD NO CHOICE. HAD TO DO IT. MY ACTIONS SAVED LIVES. I'M A HERO.
SOUNDS VERY INSPIRING. HE GIVES GOOD SPEECHES.
SURE. YOU KNOW HE LOOKED RIGHT AT ME BEFORE I DID IT? HE KNEW IT WAS COMING. HE KNEW HE WAS DEAD.
SO DID YOU, RIGHT? YOU KNEW IF YOU PULLED THE TRIGGER IT WOULD KILL HIM. AND IF YOU DIDN'T... HE'D KILL YOU. OR TANKY. SO YOU FIRED. THAT'S YOUR TRAINING.
I JUST WANTED TO FLY, CAPTAIN.
IT DOESN'T GET EASIER. YOU GO TO SLEEP AT NIGHT AND THE LIVES YOU SAVE GET BLURRIER.
BUT THE ONES YOU DON'T...THEY'RE LIKE THE ONES YOU TAKE--THEY DON'T FADE. THEY SIT LIKE SCARS.
MAYBE YOU'LL HEAL... BUT YOU DON'T EVER FORGET.
DEATH IS A THING HERE.
YOU HAVE TO FIND A WAY TO BE OKAY WITH THAT.
TAKE A BREATH. LIVE WITH THE CONSEQUENCES. OTHERWISE...YOU'LL DIE WITH THEM. AND TRUST ME...THERE'S NO IN-BETWEEN.

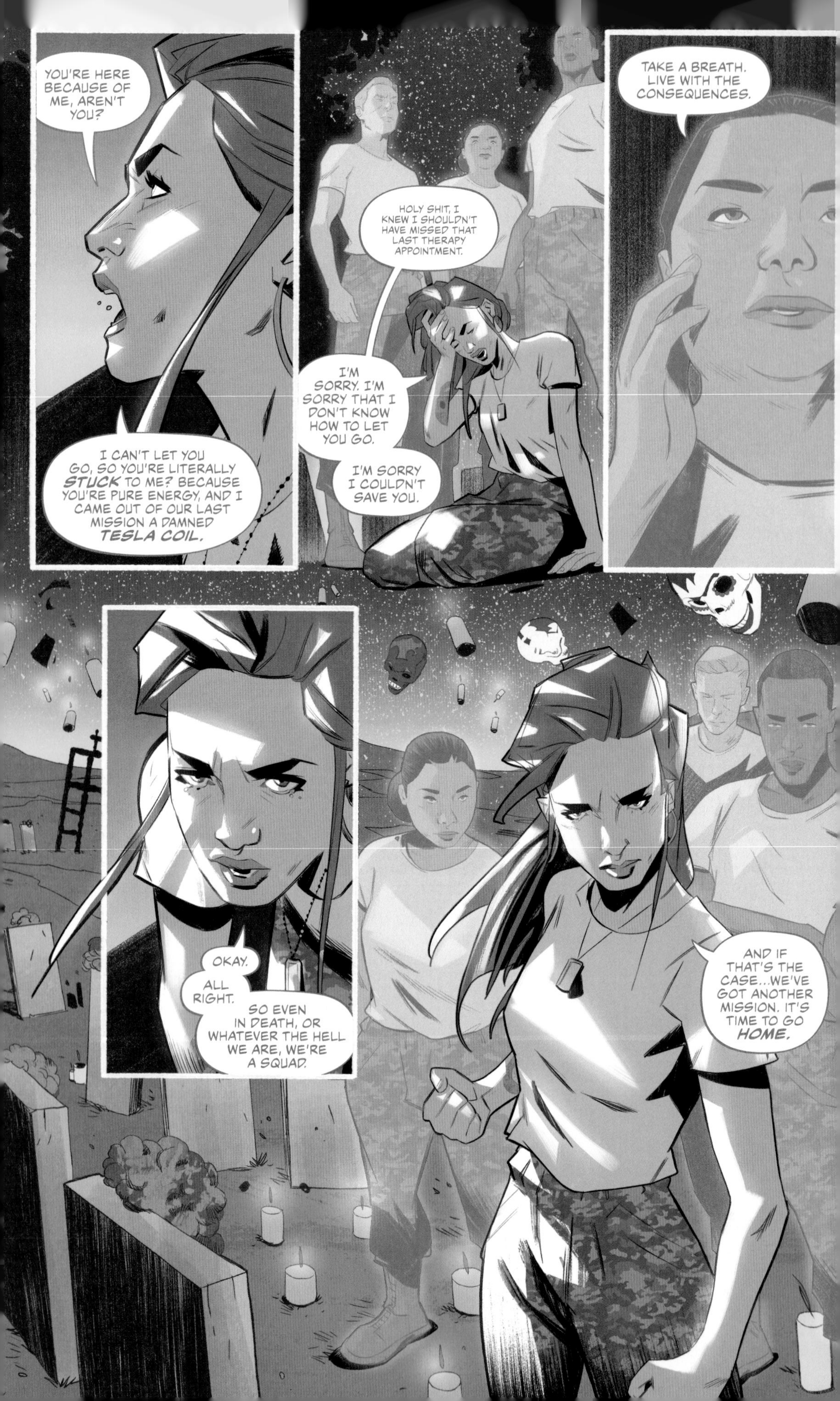
YOU'RE HERE BECAUSE OF ME, AREN'T YOU?
I CAN'T LET YOU GO, SO YOU'RE LITERALLY *STUCK* TO ME? BECAUSE YOU'RE PURE ENERGY, AND I CAME OUT OF OUR LAST MISSION A DAMNED *TESLA COIL.*
HOLY SHIT, I KNEW I SHOULDN'T HAVE MISSED THAT LAST THERAPY APPOINTMENT.
I'M SORRY. I'M SORRY THAT I DON'T KNOW HOW TO LET YOU GO.
I'M SORRY I COULDN'T SAVE YOU.
TAKE A BREATH. LIVE WITH THE CONSEQUENCES.
OKAY.
ALL RIGHT.
SO EVEN IN DEATH, OR WHATEVER THE HELL WE ARE, WE'RE A SQUAD.
AND IF THAT'S THE CASE...WE'VE GOT ANOTHER MISSION. IT'S TIME TO GO *HOME.*

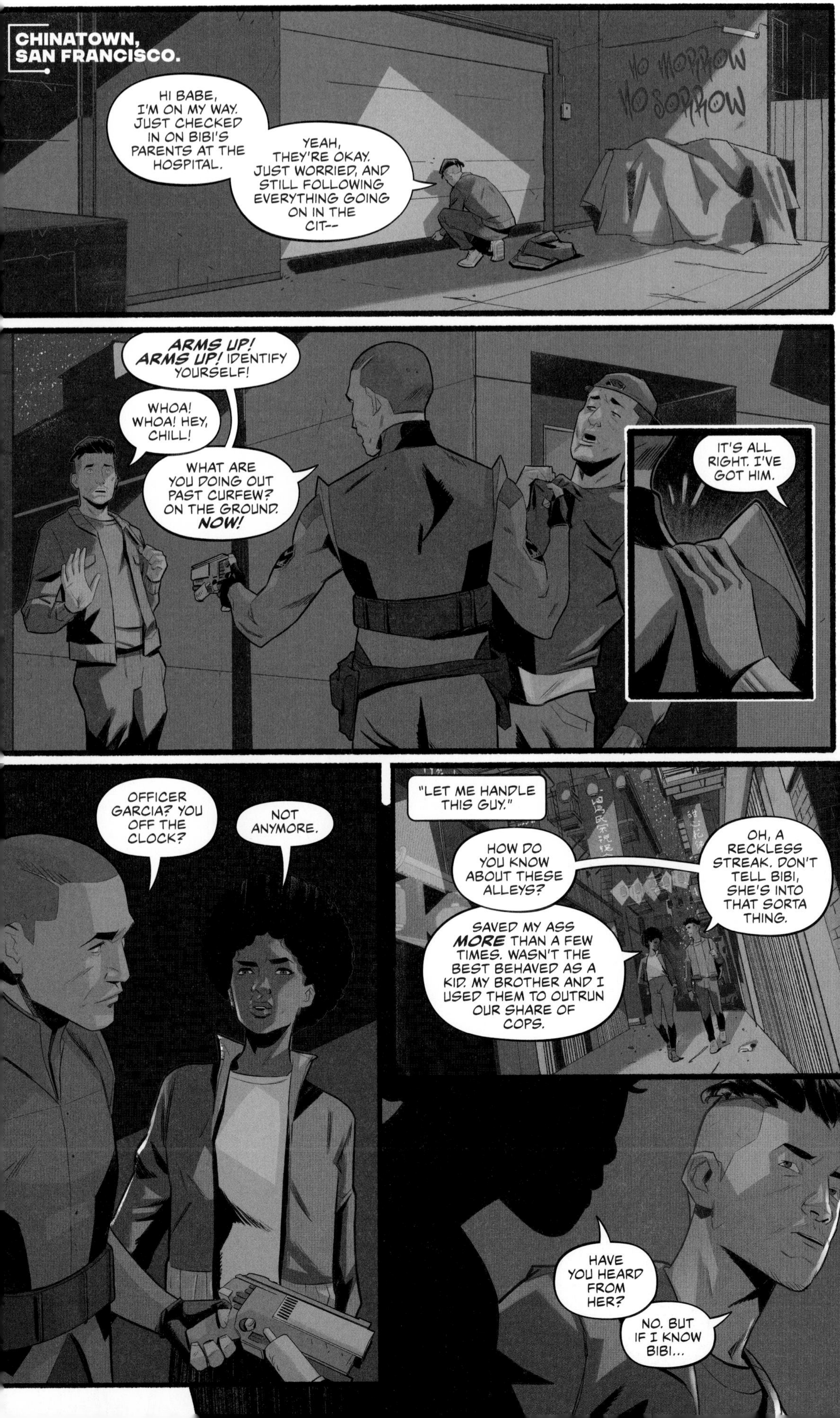
CHINATOWN, SAN FRANCISCO.
NO MORROW NO SORROW
HI BABE, I'M ON MY WAY. JUST CHECKED IN ON BIBI'S PARENTS AT THE HOSPITAL.
YEAH, THEY'RE OKAY. JUST WORRIED, AND STILL FOLLOWING EVERYTHING GOING ON IN THE CIT--
ARMS UP! ARMS UP! IDENTIFY YOURSELF!
WHOA! WHOA! HEY, CHILL!
WHAT ARE YOU DOING OUT PAST CURFEW? ON THE GROUND. NOW!
IT'S ALL RIGHT. I'VE GOT HIM.
OFFICER GARCIA? YOU OFF THE CLOCK?
NOT ANYMORE.
"LET ME HANDLE THIS GUY."
HOW DO YOU KNOW ABOUT THESE ALLEYS?
SAVED MY ASS MORE THAN A FEW TIMES. WASN'T THE BEST BEHAVED AS A KID. MY BROTHER AND I USED THEM TO OUTRUN OUR SHARE OF COPS.
OH, A RECKLESS STREAK. DON'T TELL BIBI, SHE'S INTO THAT SORTA THING.
HAVE YOU HEARD FROM HER?
NO. BUT IF I KNOW BIBI...

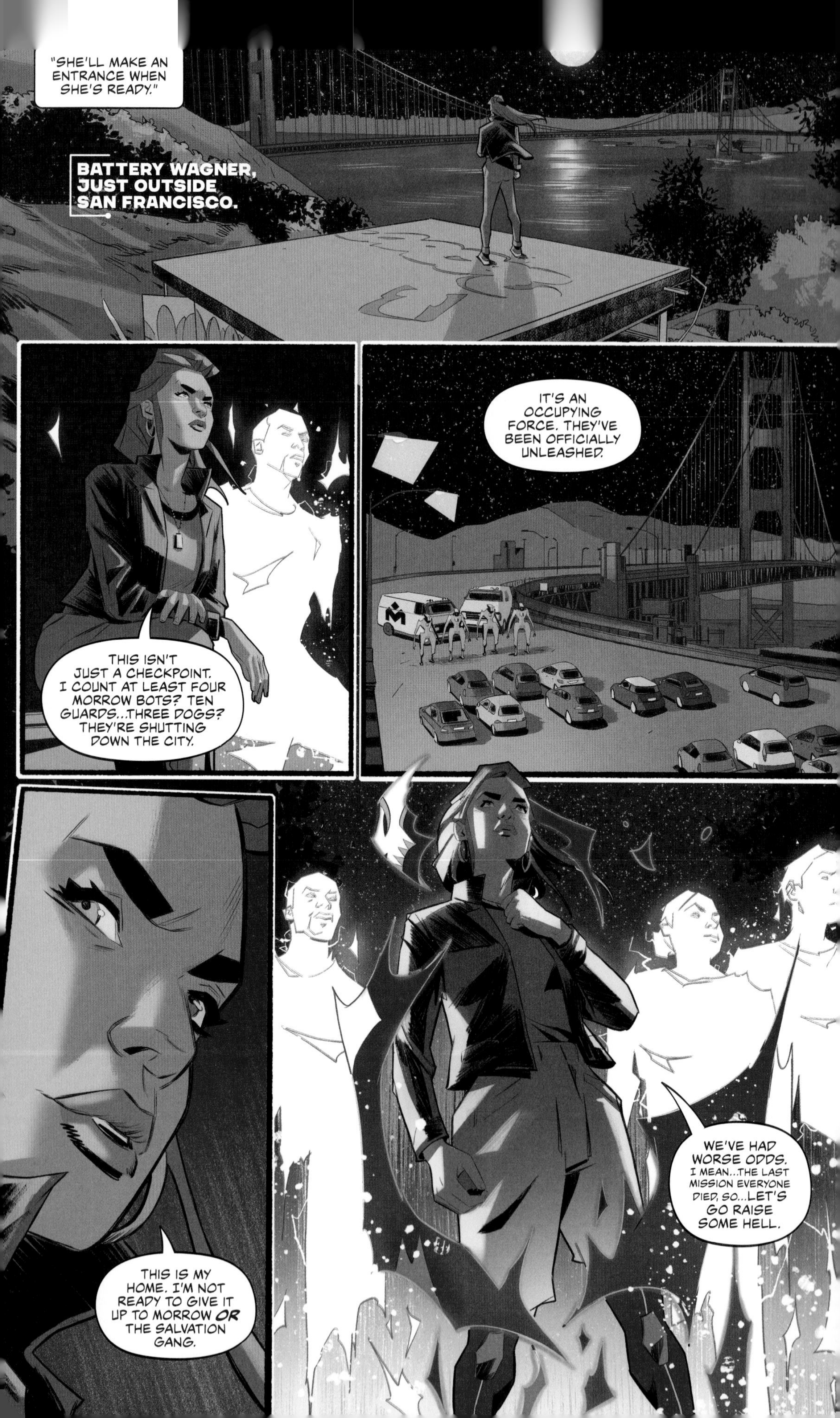
"SHE'LL MAKE AN ENTRANCE WHEN SHE'S READY."
BATTERY WAGNER, JUST OUTSIDE SAN FRANCISCO.
THIS ISN'T JUST A CHECKPOINT. I COUNT AT LEAST FOUR MORROW BOTS? TEN GUARDS...THREE DOGS? THEY'RE SHUTTING DOWN THE CITY.
IT'S AN OCCUPYING FORCE. THEY'VE BEEN OFFICIALLY UNLEASHED.
THIS IS MY HOME. I'M NOT READY TO GIVE IT UP TO MORROW OR THE SALVATION GANG.
WE'VE HAD WORSE ODDS. I MEAN...THE LAST MISSION EVERYONE DIED, SO...LET'S GO RAISE SOME HELL.

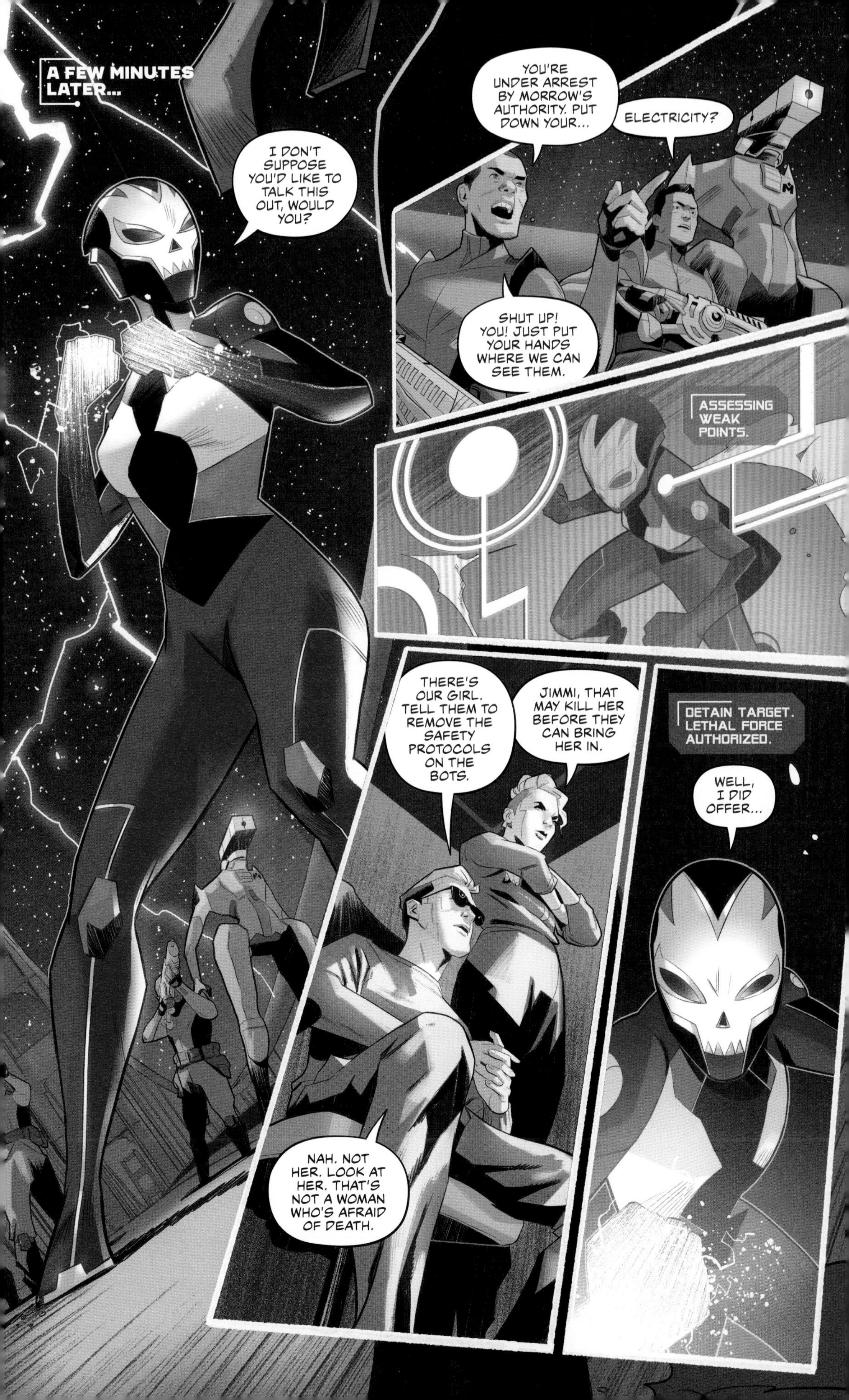

A FEW MINUTES LATER...
I DON'T SUPPOSE YOU'D LIKE TO TALK THIS OUT, WOULD YOU?
YOU'RE UNDER ARREST BY MORROW'S AUTHORITY. PUT DOWN YOUR...
ELECTRICITY?
SHUT UP! YOU! JUST PUT YOUR HANDS WHERE WE CAN SEE THEM.
ASSESSING WEAK POINTS.
THERE'S OUR GIRL. TELL THEM TO REMOVE THE SAFETY PROTOCOLS ON THE BOTS.
JIMMI, THAT MAY KILL HER BEFORE THEY CAN BRING HER IN.
NAH. NOT HER. LOOK AT HER. THAT'S NOT A WOMAN WHO'S AFRAID OF DEATH.
DETAIN TARGET. LETHAL FORCE AUTHORIZED.
WELL, I DID OFFER...

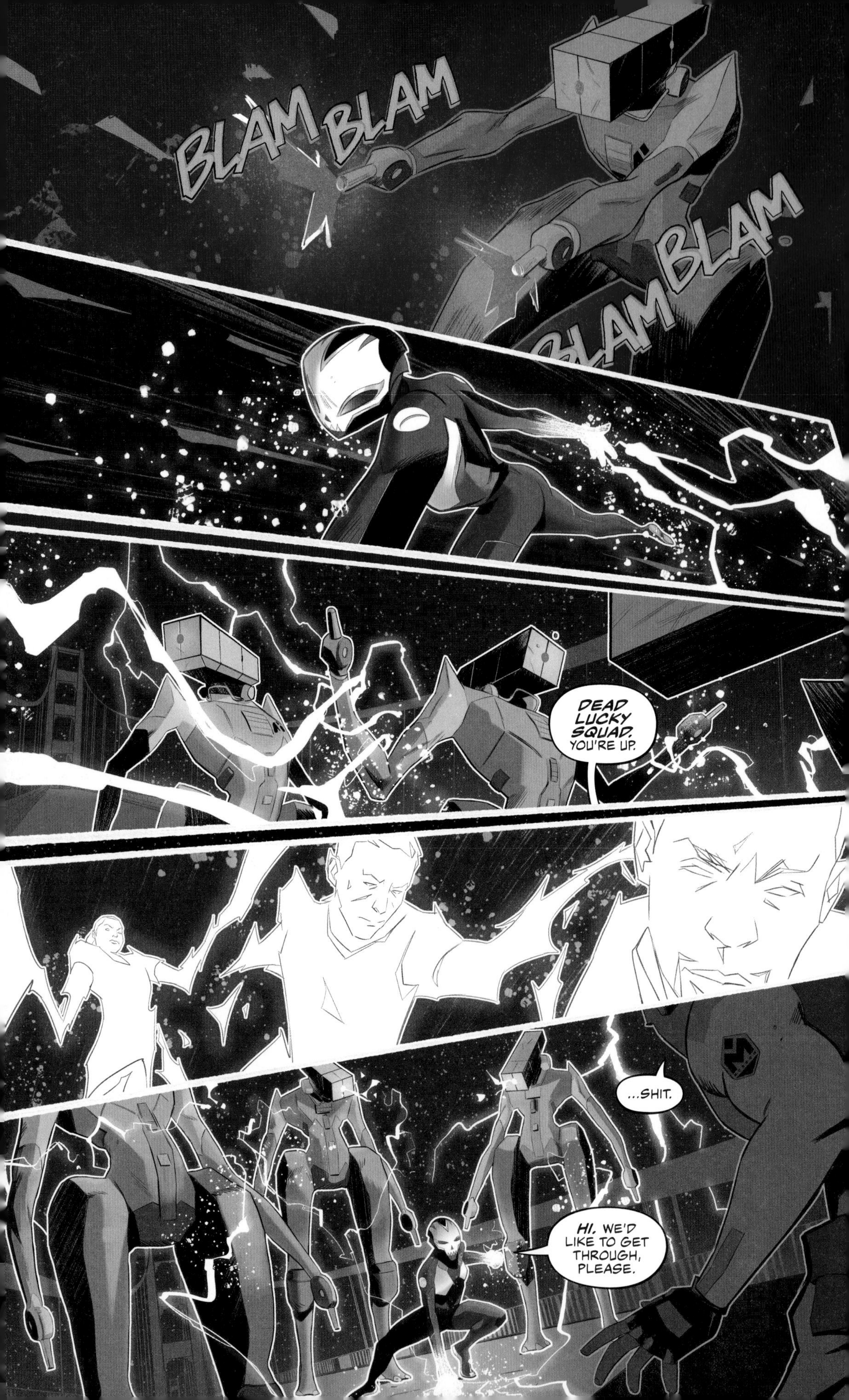
BLAM BLAM
BLAM BLAM
BLAM
DEAD LUCKY SQUAD. YOU'RE UP.
...SHIT.
HI. WE'D LIKE TO GET THROUGH, PLEASE.

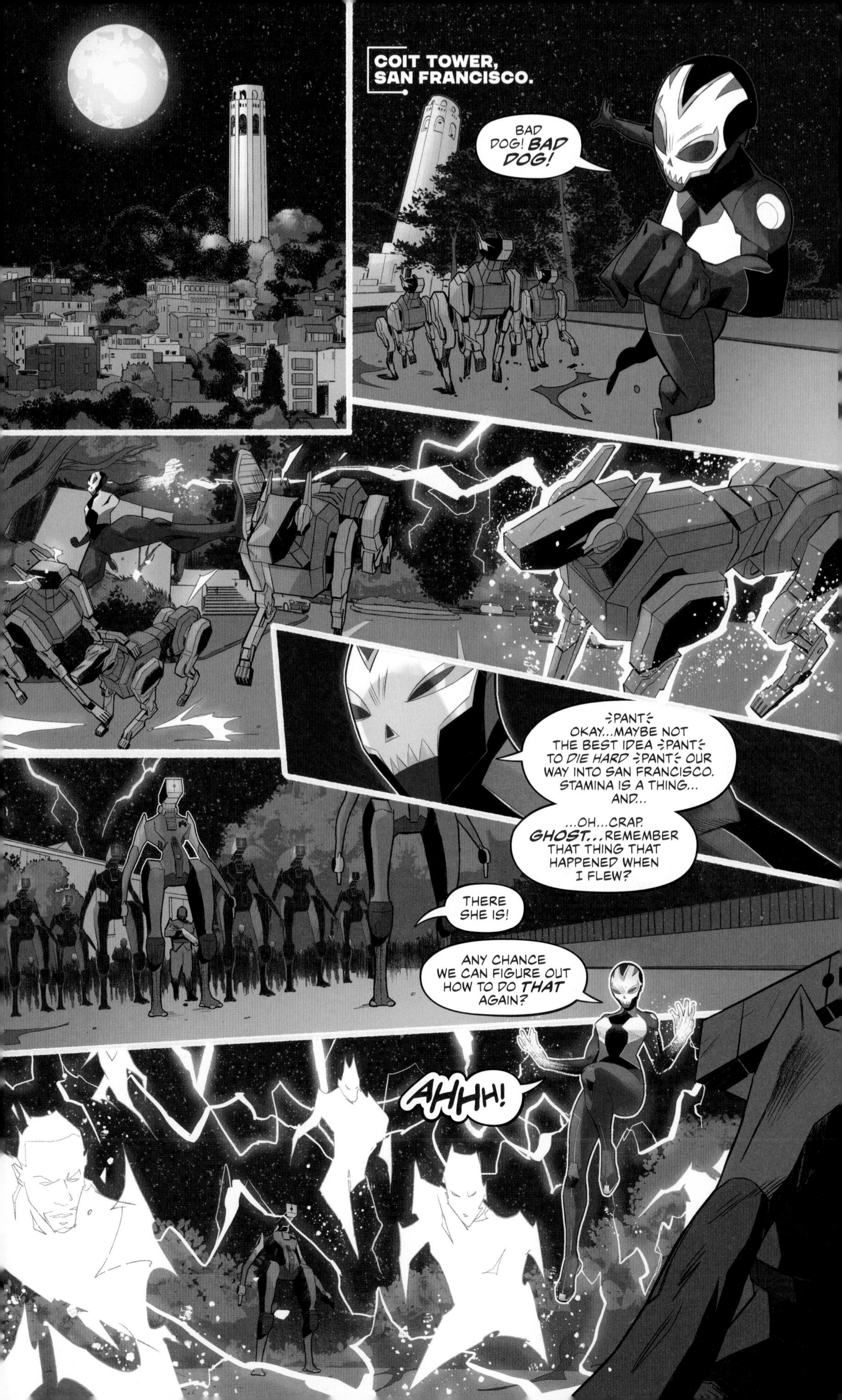

COIT TOWER, SAN FRANCISCO.
BAD DOG! BAD DOG!
≡PANT≡ OKAY...MAYBE NOT THE BEST IDEA ≡PANT≡ TO DIE HARD ≡PANT≡ OUR WAY INTO SAN FRANCISCO. STAMINA IS A THING... AND...
...OH...CRAP. GHOST...REMEMBER THAT THING THAT HAPPENED WHEN I FLEW?
THERE SHE IS!
ANY CHANCE WE CAN FIGURE OUT HOW TO DO THAT AGAIN?
AHHH!

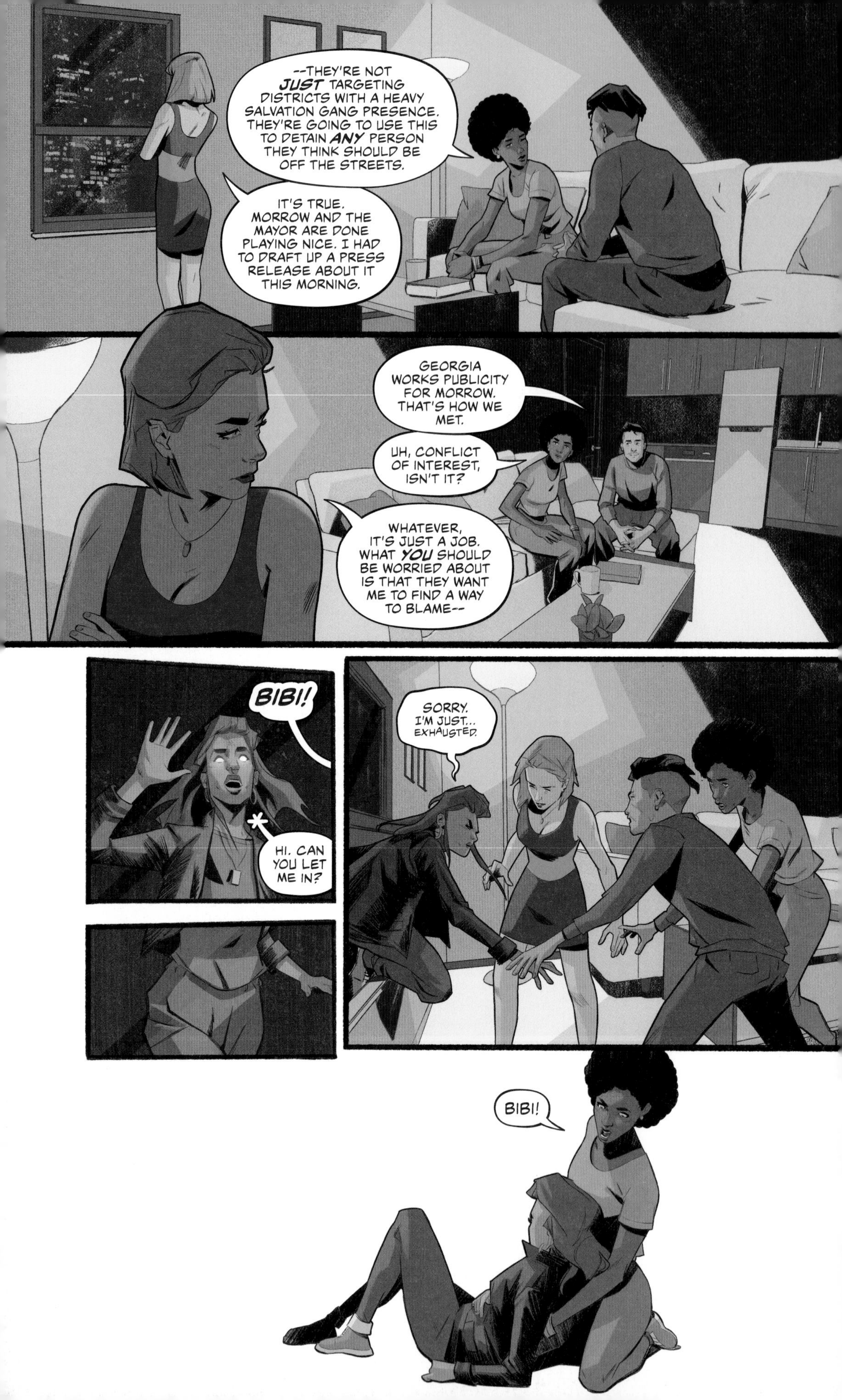
--THEY'RE NOT JUST TARGETING DISTRICTS WITH A HEAVY SALVATION GANG PRESENCE. THEY'RE GOING TO USE THIS TO DETAIN ANY PERSON THEY THINK SHOULD BE OFF THE STREETS.
IT'S TRUE. MORROW AND THE MAYOR ARE DONE PLAYING NICE. I HAD TO DRAFT UP A PRESS RELEASE ABOUT IT THIS MORNING.
GEORGIA WORKS PUBLICITY FOR MORROW. THAT'S HOW WE MET.
UH, CONFLICT OF INTEREST, ISN'T IT?
WHATEVER, IT'S JUST A JOB. WHAT YOU SHOULD BE WORRIED ABOUT IS THAT THEY WANT ME TO FIND A WAY TO BLAME--
BIBI!
HI. CAN YOU LET ME IN?
SORRY. I'M JUST... EXHAUSTED.
BIBI!

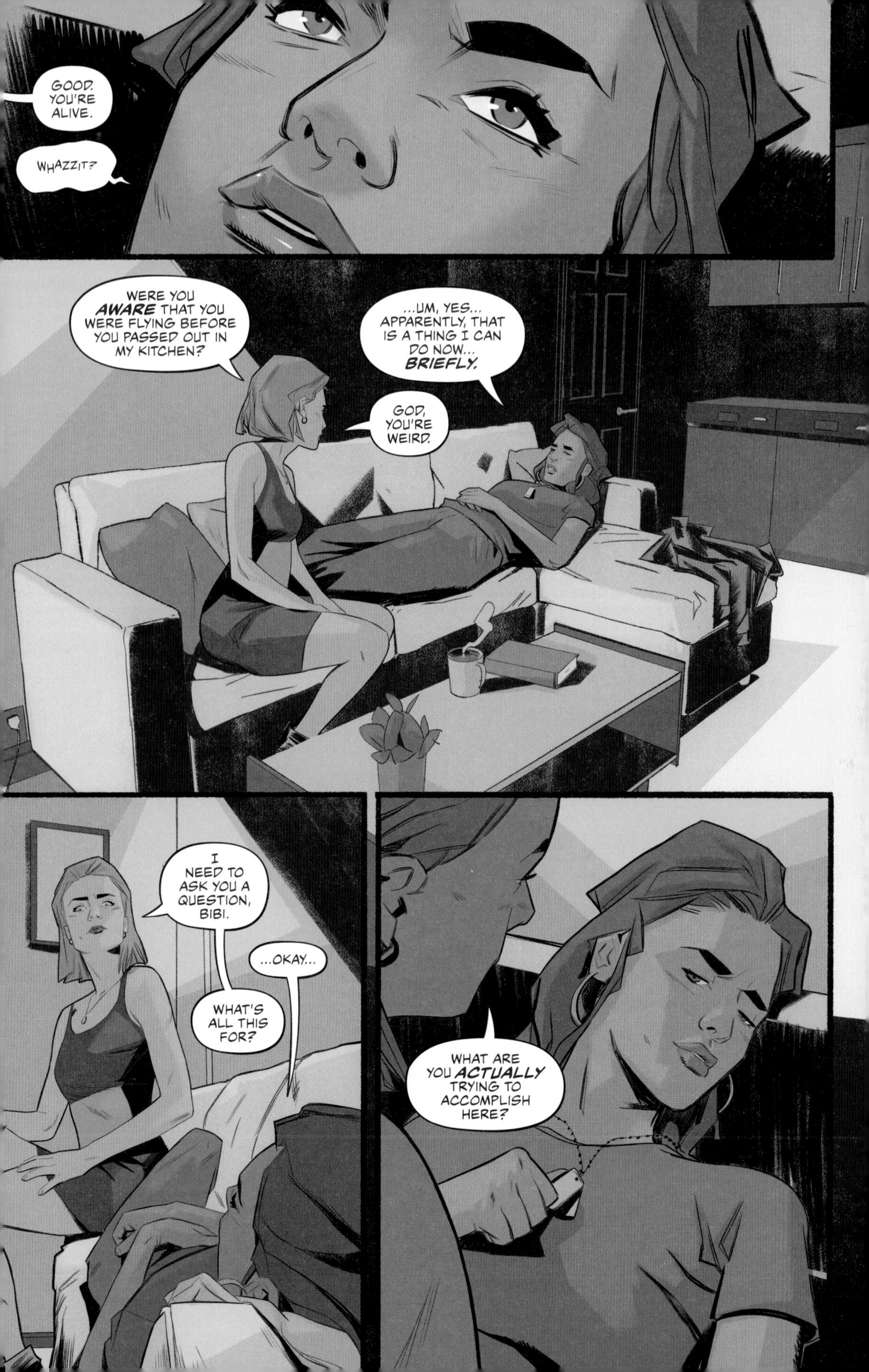
GOOD. YOU'RE ALIVE.
WHAZZIT?
WERE YOU AWARE THAT YOU WERE FLYING BEFORE YOU PASSED OUT IN MY KITCHEN?
...UM, YES... APPARENTLY, THAT IS A THING I CAN DO NOW... BRIEFLY.
GOD, YOU'RE WEIRD.
I NEED TO ASK YOU A QUESTION, BIBI.
...OKAY...
WHAT'S ALL THIS FOR?
WHAT ARE YOU ACTUALLY TRYING TO ACCOMPLISH HERE?

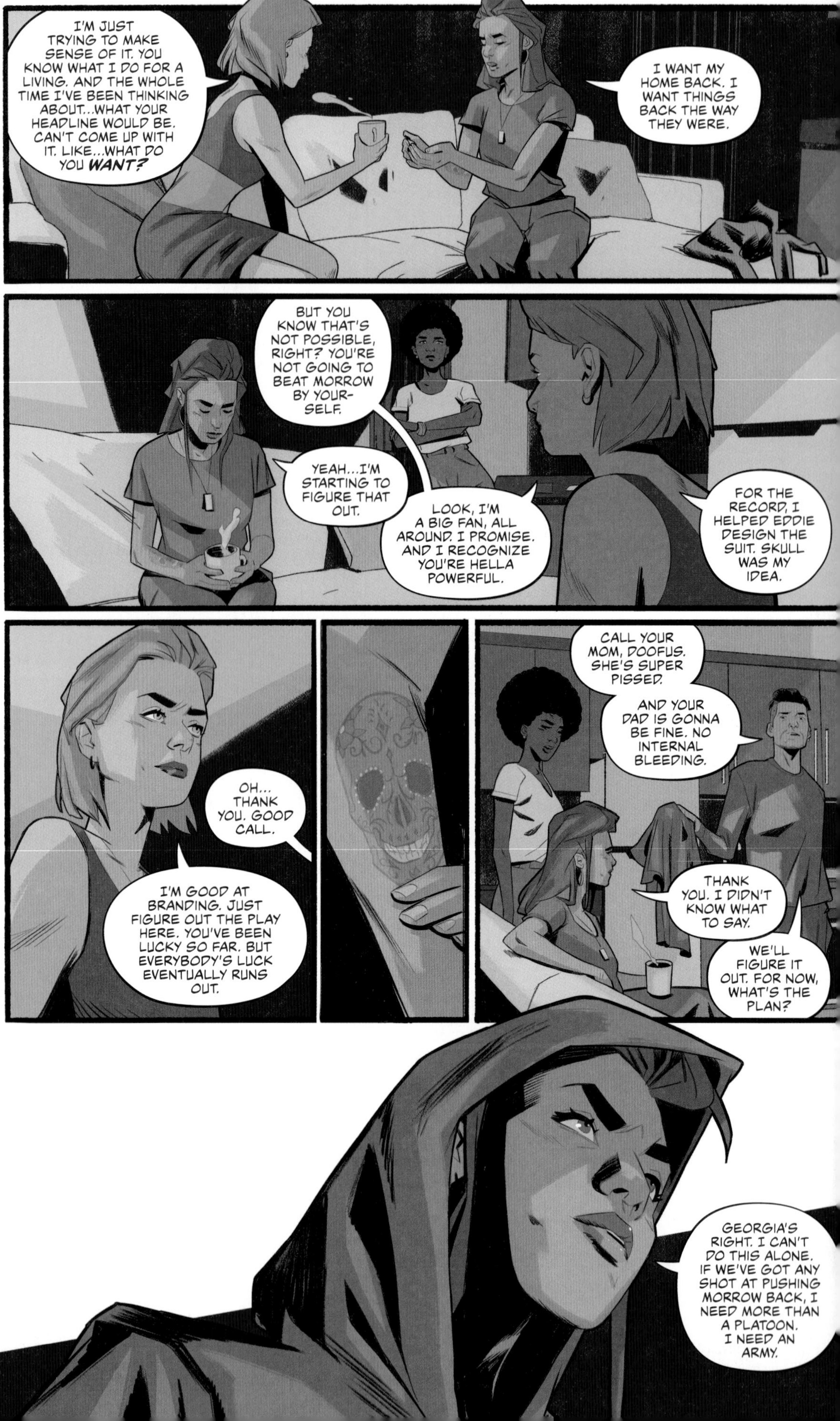
I'M JUST TRYING TO MAKE SENSE OF IT. YOU KNOW WHAT I DO FOR A LIVING. AND THE WHOLE TIME I'VE BEEN THINKING ABOUT...WHAT YOUR HEADLINE WOULD BE. CAN'T COME UP WITH IT. LIKE...WHAT DO YOU WANT?
I WANT MY HOME BACK. I WANT THINGS BACK THE WAY THEY WERE.
BUT YOU KNOW THAT'S NOT POSSIBLE, RIGHT? YOU'RE NOT GOING TO BEAT MORROW BY YOURSELF.
YEAH...I'M STARTING TO FIGURE THAT OUT.
LOOK, I'M A BIG FAN, ALL AROUND. I PROMISE. AND I RECOGNIZE YOU'RE HELLA POWERFUL.
FOR THE RECORD, I HELPED EDDIE DESIGN THE SUIT. SKULL WAS MY IDEA.
OH... THANK YOU. GOOD CALL.
I'M GOOD AT BRANDING. JUST FIGURE OUT THE PLAY HERE. YOU'VE BEEN LUCKY SO FAR. BUT EVERYBODY'S LUCK EVENTUALLY RUNS OUT.
CALL YOUR MOM, DOOFUS. SHE'S SUPER PISSED.
AND YOUR DAD IS GONNA BE FINE. NO INTERNAL BLEEDING.
THANK YOU. I DIDN'T KNOW WHAT TO SAY.
WE'LL FIGURE IT OUT. FOR NOW, WHAT'S THE PLAN?
GEORGIA'S RIGHT. I CAN'T DO THIS ALONE. IF WE'VE GOT ANY SHOT AT PUSHING MORROW BACK, I NEED MORE THAN A PLATOON. I NEED AN ARMY.

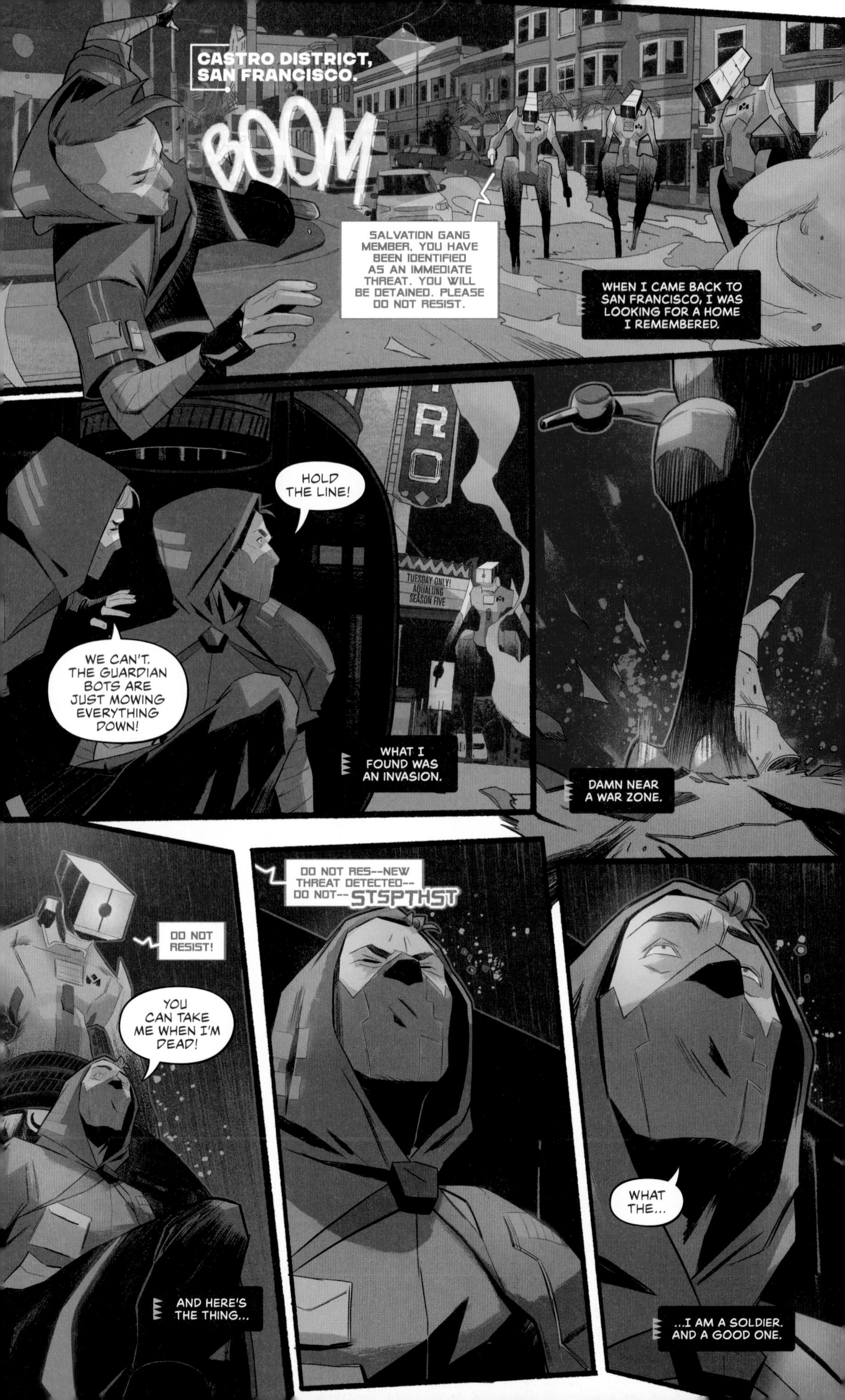
CASTRO DISTRICT, SAN FRANCISCO.
BOOM
SALVATION GANG MEMBER, YOU HAVE BEEN IDENTIFIED AS AN IMMEDIATE THREAT. YOU WILL BE DETAINED. PLEASE DO NOT RESIST.
WHEN I CAME BACK TO SAN FRANCISCO, I WAS LOOKING FOR A HOME I REMEMBERED.
HOLD THE LINE!
WE CAN'T. THE GUARDIAN BOTS ARE JUST MOWING EVERYTHING DOWN!
TUESDAY ONLY! AQUALUNG SEASON FIVE
WHAT I FOUND WAS AN INVASION.
DAMN NEAR A WAR ZONE.
DO NOT RESIST!
YOU CAN TAKE ME WHEN I'M DEAD!
AND HERE'S THE THING...
DO NOT RES--NEW THREAT DETECTED--DO NOT--STSPTHST
WHAT THE...
...I AM A SOLDIER. AND A GOOD ONE.

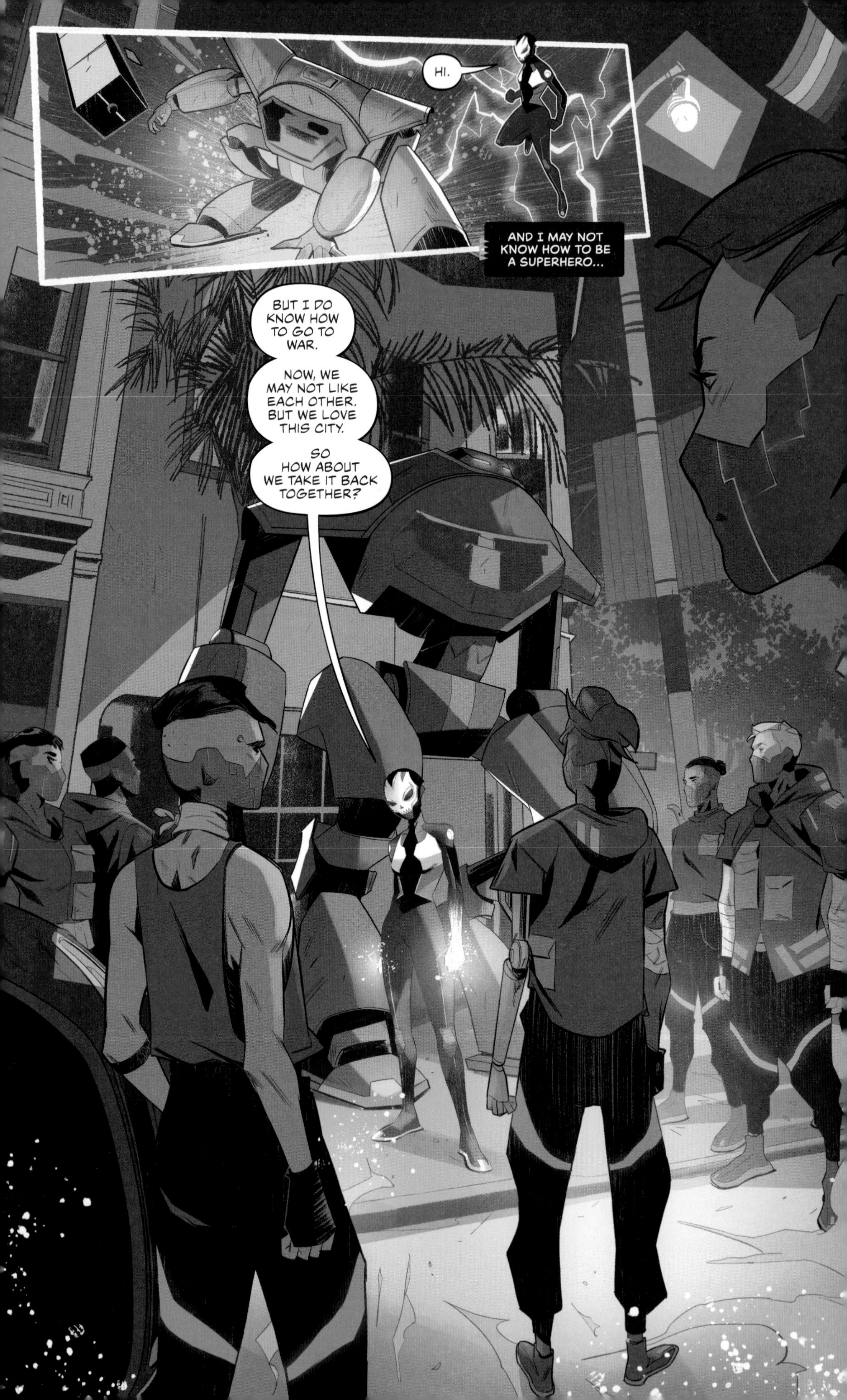
HI.
AND I MAY NOT KNOW HOW TO BE A SUPERHERO...
BUT I DO KNOW HOW TO GO TO WAR.
NOW, WE MAY NOT LIKE EACH OTHER. BUT WE LOVE THIS CITY.
SO HOW ABOUT WE TAKE IT BACK TOGETHER?

TERMINAL   _ ☓

GHOST:~ admin$ SingleIssueProfiler
Issue:
    No.: 005
    Title: A Shift in Power.

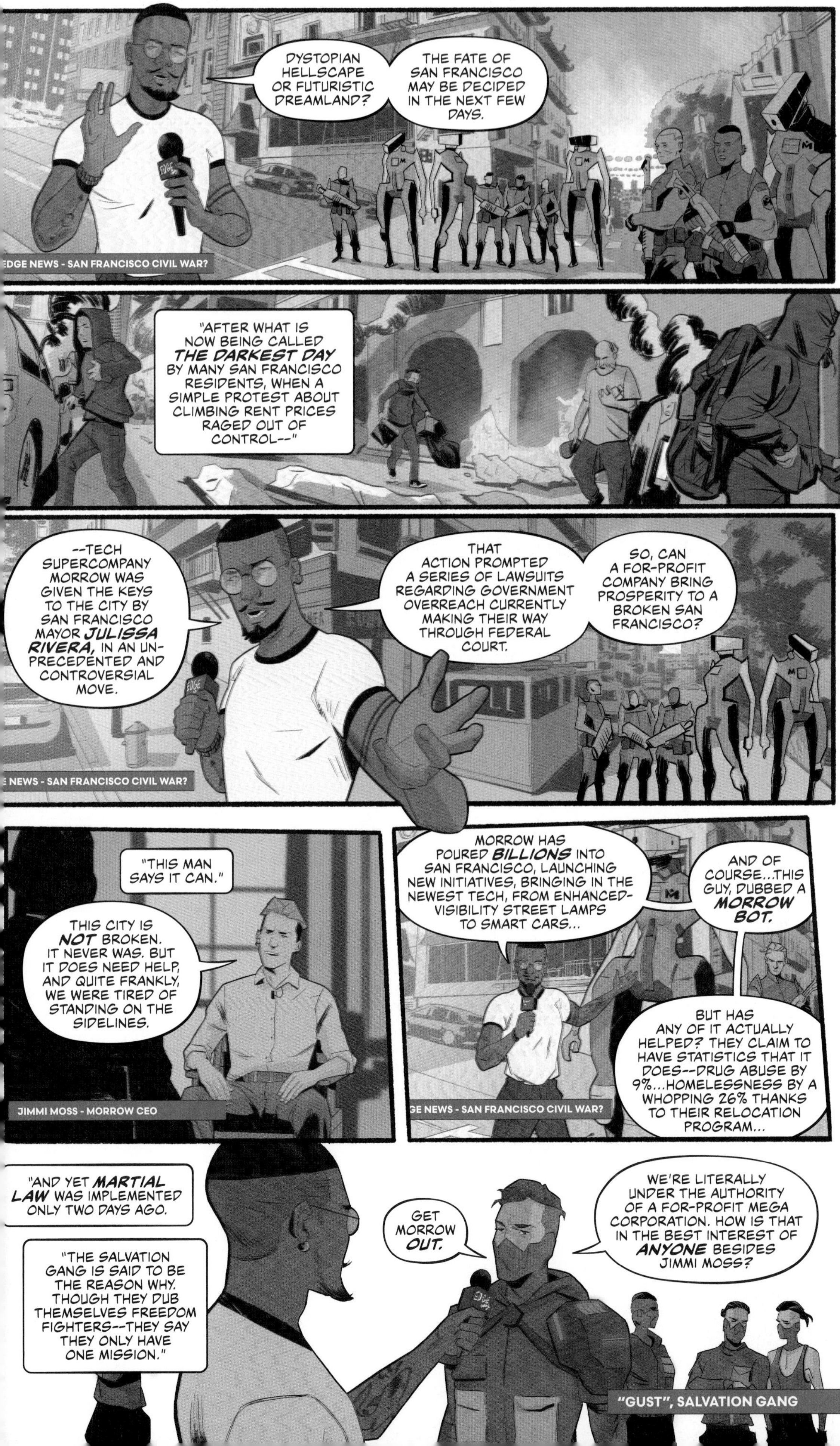
DYSTOPIAN HELLSCAPE OR FUTURISTIC DREAMLAND?
THE FATE OF SAN FRANCISCO MAY BE DECIDED IN THE NEXT FEW DAYS.
EDGE NEWS - SAN FRANCISCO CIVIL WAR?
"AFTER WHAT IS NOW BEING CALLED THE DARKEST DAY BY MANY SAN FRANCISCO RESIDENTS, WHEN A SIMPLE PROTEST ABOUT CLIMBING RENT PRICES RAGED OUT OF CONTROL--"
--TECH SUPERCOMPANY MORROW WAS GIVEN THE KEYS TO THE CITY BY SAN FRANCISCO MAYOR JULISSA RIVERA, IN AN UN-PRECEDENTED AND CONTROVERSIAL MOVE.
THAT ACTION PROMPTED A SERIES OF LAWSUITS REGARDING GOVERNMENT OVERREACH CURRENTLY MAKING THEIR WAY THROUGH FEDERAL COURT.
SO, CAN A FOR-PROFIT COMPANY BRING PROSPERITY TO A BROKEN SAN FRANCISCO?
E NEWS - SAN FRANCISCO CIVIL WAR?
"THIS MAN SAYS IT CAN."
THIS CITY IS NOT BROKEN. IT NEVER WAS. BUT IT DOES NEED HELP, AND QUITE FRANKLY, WE WERE TIRED OF STANDING ON THE SIDELINES.
JIMMI MOSS - MORROW CEO
MORROW HAS POURED BILLIONS INTO SAN FRANCISCO, LAUNCHING NEW INITIATIVES, BRINGING IN THE NEWEST TECH, FROM ENHANCED-VISIBILITY STREET LAMPS TO SMART CARS...
AND OF COURSE...THIS GUY, DUBBED A MORROW BOT.
BUT HAS ANY OF IT ACTUALLY HELPED? THEY CLAIM TO HAVE STATISTICS THAT IT DOES--DRUG ABUSE BY 9%...HOMELESSNESS BY A WHOPPING 26% THANKS TO THEIR RELOCATION PROGRAM...
GE NEWS - SAN FRANCISCO CIVIL WAR?
"AND YET MARTIAL LAW WAS IMPLEMENTED ONLY TWO DAYS AGO.
"THE SALVATION GANG IS SAID TO BE THE REASON WHY. THOUGH THEY DUB THEMSELVES FREEDOM FIGHTERS--THEY SAY THEY ONLY HAVE ONE MISSION."
GET MORROW OUT.
WE'RE LITERALLY UNDER THE AUTHORITY OF A FOR-PROFIT MEGA CORPORATION. HOW IS THAT IN THE BEST INTEREST OF ANYONE BESIDES JIMMI MOSS?
"GUST", SALVATION GANG

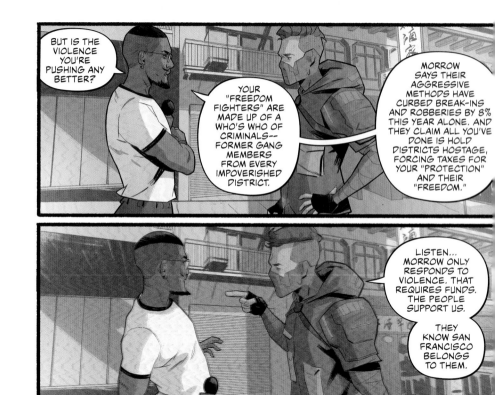

BUT IS THE VIOLENCE YOU'RE PUSHING ANY BETTER?

YOUR "FREEDOM FIGHTERS" ARE MADE UP OF A WHO'S WHO OF CRIMINALS-- FORMER GANG MEMBERS FROM EVERY IMPOVERISHED DISTRICT.

MORROW SAYS THEIR AGGRESSIVE METHODS HAVE CURBED BREAK-INS AND ROBBERIES BY 8% THIS YEAR ALONE. AND THEY CLAIM ALL YOU'VE DONE IS HOLD DISTRICTS HOSTAGE, FORCING TAXES FOR YOUR "PROTECTION" AND THEIR "FREEDOM."

LISTEN... MORROW ONLY RESPONDS TO VIOLENCE. THAT REQUIRES FUNDS. THE PEOPLE SUPPORT US.

THEY KNOW SAN FRANCISCO BELONGS TO THEM.

WHAT DOES THAT EVEN *MEAN?* SAN FRANCISCO *DOES* BELONG TO THE PEOPLE.

THE PEOPLE WHO FOLLOW THE LAW AND DON'T HIDE THEIR CRIMES BEHIND A FREEDOM FIGHTER MONIKER. THE SALVATION GANG ISN'T FOOLING ANYONE.

THEY HAVE NO FUTURE IN *OUR* SAN FRANCISCO.

WITH MARTIAL LAW NOW INSTITUTED THROUGH MUCH OF SAN FRANCISCO, MORROW SAYS THEY WON'T STOP UNTIL THEY STAMP OUT THE SALVATION GANG THREAT.

BUT THERE'S A *WILD CARD.*

"SO FAR HER IDENTITY HAS REMAINED A SECRET...BUT HER ACTIONS, AND HER FIGHTING MECH, HAVE CAUSED A RIPPLE THROUGHOUT THE CITY.

"SHE'S FOUGHT BOTH THE SALVATION GANG MEMBERS AND MORROW. SO THE QUESTION REMAINS-- WHOSE SIDE IS SHE ON?"

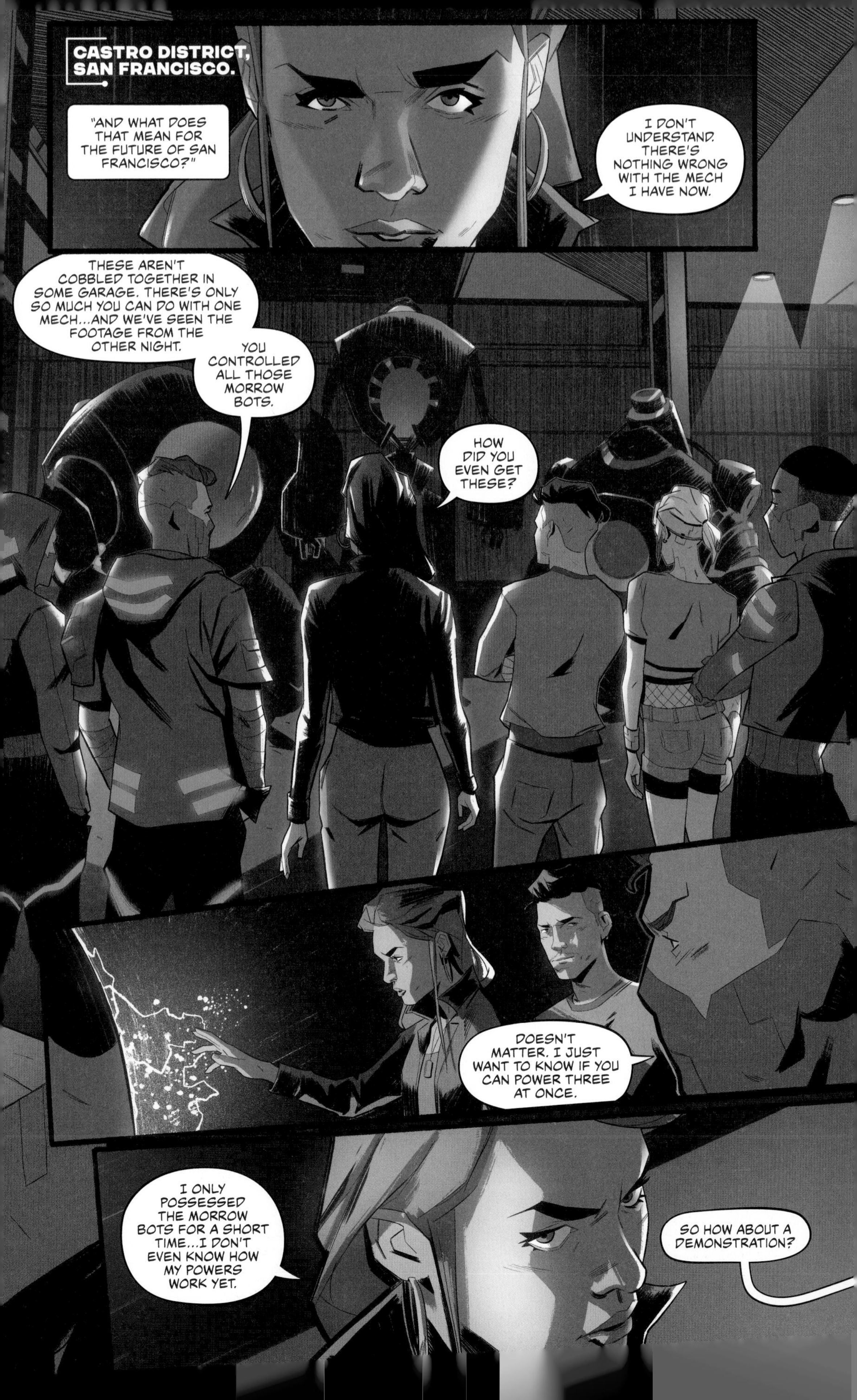
CASTRO DISTRICT, SAN FRANCISCO.
"AND WHAT DOES THAT MEAN FOR THE FUTURE OF SAN FRANCISCO?"
I DON'T UNDERSTAND. THERE'S NOTHING WRONG WITH THE MECH I HAVE NOW.
THESE AREN'T COBBLED TOGETHER IN SOME GARAGE. THERE'S ONLY SO MUCH YOU CAN DO WITH ONE MECH...AND WE'VE SEEN THE FOOTAGE FROM THE OTHER NIGHT.
YOU CONTROLLED ALL THOSE MORROW BOTS.
HOW DID YOU EVEN GET THESE?
DOESN'T MATTER. I JUST WANT TO KNOW IF YOU CAN POWER THREE AT ONCE.
I ONLY POSSESSED THE MORROW BOTS FOR A SHORT TIME...I DON'T EVEN KNOW HOW MY POWERS WORK YET.
SO HOW ABOUT A DEMONSTRATION?

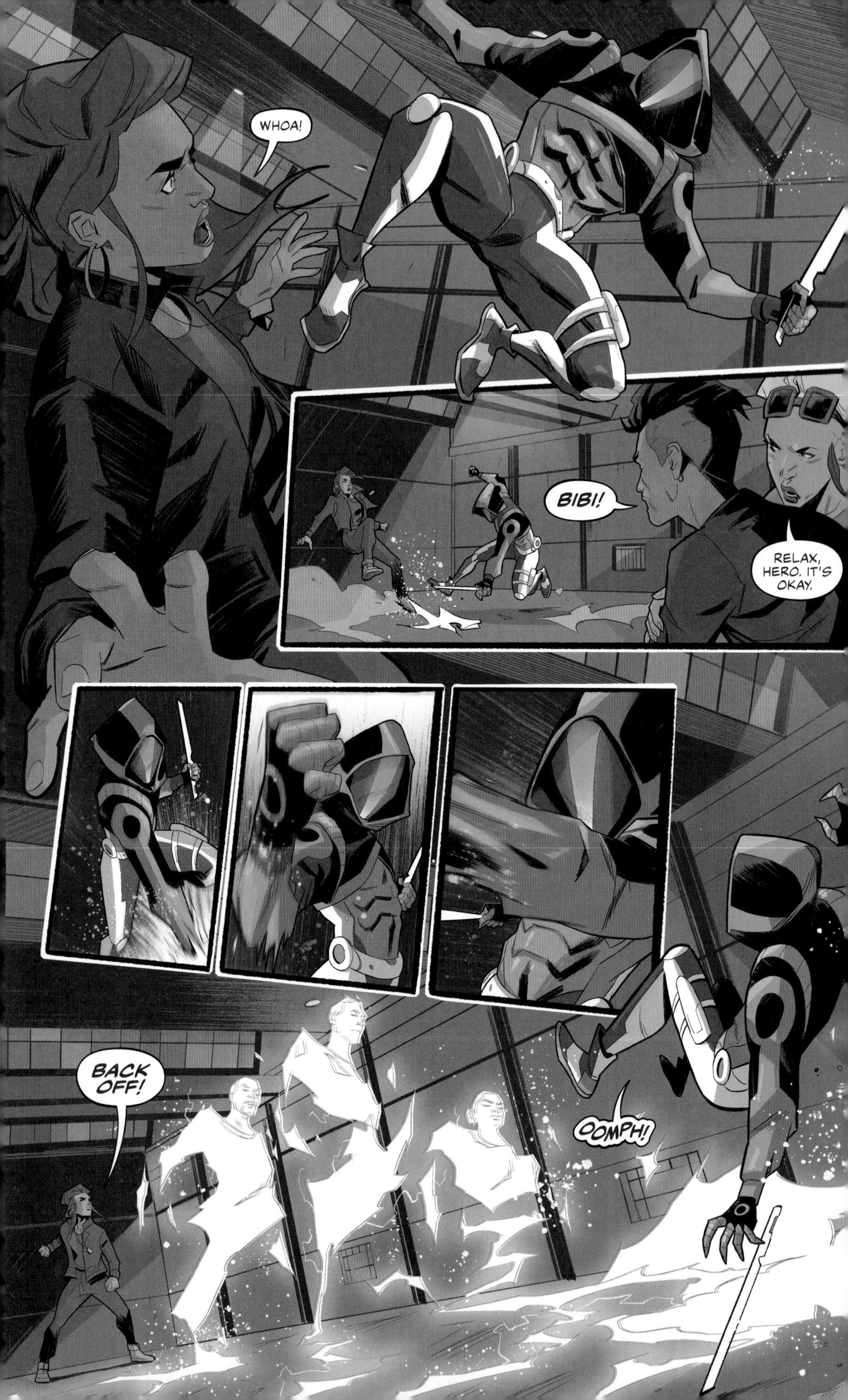
WHOA!
BIBI!
RELAX, HERO. IT'S OKAY.
BACK OFF!
OOMPH!

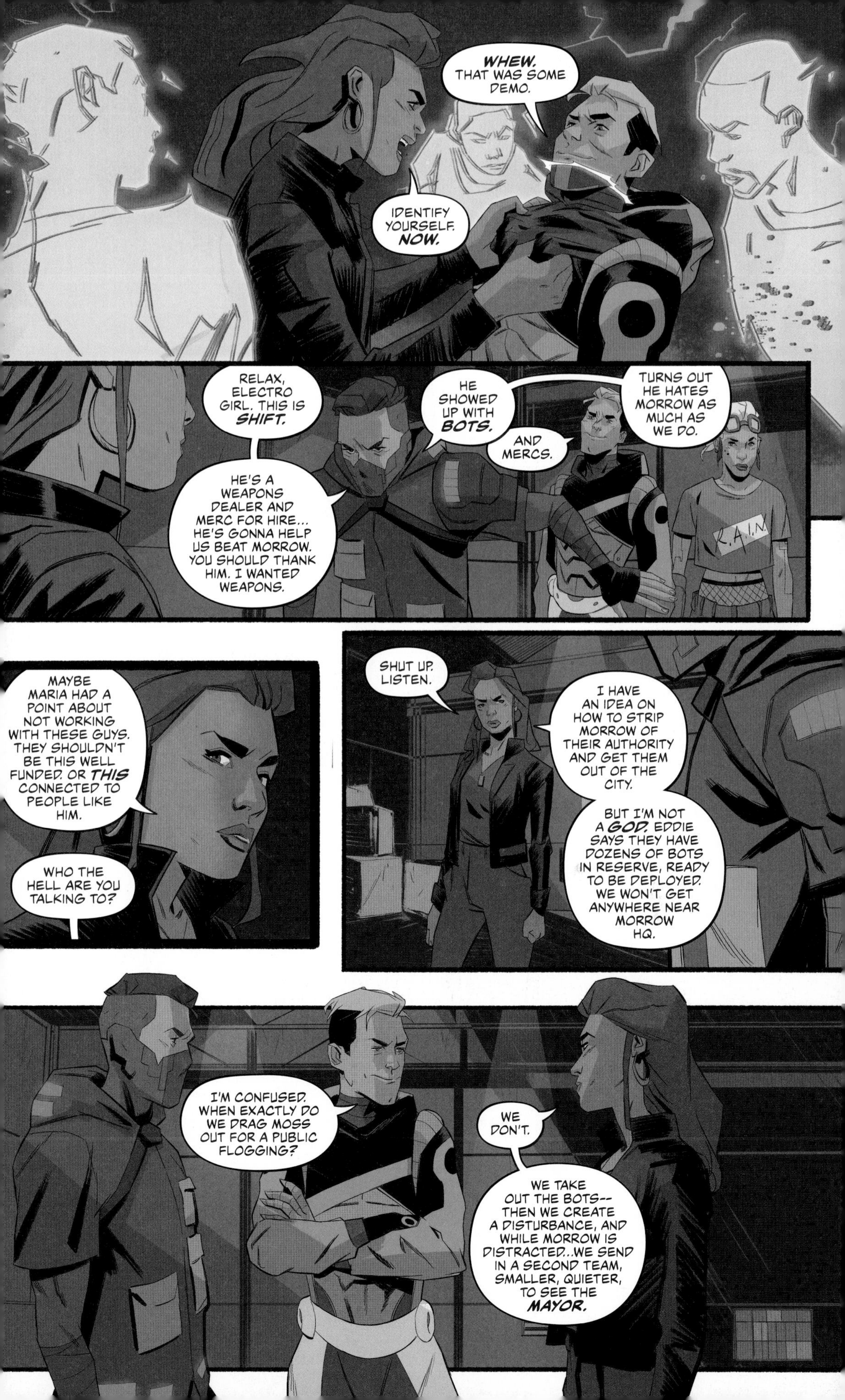
WHEW. THAT WAS SOME DEMO.
IDENTIFY YOURSELF. NOW.
RELAX, ELECTRO GIRL. THIS IS SHIFT.
HE'S A WEAPONS DEALER AND MERC FOR HIRE... HE'S GONNA HELP US BEAT MORROW. YOU SHOULD THANK HIM. I WANTED WEAPONS.
HE SHOWED UP WITH BOTS.
AND MERCS.
TURNS OUT HE HATES MORROW AS MUCH AS WE DO.
R.A.I.N.
MAYBE MARIA HAD A POINT ABOUT NOT WORKING WITH THESE GUYS. THEY SHOULDN'T BE THIS WELL FUNDED. OR THIS CONNECTED TO PEOPLE LIKE HIM.
WHO THE HELL ARE YOU TALKING TO?
SHUT UP. LISTEN.
I HAVE AN IDEA ON HOW TO STRIP MORROW OF THEIR AUTHORITY AND GET THEM OUT OF THE CITY.
BUT I'M NOT A GOD. EDDIE SAYS THEY HAVE DOZENS OF BOTS IN RESERVE, READY TO BE DEPLOYED. WE WON'T GET ANYWHERE NEAR MORROW HQ.
I'M CONFUSED. WHEN EXACTLY DO WE DRAG MOSS OUT FOR A PUBLIC FLOGGING?
WE DON'T.
WE TAKE OUT THE BOTS-- THEN WE CREATE A DISTURBANCE, AND WHILE MORROW IS DISTRACTED...WE SEND IN A SECOND TEAM, SMALLER, QUIETER, TO SEE THE MAYOR.

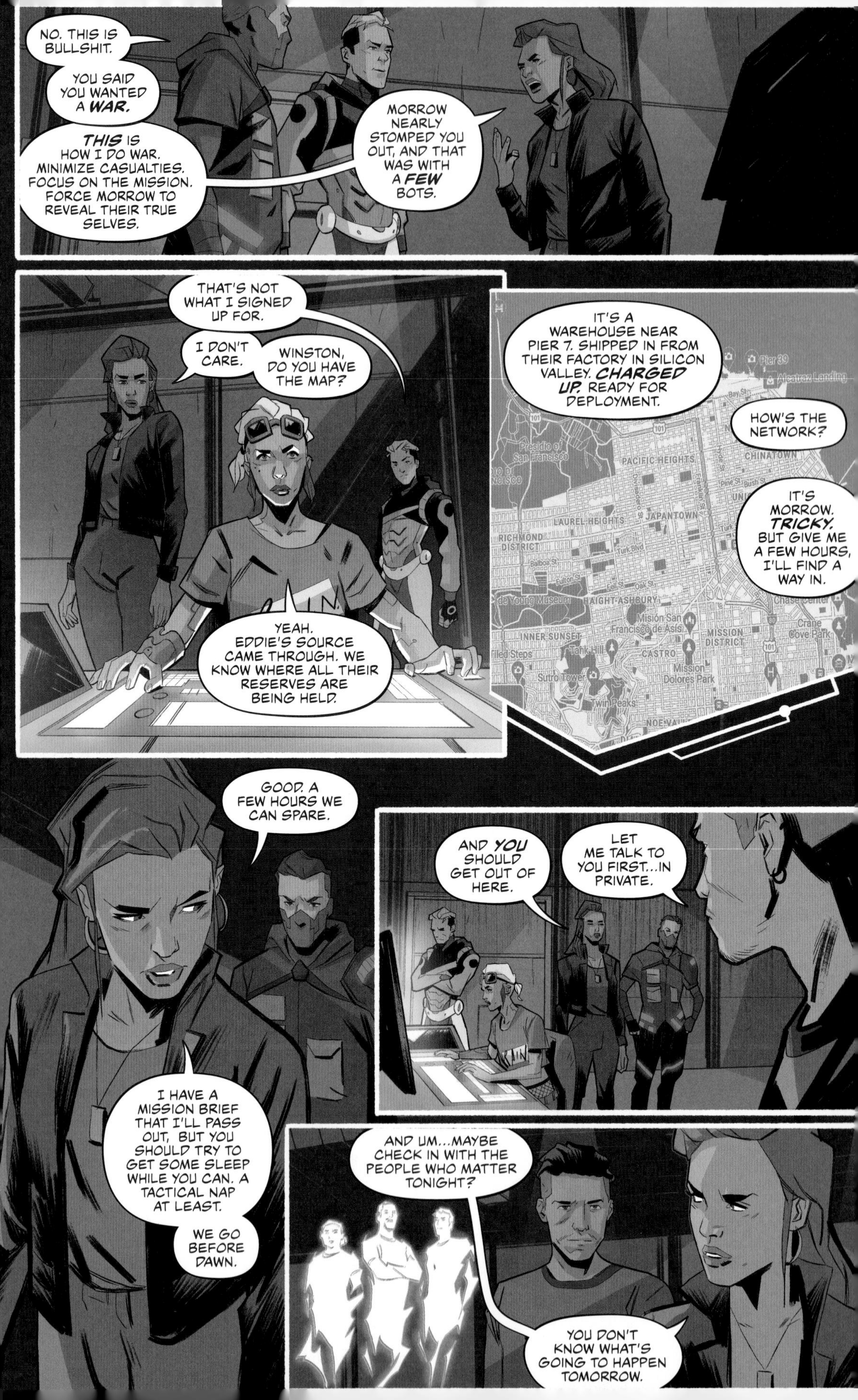

NO. THIS IS BULLSHIT.
YOU SAID YOU WANTED A *WAR.*
THIS IS HOW I DO WAR. MINIMIZE CASUALTIES. FOCUS ON THE MISSION. FORCE MORROW TO REVEAL THEIR TRUE SELVES.
MORROW NEARLY STOMPED YOU OUT, AND THAT WAS WITH A *FEW* BOTS.
THAT'S NOT WHAT I SIGNED UP FOR.
I DON'T CARE.
WINSTON, DO YOU HAVE THE MAP?
YEAH. EDDIE'S SOURCE CAME THROUGH. WE KNOW WHERE ALL THEIR RESERVES ARE BEING HELD.
IT'S A WAREHOUSE NEAR PIER 7. SHIPPED IN FROM THEIR FACTORY IN SILICON VALLEY. *CHARGED UP.* READY FOR DEPLOYMENT.
HOW'S THE NETWORK?
IT'S MORROW. *TRICKY.* BUT GIVE ME A FEW HOURS, I'LL FIND A WAY IN.
Pier 39
Alcatraz Landing
Presidio of San Francisco
PACIFIC HEIGHTS
CHINATOWN
JAPANTOWN
LAUREL HEIGHTS
RICHMOND DISTRICT
de Young Museum
HAIGHT-ASHBURY
Mission San Francisco de Asís
INNER SUNSET
MISSION DISTRICT
CASTRO
Mission Dolores Park
Sutro Tower
Twin Peaks
Chase Center
Crane Cove Park
GOOD. A FEW HOURS WE CAN SPARE.
I HAVE A MISSION BRIEF THAT I'LL PASS OUT, BUT YOU SHOULD TRY TO GET SOME SLEEP WHILE YOU CAN. A TACTICAL NAP AT LEAST.
WE GO BEFORE DAWN.
AND *YOU* SHOULD GET OUT OF HERE.
LET ME TALK TO YOU FIRST...IN PRIVATE.
AND UM...MAYBE CHECK IN WITH THE PEOPLE WHO MATTER TONIGHT?
YOU DON'T KNOW WHAT'S GOING TO HAPPEN TOMORROW.

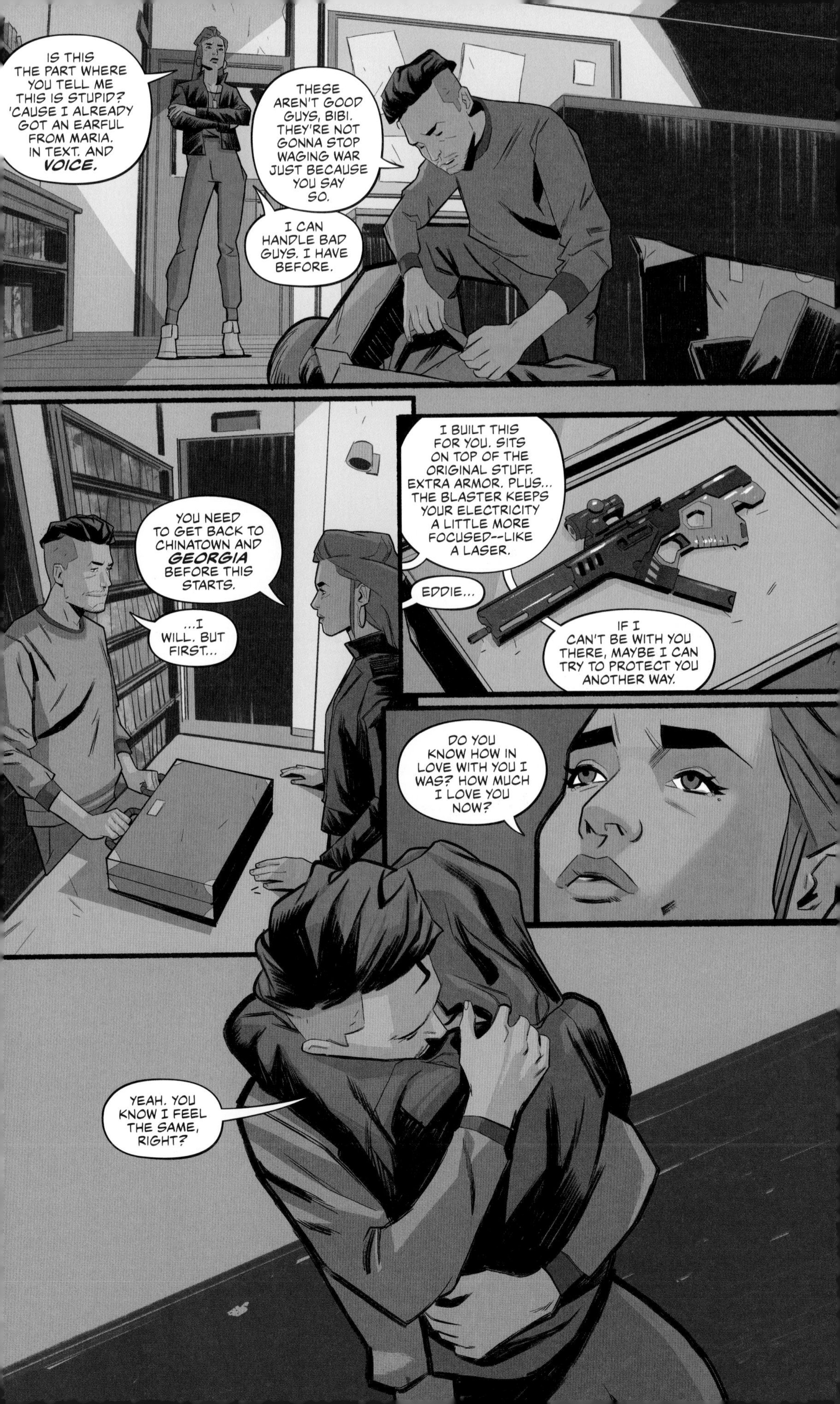
IS THIS THE PART WHERE YOU TELL ME THIS IS STUPID? 'CAUSE I ALREADY GOT AN EARFUL FROM MARIA. IN TEXT. AND **VOICE.**
THESE AREN'T GOOD GUYS, BIBI. THEY'RE NOT GONNA STOP WAGING WAR JUST BECAUSE YOU SAY SO.
I CAN HANDLE BAD GUYS. I HAVE BEFORE.
YOU NEED TO GET BACK TO CHINATOWN AND **GEORGIA** BEFORE THIS STARTS.
...I WILL. BUT FIRST...
I BUILT THIS FOR YOU. SITS ON TOP OF THE ORIGINAL STUFF. EXTRA ARMOR. PLUS... THE BLASTER KEEPS YOUR ELECTRICITY A LITTLE MORE FOCUSED--LIKE A LASER.
EDDIE...
IF I CAN'T BE WITH YOU THERE, MAYBE I CAN TRY TO PROTECT YOU ANOTHER WAY.
DO YOU KNOW HOW IN LOVE WITH YOU I WAS? HOW MUCH I LOVE YOU NOW?
YEAH. YOU KNOW I FEEL THE SAME, RIGHT?

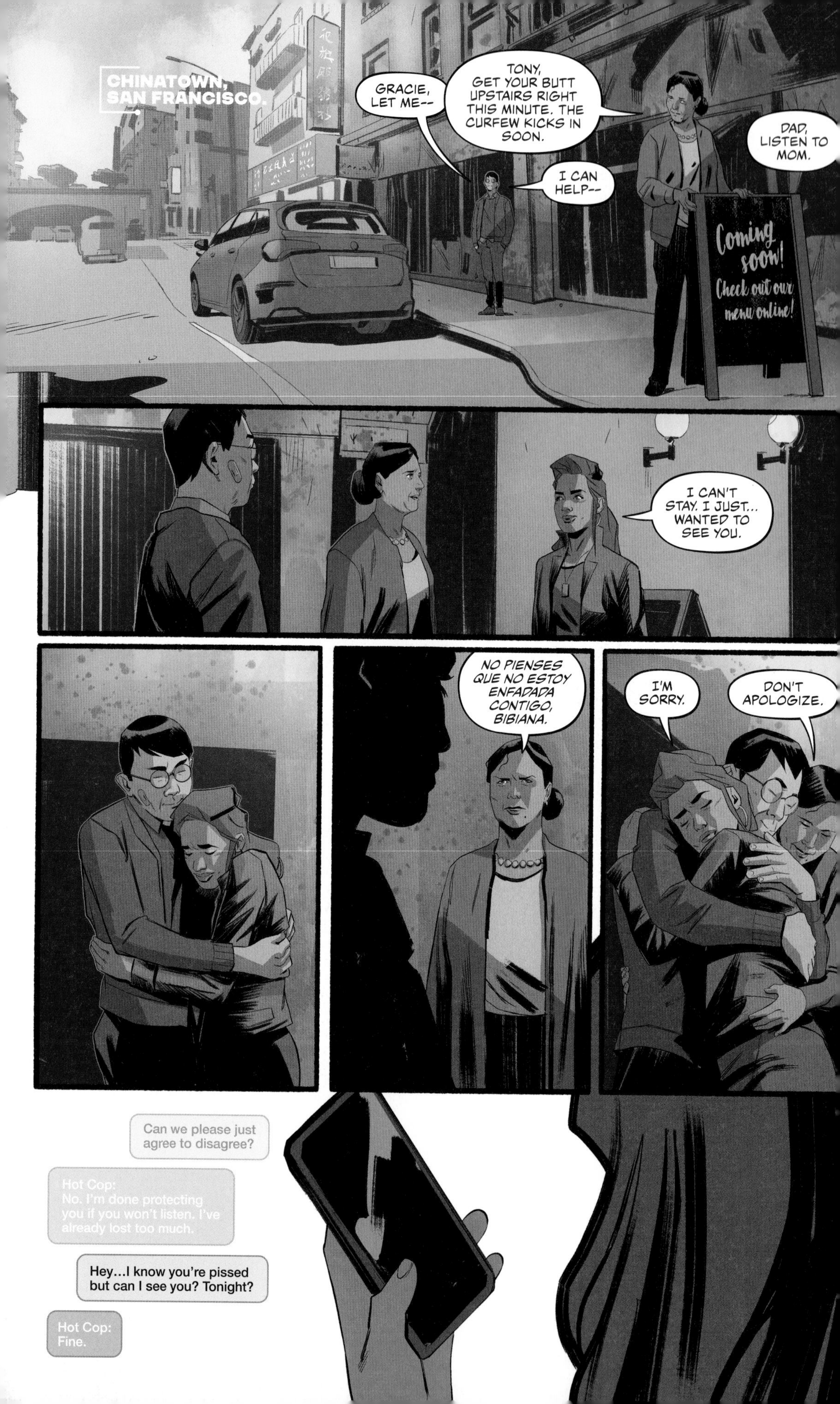
CHINATOWN, SAN FRANCISCO.
GRACIE, LET ME--
TONY, GET YOUR BUTT UPSTAIRS RIGHT THIS MINUTE. THE CURFEW KICKS IN SOON.
I CAN HELP--
DAD, LISTEN TO MOM.
Coming soon! Check out our menu online!
I CAN'T STAY. I JUST... WANTED TO SEE YOU.
NO PIENSES QUE NO ESTOY ENFADADA CONTIGO, BIBIANA.
I'M SORRY.
DON'T APOLOGIZE.
Can we please just agree to disagree?
Hot Cop: No. I'm done protecting you if you won't listen. I've already lost too much.
Hey...I know you're pissed but can I see you? Tonight?
Hot Cop: Fine.

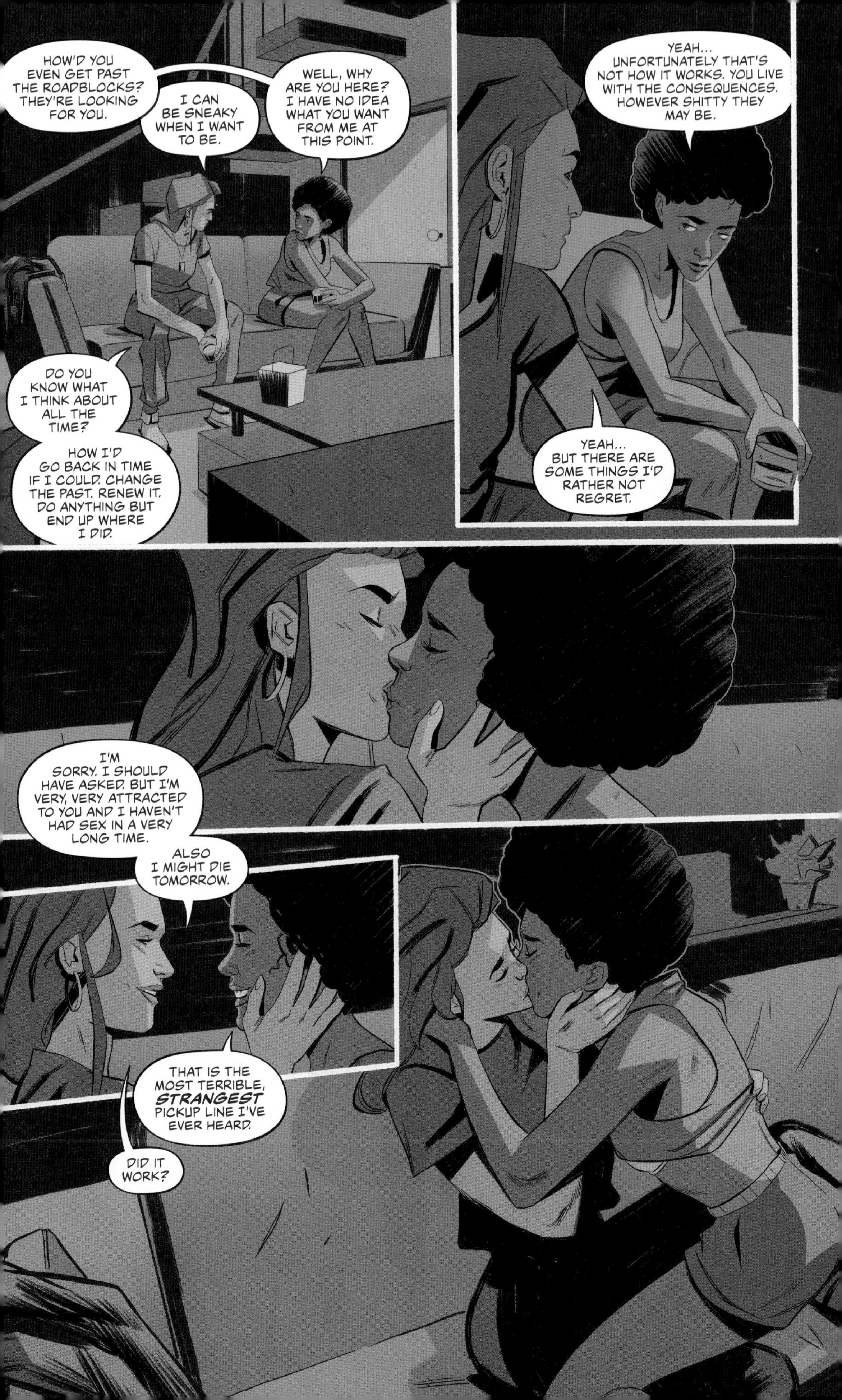

HOW'D YOU EVEN GET PAST THE ROADBLOCKS? THEY'RE LOOKING FOR YOU.
I CAN BE SNEAKY WHEN I WANT TO BE.
WELL, WHY ARE YOU HERE? I HAVE NO IDEA WHAT YOU WANT FROM ME AT THIS POINT.
DO YOU KNOW WHAT I THINK ABOUT ALL THE TIME?
HOW I'D GO BACK IN TIME IF I COULD. CHANGE THE PAST. RENEW IT. DO ANYTHING BUT END UP WHERE I DID.
YEAH... UNFORTUNATELY THAT'S NOT HOW IT WORKS. YOU LIVE WITH THE CONSEQUENCES. HOWEVER SHITTY THEY MAY BE.
YEAH... BUT THERE ARE SOME THINGS I'D RATHER NOT REGRET.
I'M SORRY. I SHOULD HAVE ASKED. BUT I'M VERY, VERY ATTRACTED TO YOU AND I HAVEN'T HAD SEX IN A VERY LONG TIME.
ALSO I MIGHT DIE TOMORROW.
THAT IS THE MOST TERRIBLE, STRANGEST PICKUP LINE I'VE EVER HEARD.
DID IT WORK?

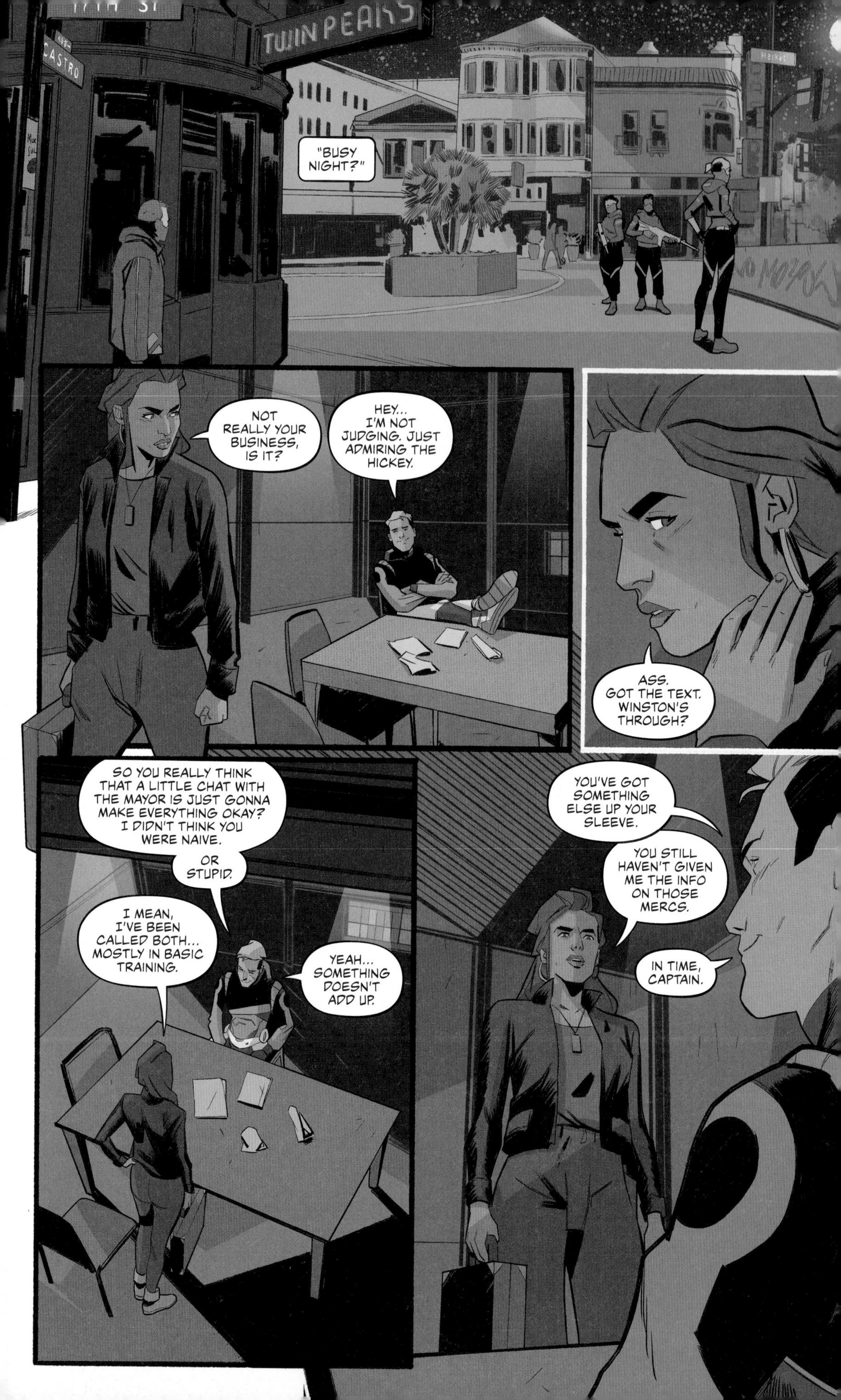

17TH ST
CASTRO
TWIN PEAKS
Market
"BUSY NIGHT?"
NOT REALLY YOUR BUSINESS, IS IT?
HEY... I'M NOT JUDGING. JUST ADMIRING THE HICKEY.
ASS. GOT THE TEXT. WINSTON'S THROUGH?
SO YOU REALLY THINK THAT A LITTLE CHAT WITH THE MAYOR IS JUST GONNA MAKE EVERYTHING OKAY? I DIDN'T THINK YOU WERE NAIVE.
OR STUPID.
I MEAN, I'VE BEEN CALLED BOTH... MOSTLY IN BASIC TRAINING.
YEAH... SOMETHING DOESN'T ADD UP.
YOU'VE GOT SOMETHING ELSE UP YOUR SLEEVE.
YOU STILL HAVEN'T GIVEN ME THE INFO ON THOSE MERCS.
IN TIME, CAPTAIN.

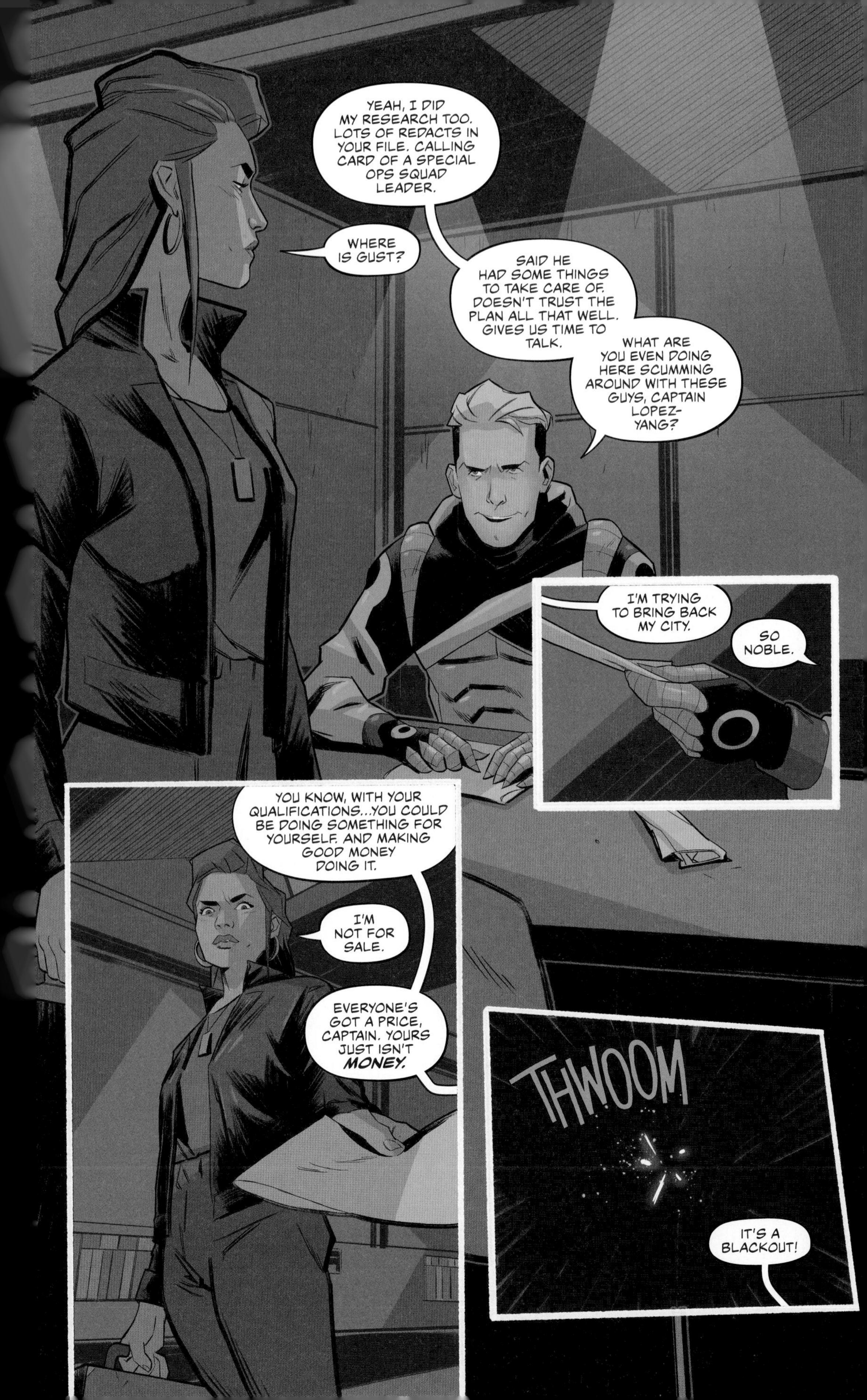
YEAH, I DID MY RESEARCH TOO. LOTS OF REDACTS IN YOUR FILE. CALLING CARD OF A SPECIAL OPS SQUAD LEADER.
WHERE IS GUST?
SAID HE HAD SOME THINGS TO TAKE CARE OF. DOESN'T TRUST THE PLAN ALL THAT WELL. GIVES US TIME TO TALK.
WHAT ARE YOU EVEN DOING HERE SCUMMING AROUND WITH THESE GUYS, CAPTAIN LOPEZ-YANG?
I'M TRYING TO BRING BACK MY CITY.
SO NOBLE.
YOU KNOW, WITH YOUR QUALIFICATIONS...YOU COULD BE DOING SOMETHING FOR YOURSELF. AND MAKING GOOD MONEY DOING IT.
I'M NOT FOR SALE.
EVERYONE'S GOT A PRICE, CAPTAIN. YOURS JUST ISN'T ***MONEY.***
THWOOM
IT'S A BLACKOUT!

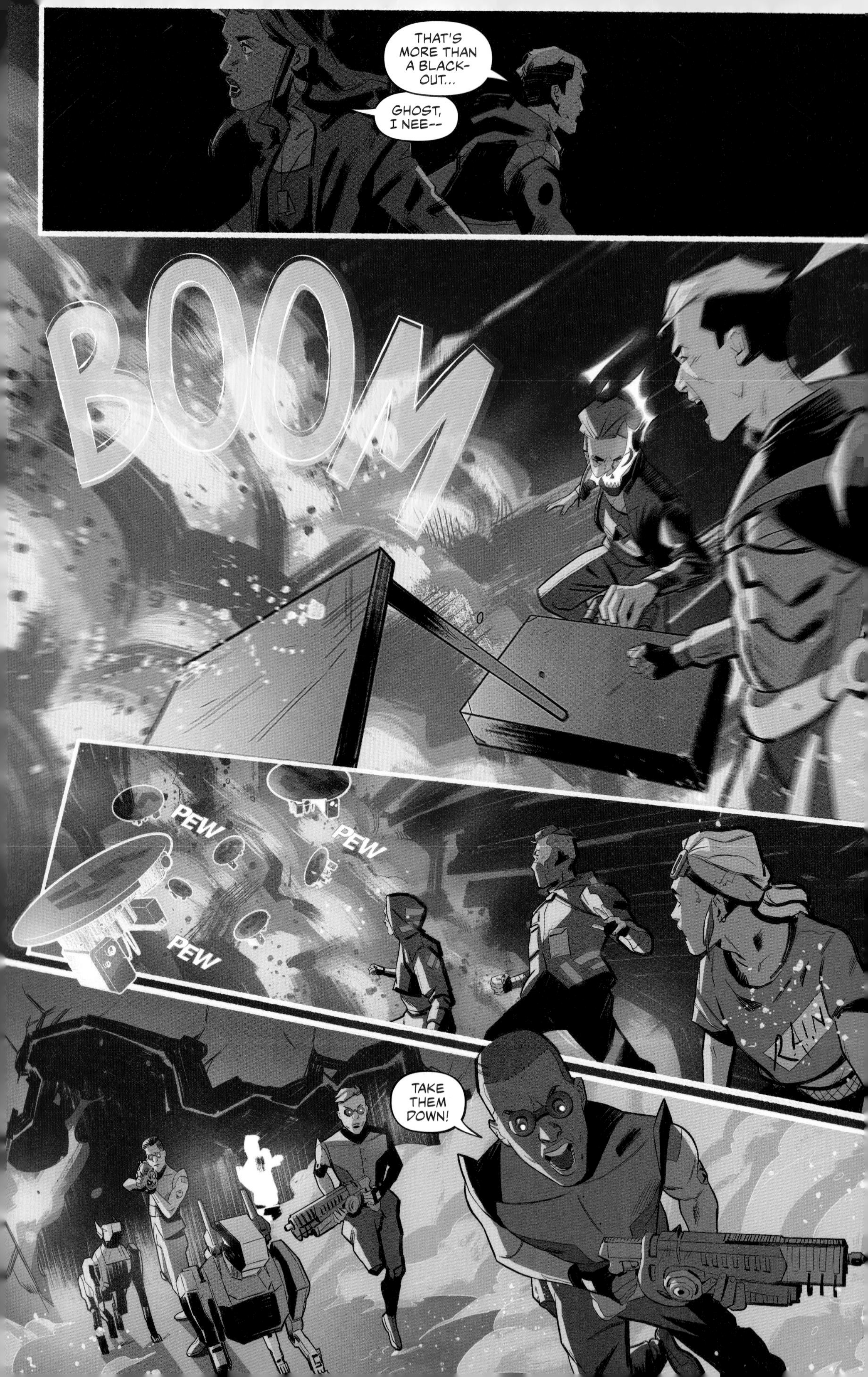
THAT'S MORE THAN A BLACK-OUT...
GHOST, I NEE--
BOOM
PEW
PEW
PEW
R.A.I.N.
TAKE THEM DOWN!

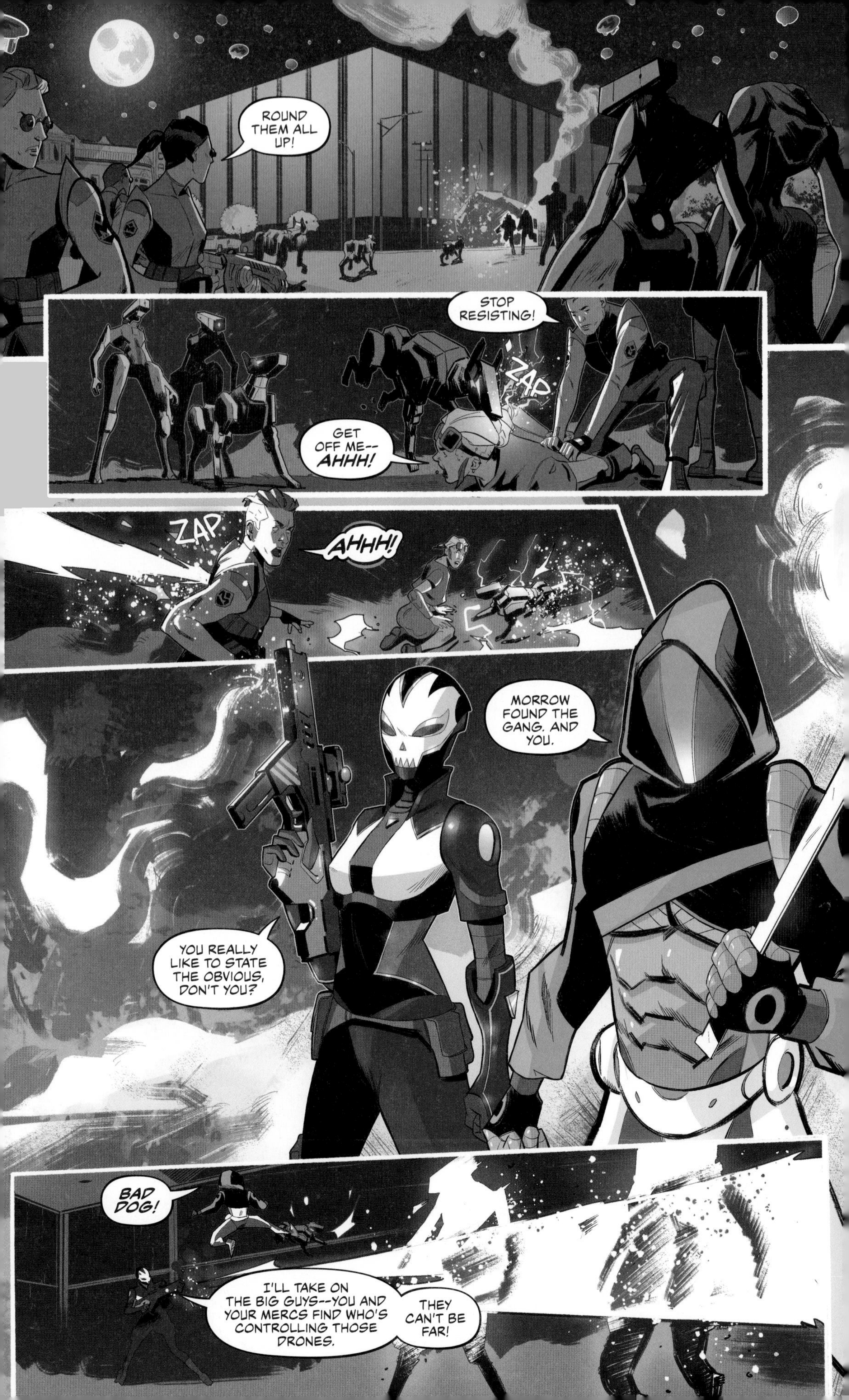
ROUND THEM ALL UP!
STOP RESISTING!
ZAP
GET OFF ME-- AHHH!
ZAP
AHHH!
MORROW FOUND THE GANG. AND YOU.
YOU REALLY LIKE TO STATE THE OBVIOUS, DON'T YOU?
BAD DOG!
I'LL TAKE ON THE BIG GUYS--YOU AND YOUR MERCS FIND WHO'S CONTROLLING THOSE DRONES.
THEY CAN'T BE FAR!

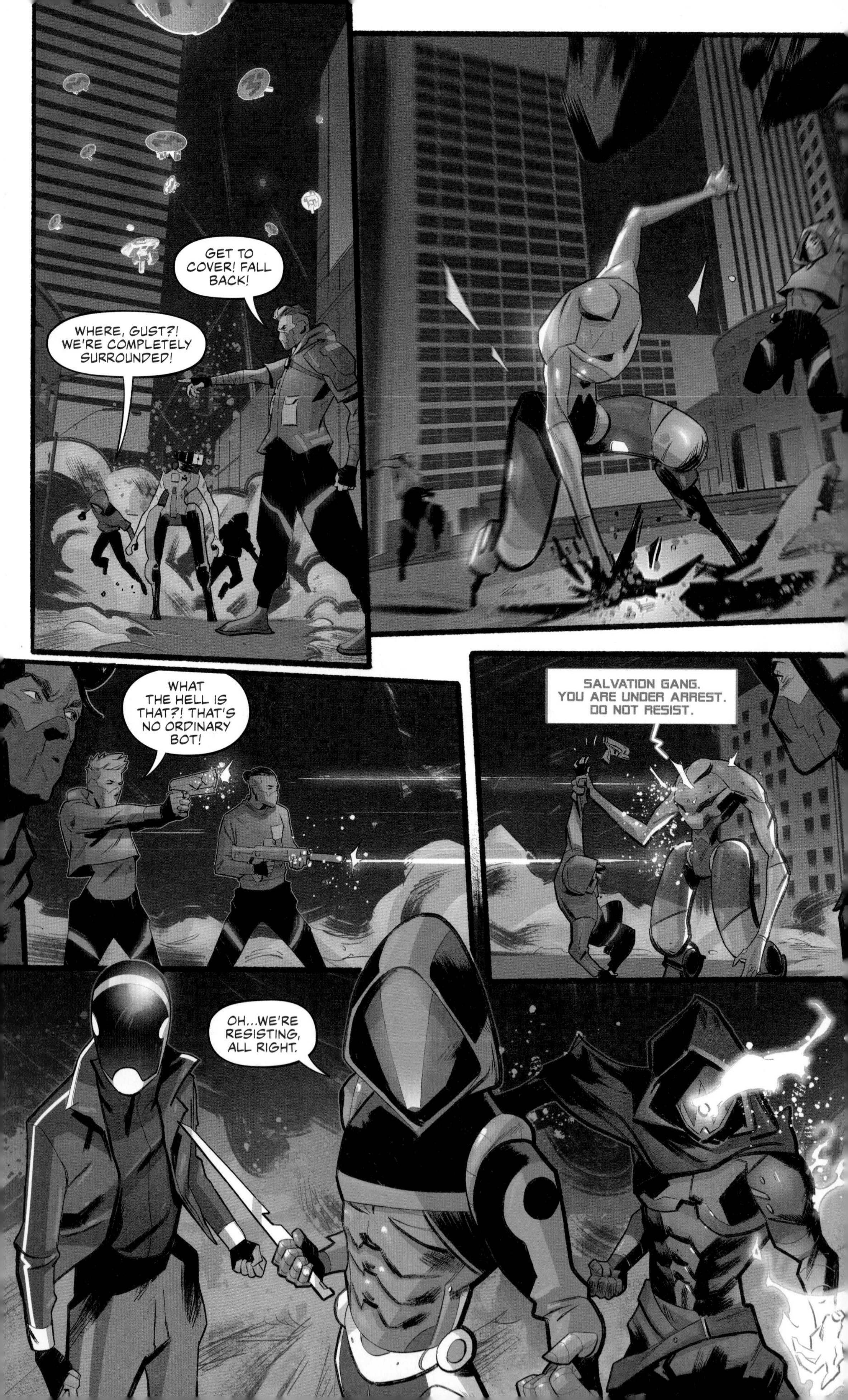
GET TO COVER! FALL BACK!
WHERE, GUST?! WE'RE COMPLETELY SURROUNDED!
WHAT THE HELL IS THAT?! THAT'S NO ORDINARY BOT!
SALVATION GANG. YOU ARE UNDER ARREST. DO NOT RESIST.
OH...WE'RE RESISTING, ALL RIGHT.

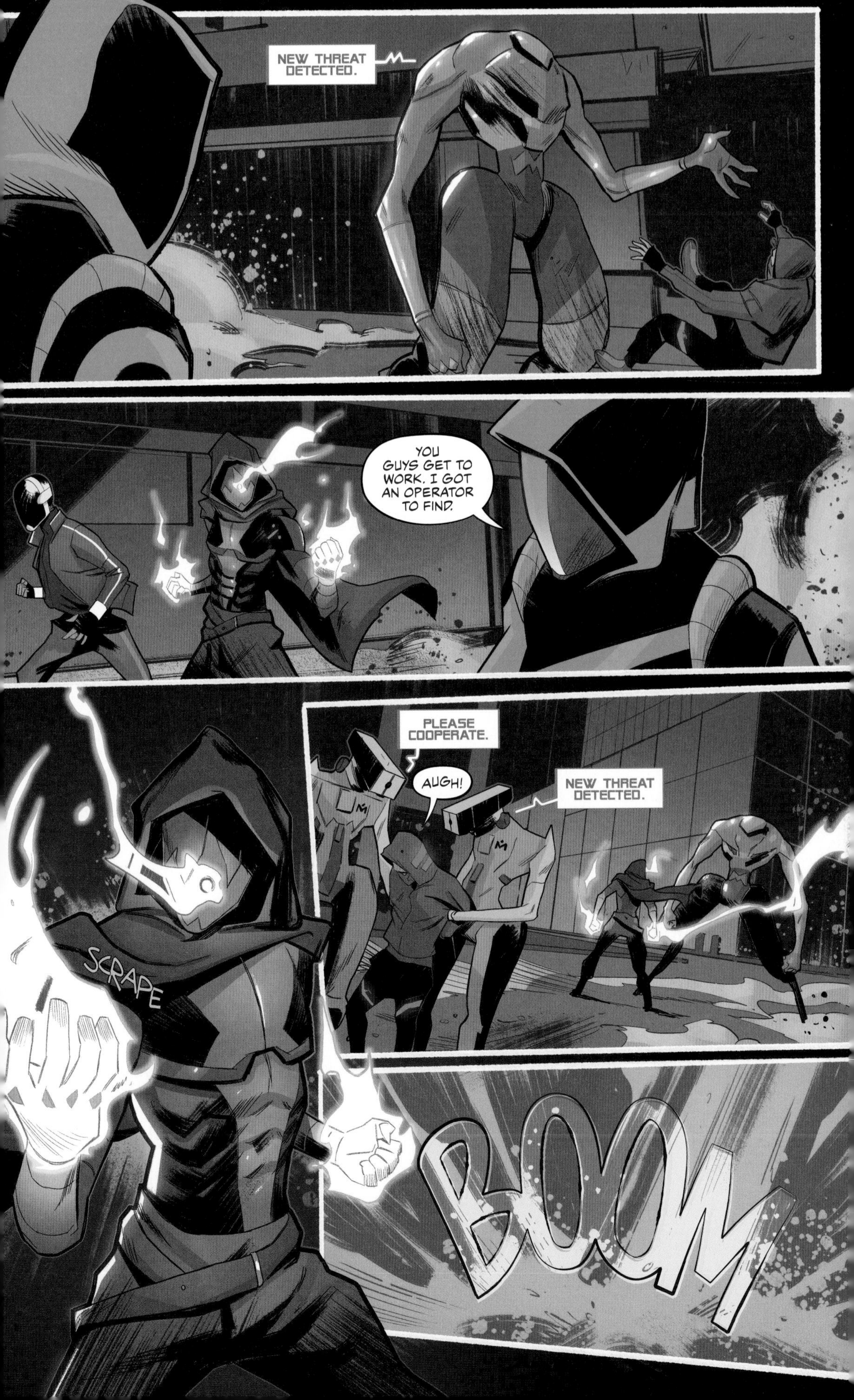
NEW THREAT DETECTED.
YOU GUYS GET TO WORK. I GOT AN OPERATOR TO FIND.
SCRAPE
PLEASE COOPERATE.
AUGH!
NEW THREAT DETECTED.
BOOM

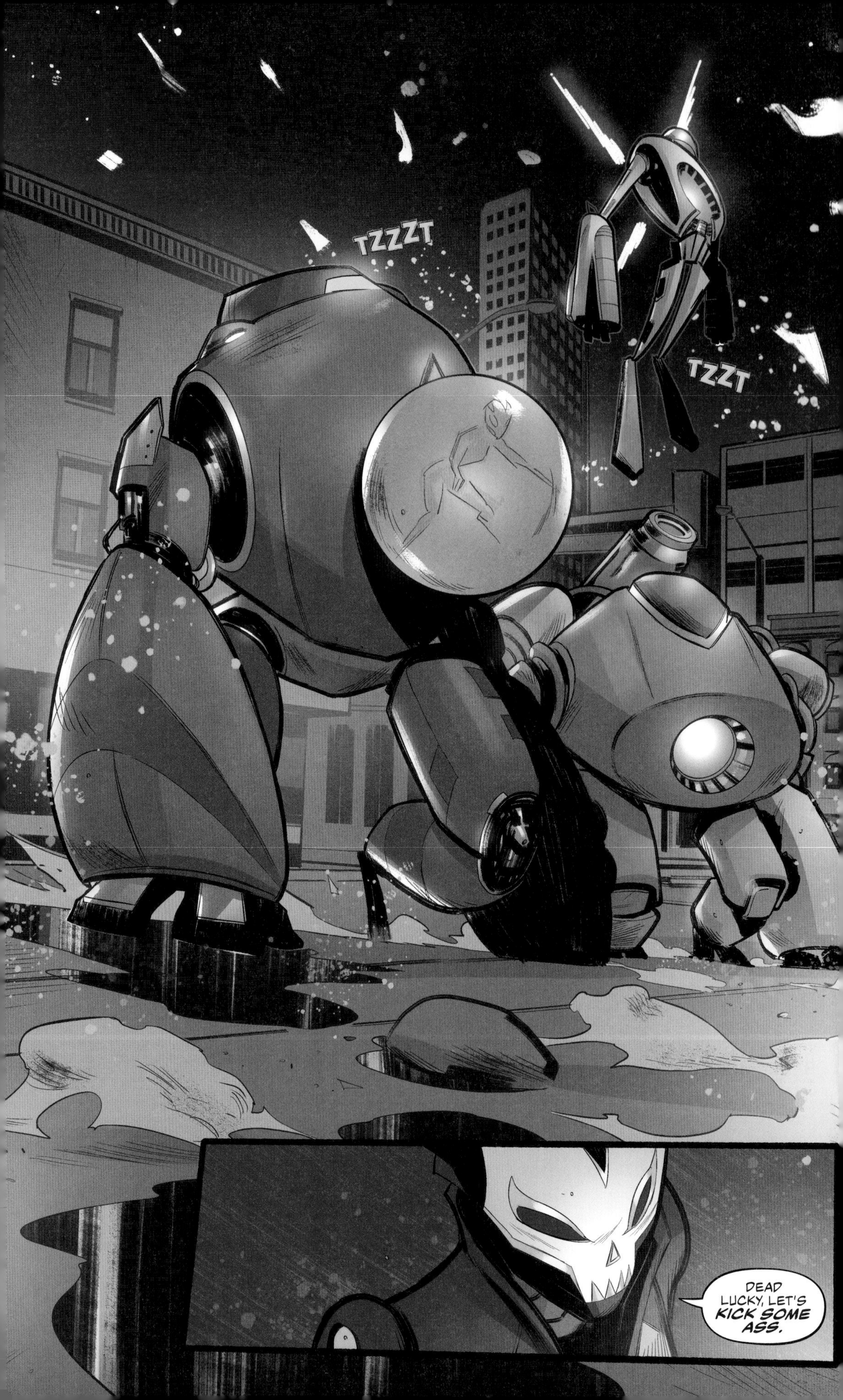
TZZZT
TZZT
DEAD LUCKY, LET'S KICK SOME ASS.

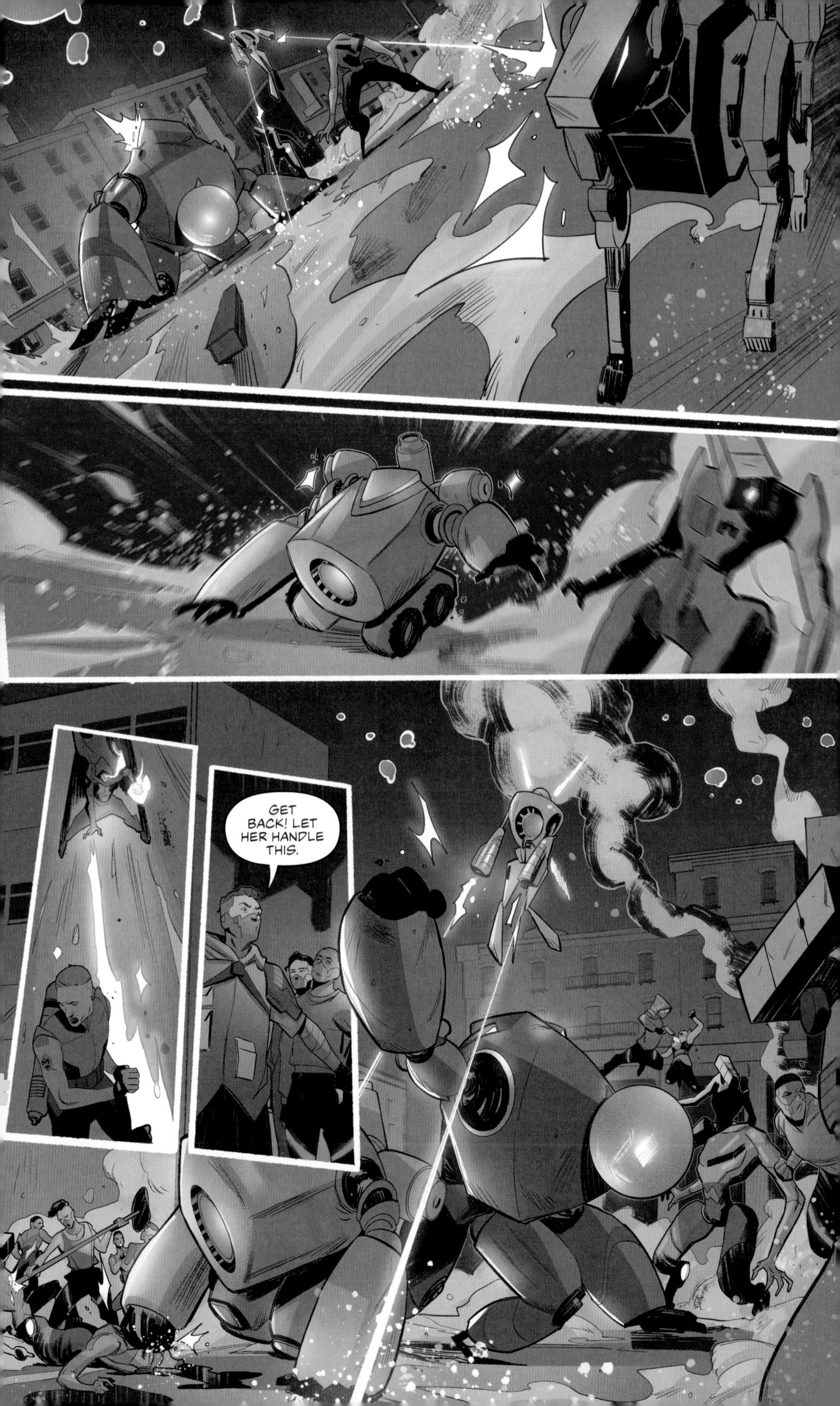
GET BACK! LET HER HANDLE THIS.

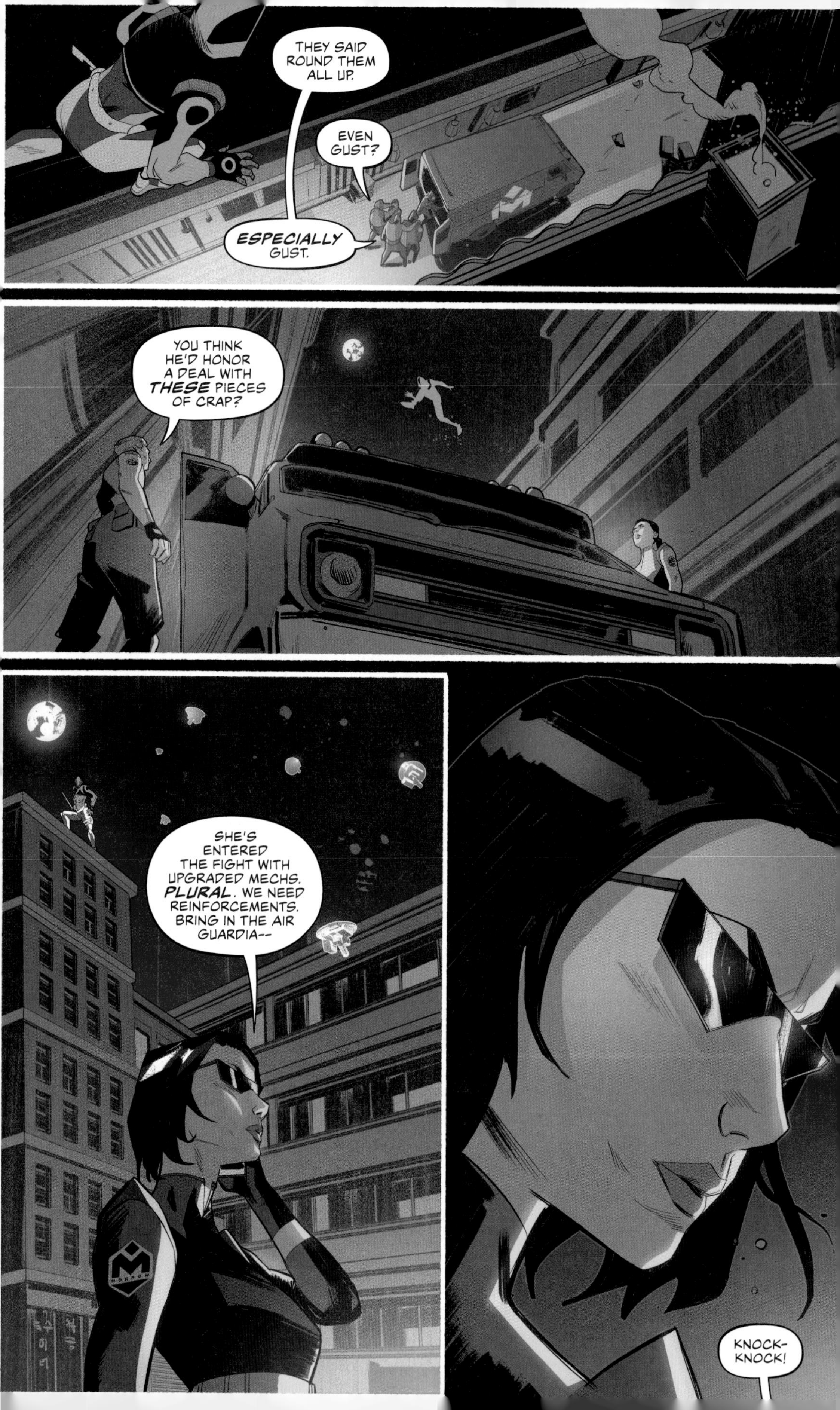

THEY SAID ROUND THEM ALL UP.
EVEN GUST?
ESPECIALLY GUST.
YOU THINK HE'D HONOR A DEAL WITH THESE PIECES OF CRAP?
SHE'S ENTERED THE FIGHT WITH UPGRADED MECHS. PLURAL. WE NEED REINFORCEMENTS. BRING IN THE AIR GUARDIA--
KNOCK-KNOCK!

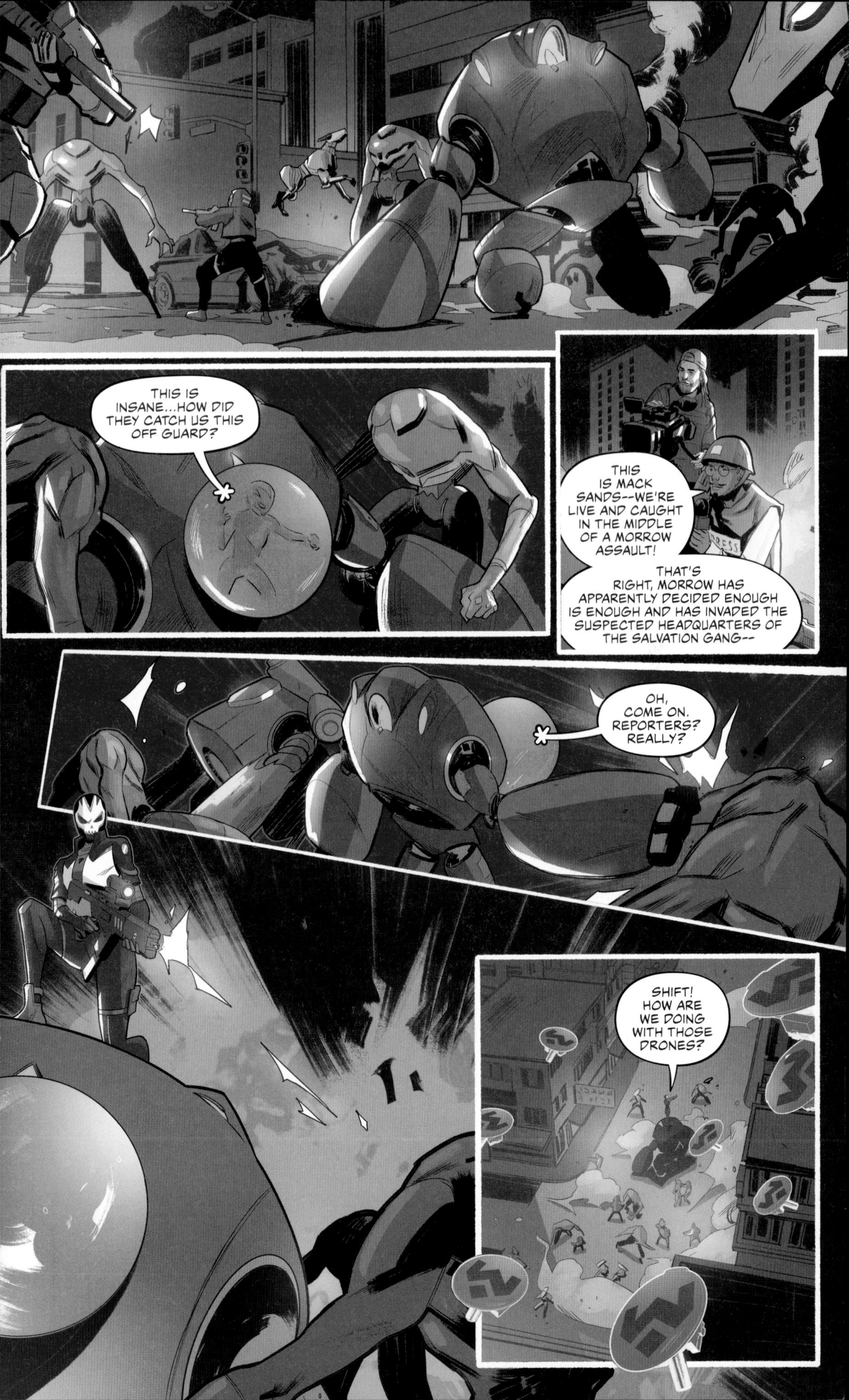
THIS IS INSANE...HOW DID THEY CATCH US THIS OFF GUARD?
THIS IS MACK SANDS--WE'RE LIVE AND CAUGHT IN THE MIDDLE OF A MORROW ASSAULT!
THAT'S RIGHT, MORROW HAS APPARENTLY DECIDED ENOUGH IS ENOUGH AND HAS INVADED THE SUSPECTED HEADQUARTERS OF THE SALVATION GANG--
OH, COME ON. REPORTERS? REALLY?
SHIFT! HOW ARE WE DOING WITH THOSE DRONES?

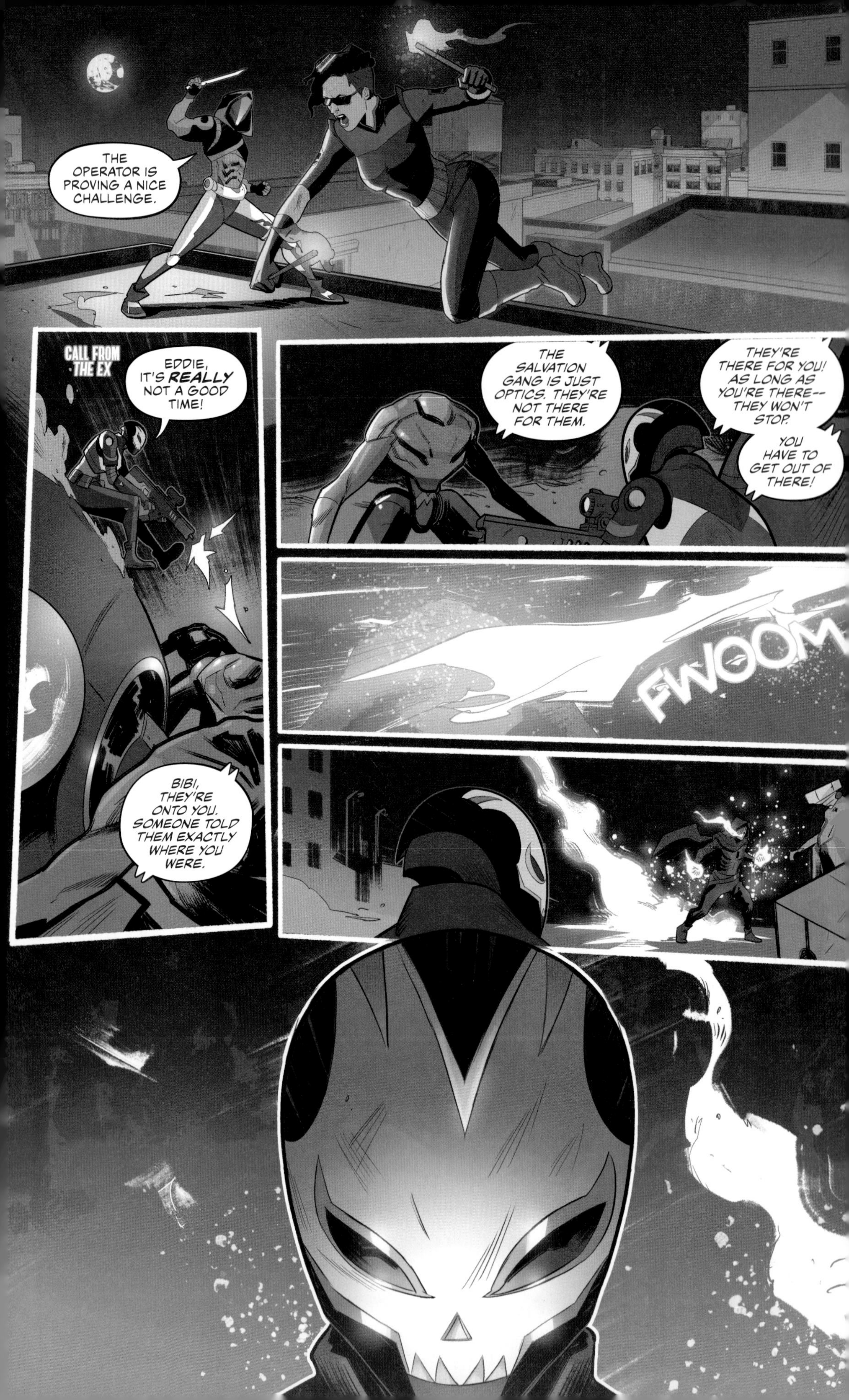

THE OPERATOR IS PROVING A NICE CHALLENGE.
CALL FROM THE EX
EDDIE, IT'S **REALLY** NOT A GOOD TIME!
BIBI, THEY'RE ONTO YOU. SOMEONE TOLD THEM EXACTLY WHERE YOU WERE.
THE SALVATION GANG IS JUST OPTICS. THEY'RE NOT THERE FOR THEM.
THEY'RE THERE FOR YOU! AS LONG AS YOU'RE THERE-- THEY WON'T STOP.
YOU HAVE TO GET OUT OF THERE!
FWOOM

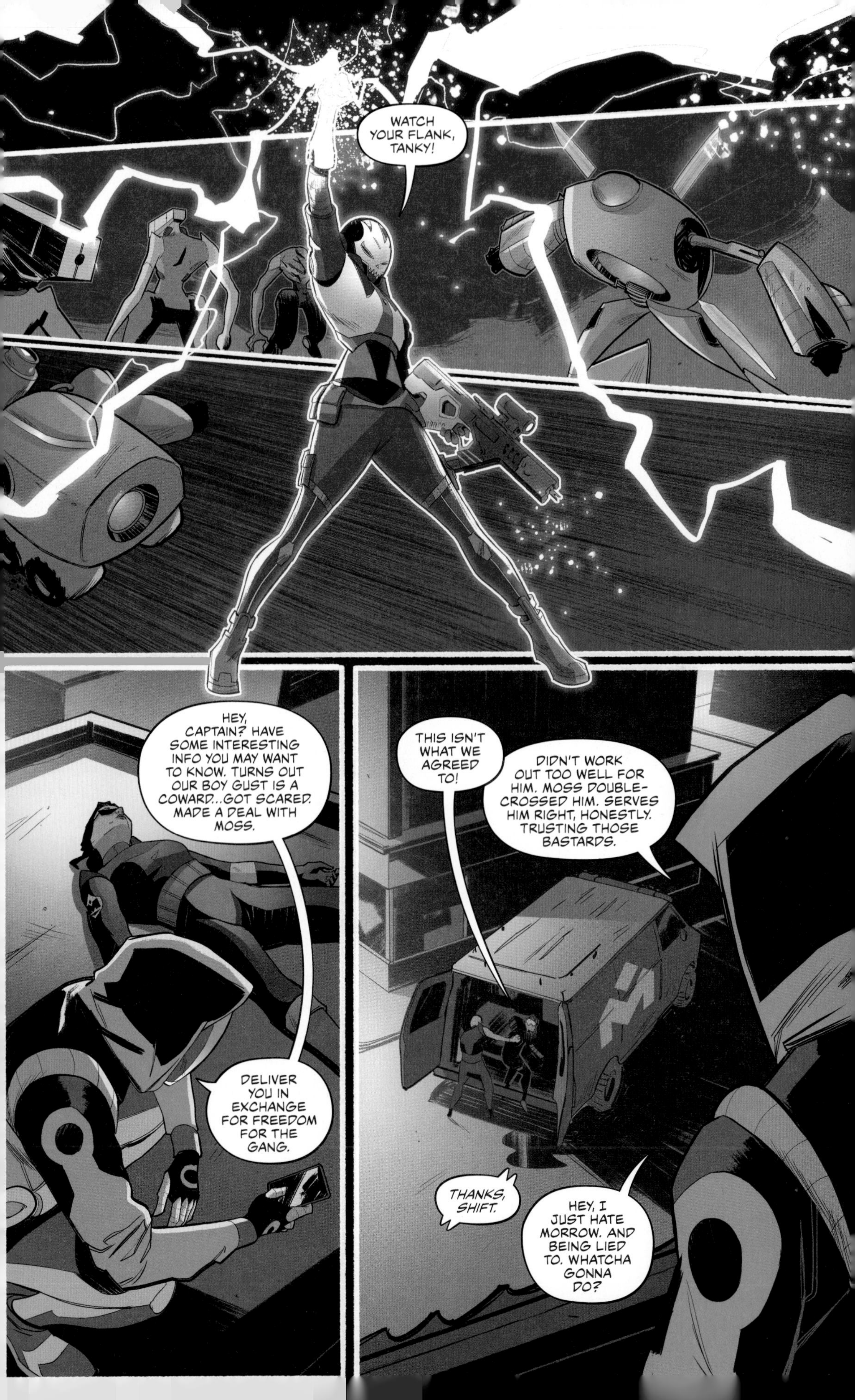
WATCH YOUR FLANK, TANKY!
HEY, CAPTAIN? HAVE SOME INTERESTING INFO YOU MAY WANT TO KNOW. TURNS OUT OUR BOY GUST IS A COWARD...GOT SCARED. MADE A DEAL WITH MOSS.
DELIVER YOU IN EXCHANGE FOR FREEDOM FOR THE GANG.
THIS ISN'T WHAT WE AGREED TO!
DIDN'T WORK OUT TOO WELL FOR HIM. MOSS DOUBLE-CROSSED HIM. SERVES HIM RIGHT, HONESTLY. TRUSTING THOSE BASTARDS.
THANKS, SHIFT.
HEY, I JUST HATE MORROW. AND BEING LIED TO. WHATCHA GONNA DO?

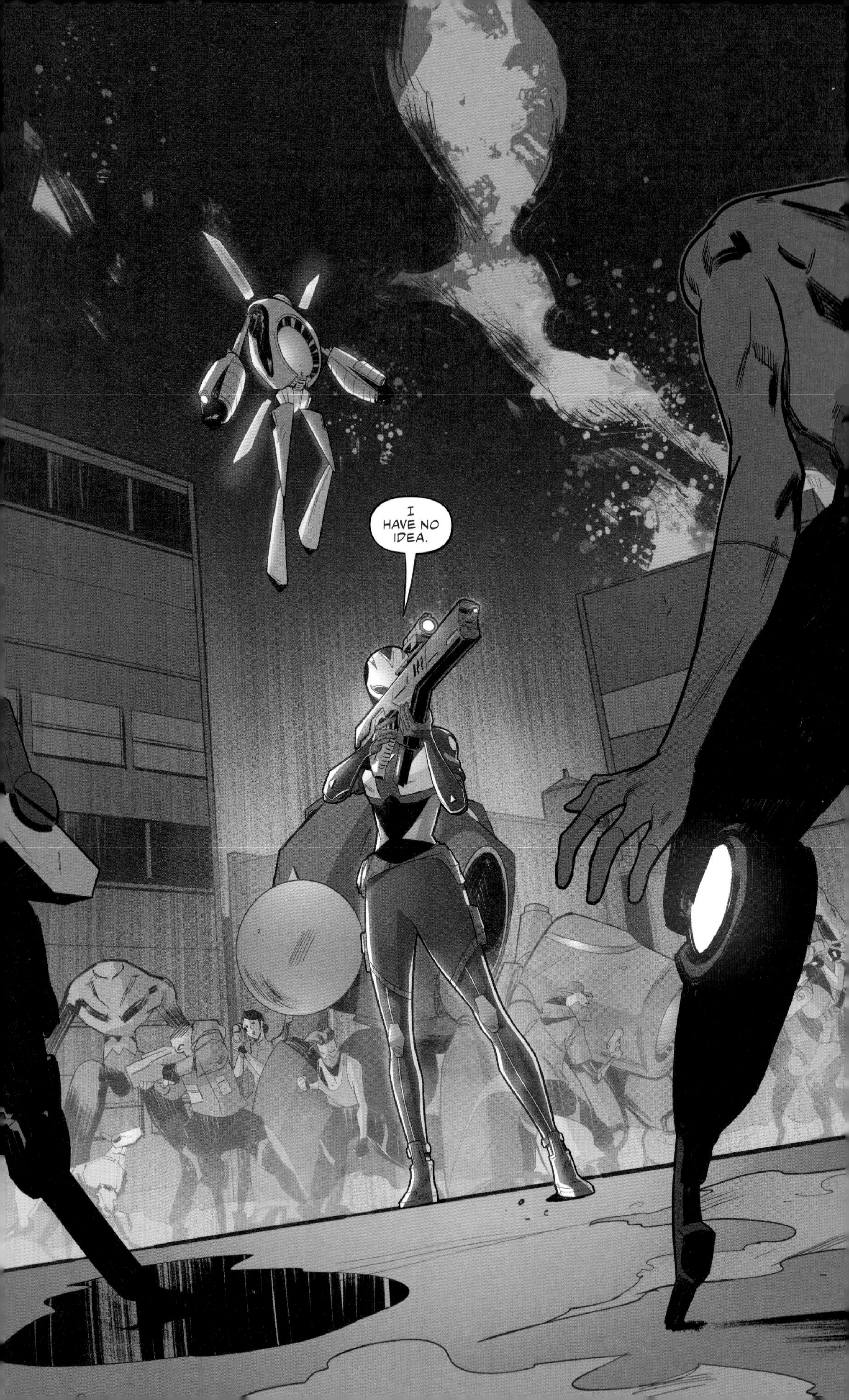
I HAVE NO IDEA.

TERMINAL — ×

GHOST:~ admin$ SingleIssueProfiler
Issue:
    No.: 006
    Title: There's No Shame In Surrender.

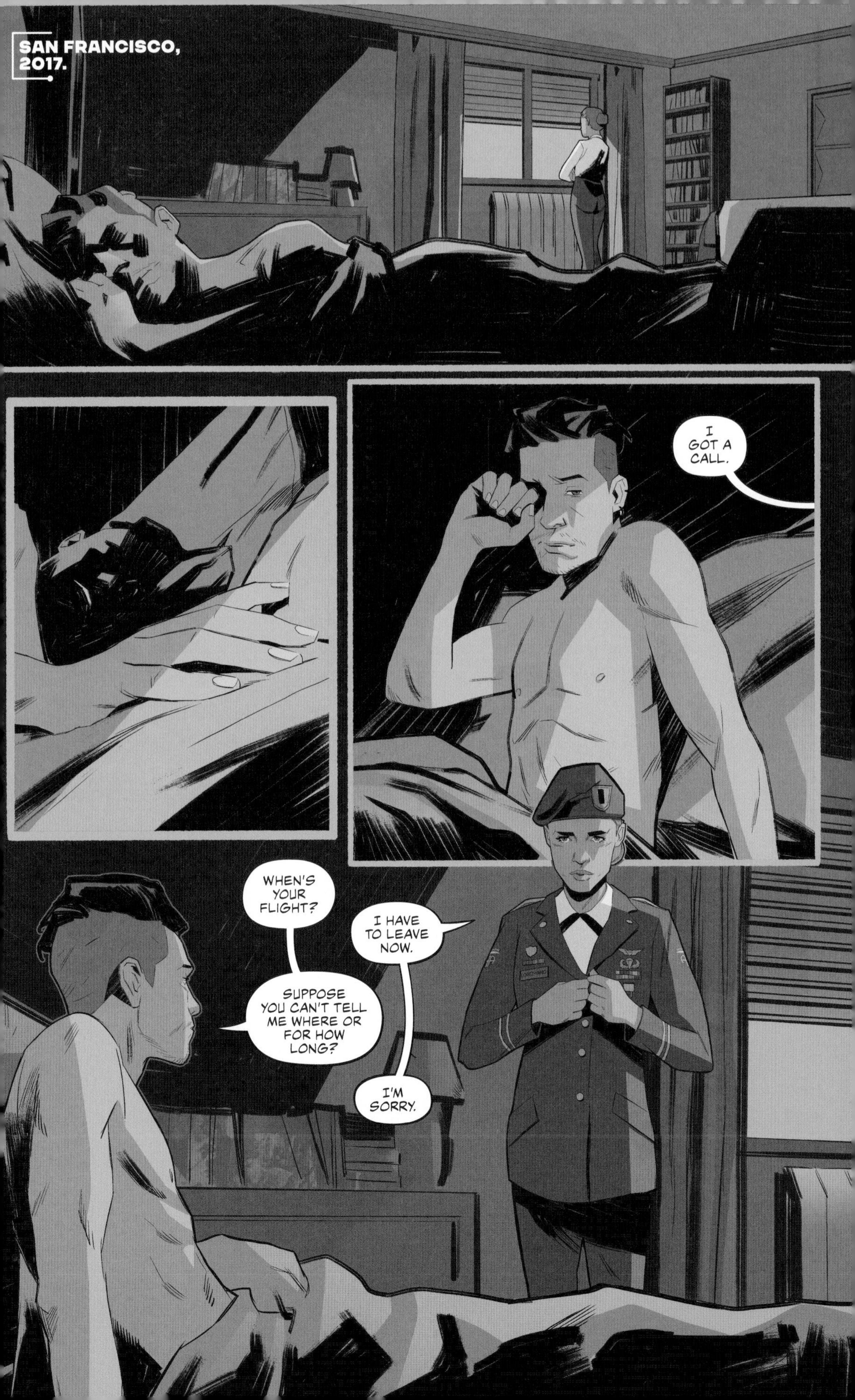
SAN FRANCISCO, 2017.
I GOT A CALL.
WHEN'S YOUR FLIGHT?
I HAVE TO LEAVE NOW.
SUPPOSE YOU CAN'T TELL ME WHERE OR FOR HOW LONG?
I'M SORRY.

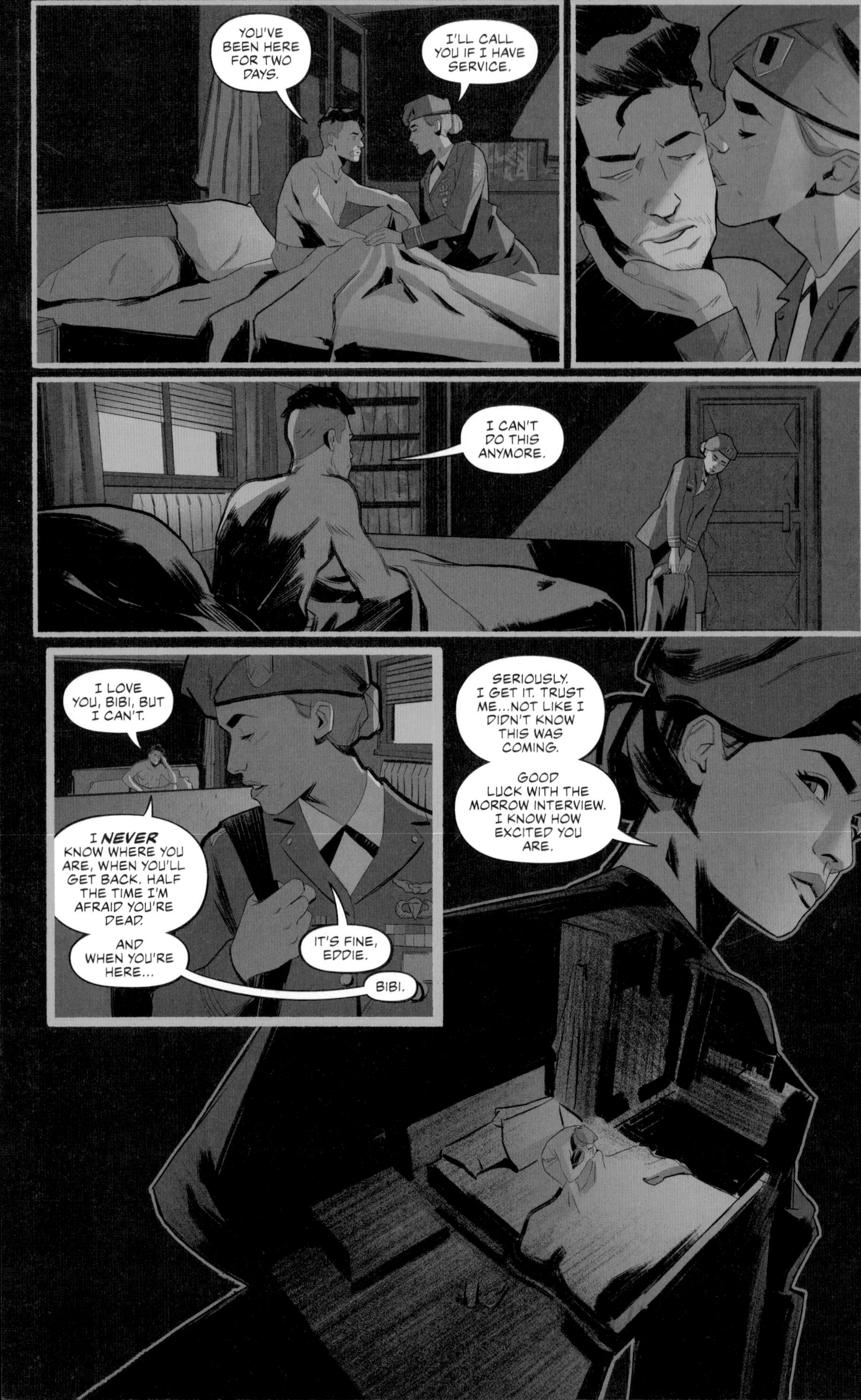
YOU'VE BEEN HERE FOR TWO DAYS.
I'LL CALL YOU IF I HAVE SERVICE.
I CAN'T DO THIS ANYMORE.
I LOVE YOU, BIBI, BUT I CAN'T.
I **NEVER** KNOW WHERE YOU ARE, WHEN YOU'LL GET BACK. HALF THE TIME I'M AFRAID YOU'RE DEAD.
AND WHEN YOU'RE HERE...
IT'S FINE, EDDIE.
BIBI.
SERIOUSLY. I GET IT. TRUST ME...NOT LIKE I DIDN'T KNOW THIS WAS COMING.
GOOD LUCK WITH THE MORROW INTERVIEW. I KNOW HOW EXCITED YOU ARE.

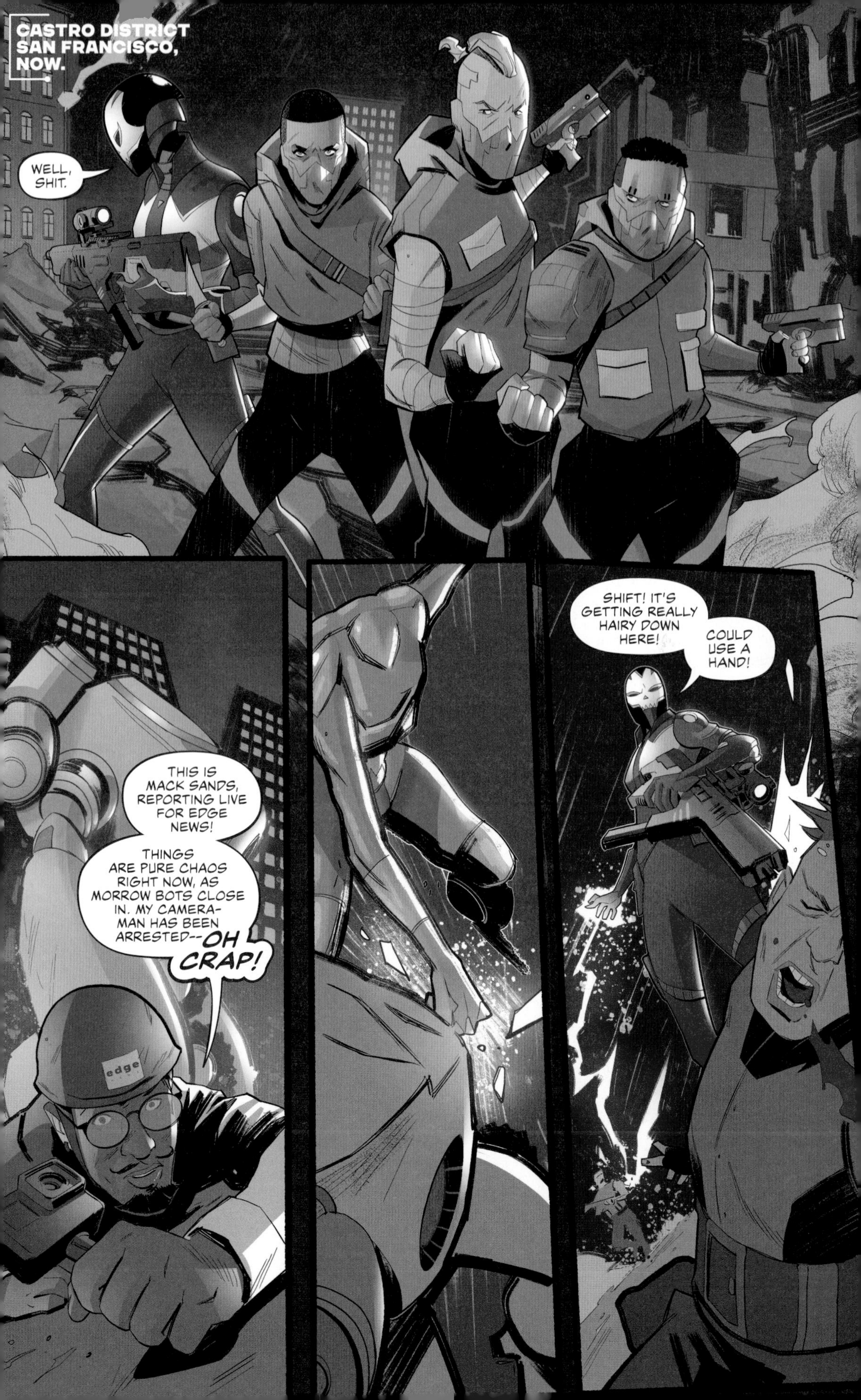
CASTRO DISTRICT SAN FRANCISCO, NOW.
WELL, SHIT.
THIS IS MACK SANDS, REPORTING LIVE FOR EDGE NEWS!
THINGS ARE PURE CHAOS RIGHT NOW, AS MORROW BOTS CLOSE IN. MY CAMERA-MAN HAS BEEN ARRESTED-- OH CRAP!
edge
SHIFT! IT'S GETTING REALLY HAIRY DOWN HERE!
COULD USE A HAND!

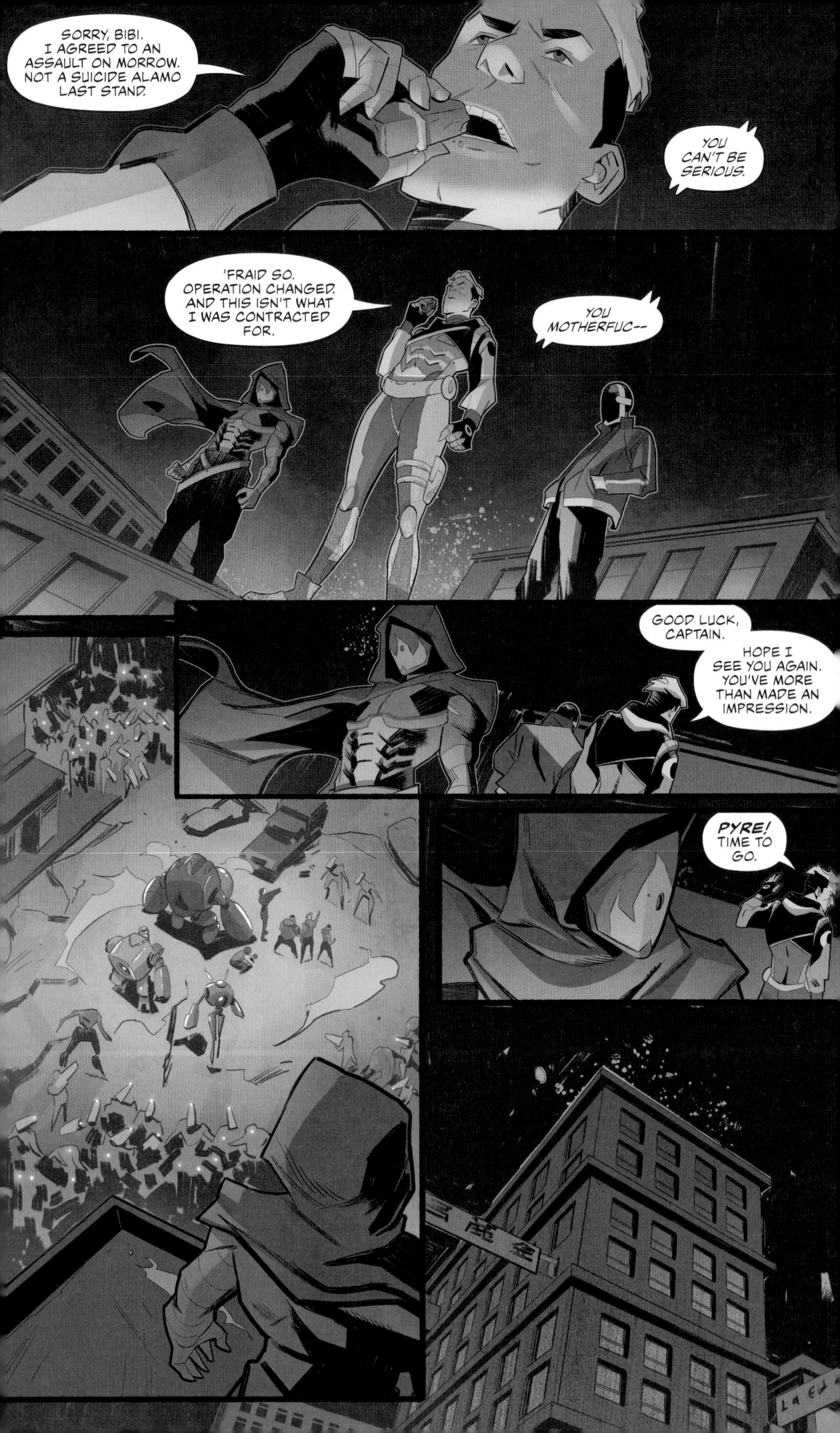
SORRY, BIBI. I AGREED TO AN ASSAULT ON MORROW. NOT A SUICIDE ALAMO LAST STAND.
YOU CAN'T BE SERIOUS.
'FRAID SO. OPERATION CHANGED. AND THIS ISN'T WHAT I WAS CONTRACTED FOR.
YOU MOTHERFUC--
GOOD LUCK, CAPTAIN.
HOPE I SEE YOU AGAIN. YOU'VE MORE THAN MADE AN IMPRESSION.
PYRE! TIME TO GO.

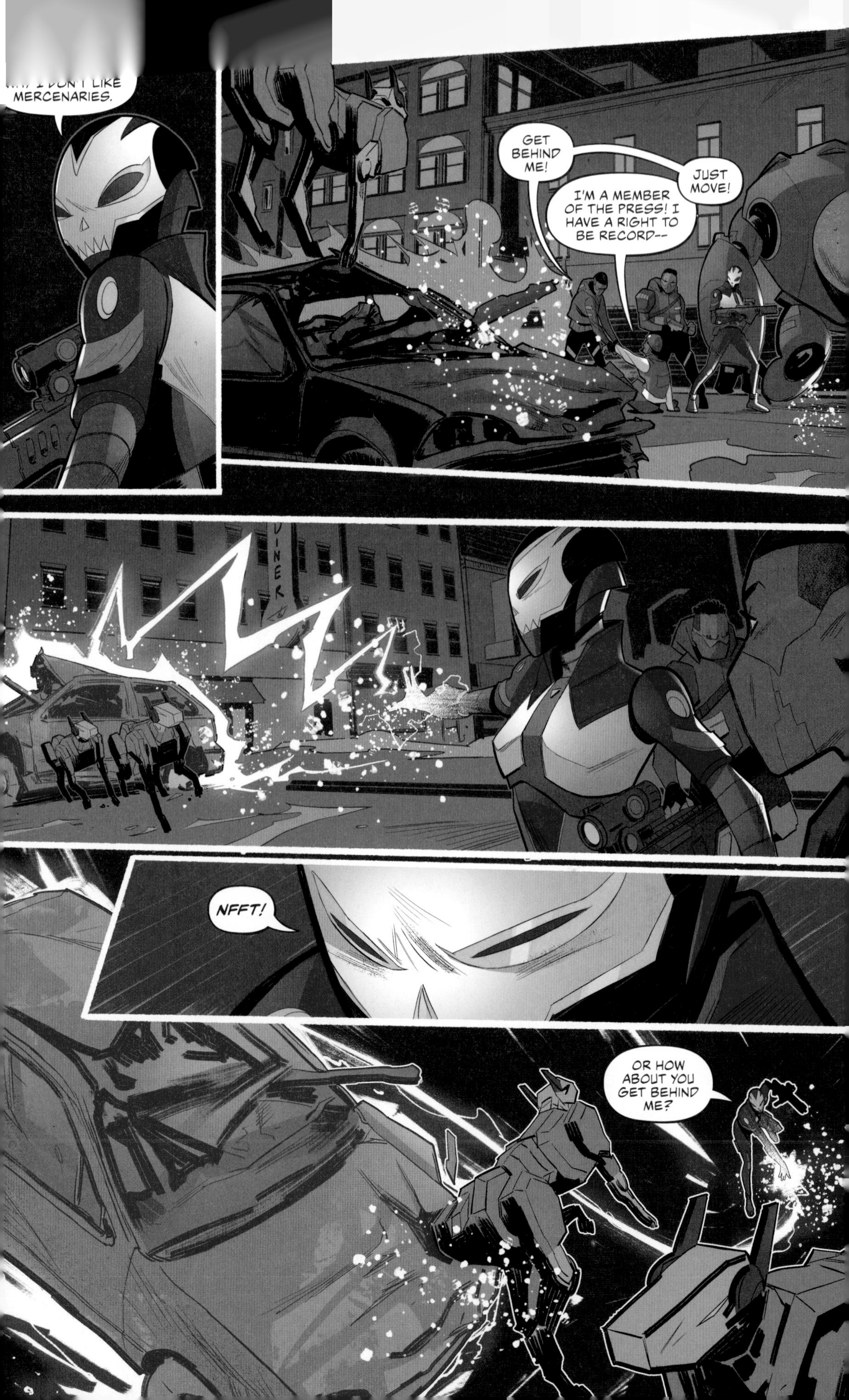
I DON'T LIKE MERCENARIES.
GET BEHIND ME!
JUST MOVE!
I'M A MEMBER OF THE PRESS! I HAVE A RIGHT TO BE RECORD--
DINER
NFFT!
OR HOW ABOUT YOU GET BEHIND ME?

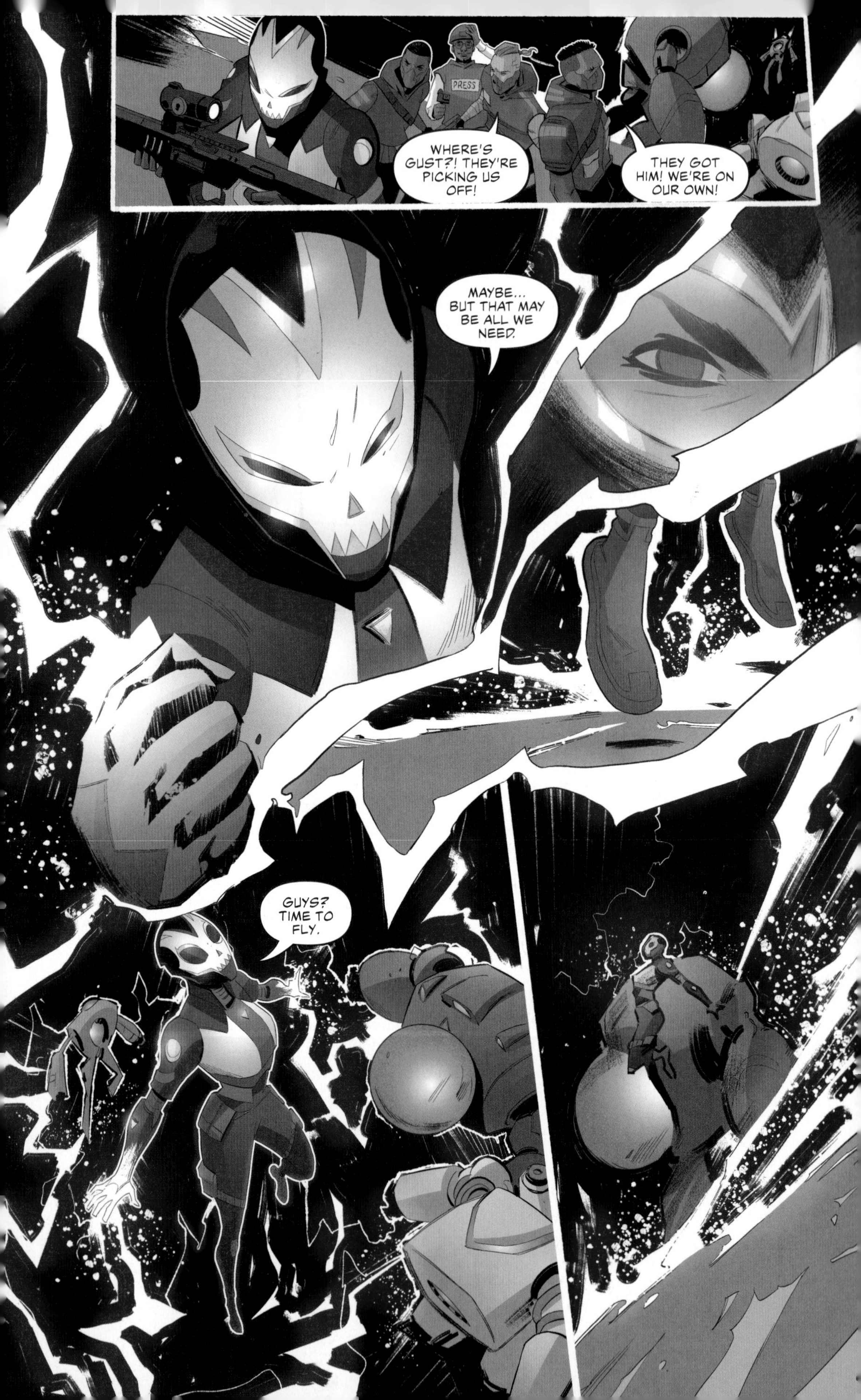
PRESS
WHERE'S GUST?! THEY'RE PICKING US OFF!
THEY GOT HIM! WE'RE ON OUR OWN!
MAYBE... BUT THAT MAY BE ALL WE NEED.
GUYS? TIME TO FLY.

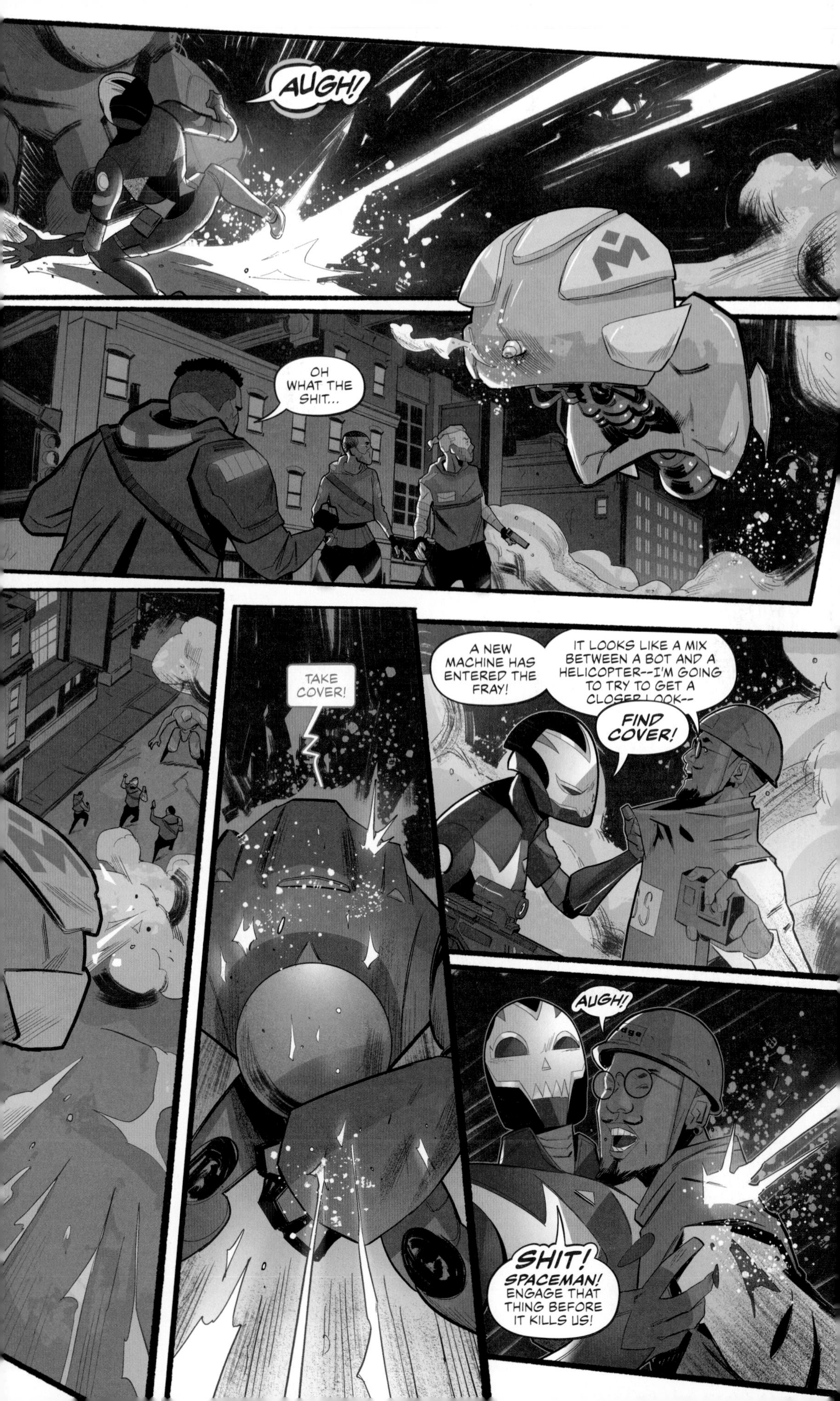
AUGH!
OH WHAT THE SHIT...
TAKE COVER!
A NEW MACHINE HAS ENTERED THE FRAY!
IT LOOKS LIKE A MIX BETWEEN A BOT AND A HELICOPTER--I'M GOING TO TRY TO GET A CLOSER LOOK--
FIND COVER!
AUGH!
SHIT! SPACEMAN! ENGAGE THAT THING BEFORE IT KILLS US!

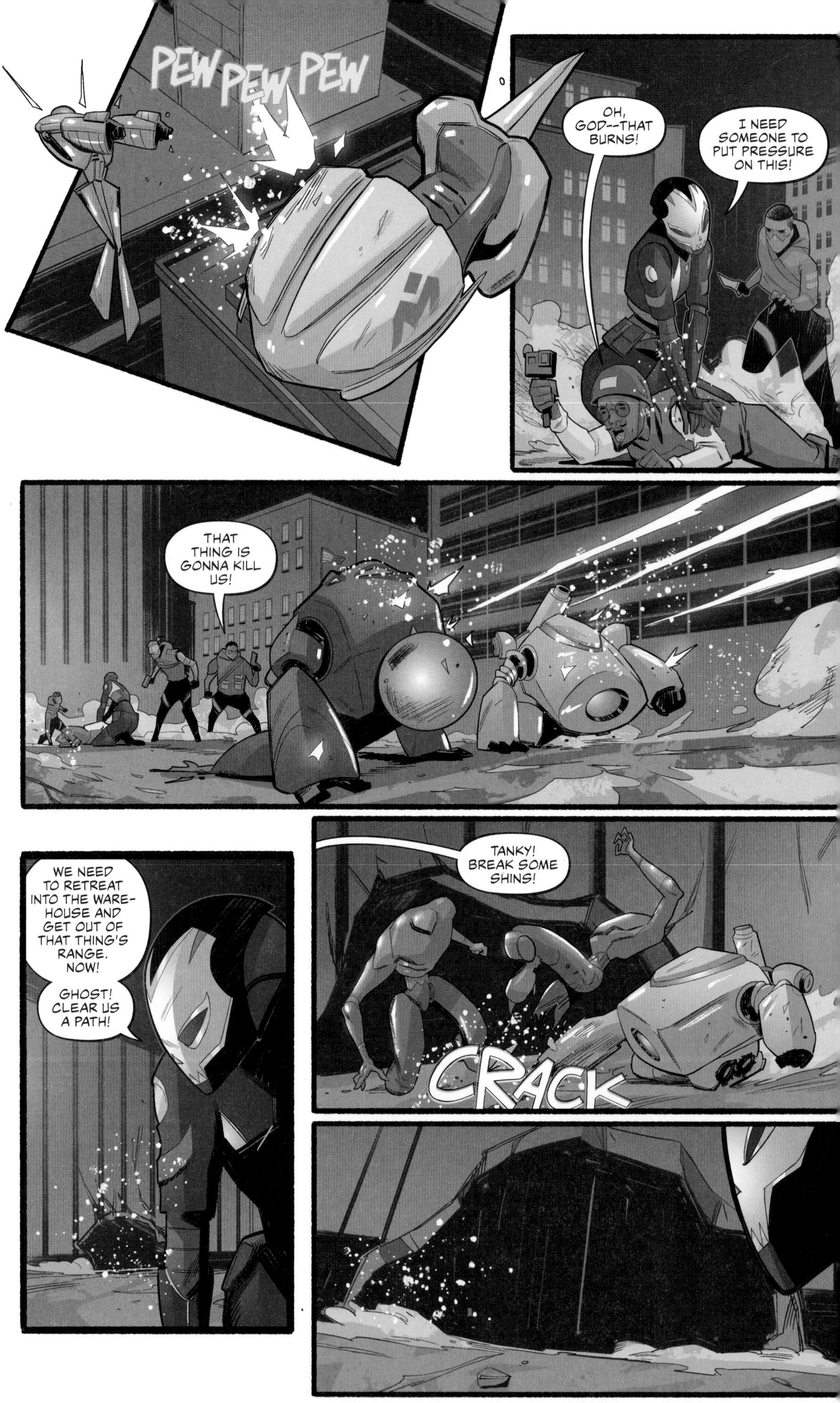
PEW PEW PEW
OH, GOD--THAT BURNS!
I NEED SOMEONE TO PUT PRESSURE ON THIS!
THAT THING IS GONNA KILL US!
WE NEED TO RETREAT INTO THE WARE-HOUSE AND GET OUT OF THAT THING'S RANGE. NOW!
GHOST! CLEAR US A PATH!
TANKY! BREAK SOME SHINS!
CRACK

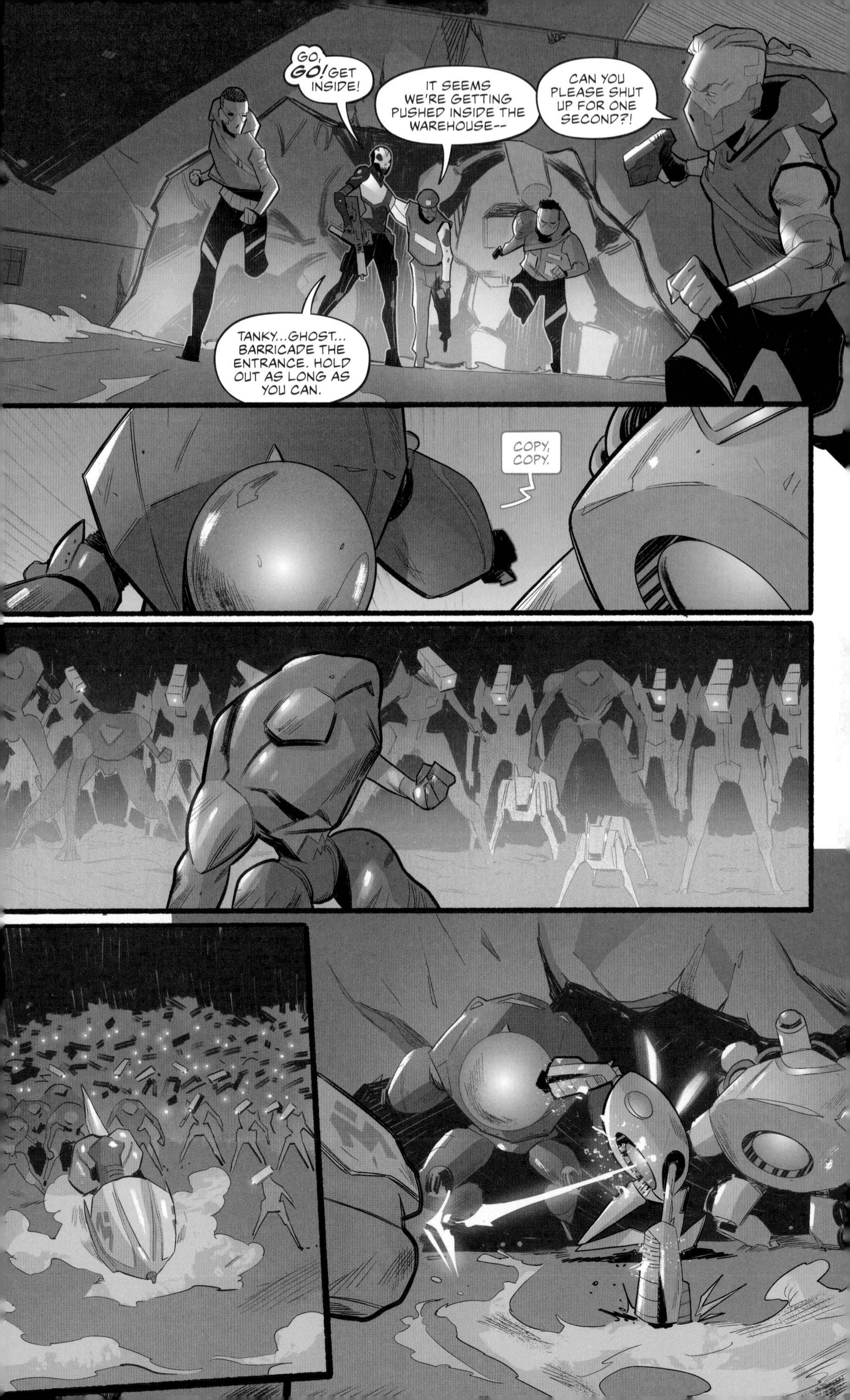
GO, GO! GET INSIDE!
IT SEEMS WE'RE GETTING PUSHED INSIDE THE WAREHOUSE--
CAN YOU PLEASE SHUT UP FOR ONE SECOND?!
TANKY...GHOST... BARRICADE THE ENTRANCE. HOLD OUT AS LONG AS YOU CAN.
COPY, COPY.

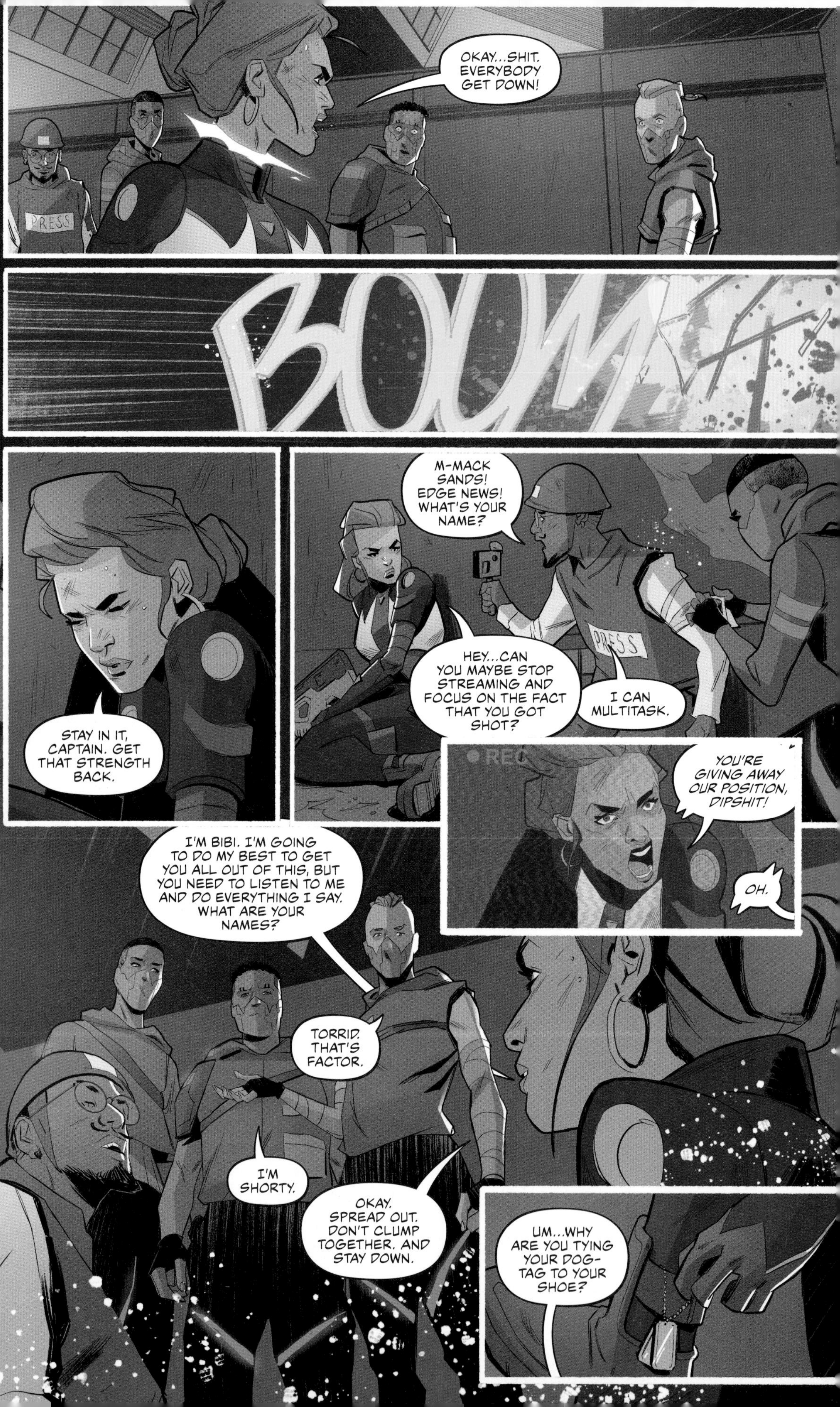
OKAY...SHIT. EVERYBODY GET DOWN!
PRESS
BOOM
STAY IN IT, CAPTAIN. GET THAT STRENGTH BACK.
M-MACK SANDS! EDGE NEWS! WHAT'S YOUR NAME?
HEY...CAN YOU MAYBE STOP STREAMING AND FOCUS ON THE FACT THAT YOU GOT SHOT?
PRESS
I CAN MULTITASK.
REC
YOU'RE GIVING AWAY OUR POSITION, DIPSHIT!
OH.
I'M BIBI. I'M GOING TO DO MY BEST TO GET YOU ALL OUT OF THIS, BUT YOU NEED TO LISTEN TO ME AND DO EVERYTHING I SAY. WHAT ARE YOUR NAMES?
TORRID. THAT'S FACTOR.
I'M SHORTY.
OKAY. SPREAD OUT. DON'T CLUMP TOGETHER. AND STAY DOWN.
UM...WHY ARE YOU TYING YOUR DOG-TAG TO YOUR SHOE?

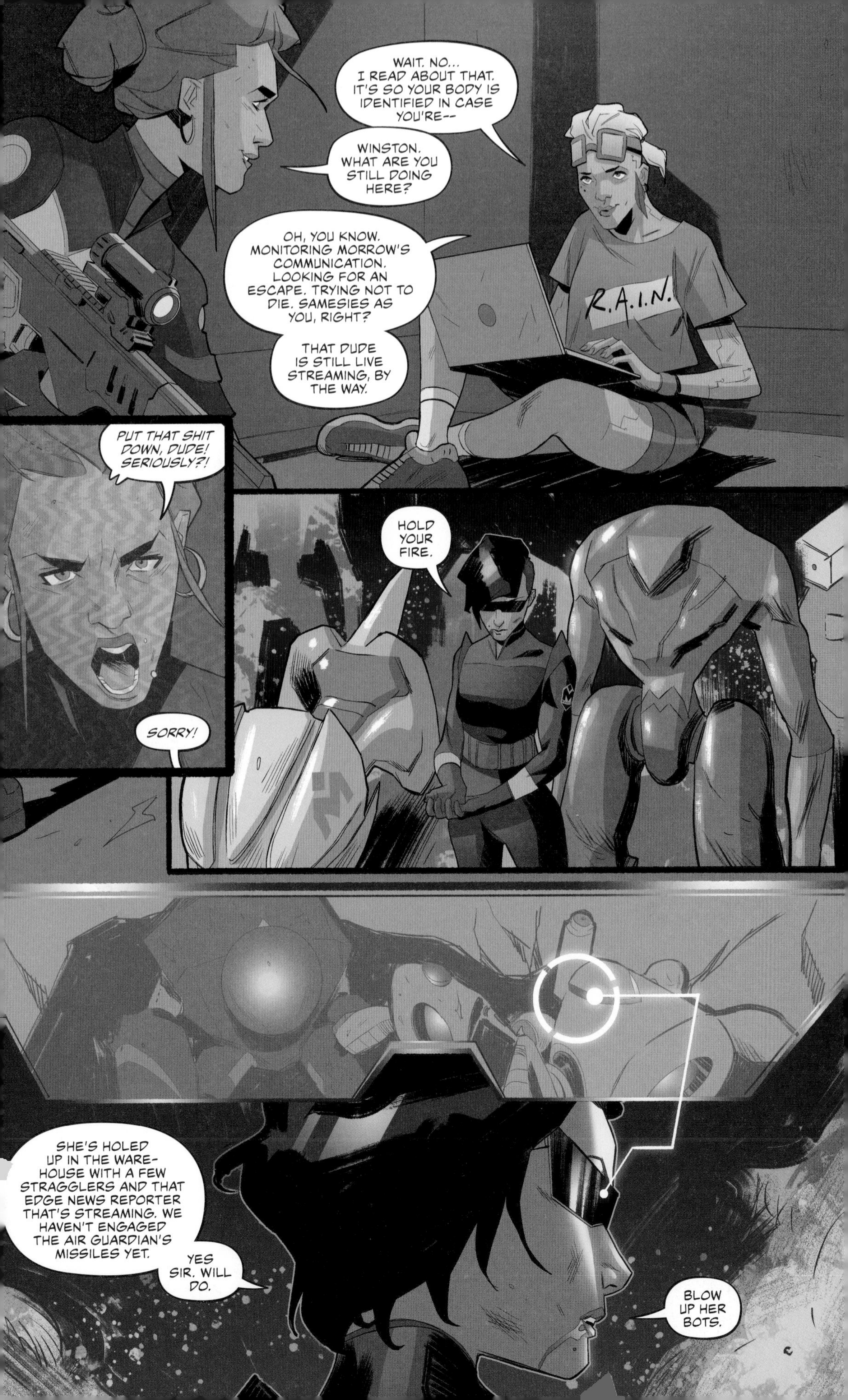
WAIT. NO... I READ ABOUT THAT. IT'S SO YOUR BODY IS IDENTIFIED IN CASE YOU'RE--
WINSTON. WHAT ARE YOU STILL DOING HERE?
OH, YOU KNOW. MONITORING MORROW'S COMMUNICATION. LOOKING FOR AN ESCAPE. TRYING NOT TO DIE. SAMESIES AS YOU, RIGHT?
THAT DUDE IS STILL LIVE STREAMING, BY THE WAY.
R.A.I.N.
PUT THAT SHIT DOWN, DUDE! SERIOUSLY?!
SORRY!
HOLD YOUR FIRE.
SHE'S HOLED UP IN THE WARE-HOUSE WITH A FEW STRAGGLERS AND THAT EDGE NEWS REPORTER THAT'S STREAMING. WE HAVEN'T ENGAGED THE AIR GUARDIAN'S MISSILES YET.
YES SIR. WILL DO.
BLOW UP HER BOTS.

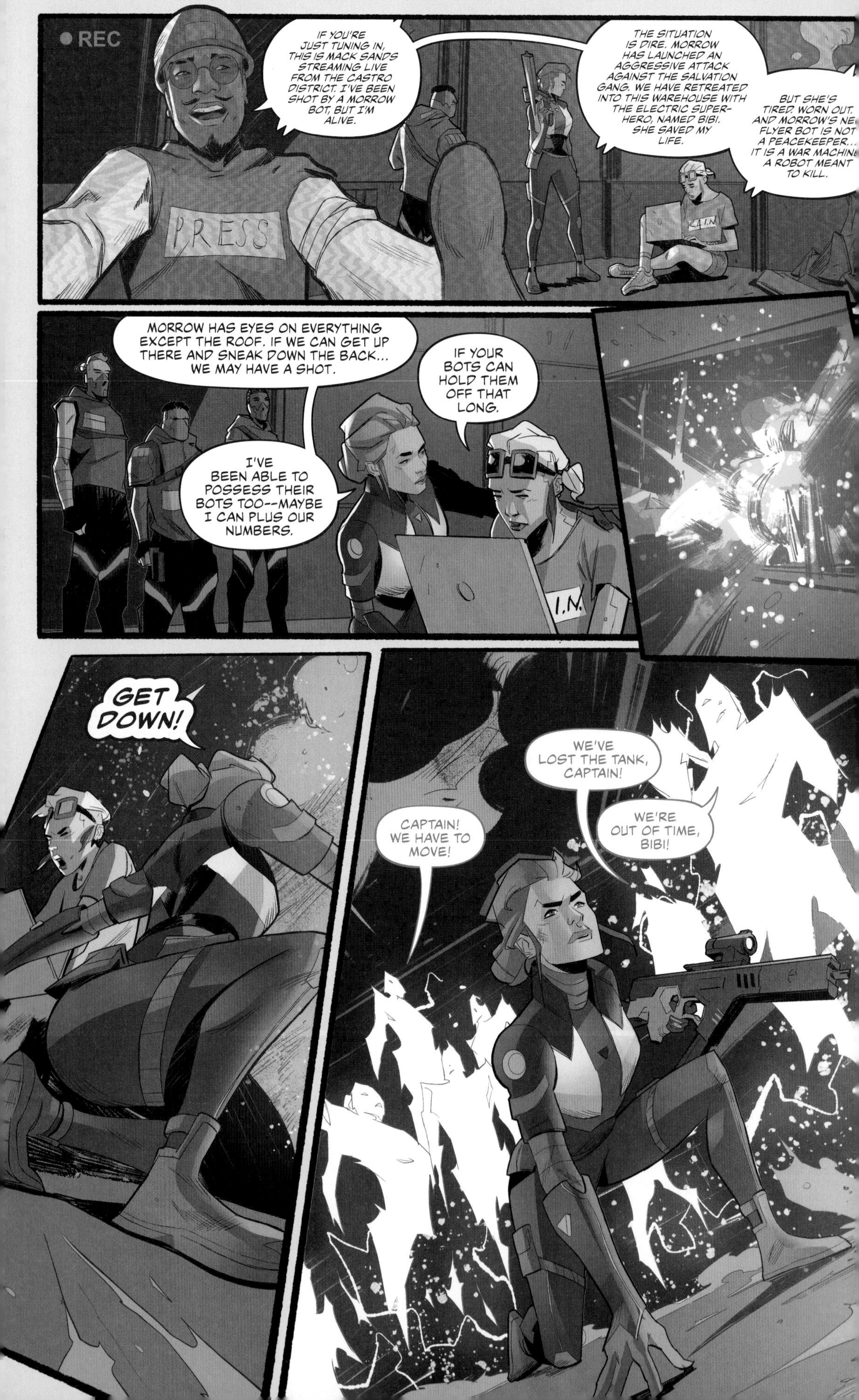
REC
IF YOU'RE JUST TUNING IN, THIS IS MACK SANDS STREAMING LIVE FROM THE CASTRO DISTRICT. I'VE BEEN SHOT BY A MORROW BOT, BUT I'M ALIVE.
THE SITUATION IS DIRE. MORROW HAS LAUNCHED AN AGGRESSIVE ATTACK AGAINST THE SALVATION GANG. WE HAVE RETREATED INTO THIS WAREHOUSE WITH THE ELECTRIC SUPER-HERO, NAMED BIBI. SHE SAVED MY LIFE.
BUT SHE'S TIRED. WORN OUT. AND MORROW'S NE FLYER BOT IS NOT A PEACEKEEPER... IT IS A WAR MACHIN A ROBOT MEANT TO KILL.
PRESS
MORROW HAS EYES ON EVERYTHING EXCEPT THE ROOF. IF WE CAN GET UP THERE AND SNEAK DOWN THE BACK... WE MAY HAVE A SHOT.
IF YOUR BOTS CAN HOLD THEM OFF THAT LONG.
I'VE BEEN ABLE TO POSSESS THEIR BOTS TOO--MAYBE I CAN PLUS OUR NUMBERS.
GET DOWN!
WE'VE LOST THE TANK, CAPTAIN!
CAPTAIN! WE HAVE TO MOVE!
WE'RE OUT OF TIME, BIBI!

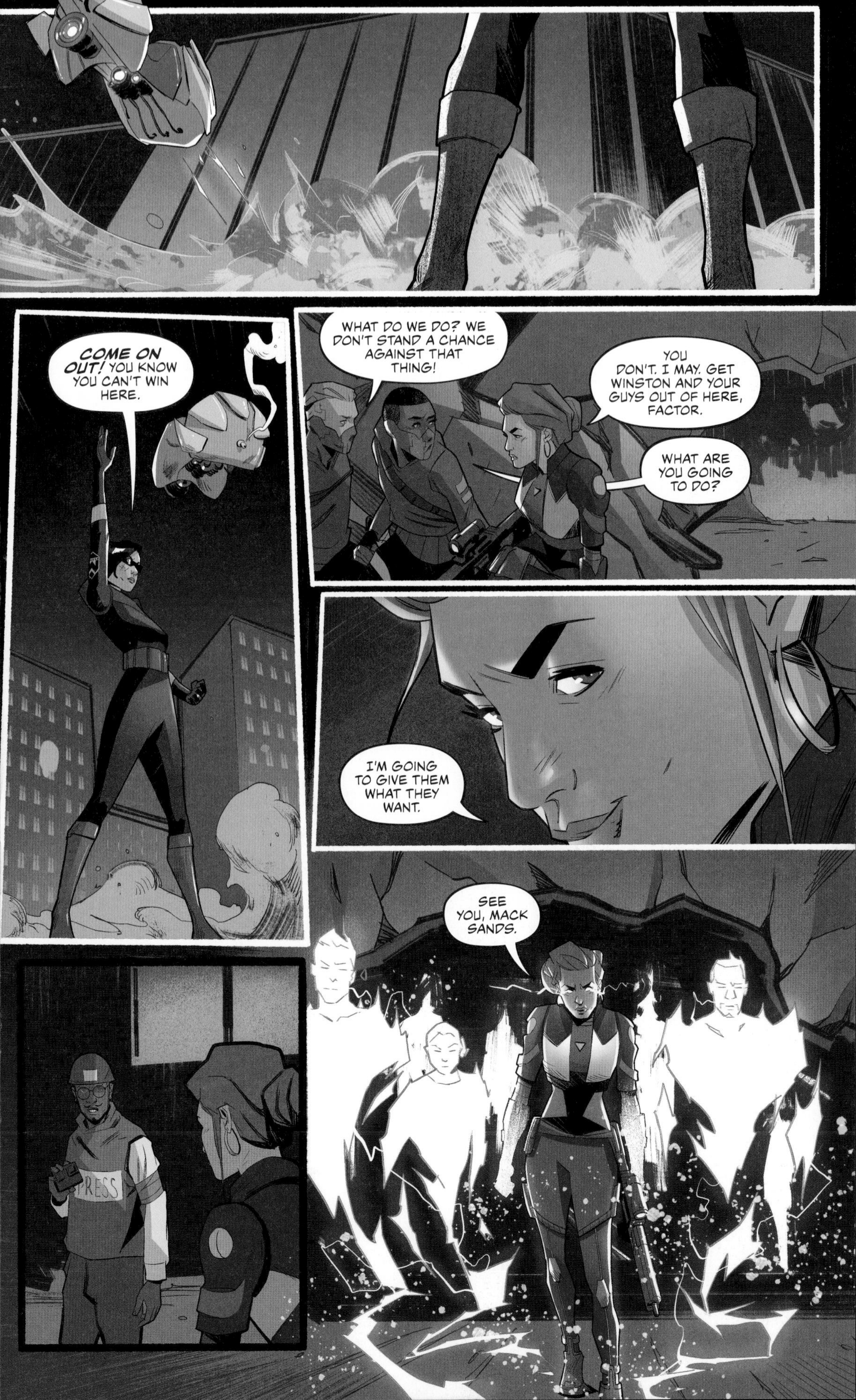
COME ON OUT! YOU KNOW YOU CAN'T WIN HERE.
WHAT DO WE DO? WE DON'T STAND A CHANCE AGAINST THAT THING!
YOU DON'T. I MAY. GET WINSTON AND YOUR GUYS OUT OF HERE, FACTOR.
WHAT ARE YOU GOING TO DO?
I'M GOING TO GIVE THEM WHAT THEY WANT.
PRESS
SEE YOU, MACK SANDS.

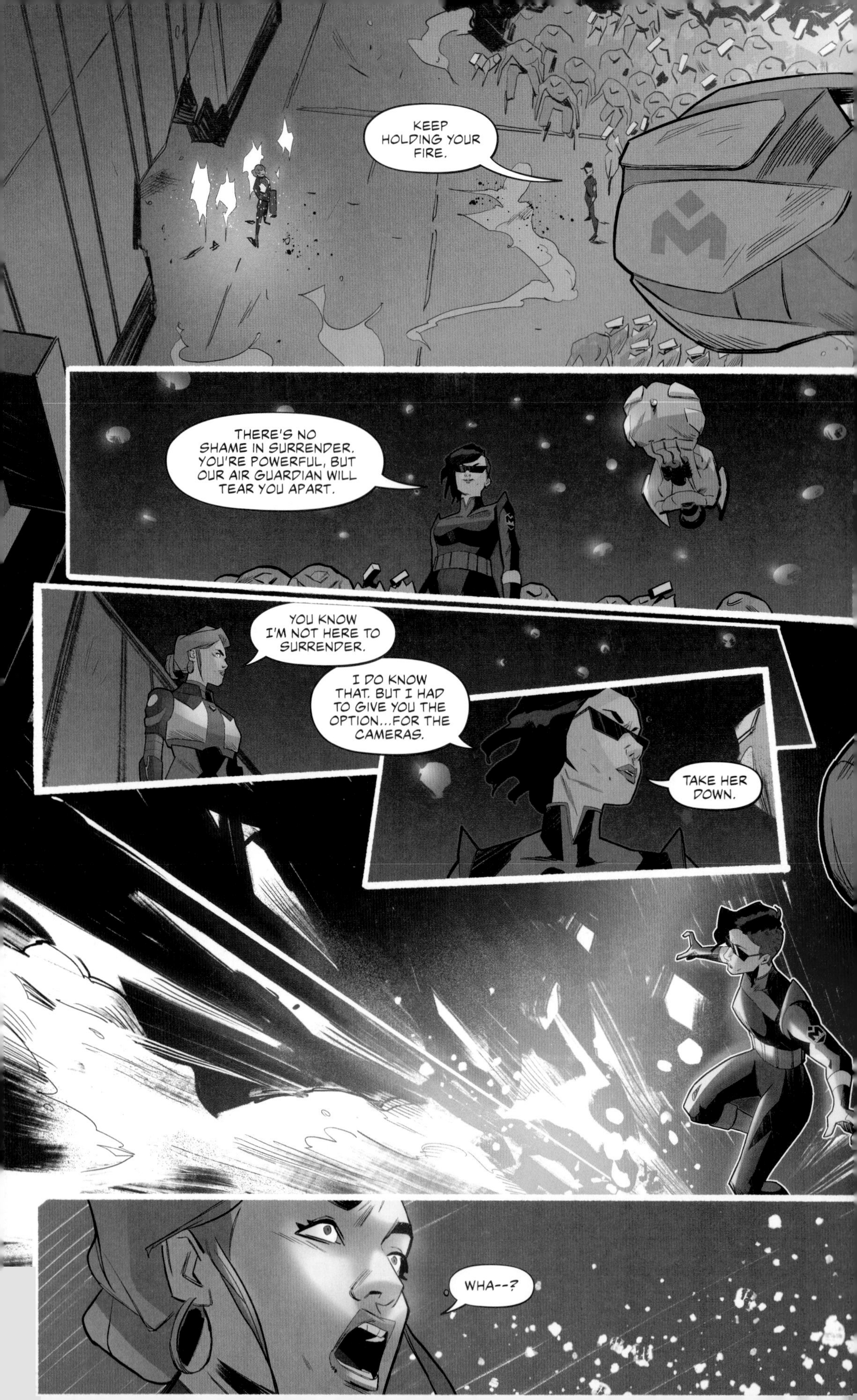
KEEP HOLDING YOUR FIRE.
THERE'S NO SHAME IN SURRENDER. YOU'RE POWERFUL, BUT OUR AIR GUARDIAN WILL TEAR YOU APART.
YOU KNOW I'M NOT HERE TO SURRENDER.
I DO KNOW THAT. BUT I HAD TO GIVE YOU THE OPTION...FOR THE CAMERAS.
TAKE HER DOWN.
WHA--?

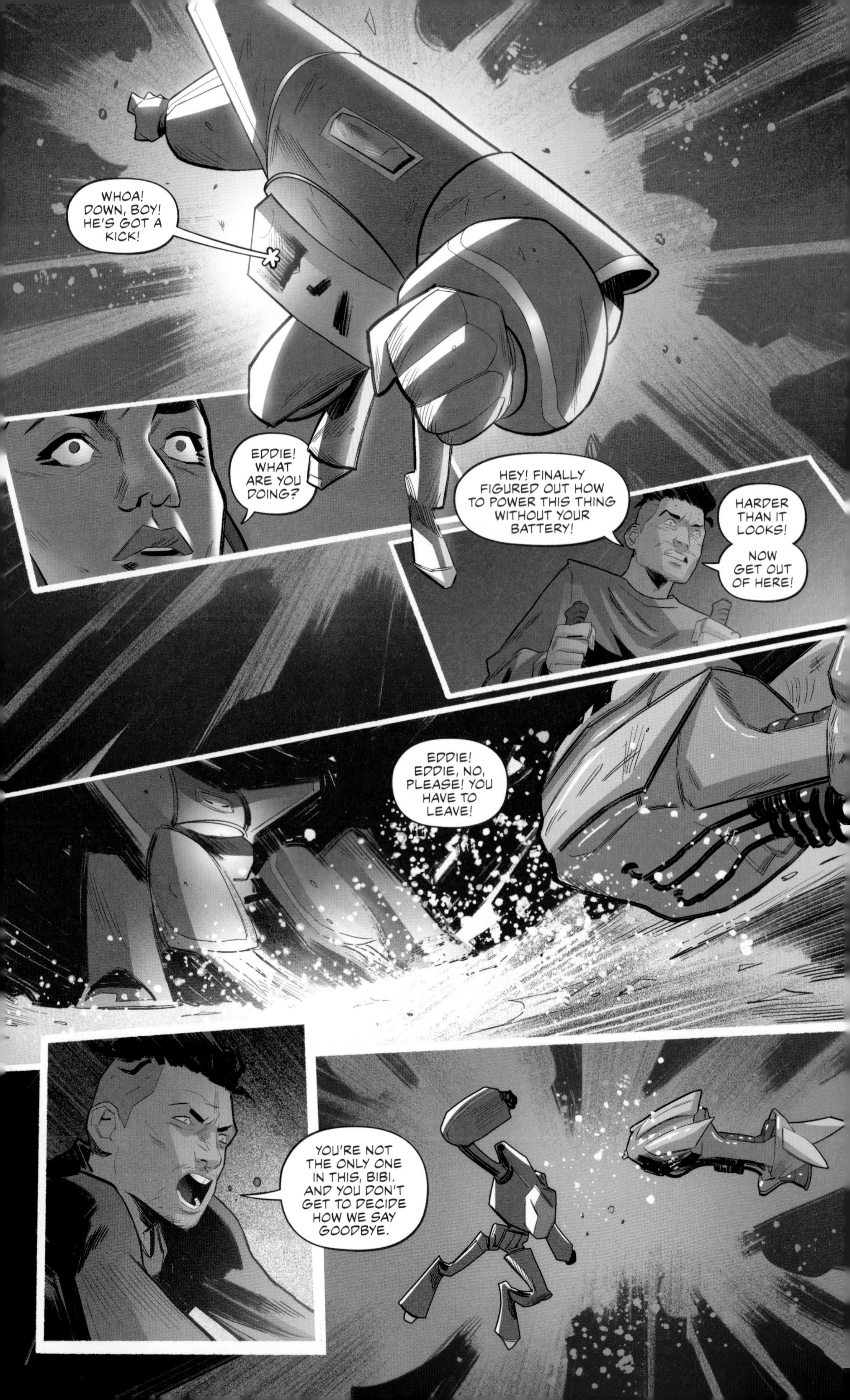
WHOA! DOWN, BOY! HE'S GOT A KICK!
EDDIE! WHAT ARE YOU DOING?
HEY! FINALLY FIGURED OUT HOW TO POWER THIS THING WITHOUT YOUR BATTERY!
HARDER THAN IT LOOKS!
NOW GET OUT OF HERE!
EDDIE! EDDIE, NO, PLEASE! YOU HAVE TO LEAVE!
YOU'RE NOT THE ONLY ONE IN THIS, BIBI. AND YOU DON'T GET TO DECIDE HOW WE SAY GOODBYE.

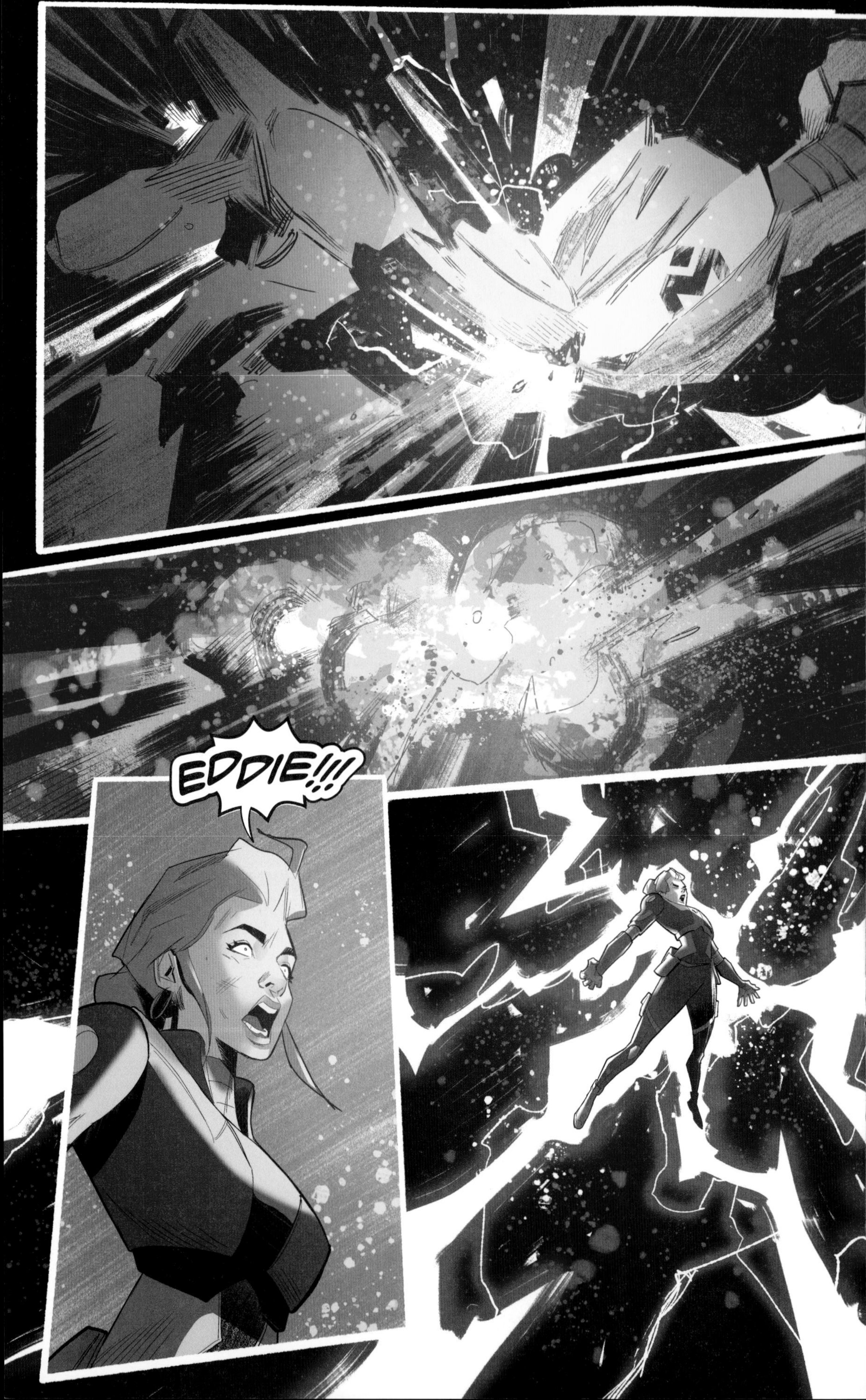
EDDIE!!!

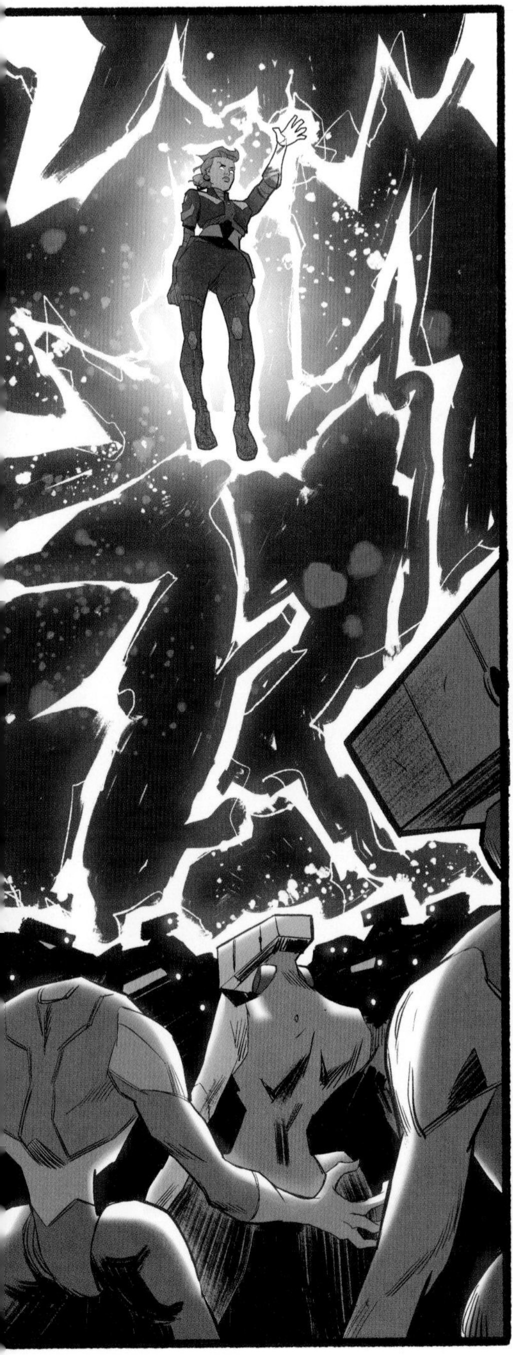

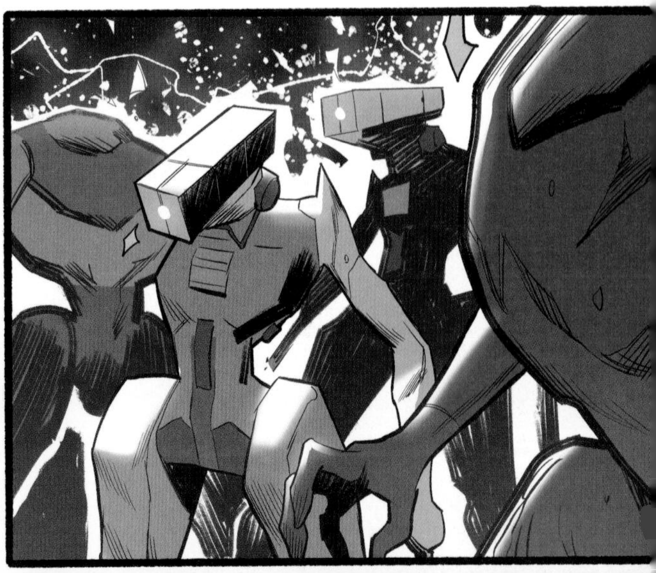

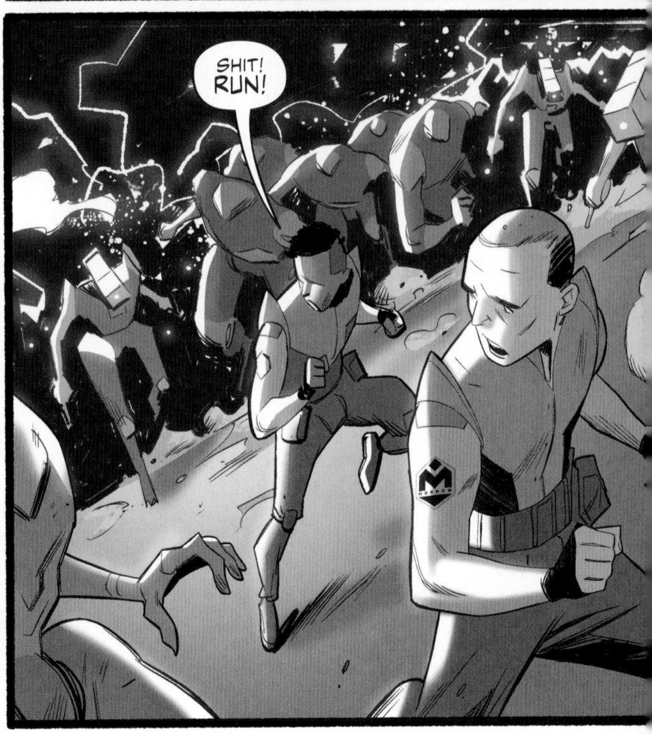
SHIT! RUN!

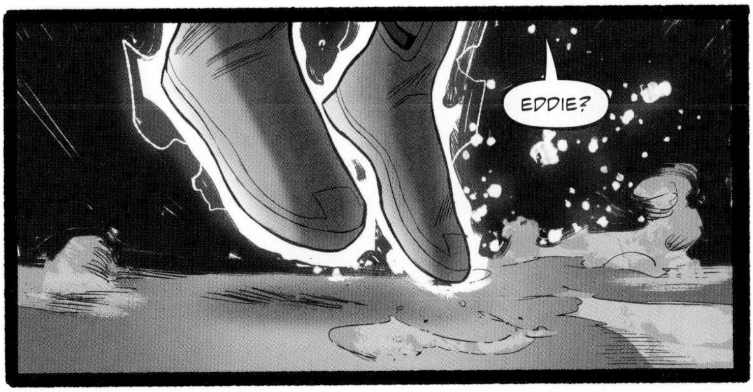
EDDIE?

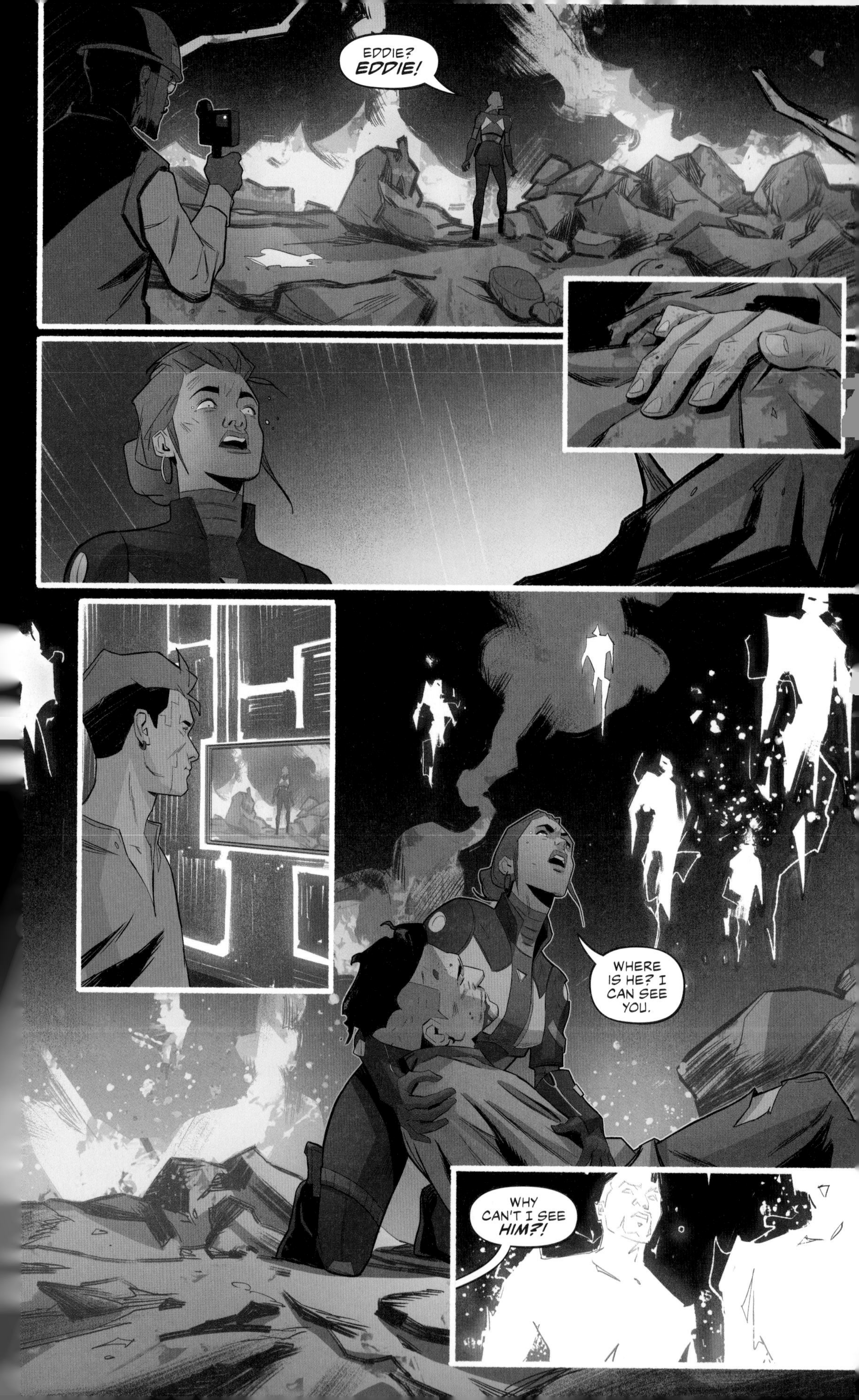
EDDIE? EDDIE!
WHERE IS HE? I CAN SEE YOU.
WHY CAN'T I SEE HIM?!

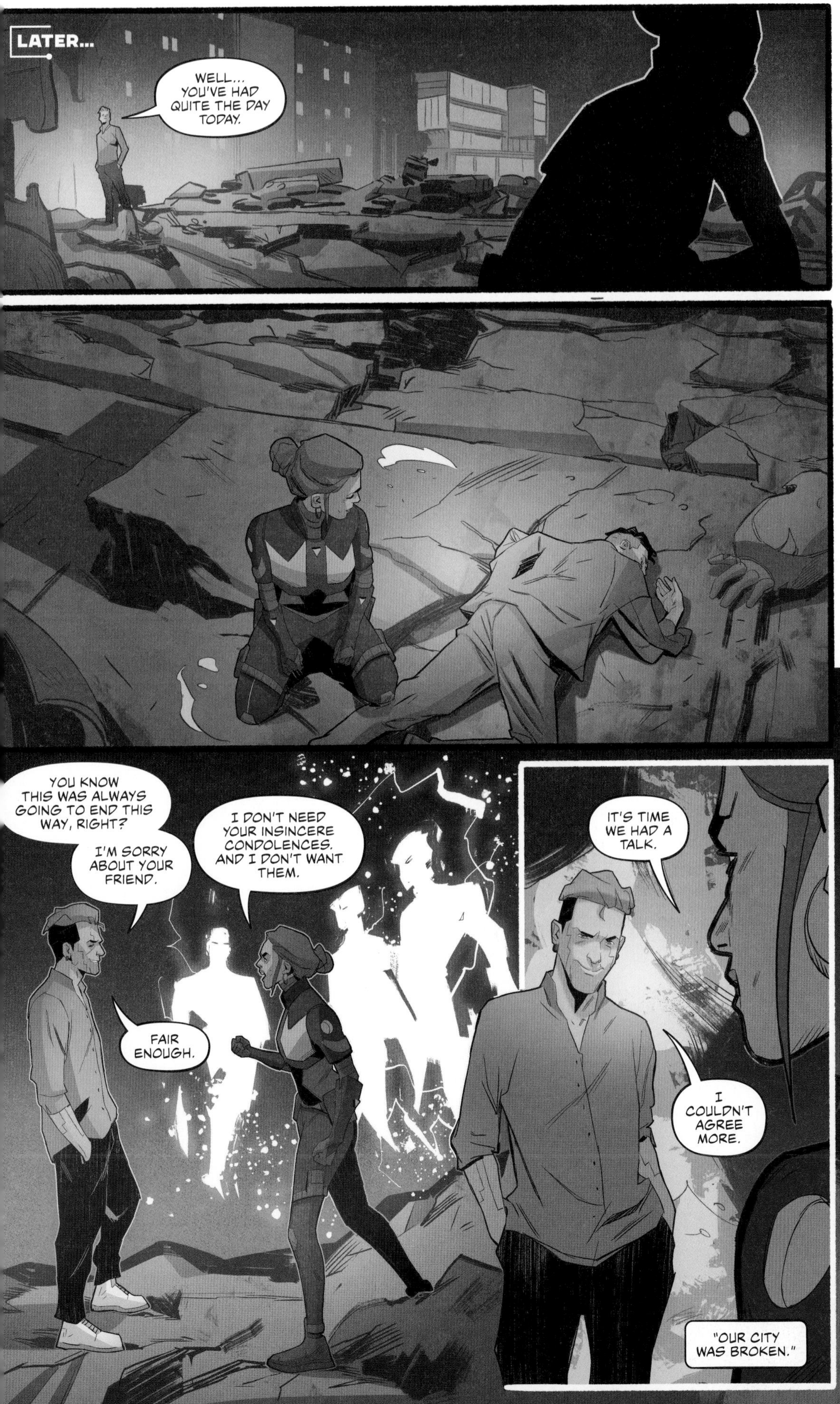
LATER...
WELL... YOU'VE HAD QUITE THE DAY TODAY.
YOU KNOW THIS WAS ALWAYS GOING TO END THIS WAY, RIGHT?
I'M SORRY ABOUT YOUR FRIEND.
I DON'T NEED YOUR INSINCERE CONDOLENCES. AND I DON'T WANT THEM.
FAIR ENOUGH.
IT'S TIME WE HAD A TALK.
I COULDN'T AGREE MORE.
"OUR CITY WAS BROKEN."

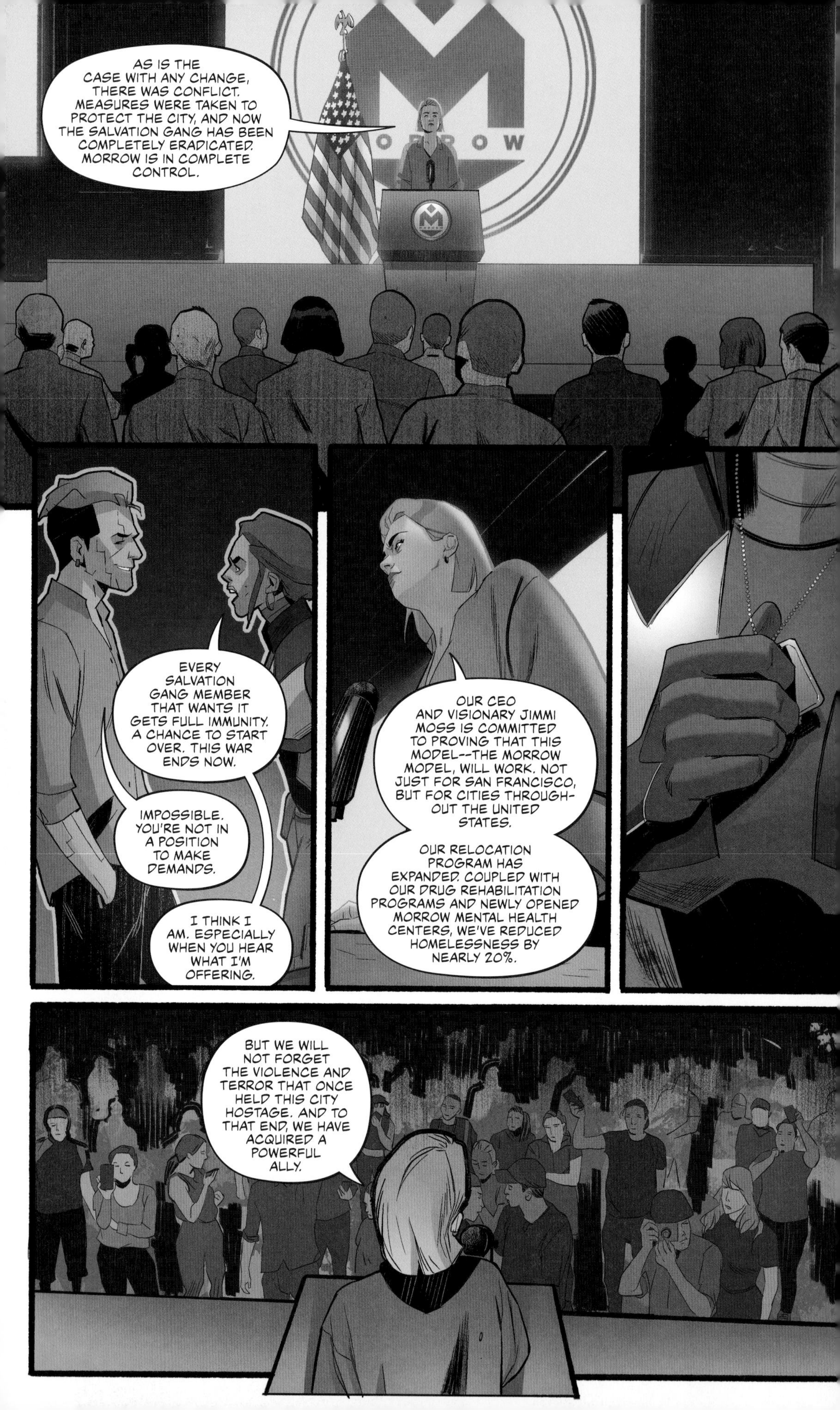
AS IS THE CASE WITH ANY CHANGE, THERE WAS CONFLICT. MEASURES WERE TAKEN TO PROTECT THE CITY, AND NOW THE SALVATION GANG HAS BEEN COMPLETELY ERADICATED. MORROW IS IN COMPLETE CONTROL.
MORROW
EVERY SALVATION GANG MEMBER THAT WANTS IT GETS FULL IMMUNITY. A CHANCE TO START OVER. THIS WAR ENDS NOW.
IMPOSSIBLE. YOU'RE NOT IN A POSITION TO MAKE DEMANDS.
I THINK I AM. ESPECIALLY WHEN YOU HEAR WHAT I'M OFFERING.
OUR CEO AND VISIONARY JIMMI MOSS IS COMMITTED TO PROVING THAT THIS MODEL--THE MORROW MODEL, WILL WORK. NOT JUST FOR SAN FRANCISCO, BUT FOR CITIES THROUGH-OUT THE UNITED STATES.
OUR RELOCATION PROGRAM HAS EXPANDED. COUPLED WITH OUR DRUG REHABILITATION PROGRAMS AND NEWLY OPENED MORROW MENTAL HEALTH CENTERS, WE'VE REDUCED HOMELESSNESS BY NEARLY 20%.
BUT WE WILL NOT FORGET THE VIOLENCE AND TERROR THAT ONCE HELD THIS CITY HOSTAGE. AND TO THAT END, WE HAVE ACQUIRED A POWERFUL ALLY.

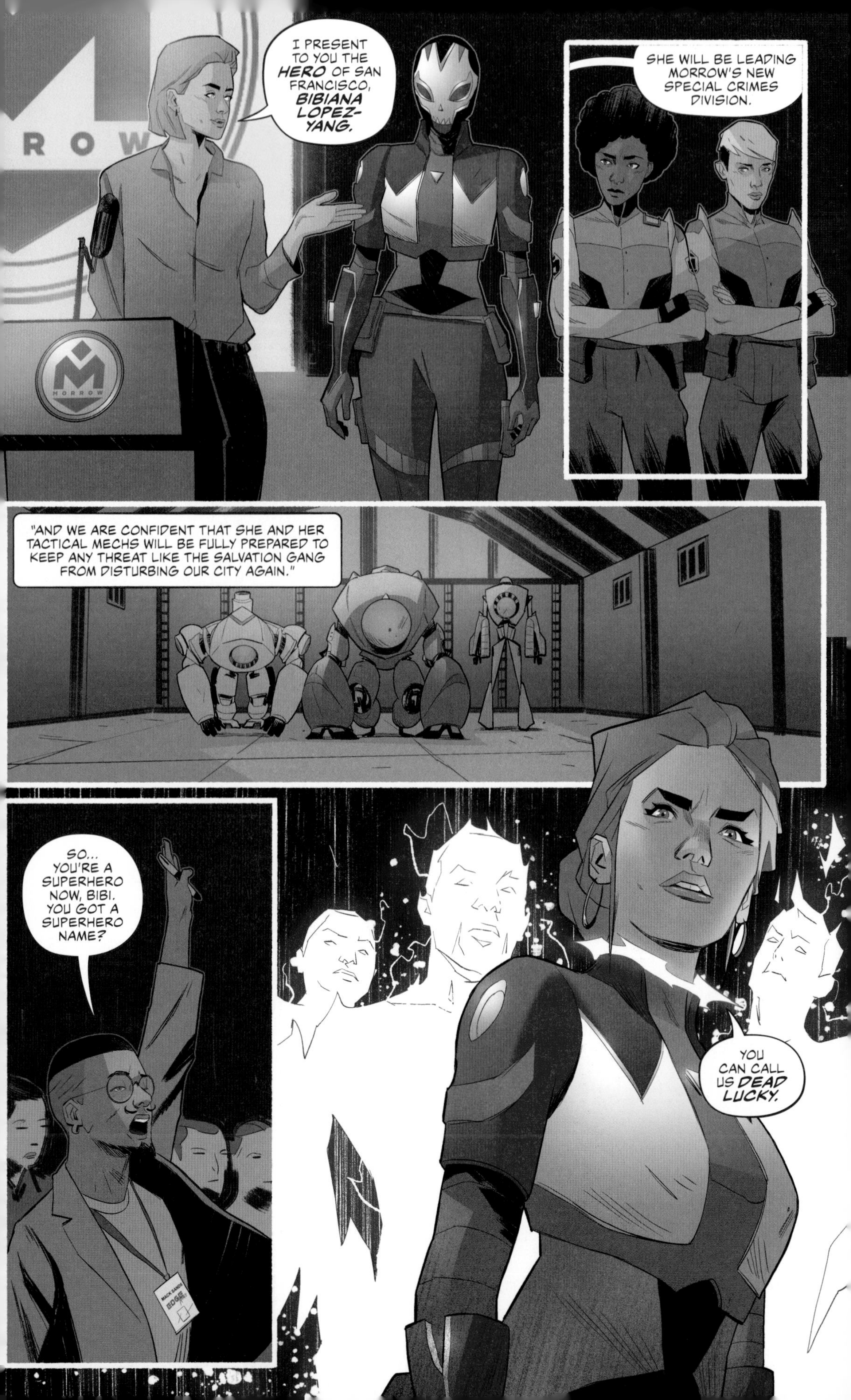

R O W
I PRESENT TO YOU THE *HERO* OF SAN FRANCISCO, ***BIBIANA LOPEZ-YANG.***
MORROW
SHE WILL BE LEADING MORROW'S NEW SPECIAL CRIMES DIVISION.
"AND WE ARE CONFIDENT THAT SHE AND HER TACTICAL MECHS WILL BE FULLY PREPARED TO KEEP ANY THREAT LIKE THE SALVATION GANG FROM DISTURBING OUR CITY AGAIN."
SO... YOU'RE A SUPERHERO NOW, BIBI. YOU GOT A SUPERHERO NAME?
YOU CAN CALL US ***DEAD LUCKY.***

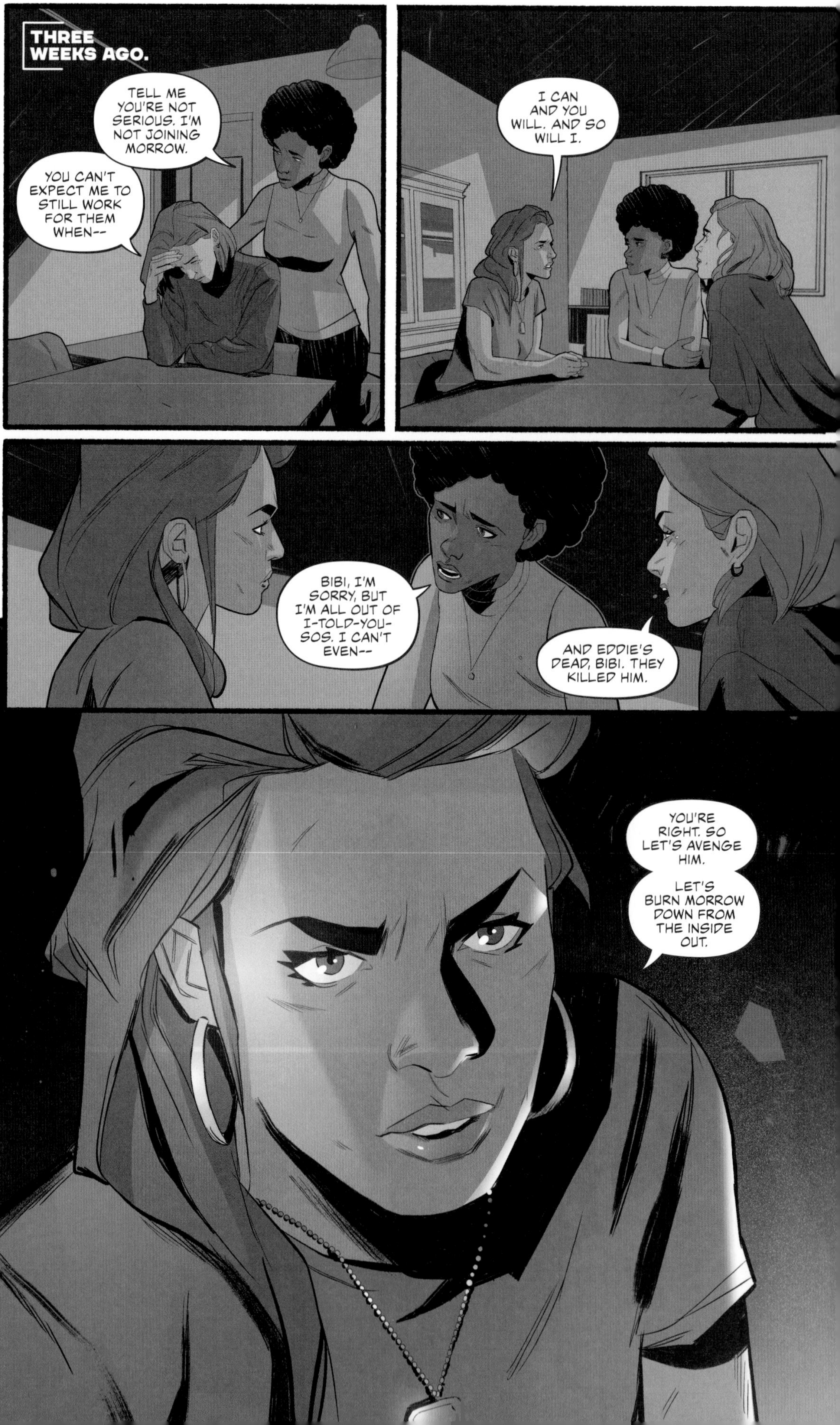

THREE WEEKS AGO.
TELL ME YOU'RE NOT SERIOUS. I'M NOT JOINING MORROW.
YOU CAN'T EXPECT ME TO STILL WORK FOR THEM WHEN--
I CAN AND YOU WILL. AND SO WILL I.
BIBI, I'M SORRY, BUT I'M ALL OUT OF I-TOLD-YOU-SOS. I CAN'T EVEN--
AND EDDIE'S DEAD, BIBI. THEY KILLED HIM.
YOU'RE RIGHT. SO LET'S AVENGE HIM.
LET'S BURN MORROW DOWN FROM THE INSIDE OUT.

TERMINAL

GHOST:~ admin$ CoverGallery
Issue:
    No.: 001-006

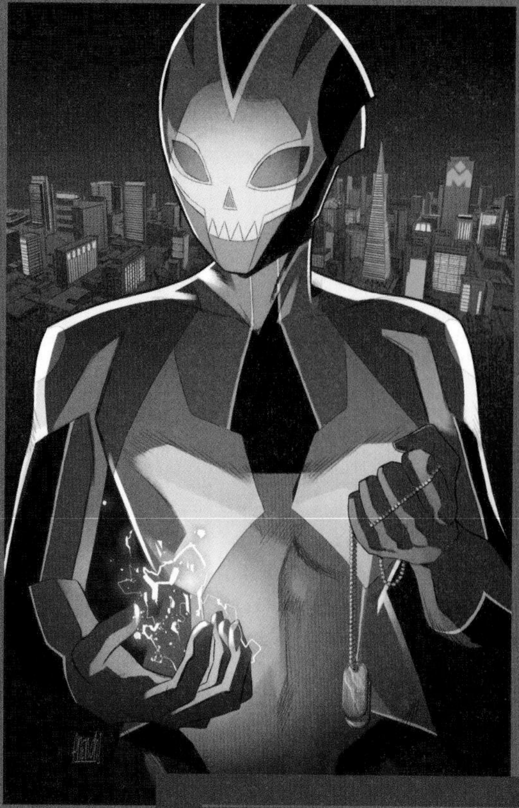

CVR: 01/A
ART: FRENCH CARLOMAGNO

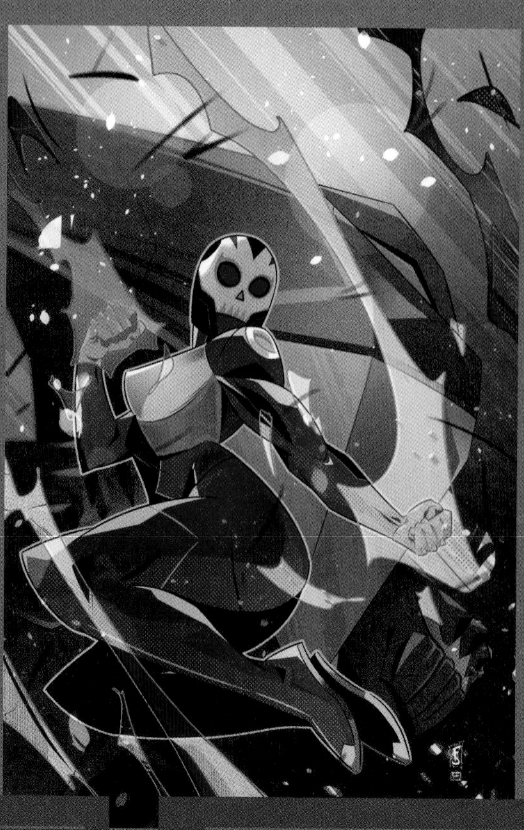

CVR: 01/B
ART: FEDERICO SABBATINI
w/ MAFURIAH

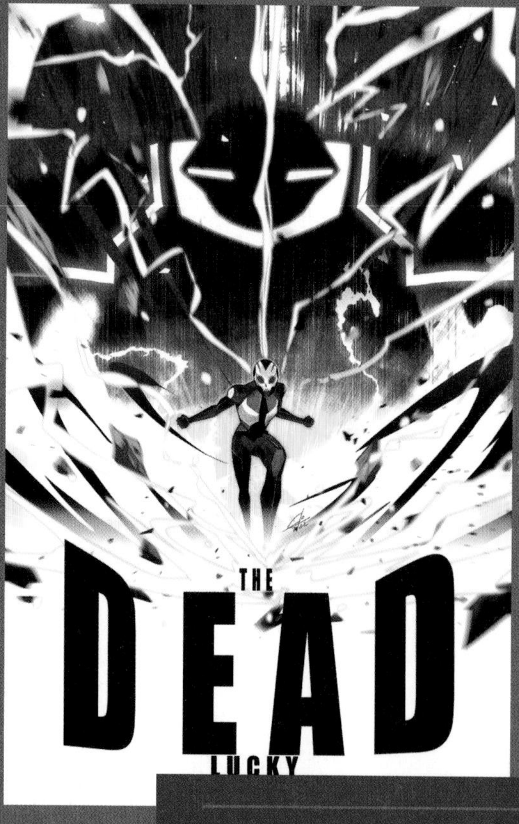
THE
DEAD

CVR: 01/C
ART: ELEONORA CARLINI

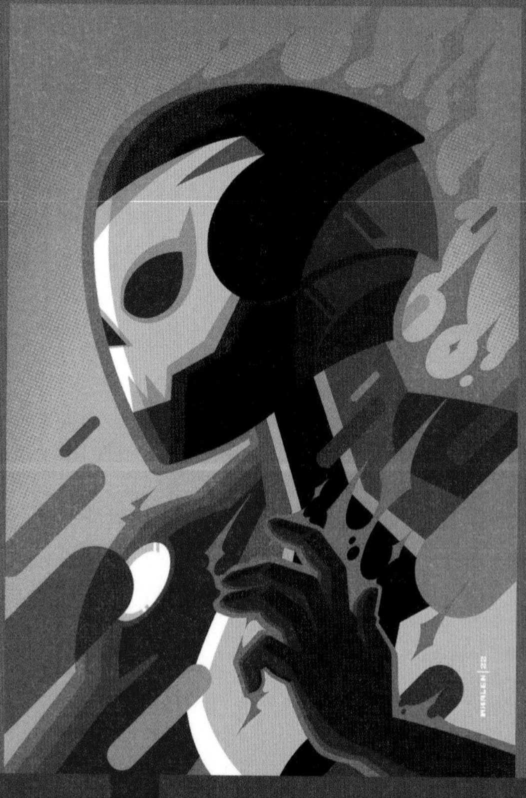

CVR: 01/D
ART: TOM WHALEN

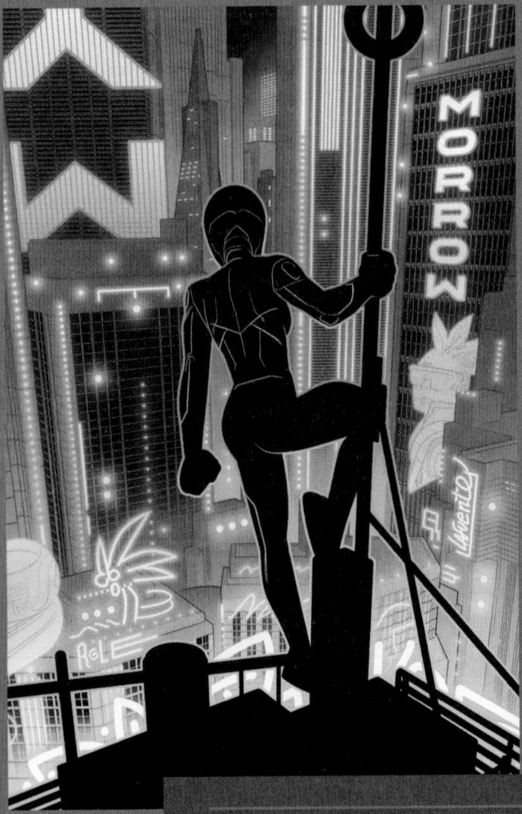
MORROW

CVR: 01/E
ART: DAVID LAFUENTE
w/ MIQUEL MUERTO

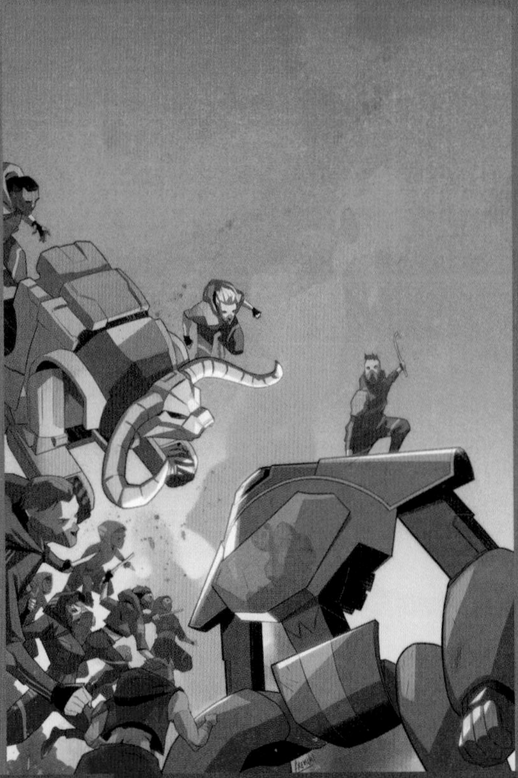

CVR: 02/A
ART: FRENCH CARLOMAGNO

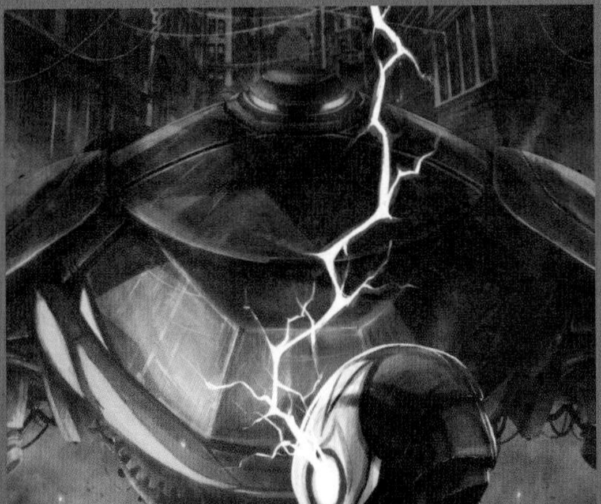

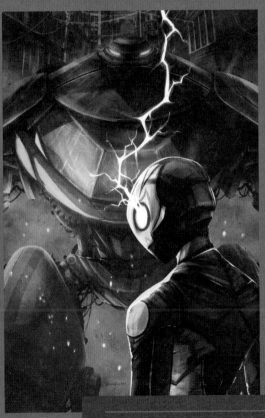

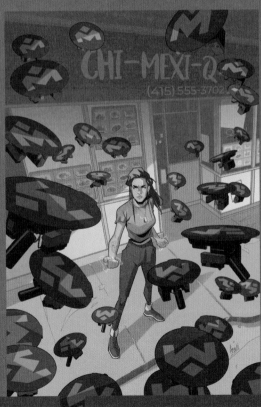

CVR: 02/B
ART: LUKE DUO ART

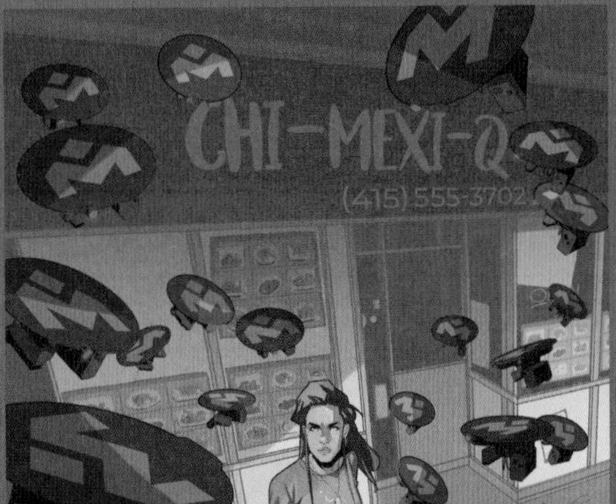
CHI-MEXI-Q
(415) 555-3702

CVR: 03/A
ART: FRENCH CARLOMAGNO

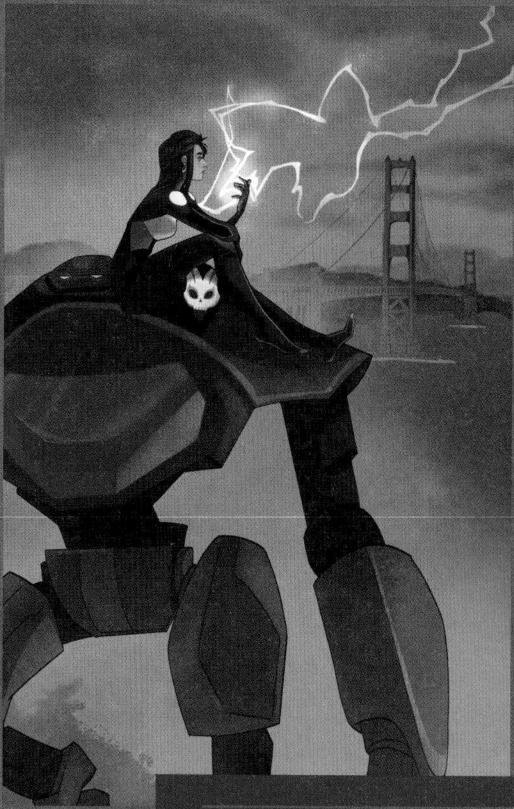

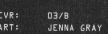

CVR: 03/B
ART: JENNA GRAY

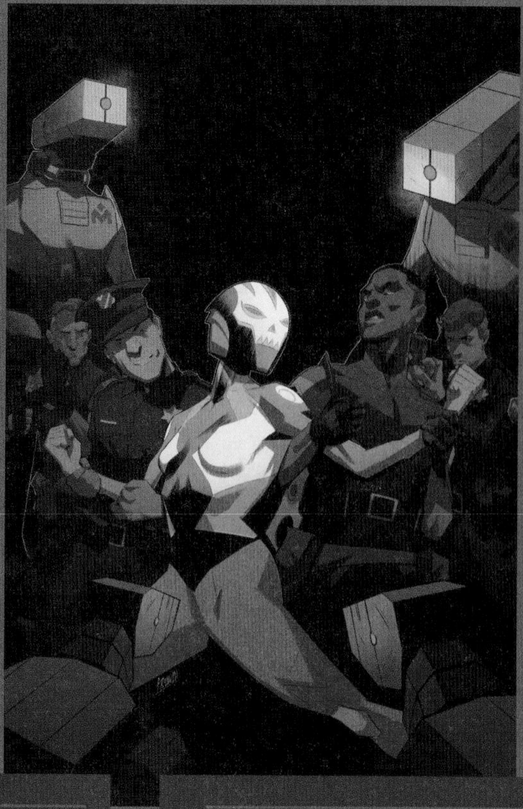

CVR: 04/A
ART: FRENCH CARLOMAGNO

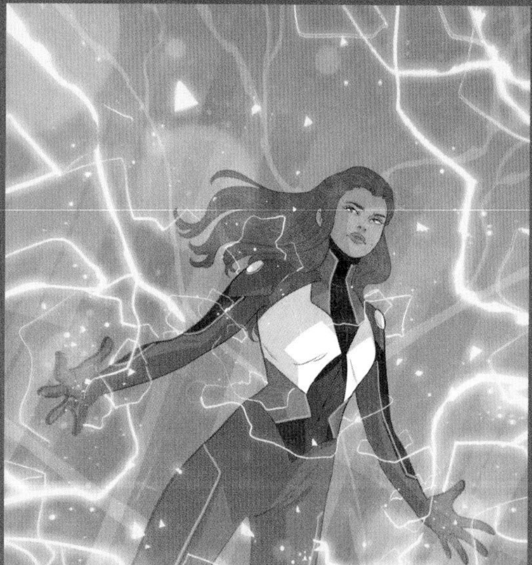

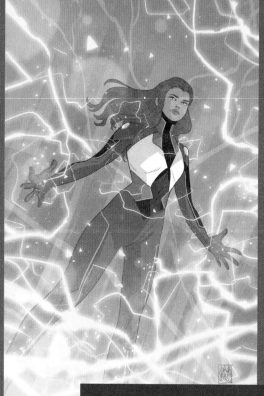

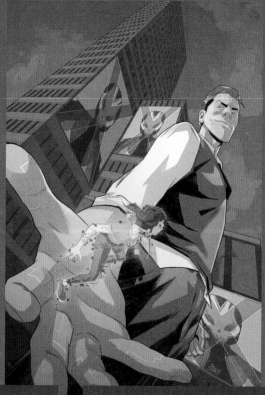

CVR: 04/B
ART: LUANA VECCHIO

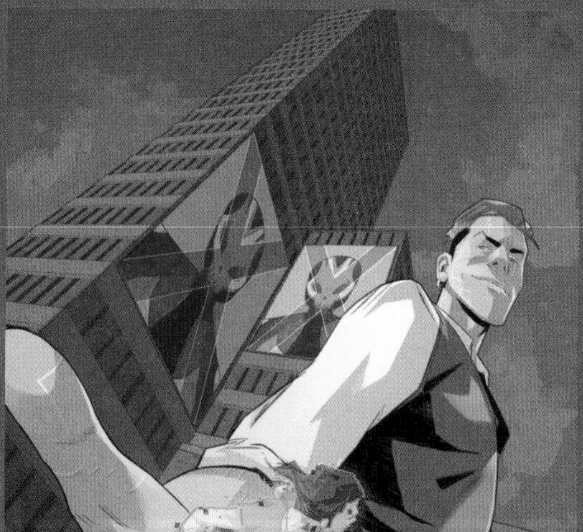

CVR: 05/A
ART: FRENCH CARLOMAGNO

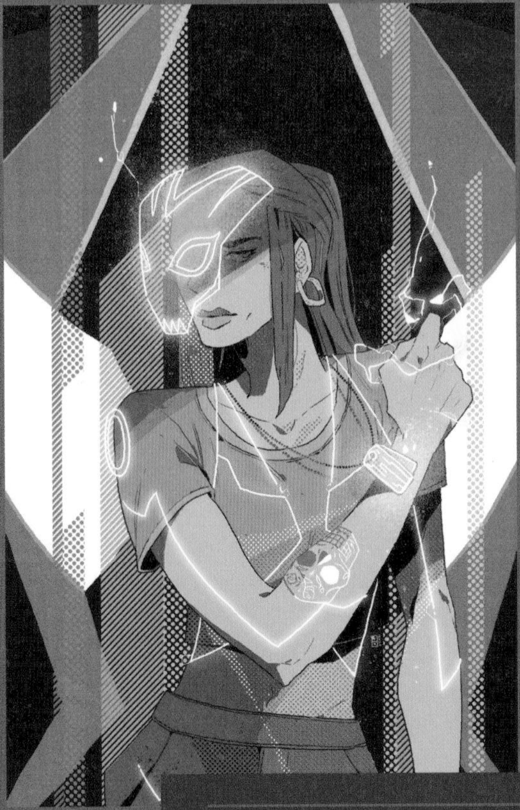

CVR: 05/B
ART: JO MI-GYEONG

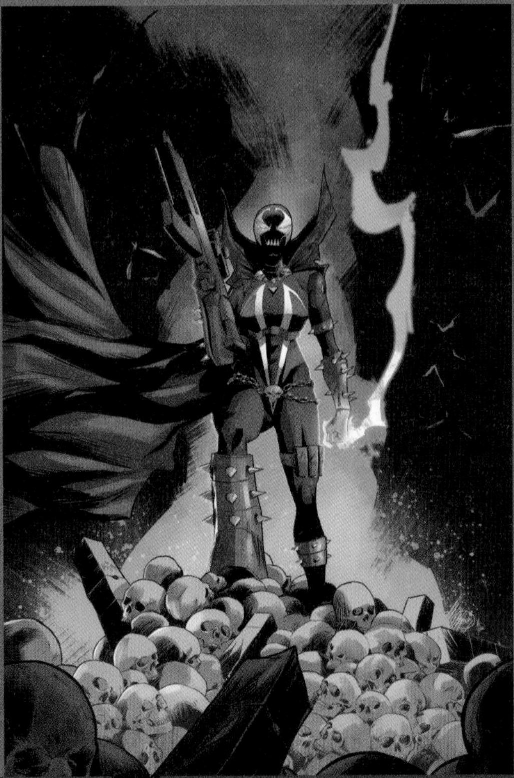

CVR: 05/C
ART: FRENCH CARLOMAGNO
w/ MATTIA IACONO

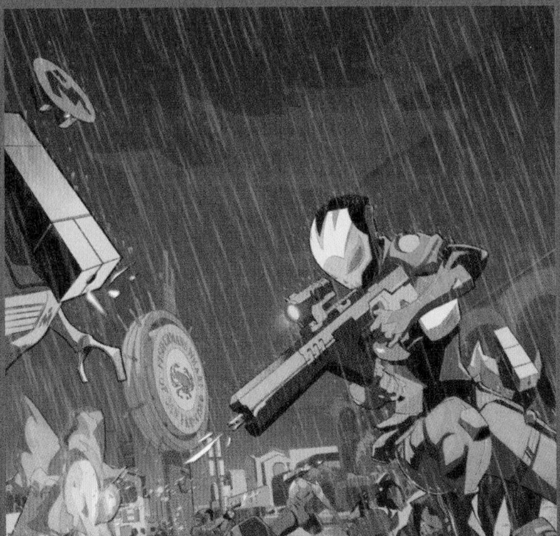

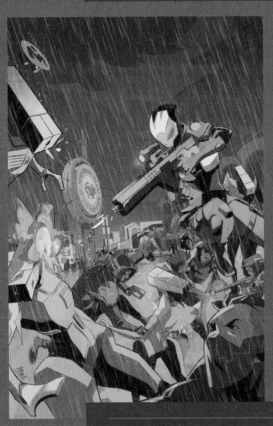

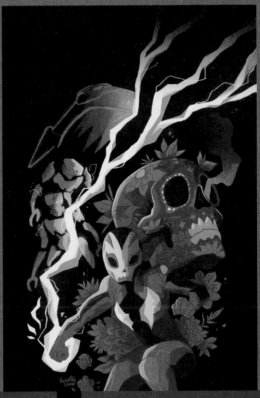

CVR: 06/A
ART: FRENCH CARLOMAGNO

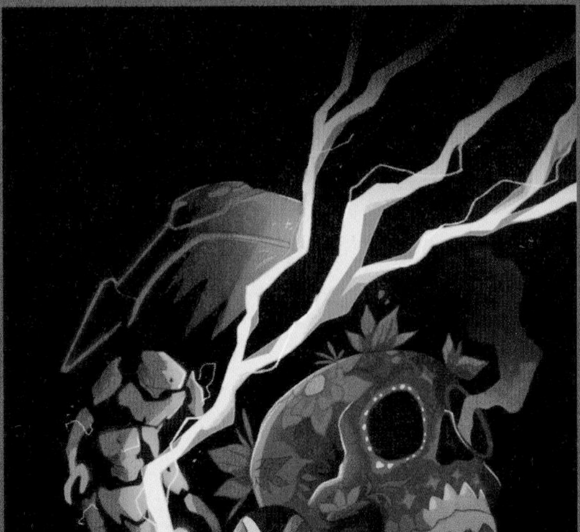

CVR: 06/B
ART: VALENTINO LASSO

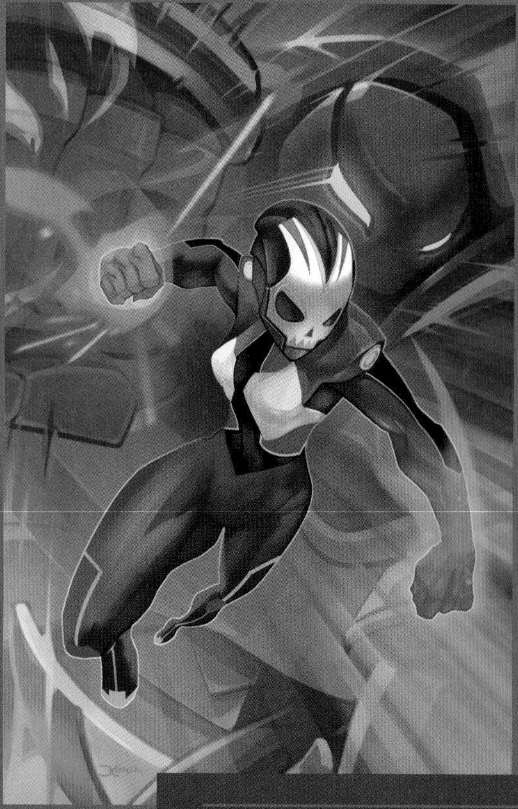

CVR: 01/TFAW
ART: MAURICIO HERRERA

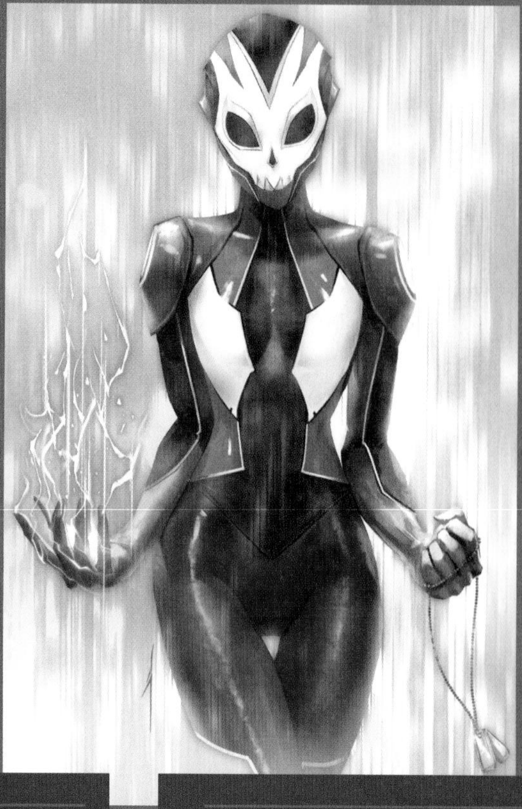

CVR: 01/RABBIT COMICS
ART: IVAN TAO

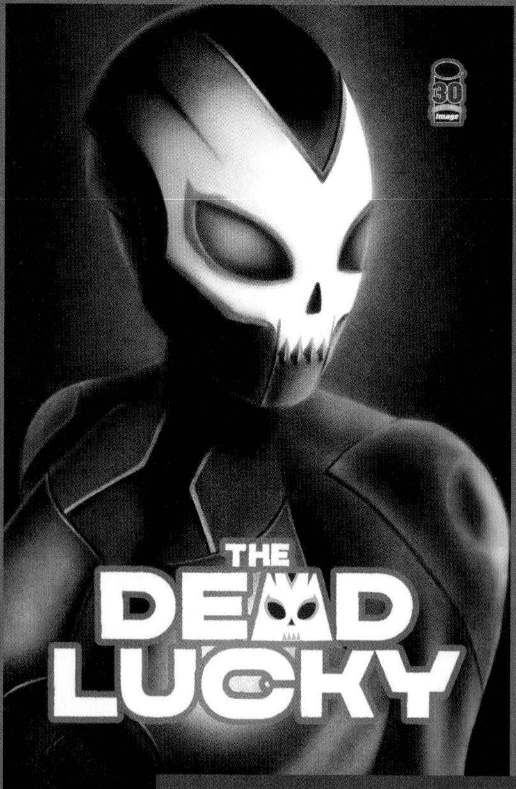
THE DEAD LUCKY

CVR: 01/GEEKED OUT & COMICS & COLLECTIBLE HQ
ART: DAVID SANCHEZ

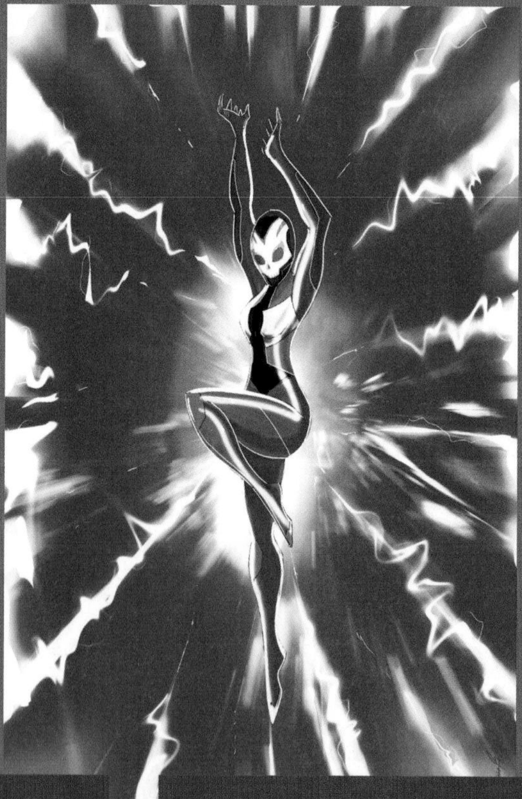

CVR: 01/GREAT WALL OF COMICS
ART: LIVIO RAMONDELLI

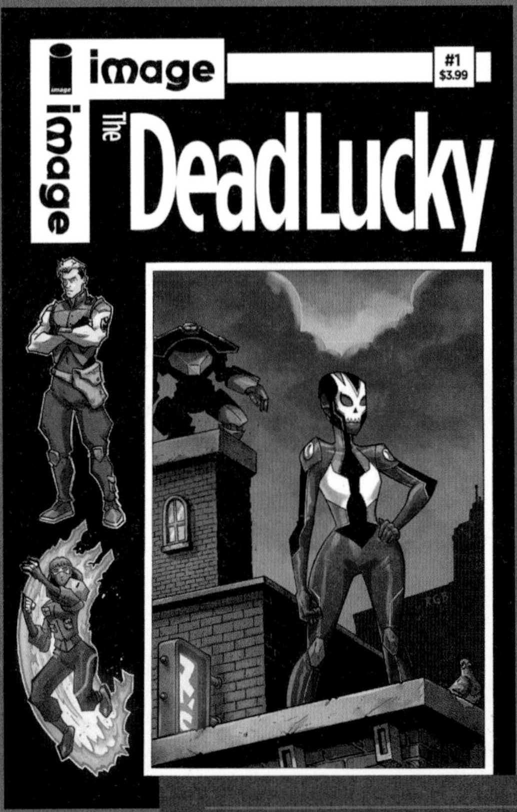
image
#1
$3.99
image
The
DeadLucky

CVR: 01/WHATNOT
ART: RYAN G. BROWNE

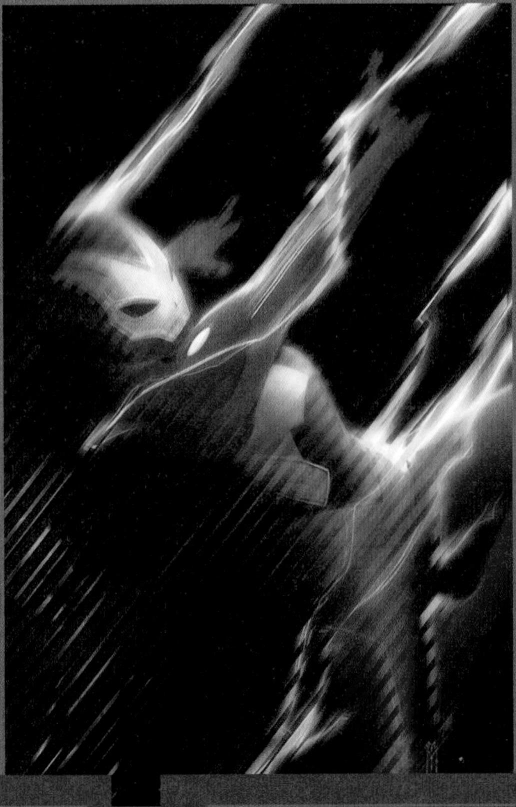

CVR: 01/SPECTRAL COMICS
ART: MIGUEL MERCADO

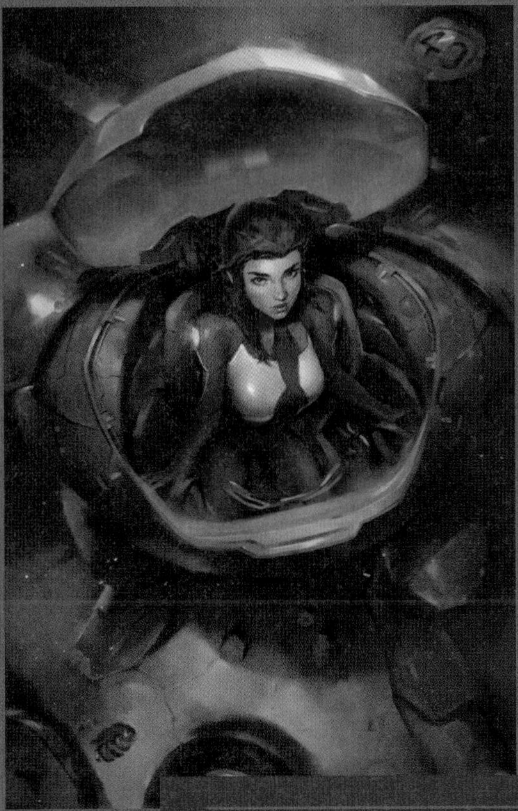

CVR: 01/BIRD CITY COMICS
ART: BROOKS KIM

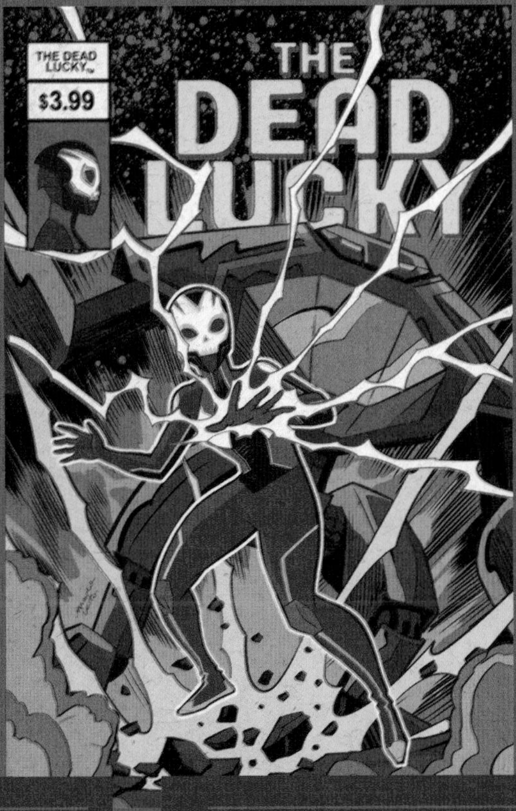
THE DEAD LUCKY
$3.99
THE
DEAD
LUCKY

CVR: 01/STADIUM COMICS
ART: MARCELO COSTA

CVR: 01/COMICS VAULT LIVE
ART: DANIELE DI NICUOLO

```
TERMINAL                                                    _  ×
_____

GHOST:~ admin$ GetRecipes
Contents:
    Birria Bao Buns
    Smoked Duck Tacos w/ Mango Habanero Sauce
    'Bibi' Breakfast Wrap
    BoBo Pudding
```

RECIPE

GHOST:~ admin$ GetRecipe
Chi-Mexi-Q's Birria Bao Buns

Birria, a stewed meat dish made famous in Jalisco, is traditionally made with goat meat, but is also often made with beef. The decadent consume that is left behind is essential for dipping. Bao are Chinese buns traditionally steamed and filled with sweet or savory filling. Bring them together, and you're in for some very sexy yummies.

FOR THE BIRRIA

2 lbs bone-in short ribs
4 lbs chuck roast
1 large onion
1 full garlic bulb
4 cups chicken broth
4 cups water
1 tsp oregano
3 bay leaves
1 tsp ground cumin
1 tsp salt
2 tsp chili powder
4 star anise pods
8 chili de árbol pods
1 large Fuji apple

FOR THE BAO

3½ cups all purpose flour or bread flour
¼ oz instant yeast
1 tbsp white cane sugar
1 pinch salt
1 cup warm water (110°F)
2 tbsp vegetable oil
1 tsp baking powder

FOR THE BIRRIA

Chop the onion and apple in half. Cut off the stem and ends of the chili de árbol and remove the seeds. Place the onion, apple, chilis and garlic in a cheesecloth and tie into a pouch.

In a large pot, add chicken broth, water and all other ingredients, including the meat and cheesecloth bundle, into the pot and bring to boil. Reduce heat to medium, stir and simmer for 30 minutes, making sure to skim off the foam from the top of the liquid. Continue to stir occasionally.

Remove the cheesecloth bundle from the broth and empty into a blender. Blend until smooth. If not smooth, add ½ cup of broth from the pot and blend.

Add the blended mixture back into the pot with the broth and stir to combine. Cover and continue to simmer for 3-4 hours until meat shreds easily with a fork, stirring occasionally.

Remove star anise pods and bay leaves from the broth.

Remove meat from the broth and shred, keeping the meat separate from the broth or consumé. Discard the bones.

FOR THE BAO

Combine sugar and yeast in 110°F water. Stir in oil and let sit for 5 minutes until the yeast blooms.

Sift flour, baking soda, and salt together.

Add yeast mixture into the dry ingredients.

Slowly add flour until not too sticky.

FOR THE BAO (CONTINUED)

Place the dough on flour surface and knead until smooth.

Place in oiled bowl and cover with a kitchen towel. Allow the dough to proof at room temperature until the dough doubles in size, which should take about two hours.

Remove the tablecloth and punch down the dough to remove the air.

With your fingers, pinch out about two inches worth of dough, and roll into a ball with your palms.

Place on a flat surface, and allow to rest for 5 minutes.

Take each ball and with the heel of your hand, flatten each ball of dough until it becomes a flat circle about ½ an inch thick.

Fold the circle to create a taco like shell, and place a small piece of parchment paper between the fold to avoid sticking.

Line a steam basket with parchment paper. Place the dough tacos on the parchment paper and steam for 8 minutes with enough room for the dough to expand.

TO COMBINE

Open up the steamed bao and add the shredded meat.

To serve, place bao with a cup of broth, now known as consumé, for dipping. Add cilantro, sliced tomato, or fermented daikon/carrot if desired.

RECIPE

GHOST:~ admin$ GetRecipe

Smoked Duck Tacos w/ Mango Habanero Salsa

Traditionally Chinese restaurants are known for their Peking Duck, a roast duck with glistening crispy caramel lacquered skin and plump succulent meat. There are many classic duck dishes in the Chinese gastronomic delights. At the Chi-Mexi-Q we like to blend our love of American BBQ and spice it up with some Latin flavor and Asian delight. Here we have the puffy smoked duck taco!

FOR THE BRINE

1/2 cup kosher salt
8 cups water

FOR THE DUCK

1 large duck
½ cup kosher salt
½ cup honey, maple syrup or birch syrup
small street taco flour tortillas
½ to 1 cup avocado oil (for frying the tortillas)
cherry and apple wood (for the smoker)

FOR THE SALSA

2 large tomatoes
2 shallots
3 habanero peppers
1 bell pepper
2 serrano peppers
1 jalapeno pepper
1 mango
2 cups cilantro, chopped
pinch of salt
1 teaspoon olive oil

BRINING INSTRUCTIONS

In a large container combine salt and water. Place duck into solution and refrigerate overnight, completely submerged. The next day, pat dry, and set in a cool area for a few hours to let the duck skin dry out.

If you did not brine your duck, then pat dry, rub with ½ cup of kosher salt, and set out in a cool place to dry out the skin.

Use a needle or knife point to gently prick holes all over the duck skin, trying not to puncture the meat.

FOR THE DUCK

This should be done in a smoker, but if required can be done on a basic BBQ grill. Have the smoker or BBQ heating to 225°-275° F while you prep the duck. Make sure the smoke is burning white to blue before putting in the duck. This process will take between 2.5 hrs and 3.5 hrs, and will require you to fire up the smoker to 500°F during the final 5 to 8 minutes.

Salt the inside cavity of the duck.

Brush the outside of the duck with the honey or syrup, and lightly sprinkle salt along the outside of the duck.

Place a drip pan under the duck to catch the fat drippings.

Set the duck on the smoker. It can be stood vertically, like beer can chicken, or laid with the breast side up.

Baste the duck every 1 hour with your honey or syrup of choice.

To crisp the skin, heat the smoker to 500°F but open up all the vents and add coal. You can remove the duck and drip pan from the smoker while you get the heat up to 500°F, or just leave the lid off. Do not leave the duck cooking in the high heat for more than 15 minutes or it will overcook and dry up.

FOR THE DUCK (CONTINUED)

Once smoker reaches 500°F, put the duck back in to allow to the skin to crisp for 5 to 8 minutes.

Remove duck from the heat and rest for 10 minutes.

Heat skillet or pan over medium-high heat and add ½ cup to 1 cup of avocado oil.

When oil reaches 350°F, slide in a tortilla and carefully baste hot oil over top of the tortilla shell. Flip the tortilla gently; in about 15 seconds, it will start getting puffy.

Remove and place on a cooling rack and drain onto paper towel.

FOR THE SALSA

Slice tomatoes into quarters and lightly oil them.

Remove stems from habaneros, serrano, and jalapenos, then slice in half length-wise. (For less heat, remove seeds.) Remove stem from bell pepper, de-seed and quarter. Peel shallots and cut in half length-wise.

Place shallots, peppers, and tomatoes in a wok or frying pan and sauté for 5 minutes in medium to high heat.

Peel and cube mango and gently sauté for 3-5 minutes with the rest of the ingredients, then allow ingredients to cool.

Place the tomatoes, peppers, shallots, and mango into the food processor and pulse, then add the cilantro and salt and process until smooth.

Transfer to a bowl, cover, and place in fridge for a few hours to allow the flavors to combine.

```
GHOST:~ admin$ GetRecipe
'Bibi' Breakfast Wrap
```

Not quite a breakfast burrito, not quite a crepe, the Bibi Wrap is a fusion of Chinese and Mexican flavors wrapped in a crispy hand-held nutritious bomb of goodness. The wrap is filled with scrambled egg, Chorizo, sesame seeds, scallions, chili sauce, hoisin sauce, and chicharrons; everything else is optional and will only enhance the texture and flavor of your Bibi wrap. Modify to your heart's content!

1 sheet rice paper or tortilla

chili sauce, to taste

hoisin sauce, to taste

1 egg

1 to 2 green scallions, chopped

1/2 teaspoon sesame seeds

5 pieces chicharron aka pork rind, crumbled

1/3 cup cooked chorizo

1/2 teaspoon poppy seeds

3 tbsp oil

OPTIONAL

cilantro

1/2 cup cooked spinach

1 avocado

Heat a nonstick griddle or frying pan on medium low heat.

Add a sheet of rice paper or a tortilla to the pan.

Brush on the chili sauce and hoisin sauce, or spread evenly with the back of a spoon.

Crack an egg on top of the rice paper, break the yolk, and spread evenly.

Sprinkle chopped scallion, sesame seed and poppy seed over the scrambled egg. Add any other toppings you'd like, such as cilantro, cooked spinach or avocado.

Add the chicharron and chorizo.

Fold in half and then in half again, forming a triangle.

Add oil to the pan, and lightly fry both sides of the wrap.

RECIPE

```
GHOST:~ admin$ GetRecipe
BoBo Pudding
```

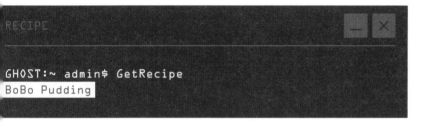

The major difference between Mexican flan and Chinese egg pudding is how you prepare it. Flan is baked, Chinese egg pudding is steamed. We've given you instructions for both, as well as our personal quick hack: the microwave! This recipe makes 8 servings.

3 eggs
12 oz can evaporated milk
14 oz can condensed milk
1 tablespoon vanilla
1 cup white sugar OR 120g rock sugar
tapioca pearls

Substitution Note: evaporated or condensed milk can each be replaced with 2 cups regular milk if required.

Melt sugar in a medium saucepan over medium-low heat. Watch the process carefully and remove from heat when sugar liquefies and turns a light golden color.

Carefully pour hot sugar syrup into a round bowl or mold, turning the dish to evenly coat the bottom and sides. Set aside.

In a blender, add condensed milk, evaporated milk, vanilla, and eggs. Blend until well mixed. If you choose, you can strain the mixture to remove bubbles.

Gently pour mixture over the sugar syrup, removing any bubbles with a small spoon.

Cook by steaming, baking, or microwave - see instructions below..

To serve, invert onto a rimmed plate, and sprinkle with a few tapioca boba. Serve warm or cold.

TO STEAM
Place bowl into the steamer and steam for 12 minutes.

Remove and allow pudding to set.

TO BAKE
Preheat oven to 350°F.

Place the bowl inside a baking pan, and add warm water to the pan to about ¾ inch.

Bake for 1 hour, then let cool to set.

TO MICROWAVE
Microwave in a microwave safe bowl at 500 watts for 3 minutes, then chill for 30 minutes in the fridge to set.

MAY 2023

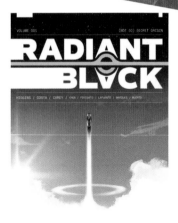

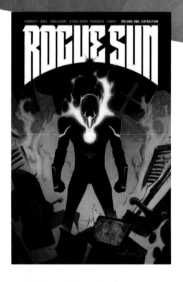

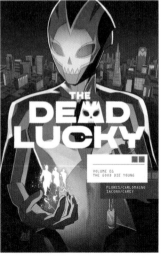

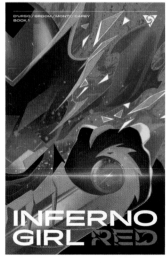

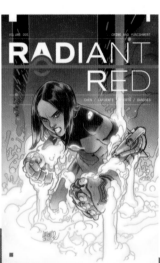

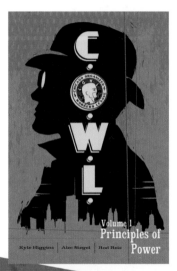